CONTENTS

THE COMPLETE
CHRISTIAN GUIDE TO
UNDERSTANDING
HOMOSEXUALITY

THE COMPLETE
CHRISTIAN GUIDE TO
UNDERSTANDING
HOMOSEXUALITY

JOE DALLAS
NANCY HECHE
GENERAL EDITORS

HARVEST HOUSE PUBLISHERS

EUGENE, OREGON

Cover by Dugan Design Group, Bloomington, Minnesota

THE COMPLETE CHRISTIAN GUIDE TO UNDERSTANDING HOMOSEXUALITY
Copyright © 2010 by Joe Dallas and Nancy Heche
Published by Harvest House Publishers
Eugene, Oregon 97402
www.harvesthousepublishers.com

Library of Congress Cataloging-in-Publication Data

The complete Christian guide to understanding homosexuality / Joe Dallas and Nancy Heche, general editors.
    p. cm.
Includes bibliographical references.
ISBN 978-0-7369-2507-5 (pbk.)
1. Homosexuality—Religious aspects—Christianity. I. Dallas, Joe, 1954- II. Heche, Nancy.
BRl15.H6C672 2009
261.8'35766—dc22

2008049215

Printed in the United States of America

10 11 12 13 14 15 16 17 18 / LB-NI / 10 9 8 7 6 5 4 3 2 1

Therefore, if anyone is in Christ, he is a new creation; the old has gone, the new has come! All this is from God, who reconciled us to himself through Christ and gave us the ministry of reconciliation: that God was reconciling the world to himself in Christ, not counting men's sins against them. And he has committed to us the message of reconciliation. We are therefore Christ's ambassadors, as though God were making his appeal through us. We implore you on Christ's behalf: Be reconciled to God.

2 Corinthians 5: 17-20 niv

INTRODUCTION

by Nancy Heche, DMin, and Joe Dallas

*It is a mark of great people to treat trifles as trifles,
and important matters as important.*

—Doris Lessing

If it doesn't matter to God, it needn't matter to us.

There are, after all, countless issues for Christians to be concerned about. So in an age marred by terrorism, poverty, violence, and corruption at every level, some would assume that sexual morality is, by its nature, a secondary matter.

And even if we do see sexual sin as an important issue, the aspect of it discussed in this book might seem tame next to others. Compare homosexuality to abortion—the taking of an innocent life—or to teen pregnancy, with its tragic repercussions; or to the wounds inflicted by molestation; or to the glaring evil of forced prostitution. Next to these, a consensual erotic relationship between two adults of the same sex can seem mild. Wrong, perhaps, but not worth verbalizing. So why bother reading (much less writing) a comprehensive book on the subject?

The answer lies in whatever motivated you to pick up this book.

If you're a pastor, priest, or lay ministry leader, you've seen how homosexuality impacts the people you serve. You've met parents whose sons or daughters have just "come out" to them, and they've got questions you're not sure how to answer. You pray with people who struggle against sexual desires for the same sex, and you want to give them counsel that's compassionate and practical. Your denomination may be debating the rightness or wrongness of homosexuality, and you want to be better equipped to take a stand. Or you simply want to give your congregation the full counsel of God on this difficult subject, so you want a good working knowledge of it. Those are all good reasons to keep reading.

Someone you love might be gay, and you're wondering how, as a Bible believing Christian, you can keep a bond with this person without compromising your moral position. You're wondering how to handle it if your loved one wants to bring a partner home for the holidays, or asks you to attend his or her same-sex wedding ceremony. And when that family member says *I was born this way, I can't change, and you need to accept it!* how do you answer? We'll cover the dilemmas faced by spouses, parents, siblings, and children of homosexuals in these pages.

Perhaps you're an educator wanting a better grasp on the academic questions the subject raises. What causes homosexuality? Is it immutable or changeable? What beliefs cause some people to embrace it, while others reject it? As a teacher, these questions matter to you, as do the homosexual students (and their parents and loved ones) whom you deal with almost daily. Much of this has been written with you and your needs in mind.

Maybe you're a counselor, psychologist, or therapist looking for insights you can incorporate into your work, so that when your patient says, "I'm a lesbian" or, "I'm a gay man," you'll better understand the issues he or she brings into your office. And if you're a Christian counselor, working with people who want to overcome homosexuality, you'll want to know what changes they can realistically expect, what steps they should take, and what challenges they'll face along the way. You'll find all these concerns addressed here.

You yourself could be a Christian who's attracted to the same sex, engaged in a lifelong struggle with feelings you neither desired nor chose, wondering what, if anything, you can do. If you abstain from homosexual sex, will you ever become attracted to the opposite sex? Is marriage an option? Where do you go for help and support when you wrestle with feelings few people can relate to?

And what about habits or bonds you've already developed? How do you cut off a relationship you know to be wrong? What do you do when you're hooked on porn? And if you're what's commonly known as a sex addict, how do you break the pattern? These and similar questions are posed, explored, and responded to in *The Complete Christian Guide to Understanding Homosexuality.*

Concerned Christians, activists, and apologists are likely to pick this book up too. Many believers see this as a cutting edge issue, one they face on the job, at school, or wherever they interact with the culture. They want to better understand the biblical perspective on homosexuality so they can persuasively articulate it, making them, in essence, apologists, activists, or both. As such they hope to reason with people, function as ambassadors for Christ, and always be ready to give an answer to anyone willing to discuss the Judeo-Christian view on this current issue. In these chapters they'll find responses to common pro-gay arguments, a history of the gay rights movement in America and its ramifications for believers, critiques of the church's response to the issue thus far, and suggestions for those wanting to take a public stand for the traditional view.

Seekers of all kinds will no doubt also be interested in the information on the following pages. Seekers are not necessarily interested in converting to a biblical perspective, but they do hope to better understand why Christians believe what they do about homosexuality in particular, and the human experience in general. Openly gay and lesbian readers seeking to know our position will scan these pages as well, and while they'll dispute much of what's written here, we hope they'll at least find it to be reasonable, clear, and respectful.

The Bible and Its Approach to Human Sexuality

To each of the foregoing groups, homosexuality is no trifle. It matters so much, and to so many. But the Scriptures indicate it also matters to God. And since this book describes itself as a Christian guide, it's written from a distinctively biblical perspective. We regard both the Old and New Testaments as authoritative, much like Paul the apostle did when he affirmed:

> All scripture is given by inspiration of God, and is profitable for doctrine, for reproof, for correction, for instruction in righteousness (2 Timothy 3:16).

So while science and psychology will be referenced in these pages as ways of explaining what *is*, the Bible—our profitable authority on all things relating to doctrine, correction, and instruction—will have the ultimate say when determining what *ought* to be, and how *we* ought to be.

For that reason, a few points on the Bible and its approach to human sexuality are in order. They help explain the reasons we're concerned—as is God—about homosexuality.

1. We are *created* beings (Genesis 2:7; Revelation 4:11). If we weren't created, and therefore answered to no creator, we might judge the rightness or wrongness of our behavior by its rightness or wrongness in our own eyes. But if we, as created beings, are accountable to our Maker, then it matters less what seems right and natural to *us*, and more what is deemed right and natural to our Creator. Christian apologist and radio host Gregory Koukl states it plainly:

> If God is there (which is what the Christian says), it doesn't matter what is preferred. It only matters what is true.[1]

2. Our Creator has *specific intentions* for our existence and behavior, which are spelled out in Scripture. This is seen most noticeably in the Mosaic Law, the Psalms and Proverbs, the prophetic books, the Gospels, and the epistles, all of which are brimming with instructions, prohibitions, and warnings, testifying to a God who is not passive or unconcerned about His creation. We were fashioned with specific purposes in mind, purposes we'll refer to as *created intent*.

3. These intentions are extended to our relationships in general and to our *sexual relationships* in particular. It should be noted that not only did our Maker create us as *human* beings, but as *sexual* beings as well. He authored our male/female distinctives and our capacity for erotic response, then looked on all He had created (human sexuality included) and said, "That's good!" (Genesis 1:26-30). Far from being prudish or antisexual, then, God is the author and original celebrator of sex. Understanding this is important when approaching the next point.

4. Sexual behaviors falling short of created intent are regarded by the Creator as serious enough to warrant public rebuke (Matthew 14:3-4) and church discipline (1 Corinthians 5:1-5), and are considered detrimental in ways that are *unique* and *severe* (1 Corinthians 6:18). God finds sexual sin abhorrent precisely because He views healthy sex as being so exquisite and meaningful. So John the Baptist lost his life for taking a stand against King Herod's immorality; the first recorded case of church discipline occurred after the Corinthian church was rebuked for allowing open immorality to be practiced in the congregation; and Paul described sexual sin as having particularly heinous impact on the person practicing it (see the scriptures listed above). While we must regard all sin as serious, sexual sin carries a severity in both its nature and its consequences.

5. The specific sexual sin of homosexuality is prohibited in both Testaments (Leviticus 18:22 and 20:13; Romans 1:26-27; 1 Corinthians 6:9; 1 Timothy 1:10) and is regarded as one of many sexual behaviors falling short of created intent, along with adultery, fornication, prostitution, and incest. If we are indeed created with and for specific intentions; and if sin falls short of those intentions; and if sexual sin falls short in ways that especially offend our Creator and wreak havoc in our lives; and if homosexuality constitutes sexual sin, then homosexuality clearly matters. It matters to God, it matters to the church, it matters to the culture, and it matters to us.

"Us" includes the two of us who edited, and contributed to, *The Complete Christian Guide to Understanding Homosexuality.* We've both spoken extensively on this subject at churches and conferences, and both of us have spent years counseling women and men who've been directly impacted by it. More importantly, *we've* been impacted by it—hugely!—so we approach this topic with insights and passion born of our own experiences.

Nancy's Story

My interest in homosexuality can be traced to my 25-year marriage to a man who, unbeknownst to me, was living a secret second life as a homosexual. It was his AIDS diagnosis (and eventual death) that finally brought out the truth. Years later, I would be dealing with this issue again from a more public perspective as my daughter, actress Anne Heche, embarked on a well-publicized lesbian affair. I have recounted these experiences more fully in my book *The Truth Comes Out.*

When I reflect on some of my own history with the GLBT (Gay, Lesbian, Bisexual, Transgender) community I think of myself as having been very much like the priest and the Levite in the story of the Good Samaritan—I walked on the other side of the street. I wouldn't go to a hair salon where the stylists were gay. I didn't want to be served in a restaurant where the servers were gay. I avoided homosexuals any way I could.

I had been so hurt by my experience, I was fully convinced that my husband could never be in heaven, even though I was told by a godly pastor that he had repented and left his homosexual practices. Frankly, I didn't *want* him to go to heaven.

I was angry at the homosexual community, a phantom world I had made up in my mind that had "done me wrong." They had raped my marriage, broken up my home, and left me in despair. As a result, my attitude needed an "extreme makeover." I needed to move out of my fear and anger and confusion into a place of love and respect where God's truth and grace could overcome my bitterness. I needed to understand God's heart toward a community from which I was deliberately estranged. And so God began His gentle, persistent work to give me His perspective and pour His heart into my heart toward these people I so disliked.

My first big "aha!" was the realization that there was a bigger picture for my life than my anger would allow. God meant there to be a design, a plan, and a purpose that far exceeded my intentional separation from and rejection of individuals in the GLBT community. The truth was, I had known a small taste of the homosexual life with my husband and my daughter. But there was to come a new life for me with the GLBT community.

The next "aha!" came when I realized I could choose what kind of person I would be: I could either live my life in fear and anger for the way homosexuality had come into my life or I could choose to live in a way that manifests love and respect for others.

Another "aha!" came as result of attending a conference where men and women who had lived homosexually were now finding God's purpose for their lives in holy, obedient lives. I learned that my journey on this path is not about changing anyone else. It's about changing *me.*

Homosexuality will not go away. But, one by one, God is bringing many who struggle with same-sex attraction into a new life of surrender to and pursuit of Jesus Christ. He is also bringing His church to a place of ministry to homosexuals, not condemnation. God has a winning strategy regarding homosexuality. That strategy is *love trumps everything.* As a result, my present hope is in the power of the God who seeks, invites, saves, and heals us one by one by His Spirit in secret ways and secret places far beyond our personal hopes or dreams or imaginations.

Joe's Story

From boyhood I was aware of my same-sex desires, at the time when the only word for them was "queer." I'm a product of the turbulent 1960s, and in those days being known as a queer didn't open many doors. So when I was molested as a boy by a stranger in a movie theater, I told no one. Nor did I confide in anyone when I experimented with both sexes as a junior high student, or when I began random relationships with adult men as a high school junior. To friends and schoolmates, I was known as a fairly normal California boy who never lacked for girlfriends or typical social outlets. I would often, in fact, attend high school football games on Friday nights with my jock friends, a pretty girl on my arm, then sneak out the next evening to meet adult males. Today we call that kind of secrecy the "closet," but then it was called "survival."

Yet I'd always been attracted to girls as well. One in particular, a lovely Christian named Ann, invited me to a "girls ask boys" dance, and a romantic relationship began. She gradually invited me to church with her and, more out of curiosity than faith, I went. The church was Calvary Chapel of Costa Mesa; the pastor was well-known Bible teacher Chuck Smith. Never had I heard the gospel presented so plainly, and I spent the subsequent three months wrestling with fierce conviction. Finally, in the spring of 1971, I received Christ, was born again, and assumed—mistakenly—that conversion would relieve me of all my wayward sexual desires.

I established myself firmly in the life of the church, eventually entering full-time ministry with a separate, newly formed church which became a vibrant, thriving ministry. But with its growth came increased problems—commercialism, infighting, greed—so in 1975 I left it, disillusioned and bitter.

Homosexual fantasies, which had been largely dormant for years, started re-emerging with a vengeance. I became curious about the new phenomenon of adult bookstores, which were springing up all around my city. Not having viewed pornography for years, I was drawn to, and eventually entered, a porn shop. A quick downward spiral ensued, including an affair with a good friend's wife culminating in an aborted child, the use of prostitutes, heavy drinking, and a yearlong affair with the owner of a local gay bar. I was by then remarkably back-slidden and jaded, but still hungry for God and the fellowship I now missed so badly. But how could I, in my present state, return to church? I was unwilling to repent of homosexuality, but also unable to fully reject Christianity.

It was then—the fall of 1978—that I heard of a church where one didn't need to choose between homosexuality and God. So I attended a service and heard for the first time a pro-homosexual interpretation of Scripture. And while this interpretation seemed full of holes to me, it also offered a quick remedy to my dilemma. If, after all, the Bible could be read in a way that justified homosexuality, then I could be gay *and* Christian—problem solved, conflict over.

But I'd been grounded in sound doctrine too long to permanently believe this distortion. So after six years of unsuccessfully trying to convince myself that the Bible condoned homosexuality, I did what the prodigal must eventually do. I woke up to my brokenness, repented, and headed for home.

Within weeks I'd relocated to another county, found a good Christian counselor, and settled into a Bible-believing church where I met a lovely young woman who I began dating and, three years later, married. By then I'd also begun ministering, as a pastoral counselor and speaker, to Christian men struggling with pornography, adultery, and homosexuality. The honor of serving such men and their families over the past two decades has been indescribable.

High Hopes

Obviously, then, we both bring our own pain, struggles, and hopes to this book, so when Harvest House asked us to write and edit it, we were thrilled. "Wouldn't it be great if...?" became a question we repeated, over and over, as we considered the directions it could take.

"Wouldn't it be great if this book could be a one-stop resource?" So we selected the main topics associated with homosexuality—theological, clinical, social, political, and familial—then solicited contributions from a variety of authors with specific expertise. The result is a comprehensive guide providing biblically based insights into the many issues the subject raises. And, oh, how we argued about the title, *The Complete Christian Guide to Understanding Homosexuality*! Because we realize, of course, that no one book can cover all the aspects of such an enormous topic. Still, we do feel this one addresses most if not all of the primary questions and concerns the average Christian reader will have.

"Wouldn't it be great if we could equip Christians to discuss this subject intelligently and with confidence?" So we've provided the most common pro-gay arguments the reader is likely to hear, and offered clear, simple, and practical responses. We know this is a classic "hot button" issue, the controversy about which leads many Christians to avoid speaking about it for a number of reasons: fear of offending, uncertainty of what to say or how to say it, or wariness of being deemed "politically incorrect." We'd like to change that, because we feel no one should have to apologize for having an opinion, holding to a truth, or expressing that truth in any setting. The subject and the times call for Christian boldness, tempered with consideration, compassion, and wisdom. So by anticipating many of the opportunities the reader will have for dialogue, we've tried to equip him/her with conversational "dos and don'ts" that are both user-friendly and effective.

"Wouldn't it be great if the reader gained a deeper respect and empathy for homosexual friends and loved ones, without compromising truth?" So we've included chapters written by people who've wrestled with their own homosexuality, hoping to help readers walk a mile in the shoes of someone whose journey has been quite different from their own. We're convinced that deeper understanding leads to more effective ministry, better relationships, and a more Christlike compassion.

All these "wouldn't it be great if…" questions raised our hopes considerably. So we offer *The Complete Christian Guide to Understanding Homosexuality* hoping it will equip believers to speak, serve, and love. We hope a Christian father who reads these pages will better communicate with his gay son, improving both their relationship and his ability to explain biblical truth. We hope the pastor who picks this up will preach more clearly and fervently on the subject, and that the counselor or educator who buys it will find ways to put its theories and suggestions into practice. We hope the Christian activist reading this in preparation for an interview or public debate will be empowered to field the tough questions and arguments that'll be thrown his way. We hope the Christian wrestling with his own sexual conflicts will find resolution here, and we hope the gay activist reader will better understand the position he's rejected, walking away with a more accurate picture of the Christians he disagrees with.

But our hopes are aimed beyond this book and its readers. They extend, in fact, to the body of Christ everywhere, and to its future effectiveness and health.

We hope churches will see the current misguided widespread acceptance and promotion of homosexuality as an opportunity to begin fresh, vibrant dialogues on human sexuality, and by what standards we should express it. We hope families with gay loved ones will seize the opportunity, however painful the situation, to open up more honesty and clarity in their relationships. We hope concerned Christian citizens will see the gay rights movement as an opportunity to challenge the increased secularism of our times by reminding the American culture of its Judeo-Christian traditions.

Most of all we hope for the remnant—those who will, regardless of prevailing trends and practices, respond to the gospel's calling and promise. While recognizing a growing resistance to traditional Christian viewpoints in all aspects of culture, we remember that God's sovereignty cannot be restricted, nor can the Holy Spirit be bound. So there will always be those who say "no" to what the world says "yes" to, just as there will always be those willing to say what is unpopular but redemptive, standing for what is controversial but true, even when truth is being relentlessly, systematically obscured.

And so it is with these high hopes, and deepest gratitude, that we've labored to produce this book. We're indebted to Harvest House Publishers, our editor Nick Harrison, our patient families, and the readers who'll take the time to invest in this material. May it be used to work God's purposes in all.

Nancy Heche, DMin
Joe Dallas
July 2010

NOTES

1. Gregory Koukl, "Preference or Truth?" *Stand to Reason* program transcript, 1994, www.str.org/site/News2?page=NewsArticle&id=5503.

PART ONE

THE CHURCH IN CRISIS, PART 1
Truth Revised

by Joe Dallas

*When written in Chinese the word "crisis" is
composed of two characters—one represents danger,
and the other represents opportunity.*

—JOHN F. KENNEDY

*C*risis is an overused word. Family crisis, financial crisis, emotional crisis, energy crisis, nothing-to-wear crisis—its force gets watered down when it's heard too often.

I noticed this when traveling after 9/11. Terror alert threat levels were established after the attacks, letting airline passengers know whether today's likelihood of another one was low, elevated, or severe. Airports began announcing them over the loudspeakers, so to fly meant to hear, at regular intervals, the current "Terror Alert" status. The phrase chilled me the first time I heard it, caught my attention the next few trips, then finally, for no reason other than repetition, it lost its punch. To my knowledge the threats were no less real; I'd simply gotten used to hearing about them.

So it is with "crises." If your name's out there on Christian mailing lists, I'll bet you receive any number of letters from organizations describing a problem, the crisis it creates, the ways they can avert the crisis, and the reasons you must send money to help them do so. I trust most of these groups are sincere and the problems they address are serious, but after a while, the sheer volume of crisis-oriented mailings can dull the word's edge.

Besides which, has there ever been a time the church *didn't* face a crisis? Everything dire that's happened in civilization since Christianity was birthed, whether natural disaster, social upheaval, or war, required a response from the church. And internally, from the time the New Testament was written to the present, schisms and conflicts among believers have been business as usual.

So the church has, does, and always will face crisis, from without or within. The question for us, then, is not whether the church faces crisis, but rather, what types does she face today, and is homosexuality one of them?

A Crisis of Truth

Webster's definition of "crisis" includes

1. a point of time made critical by a concurrence of circumstances.
2. a situation that has reached a critical phase.

By that definition, I would argue that a concurrence of circumstances, including the issues raised by homosexuality, the challenges they present the church, and the church's handling and (at times) mishandling of the matter, have combined to create, as Webster puts it, "a situation that has reached a critical phase."

I see this concurrence of circumstances as a deterioration, in both the church and the culture, seen noticeably from the 1960s onward, and having much to do with our commission to know, express, and properly handle truth. It looks something like this (see following diagram):

In this chapter, we'll focus on the downward progression occurring among churches influenced by the culture (left column) and in the following chapter, we'll examine the problems raised by churches who hold to the truth (right column) but often in the wrong way. In both cases, the end results are the denigration, distortion, and finally, the prohibition of truth, leading to crisis.

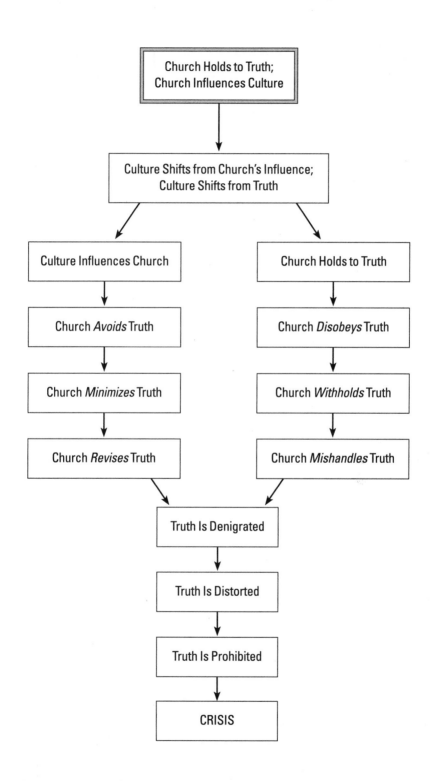

Let's walk through this step-by-step, beginning with the concept of objective truth, and the church's stewardship of it.

> **Church Holds to Truth;**
> **Church Influences Culture**

Four obvious points about truth should be considered:

1. Truth *is*, and it matters. It's part of what defines God's nature ("...in hope of eternal life which God, *who cannot lie,* promised before the world began"—Titus 1:2), and its opposite—falsehood—is so abhorrent to Him that Jesus referred to Satan as the father of lies (John 8:44). The fall of the human race is, in fact, largely attributed to the power of deception (Genesis 3:1-5; 1 Timothy 2:14), all of which says much about God's love of truth and hatred of anything veering from it.

2. Truth is both revealed to, and commissioned to, the church. Since the New Testament references believers collectively as the *ekklesia* (Greek for "church," meaning those "called out"), and since Jesus Himself confirmed that no one comes to Him unless drawn by God ("No one can come to me unless the Father who has sent me draws him"—John 6:44), we know God "calls out" His people, revealing Himself and His truth to them. This "revealing" comes first with our salvation, then continues through our ongoing spiritual growth (2 Corinthians 3:18). But having revealed truth to the church, God then commissions the church to reveal it in turn, through preaching, teaching, and disciple-making, to the world He loves. Thus the great commission:

> Go therefore and make disciples of all the nations, baptizing them
> in the name of the Father, and of the Son, and of the Holy Spirit,
> teaching them to observe all that I have commanded you (Matthew
> 28:19-20).

3. The great commission requires the church to speak clearly on the nature of humanity, God, and life. It requires teaching the nature of humanity, because we cannot preach the cross without showing the need for it, so we're compelled to teach the truth of human value and its sinfulness. ("For God so loved the world..."—John 3:16; "For all have sinned and fall short of the glory of

God"—Romans 3:23.) Nor can we evangelize without describing the nature of a loving God who is willing to forgive ("…that whoever believes in Him should not perish…"—John 3:16) but fearful in judgment ("It is a fearful thing to fall into the hands of the living God"—Hebrews 10:31). And the nature of eternal life—whether heaven with God or hell without Him—is a vital if unpleasant part of the church's message as well, one emphasized more by Jesus than by anyone else in Scripture (Matthew 18:9; 23:33; Luke 12:5). Remove any of these three elements—the truth about humanity, God, or life—and you have an inadequate, incomplete gospel.

4. The church cannot make disciples without knowing and teaching all three elements as well. These three points—the truth about humanity, God, and life—are not only required when evangelizing, but also when discipling. If Christians are to, as Peter encouraged, "grow in grace and in the knowledge of our Lord and Savior Jesus Christ" (2 Peter 3:18), then they have to be taught about themselves, and about Him.

Spiritual growth calls for understanding a myriad of concepts about the believer's life: the struggle between the flesh and the spirit (Galatians 5:16-25), the sanctity of the body (1 Corinthians 6:19-20), the responsibility to make use of our God-given gifts (Matthew 25:14-29), and the moral and sexual boundaries God has established, since any ambiguity on that topic is an invitation to chaos (1 Corinthians 6:18).

We need both to teach and to be taught what's revealed in Scripture about the nature of God and eternity as well, knowing the confidence we have in Him ("If God is for us, who can be against us?"—Romans 8:31), the standards required of anyone naming the name of Christ ("'The Lord knows those who are His,' and, 'Let everyone who names the name of Christ depart from iniquity'"—2 Timothy 2:19), and the fact of our own "day of reckoning" when we stand before Christ to receive eternal gain, or loss, of rewards ("We must all appear before the judgment seat of Christ, that each one may receive the things done in the body, according to what he has done, whether good or bad"—2 Corinthians 5:10).

For disciples to be made and nurtured, clear teaching on the nature of God, humanity, and life is required. So when functioning at its best, the church holds to these truths, teaches them clearly, and positively influences the culture as a result.

So Whatever Happened to Truth?

Historically, objective moral truth was acknowledged in America as something that could be found in, and drawn from, the Bible. We were no theocracy; citizens were not required to be Christian, nor did everyone believe the Good Book was divinely inspired. But it was revered, both by the general public and its leaders, and its sway was felt in law, literature, customs, entertainment, and common speech.[1] The body of Christ worldwide is challenged to respond to this issue, and while the acceptance of homosexuality has accelerated in some nations while lagging behind in others, the fact remains that Christians in all countries face the challenge of responding with love and truth to all homosexuals.

Our first president, George Washington, said, "It is impossible to rightly govern the world without God and the Bible." Five administrations later, President John Quincy Adams admonished his son: "It is essential…that you should form and adopt certain rules or principles, for the government of your own conduct and temper…It is in the Bible, you must learn them, and from the Bible how to practice them." President Theodore Roosevelt declared that "a thorough knowledge of the Bible is worth more than a college education." And President Hoover shared Roosevelt's high regard when he insisted that "the whole inspiration of our civilization springs from the teachings of Christ and the lessons of the prophets. To read the Bible for these fundamentals is a necessity of American life."[2]

The Bible, then, was viewed in this society as inspired and inspiring; foundational to a basic education, and an invaluable moral guide. The church, in turn, exerted no small influence in public thought and standards, leaving this principle intact:

> Church Holds to Truth;
> Church Influences Culture

Dr. Woodrow Kroll, recalling the Bible's influence on the American public, remarks that

> the early history of America reads like a Bible story. The men and women who settled in this country came to the United States because they were strong advocates of God's Word. They read the Bible, they

believed it, they cherished it, they lived by it. And that makes the comparison with Americans today all the more striking.[3]

Our history from the early twentieth century shows a continuation of the biblical influence Kroll describes. "Up until the 1960s," writes Professor Joanne Beckman of Duke University in her essay on politics and religion in the U.S., "the 'Protestant establishment' dominated the religious scene." Acknowledging intermittent challenges to religion in the 1920s, she correctly describes church and family as being "the twin pillars of security and respectability" in recent U.S. life.[4]

> ## Culture Shifts from Church's Influence; Culture Shifts from Truth

Yet in the 1960s, the symbiotic relationship between church and society deteriorated for a number of reasons, resulting in a cultural shift that would permanently alter Judeo-Christian influence in America and the very definition, culturally and theologically, of truth:

> In the late 1960s and early 1970s, religion itself was not rejected so much as was institutionalized Christianity…a new vista of lifestyle options was introduced into mainstream America. In the religious sphere, this meant that mainline Protestantism or even the tripartite division of Protestant-Catholic-Jew no longer represented all of society's spiritual interests.[5]

This was the era of Vietnam, women's liberation, Woodstock, and the hippie movement with its "drugs, sex, and rock 'n' roll" ethic. So while Christianity still offered truth, much of the culture was demanding a "new truth," removing itself from the authority and influence the church had enjoyed. The Bible, with its moral absolutes and sexual prohibitions, became irrelevant in the minds of many, making the next step inevitable.

"The change of Christianity's position in the place of America's soul from the 1950s to the 1960s (and thereafter) could not be more dramatic," notes former political science professor Miles Hodges in his writings on American government:

The 1960s was fast moving to a point of belonging to the university educated American—our new intellectual elite. The very idea of such divine dependency seemed to these new elite to be darkly superstitious…And so they set out to correct…this debilitating spiritual dependency on the God of middle America.[6]

That "correction" drove quite a wedge between Christian thinking and popular opinion. Things were changing outside the church, certainly, as new philosophies and ideals filled the void that was created where biblical concepts were rejected. Transcendental meditation, LSD-induced ecstasy, and Eastern philosophies came into vogue, paving the way for the variety of spiritual approaches that would come years later under the New Age umbrella. "Man is a being born to believe," wrote British statesman Benjamin Disraeli, "and if no church comes forward with the title deeds of truth, he will find altars and idols in his own heart and his own imagination."[7]

But things were changing *inside* some churches as well. Many held firm in their convictions despite the trends, and in light of a Christian influence that would show itself prominently in the following decades (via the Moral Majority and the Christian Coalition, for example) one could hardly say the 1960s muted their voice. But other voices crept into some congregations and denominations as well. Once influential in society, they now, whether out of doctrinal weakness, a desire to please the world, or both, were becoming the *influenced* rather than the *influencers*. A choice was being made, and not for the first time. Either the church would hold to essential truths despite a significant cultural shift away from those truths, or it would allow the culture's new ethic to shape its own. And while societal rejection of its teaching doesn't prove the church failed, when the church, in response to that rejection, starts taking its moral and doctrinal cues from the culture, then it is, indeed, deteriorating.

Culture Influences Church

Since the upheaval of the 1960s, many religious leaders have unabashedly endorsed a rethinking of long held, biblically based assumptions, citing the need for guidance from secular resources. So Troy Perry, the openly homosexual founder of the pro-gay Universal Fellowship of Metropolitan Community Churches, had this to say when discussing the role culture plays when influencing the church:

> Scientific information, social changes and personal experience are the greatest forces for change in the way we interpret the Bible.[8]

Popular author and Emergent Church leader Brian McLaren seems to share Perry's view that secular disciplines trump—or are at least equal in authority to—the Scriptures. When discussing how the church should address homosexuality, McLaren told *Christianity Today*'s online *Leadership Journal* that he recommends

> "...a five year moratorium on making pronouncements" about homosexuality, during which we should "keep our ears attuned to scholars in biblical studies, theology, ethics, psychology, genetics, sociology and related fields."[9]

When prominent church leaders allow secular guidance to trump biblical teaching, then the world can rightfully boast of having become the light of the church, reversing the formula Jesus prescribed (*"You* are the light of the *world"*). Apologist Dr. Ron Rhodes notes:

> The culture-forming energies of Christianity depend upon the church's ability to resist the temptation to become completely identified with, or absorbed into, the culture.[10]

The late Dr. Greg Bahnsen is blunter when he asserts:

> When the church begins to look and sound like the world, there is no compelling rationale for its continued existence.[11]

To which we might add, when the church begins to look and sound like the world, three things are likely to happen. First:

Church *Avoids* Truth

That is, segments of the church show an increasing reluctance to take clear positions on essential matters, avoiding truth in lieu of unity. (We'll discuss "essentials" and how we can best define and address them in chapter 6, "Understanding Pro-Gay Theology.") In America, we find this trend in leaders and laity as well, attested to by pollster George Barna's surveys, which reveal a generally cavalier attitude toward truth:

> In spite of the fact that most Americans consider themselves to be Christian, very few adults base their moral decisions on the Bible, and surprisingly few believe that absolute moral truth exists.[12]

Those "very few" include self-identified believers:

> In 1991, more than half (52 percent) of born-again respondents sided with the secular culture in agreeing *There is no such thing as absolute truth.* In 1994, it was even higher (62 percent). Clearly, believers cannot present a credible defense of biblical truth when more than half don't even believe in real truth.[13]

It stands to reason, then, that the segments of the church influenced by the culture will adopt its insistence that there is no absolute truth. (Though, ironically, that very statement *is* an absolute!) Essential truths about the nature of humanity, God, and life will thus be avoided in teaching and ministry, leading to the next step:

Church *Minimizes* Truth

After all, if we can't be certain about salvation or the difference between the Christian spiritual rebirth and all other spiritual experiences, then how important can sound doctrine—absolute truth—really be? How certain can we then be about God's approval or prohibition of homosexuality? And even if we are certain about its rightness or wrongness, all truth supposedly being relative, how much can it really matter?

Paul, of course, saw the importance of sexual morality among Christians a bit differently:

I have written to you not to keep company with anyone named a brother, who is sexually immoral, or covetous, or an idolater, or a reviler, or a drunkard (1 Corinthians 5:11).

Neither fornicators, nor idolaters, nor adulterers, nor homosexuals, nor sodomites, nor thieves…will inherit the kingdom of God (1 Corinthians 6:9-10).

Fornication and all uncleanness or covetousness, let it not even be named among you, as is fitting for saints (Ephesians 5:3).

Former President Jimmy Carter sees it differently. Addressing the Cooperative Baptist Fellowship in 2006, he minimized homosexuality's importance, comparing it to other secondary issues that "in God's eyes, fade into relative insignificance, as did circumcision in the first days of the early church.[14] Grammy award-winning gospel singer Cynthia Clawson concurs, stating that her decision to sing at pro-gay churches is valid, because "Jesus never said anything about gay people. How important could it have been to Him if He did not mention it?"[15] And Dr. Robert Schuller, when asked about the sin nature in general, minimized its importance, suggesting it could actually be damaging to challenge people's love of self, even though Paul warned against it:

Questioner: Why should we do anything to encourage people to become "lovers of themselves" if Paul in fact warned others that that would be the state of godlessness in the last days?

Schuller: I hope you don't [preach this] because you could do a lot of damage to a lot of beautiful people…Just because it's in the Bible doesn't mean you should preach it.[16]

When biblical truth is minimized by a former United States president, an award-winning Christian artist, and one of the world's most renowned preachers, it's easy to see why it's also minimized in many local congregations as well. Predictably, the deterioration continues when Christian thinking is influenced more by this present world than the next.

Church *Revises* Truth

When Jesus addressed seven different churches in the book of Revelation, He took into account each one's unique strengths and weaknesses. So He rebuked the Laodicean church for its lukewarm state without accusing the other churches of being lukewarm, and commended the Philadelphians for their faithfulness without assuming all other churches stood as firm. He knew then, as now, that the faults or assets of one church differs from those of another, so most blanket statements about the church's condition won't apply to *all* of the church. Likewise, when we discuss the problem of churches who've been influenced by the culture, and who then avoid, minimize, or revise the truth, we're referring to *some* parts of Christ's body, not all.

Yet those "some parts" constitute a large and growing number of Christian individuals, congregations, and even denominations, who've not been content to simply avoid or minimize the truth. They've revised it as well, and on no topic is this revision more glaring and audacious than the topic of homosexuality.

"Gay Christian" is a label being adopted by many believers who privately struggled with homosexual temptations, made significant contributions to the church and society even in the midst of their struggles, then reached a point of surrender, saying, in essence, "I can't change my sexual feelings, so God must have intended them!" Every year another group of women and men join their ranks, and in the future we can surely expect more of the same. Examples include the following:

- Christian composer and singer Ray Boltz, whose song "Thank You" became a Christian classic when released in 1994, announced his homosexuality in 2008, stating that he had retired from the Christian music industry, fearing no one would accept him if they knew he was gay. But having attended a pro-gay church, he claimed to have found peace with both God and his homosexuality and has resumed his singing career as a gay believer.[17]

- Mel White, author, former pastor, and ghostwriter for Billy Graham, Jerry Falwell, and Oliver North, declared himself openly gay in 1994 after trying for years to change. He then began systematically confronting leaders of the "Religious Right" and eventually formed Soulforce, an organization committed to changing the minds of conservative Christians regarding homosexuality.[18]

- *American Idol* finalist Clay Aiken, already established as a pop star and an actor, disclosed his homosexuality in 2008 shortly after the birth of his son by artificial insemination. Referring to his Southern Baptist upbringing, he identified himself as a born-again, openly gay Christian who had not rejected Christianity, but only the traditional Christian position on homosexuality.[19]

- Marsha Stevens, who composed "For Those Tears I Died" (often referred to as the anthem of the Jesus Movement in the 1970s) was part of the music group Children of the Day in the '70s and early '80s. Her group played a significant role in the early years of Calvary Chapel in Costa Mesa, California, and under pastor Chuck Smith's leadership, she contributed hugely to the formative days of contemporary Christian music. After coming out as a lesbian in the 1980s, she formed BALM (Born Again Lesbian Music) and continues to perform at pro-homosexual churches around the country, promoting a "gay-friendly" interpretation of Scripture.[20]

But prominent heterosexual Christian leaders are joining in the revision as well:

- Jay Bakker, son of PTL founders Jim and Tammy Faye Bakker, pastors a New York congregation and is an advocate for same-sex marriage. In 2008 he traveled the country with Soulforce, visiting selected megachurches, hoping to persuade influential pastors to adopt and incorporate a pro-gay stance in their congregations.[21]

- Grammy award-winning gospel artist Reba Rambo-McGuire, daughter of the late gospel music giant Dottie Rambo, has, along with her husband, Donny, adopted the position that gay and Christian are compatible, and that the church's traditional approach to homosexuality is not only wrong, but damaging. In November of 2005, she and her husband participated in a worship service at Glory Tabernacle MCC (an openly pro-gay church in Long Beach, California) and closed the meeting by inviting any gay pastors who were present to come forward so she and her husband could wash their feet, while apologizing for the way Christians have "maligned God's work in gay churches."[22]

- Similarly, Peggy Campolo, wife of well-known author Tony Campolo, has spent years advocating for the pro-gay interpretation of scriptures); Anne Rice, author of The Vampire Chronicles and a recent convert to Christianity, testifies to both her newfound faith in Christ and her conviction that homosexuality is not only biblically condoned, but is a gift as well; and world-famous pop star and Christian artist Sir Cliff Richard has chided the church for not accepting openly homosexual ministers.[23]

All of this constitutes a revision of scriptures in both Testaments that plainly condemn homosexuality, along with a number of other sexual behaviors, in unmistakable terms. But the revision is a popular one, enjoying success among whole denominations, constituting some of the modern church's most vociferous, relentless controversies.

The 218th General Assembly of the Presbyterian Church voted in 2008 to delete the denomination's requirement that clergy live in "fidelity within the covenant of marriage between a man and a woman, or chastity in singleness." Whether the denomination as a whole will ratify the change remains to be seen as of this writing, but the general assembly's endorsement of it speaks volumes.[24]

Likewise, the Churchwide Assembly of the Evangelical Lutheran Church of America voted in August of 2009 to "open the ministry of the church to gay and lesbian pastors and other professional workers living in committed relationships."[25] On July 4, 2005, the United Church of Christ became the first mainstream Christian denomination to officially support gay marriages, when its general synod passed a resolution affirming "equal marriage rights for couples regardless of gender";[26] and the Episcopal Church's House of Bishops voted in 2003 to confirm Gene Robinson as the Episcopalians' first openly homosexual bishop.[27]

Some would call this progress; others might say it's a pragmatic way of adjusting to the times. But journalist Russell Baker's comments on progress seem more applicable to this particular and widespread revision of truth:

> Usually, terrible things that are done with the excuse that progress requires them are not really progress at all, but just terrible things.[28]

When we consider Peter's call to repentance on the day of Pentecost, when he insisted his listeners were doomed without Christ and there was no other way to salvation (Acts 2:14-40), we conclude the truth about salvation cannot be revised. When we remember Paul's call to repentance, made to the Corinthians when they were condoning open fornication (1 Corinthians 5: 1-12), we conclude the truth about sexual morality to be nonnegotiable. And when we read Christ's call to repentance, extended to the churches He rebuked in Revelation for their compromises (Revelation 2–3), we conclude that fidelity to truth, both in doctrine and behavior, is no more optional to a healthy church than food and water are to a healthy body.

Truth revised is, in the end, truth discarded. But if the revision of truth regarding homosexuality contributes to our current crisis, it does so in tandem with those who maintain the right position with the wrong attitude, manner, and approach. In chapter 2, we'll continue this two-part examination of the church in crisis as it wrestles with homosexuality.

CHAPTER ONE

THE CHURCH IN CRISIS, PART 1

○—KEY POINTS—○

1. The growing acceptance of homosexuality in both the culture and the Christian population constitutes a crisis for the church.
2. Truth—objective truth founded in and provided by the Bible—has been both *revealed* to the church and *commissioned* to the church.
3. For the church to effectively fulfill the Great Commission to preach the gospel and make disciples, it must know and affirm the truth about God, humanity, and life, both eternal and temporal.
4. America historically has recognized that truth can be found in the Bible. Accordingly, all aspects of culture were significantly influenced by the church and its teaching.
5. The turbulence of the 1960s brought about a shift in secular thought, by which large segments of the culture rejected traditional Christian teaching and turned to other sources for enlightenment and guidance.
6. Many churches began to be noticeably influenced by the culture as a result of the shift away from biblical authority in the 1960s.
7. A number of churches and prominent Christian leaders have *avoided* the concept and promotion of objective biblical truth.

8. A number of churches and prominent Christian leaders have *mini-mized* the concept of objective biblical truth, especially as it relates to homosexuality.

9. A number of churches, denominations, and prominent Christian leaders have *revised* biblical truth, especially as it relates to homosexuality.

10. When truth is avoided, minimized, or revised by the church, it will inevitably be denigrated, revised, and ultimately prohibited in the culture.

RESOURCES

The Light and the Glory by Peter Marshall, Revell Publishers, 1980.

The Great Evangelical Disaster by Francis Schaeffer, Crossway Books, 1984.

The Great Compromise by Greg Laurie, Kerygma Publishing, 2004.

ONLINE RESOURCES

"Christian History," www.christianitytoday.com/history.

NOTES

1. For a full treatment of Christianity's early role in American thought and development, Peter Marshall's book *The Light and the Glory* (Old Tappan, NJ: Revell Press, 1980), is an excellent beginner's source. *Christianity Today*'s online "Christian History" at www.christianitytoday.com/history also provides updated articles, timelines, and overviews of the subject.

2. Sources for quotations are as follows: As quoted in *Haley's Bible Handbook*, p. 18; L.J. Capon, ed., *The Adams-Jefferson Letters* (Chapel Hill, NC: University of North Carolina Press, 1959), 2:412; Alfred Armand Montapert, *Distilled Wisdom* (Englewood Cliffs, NJ: Prentice Hall, 1965), p. 36; Charles E. Jones, *The Books You Read* (Harrisburg, PA: Executive Books, 1985), p. 116.

3. Radio interview with Dr. Woodrow Kroll, "The Bible's Influence on Early America," www.backtothebible.org/index.php/Back-to-the-Bible-Radio-Program/The-Bible-s-Influence-on-Early-America.html.

4. Joanne Beckman, "Religion in Post–World War II America," http://nationalhumanitiescenter.org/tserve/twenty/tkeyinfo/trelww2.htm.

5. Beckman.

6. Miles Hodges, "American Government," www.newgenevacenter.org/03_AmericanGovernment/00_Introduction/00_Introduction.htm.

7. www.quoteworld.org/category/men/author/benjamin__dizzy__disraeli.

8. Troy Perry, *Don't Be Afraid Anymore* (New York: St. Martin's Press, 1990), p. 39.

9. "Brian McLaren on The Homosexual Question: Finding a Pastoral Response," Leadership Journal .net, blog; christianitytoday.com/mt-tb.cgi/43.

10. Ron Rhodes, *The Culting of America* (Eugene, OR: Harvest House Publishers, 1994), p. 27.

11. Greg Bahnsen, quoted in *Penpoint Journal,* June 1991, p. 1.

12. "Most Adults Feel Accepted by God But Lack a Biblical World View," *The Barna Update,* August 9, 2005, www.barna.org/FlexPage.aspx?Page=BarnaUpdate&BarnaUpdateID=194.

13. "Apologetics for the Church: Why Christians Are Losing the Culture War," cited in the *Christian Research Journal,* www.equip.org/atf/cf/%7B9C4EE03A-F988-4091-84BD-F8E70A3B0215%7D/DA311.pdf.

14. Cited in *The Record: A Newsletter of Evangelicals Concerned,* Winter 2006, www.ecinc.org.

15. Quoted in *Gay Christian Movement Watch,* http://gcmwatch.wordpress.com/2008/05/14/cynthia-clawson/.

16. From radio interview conducted in November 1992, cited at www.rapidnet.com/~jbeard/bdm/exposes/schuller/general.htm.

17. See www.rayboltz.com for details.

18. See www.soulforce.com for details.

19. "Clay Aiken—'I'm a Gay Dad,'" *People* magazine, September 24, 2008.

20. See www.balm.com for details.

21. "Punk Jay Bakker on a Mission from God" from *Times Online,* www.timesonline.co.uk/tol/news/world/us_and_americas/article4596825.ece.

22. www.soulforce.org/forums/showthread.php?t=275.

23. Respectively: www.mckinneyspeakers.com/speakers/Peggy_Campolo; "Mother Son Bond," *Washington Blade,* March 21, 2008, http://washblade.com/2008/3-21/outindc/cover/12278.cfm; www.religiousintelligence.co.uk/news/?NewsID=2764.

24. *The Christian Post,* www.christianpost.com/article/20080628/pcusa-assembly-approves-deleting-gay-clergy-ban_pageall.htm.

25. The ELCA and Homosexuality, from the Minnesota Family Council website at: http://mnfamilycouncil.blogspot.com/2008/06/elca-and-homosexuality.html.

26. "United Church of Christ and Gay Marriage," http://lesbianlife.about.com/od/spirituality/a/UCC.htm.

27. "Episcopalians approve gay bishop," CNN.com.us, August 6, 2003.

28. Cited at Quotes.net at http://quotes.net/quote/4695

THE CHURCH IN CRISIS, PART 2

by Joe Dallas

There has been grave error.
I do not mean so much error of
doctrine as error of emphasis.

—A.W. TOZER

Truth has been revealed to the church through the preaching of the gospel, the regenerative work of the Holy Spirit, and the Old and New Testaments. Having received this truth, the *ekklesia* (Greek for "church," meaning those who are "called out") is then commissioned to express and promote it, especially as it relates to God, humanity, and life, both temporal and eternal. These three aspects of truth are required elements for the preaching of the gospel to the world, and the making of disciples within the church body.

When those commissioned with biblical truth become influenced by sources that are at odds with that truth, they may err by either avoiding, minimizing, or revising that truth. In chapter 1 we discussed the downward spiral experienced by churches and individuals who receive truth and yet, when unduly influenced by the culture, tend toward all three errors (avoiding, minimizing, or revising essential truths) all of which are serious and consequential.

It is possible, though, to hold to the truth, yet still be in error. In this chapter, we'll discuss how many have rightfully avoided being unduly influenced by secular trends, maintaining doctrinally sound beliefs and positions, but have been wrong in their *attitude* or *approach* while being right in their *beliefs*. This, too, contributes to the crisis the church faces today as it seeks to address homosexual people and the gay rights movement.

Church Holds to Truth

Without question, even as large numbers of believers and denominations have been swayed toward serious distortions of essential Christian doctrines, there have always been congregations, denominations, and individuals who've steadfastly retained a high view of Scripture, and, correspondingly, of truth as well. Many have retained the right position, a proper attitude, and a responsible approach, fulfilling Paul's formula to Timothy:

> A servant of the Lord must not quarrel but be gentle to all, able to
> teach, patient, in humility correcting those who are in opposition,
> if God perhaps will grant them repentance, so that they may know
> the truth (2 Timothy 2:24-25).

But while damage has certainly been done by the watering down of truth, immeasurable damage has also been done when truth has been preached but not lived, believed but withheld, or spoken without love. In this chapter we'll examine these three errors in hope of recognizing, correcting, and avoiding them.

Church *Disobeys* Truth

"Do as I say, not as I do" is a message no responsible parent gives their child, for obvious reasons. One could hardly expect a child to respect, much less obey, mothers and fathers who blatantly disregard the standards they impose on their offspring. Granted, no one perfectly lives up to every ideal they teach, but in healthy families, parents will generally live in consistency with the values and boundaries they promote in the home. To do anything less would be to sacrifice credibility and, in the end, the ability to influence.

So it is with the church, which is commissioned not only to promote biblical standards, but to live by the standards it promotes. To do less would be, as with parents who "say but don't do," an abdication of credibility and influence. And here we must own, with all due grief, that we've fallen horribly short.

While a large percentage of the Christian population maintains the right position on sexual morality—that is, that any sexual contact apart from heterosexual marriage falls short of God's will—within that population, there's a scandalously high number of believers who are, in essence, "saying but not doing."

Consider some bleak statistics: 37 percent of pastors surveyed by Christianity Today's *Leadership Journal* admitted that cyberporn use was, for them, a "current struggle"; and four in ten pastors had visited a porn site.[1]

Further, a poll by Focus on the Family suggested that 17.8 percent of all "born-again" Christian adults in America have visited sexually oriented websites; 63 percent of men attending a marriage seminar in 2000 admitted to struggling with porn in the past year (two-thirds of whom were in church leadership and 10 percent of whom were pastors); and *Today's Christian Woman* magazine found that 34 percent of its female readership admitted that they had intentionally sought out pornography on the Internet.[2]

Pollster George Barna found the divorce rate among Christians to be essentially the same as among nonbelievers,[3] and Regis Nicoll nicely summed up the inconsistency of condemning homosexual sin while winking at such appalling, widespread moral lapses when he wrote:

> While evangelical Christians are known for their high view of Scripture, their acceptance of certain behaviors at odds with that standard has not gone unnoticed. As Robert Hart writes, "[Christians] have become more and more accepting of sexual relations that fall far below Christian belief in chastity, to the point where many churches accept unmarried couples, as long as they are not homosexual."[4]

"Thou Art the Man"

After King David's adultery with Bathsheba, and his subsequent indirect murder of her husband, he was confronted by the prophet Nathan, who told him a brief story. He described a poor man who had a lamb he loved very much, even to the point of treating it like a family member. A rich man with flocks of sheep was entertaining his friends and, unwilling to sacrifice one of his own sheep though he had many, forcibly took the poor man's only lamb and killed it to feed his guests. David, oblivious to the fact Nathan was detailing his own sins, reacted furiously, indignant that anyone would commit such a heinous act. And in one of the Bible's most chilling statements, Nathan holds up a mirror to the guilty king and pronounces, "Thou art the man" (2 Samuel 12:1-7 KJV).

Jesus expressed a particular hatred for hypocrisy. His strongest denunciations, in fact, were reserved for religious leaders who preached one ethic and lived another. (See, for example, Matthew 23.) That is not to say He didn't also speak against a number of vices, both sexual and nonsexual, and His teaching on morality throughout the gospels is strict and unwavering. But His revulsion toward hypocrisy among the religious is clear, and is echoed in Paul's rhetorical questions to those who congratulate themselves simply for holding God's standards in high regard:

> You, therefore, who teach another, do you not teach yourself?...
> You who say, "Do not commit adultery," do *you* commit adultery?
> (Romans 2:21-22).

And when describing the credibility gap created by hypocrisy, he notes:

> You who make your boast in the law, do you dishonor God through breaking the law? For "the name of God is blasphemed among the Gentiles because of you" (Romans 2:23-24).

A similarly pertinent question to many conservative Christians, then, might be, "You who say immorality is wrong, do *you* commit immoral acts? You who say marriage is sacred, do you yourselves dishonor marriage?"

Think about it. A high number of Bible-believing Christians are vocally, and rightfully, concerned about the prevalence of homosexuality and its widespread approval. Citing the sanctity of marriage, they protest pro-gay legislation, support laws prohibiting the legitimization of same-sex marriage, and decry homosexuality as a symptom of general depravity. And yet, among this same vocal group holding the correct biblical view, there's an epidemic of unclean behavior, ranging from the secret use of pornography to more blatant problems of adultery, fornication, and casual divorce. What must people think when they hear our pronouncements against same-sex marriage, then read about yet another Christian leader caught in adultery? Or when they hear us rail against the excesses of the "gay lifestyle," then read statistics citing the excesses of sexual sin among those who allegedly oppose it? Would they not, as did Paul himself, rightfully protest, "For this cause the name of God is blasphemed among the unbelievers because of you!"?

Holding to the truth is critical, and commendable, but only when it is held to in our behavior as well as our profession. It's even a good thing to fight, when necessary, for the truth. Yet the philosopher Alfred Adler reminds us that "it is always easier to fight for our principles than it is to live up to them." To which we should add, our failure to live up to what we've defended has severely undermined our credibility; a credibility that can only be regained when we show harmony between what we believe and what we do, both publicly and privately, because we cannot hope to influence a culture that sees us ignore the values we aggressively promote. So James, pointing out the folly of knowing the truth yet disobeying it, puts it plainly:

> Be ye doers of the word, and not hearers only, deceiving your own selves (James 1:22 KJV).

To do anything less is, indeed, to deceive ourselves. But no one else.

Church *Withholds* Truth

Dr. Martin Luther King Jr. made a pertinent observation about the church's role in the culture:

> The church must be reminded that it is not the master or the servant of the state, but rather the conscience of the state. It must be the guide and the critic of the state, and never its tool. If the church does not recapture its prophetic zeal, it will become an irrelevant social club without moral or spiritual authority.[5]

The conscience of the state; the guide, the critic, operating with prophetic zeal. To function in this way requires clarity. If the church is indeed the conscience of the state, then the state should be able to read clearly what its conscience is saying, since a conscience that is muted or nonspecific is virtually inoperative.

Plainly put, the church must hold, but never *with*-hold, the truth. To do so would be akin to a conscience withholding its message, rendering it useless. Here churches and believers should take note, as one of the greatest temptations for the modern church will be to shun its prophetic role when speaking to the culture about homosexuality. If current trends continue, the repercussions for maintaining (much less promoting) the biblical view will be such that many will be tempted to appease, rather than oppose, the normalization of homosexuality. And since that appeasement will constitute a withholding of essential truth, it will likewise constitute a betrayal of the church's function as the conscience of the state.

The Dark Side of a Movement

It's not a stretch to say there's an intolerant, heavy-handed element of the modern gay-rights movement that seeks not only to normalize homosexuality, but to also silence anyone who resists their efforts. And that silencing is already happening, internationally and domestically, with astonishing success.

In Sweden, for example, after the Swedish government added "sexual orientation" to its "hate crime" law in 2003, Pastor Ake Green was arrested and served jail time for preaching a sermon pointedly condemning homosexual behavior while commending love for homosexual people. (It's notable that the public prosecutor stated, when accusing Green to the court, that "collecting Bible verses on [homosexuality] makes this hate speech.") In New Zealand, a Christian video criticizing aspects of the gay rights movement and advocating a traditional approach to sexuality was confiscated and, initially, banned as "homophobic" and "damaging."

And in Canada, free speech was dealt a lethal blow when C-250, the country's new "hate crimes" law, was enacted, reading: "Everyone who, by communicating statements, other than in private conversation, willfully promotes hatred against any identifiable group is guilty of...an indictable offense and is liable to imprisonment for a term not exceeding two years."[6]

It would be nice to say such trends aren't seen in the Land of the Free, but they've been cropping up in America for years:

- In 1989 the AIDS activist group ACT UP (Aids Coalition to Unleash

Power) invaded St. Patrick's Cathedral in New York City while mass was being celebrated, throwing themselves into the aisle in protest of Cardinal O'Connor's views on homosexuality and, to the horror of the congregation, trampling on the consecrated communion wafer.[7]

- At Hamilton Square Baptist Church in San Francisco, when a conservative speaker known for his antihomosexuality views was scheduled to address the evening service, gay activists surrounded the church, physically refusing entrance to people trying to get inside, vandalizing the building, and terrorizing the worshippers. When the police were notified of (and, in fact, witnessed firsthand) clear violations of the law, they refused to intervene, telling the pastor who called on them for help, "You know, this is San Francisco."[8]

- And in Lansing, Michigan, in November of 2008, a gay "anarchist" group called Bash Back invaded the Mt. Hope Church, throwing condoms and other objects in the sanctuary, taking over the service and kissing in front of the altar, stating they were punishing the church for its "homophobic" stance.[9]

Small wonder, then, some churches are reluctant, in the face of these sort of disruptions, to take a clear stand, when taking a stand can cost so dearly. Years ago, one of the largest churches in Southern California invited me to speak on homosexuality. I accepted the invitation but, when discussing details with the administrator, I was told the pastor didn't want to bring me onto the church property for fear of gay protestors. Instead, they decided to rent a separate hall, off church grounds, so as not to antagonize gay activists. When I reminded the administrator that the church was private property and that they were entitled to host whoever they chose, he replied, "Yes, but we don't take too clear a position on this subject, because we don't want the gay community to think badly of us and cause trouble." The truth, a liability in volatile times, was being withheld.

Likewise, a professor of one of the largest Christian universities in the country asked me to speak on campus, then rescinded the invitation a week later when the university president told him it would be too much trouble if word got out that an "anti-gay" speaker was lecturing. (Even though that same university had hosted a group of gay activists, inviting them to come on campus—a Christian, Bible-believing campus—and present their views.) Hosting pro-gay speakers was safe; hosting someone promoting the traditional view was too risky.

The truth, though written into this university's code of conduct, was too risky to promote on campus and had to be withheld.

There is a place for discretion, to be sure, and there's no virtue in being needlessly controversial. Yet the cult apologist Dr. Walter Martin pointed out, "Controversy for its own sake is a sin, but controversy for the sake of the truth is a divine mandate."

The church has, at times, a divine mandate to be controversial for the sake of the truth. And to shun that responsibility is to say, by our silence, that truth is not valuable enough to take a risk for; not essential; and, finally, optional. And when truth is optional, it can no longer, with integrity, be called truth.

Church *Mishandles* Truth

There is, finally, the error of holding to the truth, obeying it as well as professing it, but *mishandling* it. Paul gives a twofold command to truth-tellers: "Speaking the truth *in love*" (Ephesians 4:15). It is good, but never enough, to simply say the right thing. It has to be said in the right way, from the right heart. To neglect this part of truth telling is to make the truth more of a weapon than a tool, and even the best tool, when misused, can be destructive.

Jonah was a prophet called to speak truth to the Ninevites, a people he feared and loathed. While the most widely known part of his story has to do with God's intervention when Jonah tried to get out of preaching to Nineveh (having been thrown overboard during a storm, he found himself swallowed by a large fish, from whose stomach he prayed and was amazingly delivered) a noteworthy part of his story has to do with what happened after he was expelled from the fish.

His message was one-dimensional: "Destruction's coming!" And having delivered that one-line sermon, he waited and watched, anticipating Nineveh's destruction. To his surprise and evident disappointment, Nineveh repented and God's judgment was averted. And yet Jonah, the prophet, seemed to resent their redemption. Here was a man eager to see a people judged, but loathe to see them saved. And while some might see Nineveh's repentance as a validation of Jonah's approach, it should be pointed out that the wrong approach may, by God's grace, still yield good results. But it remains the wrong approach.

When listening to many Christians talk about homosexuals, I can't help but wonder if the Jonah Syndrome isn't still evident today. I recall listening to a Christian psychologist being interviewed on television during the early days of the AIDS epidemic, telling the viewers that if they or someone they loved got AIDS through a transfusion, then they had been *murdered* by a homosexual, as homosexuals were to blame for the AIDS epidemic. In those days it was common to hear Christian ministers denouncing homosexuals with a contempt and vehemence they certainly avoided when discussing other sexual sins. And the "judgment of God" approach to AIDS was widespread as well, famously enunciated by the late Dr. Jerry Falwell, who said, "AIDS is not just God's punishment for homosexuals; it is God's punishment for the society that tolerates homosexuals."[10]

To his credit, Dr. Falwell later apologized for some of his intemperate remarks without compromising his basic position. Would that others had followed his example. Christian artist Shelia Walsh writes about a young man who contacted her when she was co-hosting *The 700 Club* television show. After inviting any homosexual viewers to pray with her to receive Christ, she said, "If you are a homosexual who just prayed with me, then please go to your local church and tell the pastor what you just did, and ask him what to do next." The young man did so, and was told by the pastor, "There's no room for fags in this church."[11] And in one of the most egregious displays of the Jonah Syndrome, evangelist and faith healer Benny Hinn announced during one of his meetings:

> The Lord also tells me to tell you in the mid-90s, about '94-'95, no later than that, God will destroy the homosexual community of America. But He will not destroy it with what many minds have thought Him to be, He will destroy it with fire. And many will turn and be saved, and many will rebel and be destroyed. [12]

What followed Hinn's statement was chilling:
The audience broke out into applause.

It's worth considering the effect this could have on any homosexual listening to the recording of that message (which is still available, widely played and referred to often). One can only speculate as to what a homosexual man would think about a group of Christians who broke out into applause when informed that he would be killed by fire. And one can only imagine what that same person would think the next time a Christian said to him, "Oh, I love you, really. I just hate your sin!"

When truth is mishandled, it's easily rejected. Worse, the credibility of the entire church is crippled when a minority of vocal Christians speak truth, but without love, reducing their message to the homosexual to a series of clangs and clashes from bells that were meant to ring, but instead, merely omit sounds that are utterly offensive and entirely ineffective.

A general deterioration is unavoidable when truth is disobeyed by its promoters, or withheld by its agents, or mishandled by the ones it was entrusted to. Whether watered down by believers who allowed the culture's influence to reshape truth, or expressed irresponsibly by Christians with enough boldness to rebuke but not enough love to weep for sinners, truth is ultimately denigrated in the culture as irrelevant or untrue; revised in a culture that comes to view it as relative and flexible; then finally prohibited by a culture that, as Paul predicted, will no longer endure sound doctrine (2 Timothy 4:3). All of which spells, boldly and bleakly, *crisis*.

Yet when revisiting President Kennedy's assessment of the word, we're reminded that only half of it symbolizes danger. The other half, opportunity, will be the focus of our attention in the rest of these chapters. Having assessed the crisis we find ourselves in, we'll now turn to a variety of authors and teachers who will explain the many issues related to homosexuality, and offer methods and insights to enhance our ability to express both the heart and mind of God on this difficult and critical issue.

CHAPTER TWO

THE CHURCH IN CRISIS, PART 2

○—KEY POINTS—○

1. It is possible to hold the right position in the wrong way, thus discrediting the position itself.

2. When the truth is *disobeyed*, its promoters profess a standard they themselves are not living up to. This constitutes a hypocrisy that discredits the church and the gospel.

3. Before the church can effectively address immorality in the culture, it must first address whatever immorality exists within its own ranks.

4. When the truth is *withheld*, its promoters withhold vital information because the information may be volatile and provoke controversy and opposition.

5. The church has a divine mandate to at times be controversial for the sake of the truth.

6. When the truth is *mishandled*, its promoters express the right position in the wrong way, and with the wrong attitude. Like the prophet Jonah, their opposition to a group overrides their compassion for the individuals themselves.

7. If truth is spoken without love, the speech will be ineffective and the truth will be ignored.

ADDITIONAL RESOURCES

God's Grace and the Homosexual Next Door by Alan Chambers, Harvest House Publishers, 2006.

The Homosexual Agenda by Alan Sears and Craig Osten, Broadman and Holman, 2003.

NOTES

1. *Christianity Today,* Leadership Survey, December 2001.

2. Respectively: Zogby survey conducted for Focus on the Family, 2000; *Pastor's Family Bulletin,* Focus on the Family, March 2000; From "A Woman's Struggle, Too," *AFA Journal,* March 2004, www.afajournal.org/2004/march/304pornography.asp.

3. "Born Again Christians Just As Likely to Divorce As Are Non-Christians," *The Barna Update,* www.barna.org/FlexPage.aspx?Page=BarnaUpdateNarrow&BarnaUpdateID=170.

4. Regis Nicoll, "The Mercy of Intolerance," BREAKPOINT website, January 4, 2008.

5. Martin Luther King Jr., *Strength to Love* (Cleveland: World, 1963), p. 64.

6. Mattias Karen, "Swedish Pastor Defends Anti-Gay Sermon," Associated Press, November 9, 2005, at http://abcnews.go.com/International/wireStory?id=1295029; http://www.hrc.co.nz/report/chapters/chapter08/expression03.html#10; "A Call to Prayer: Swedish Pastor Faces PRISON for So-Called 'Hate Speech' in Sermon," *Alliance Defense Fund Weekly Alert,* November 8, 2005.

7. Ed Magnuson, "In a Rage over AIDS: A Militant Protest Group Targets the Catholic Church," *Time,* December 25, 1989, cited in Alan Sears and Craig Osten, *The Homosexual Agenda* (Nashville, TN: Broadman and Holman, 2003), p. 117.

8. "Official Statement by Dr. David Innes," www.hsbchurch.org/riot1.html. "Gay Anarchist Action Hits Church," *City Pulse* (Lansing, MI), November 11, 2008,

9. www.lansingcitypulse.com/lansing/article-2302-gay-anarchist-action-hits-church.html.

10. Jerry Falwell, cited in http://en.thinkexist.com/quotes/jerry_falwell/.

11. Sheila Walsh, in foreword to Dan Wooding, *He Intends Victory* (Irvine, CA: Village Books, 1994), p. i.

12. Benny Hinn, transcript of 1989 message, www.sherrytalkradio.com/hinn/index.htm.

Homosexuality and Truth
A Time to Speak
by Paul Copan, PhD

*It is better to be divided by truth
than united in error.*

—Adrian Rogers

While I was in high school, I was first exposed to Christian apologetics. It was during this time that I began to realize that the Christian faith had excellent reasons for being true and publicly accessible (for example, the historicity of the resurrection of Jesus and the utter failure of naturalistic accounts to make sense of an empty tomb, the transformation of the disciples, the transformed picture of the cross as one of glory rather than shame). The Christian faith isn't a matter of our having a private conversation with God and no one else can get in on it. Rather, as Paul says to Festus and Agrippa about the Christ-event and Paul's own testimony, "This thing was not done in a corner" (Acts 26:26). I began to realize that the faith my parents had was one that I too could intellectually—not just emotionally—embrace.

Since those days, it's been sobering at least—and frightening at most—to observe how casually both the culture and the church are taking the concept of objective, verifiable truth and moral facts. According to the Barna Group's 2002 survey, 83 percent of American teenagers claimed that moral truth depends on circumstances; only 6 percent of teens said that objective moral values exist; and 75 percent of adults between 18 and 35 claimed to embrace moral relativism. The Barna Group concluded, "Thus, it appears that relativism is gaining ground, largely because relativism appears to have taken root with the generation that preceded today's teens."[1]

Basic Issues with Relativism

Relativism—whether pertaining to truth or morality—maintains that a belief can be true for one person (or culture) but not another. People tend to be relativists not because they've thought through their position, but because of a pursuit of personal autonomy. The atheist philosopher John Searle at the University of California, Berkeley, notes:

> I have to confess…that I think there is a much deeper reason for the persistent appeal of all forms of anti-realism [for example, relativism] and this has become obvious in the twentieth century: it satisfies a basic urge to power. It just seems too disgusting, somehow, that we should have to be at the mercy of the "real world."[2]

Nevertheless, this philosophy tends to assume certain unchanging truths in order to get along. That is, it's selective. People may be relativists when it comes to sex or to cheating on exams or income taxes. But they won't be relativists when someone steals their property or violates their rights. When I speak to certain audiences I suspect are relativistic, instead of telling them that objective moral values (real right and wrong) exist, I will ask them, "Is there anything that is wrong all the time for all people?" I'll get answers such as "Rape is always wrong" or "Racism is never right." Self-proclaimed relativists also consider their cardinal virtue to be "tolerance." Their absolute is, "Intolerance is always wrong." If they were consistent, they'd have to admit that they do believe in some absolutes. Relativism is completely inconsistent with the notion of human or civil rights, but most relativists will often trumpet "their right" to this or that.

But all in all, even the relativistically minded, when push comes to shove, recognize that tyranny, racism, and bigotry are really wrong. This can be the starting point for a fruitful dialogue. All human beings are God's image-bearers, and we are designed to function properly when we are living according to the way God has designed us. With that as a starting point, let's look at some "ground rules" regarding the promotion and parameters of objective truth and morality.

The unsustainable "You can't legislate morality" view. The "you can't legislate morality" claim is itself a moral one: such a thing *ought not* to be done. But where does *that* standard come from, and what is to be done with those who reject it? Indeed, we can and should "legislate morality" at a fundamental level—when it concerns, say, the safety and security of individuals and promotes the public good by preserving the fundamental rights of all. The rightness of legislating morality against rape, murder, wife or child abuse, robbery—or of outlawing slavery, apartheid, or Jim Crow laws—seems inescapably clear. We don't have to wonder "whose morality?" since we tend to have a good idea of these moral basics.

Legislating morality does *not* mean advocating "positive law," which equates the legal with the moral. These two are distinct: some things that are legal (for example, adultery, pornography) are immoral, and certain practices that had been (and in some places, still are) legal (for example, slavery, racial discrimination) are still immoral. Any recognition of human dignity and worth requires legislating morality. Indeed, such dignity and worth are not *bestowed* by human governments, but rather *recognized* by them. Rights are granted because of inherent human dignity, which has been granted by God, who made humans in His image. The Declaration of Independence gets it right in affirming that we have been "endowed by our Creator with certain unalienable rights." We can rightly wonder where human dignity and worth come from if no good, personal God exists.

The myth of neutrality. This is an important point that figures into the discussion on key themes such as abortion or homosexual marriage. Citizens cannot be neutral about these issues, and neither can the government. Indeed, the claim that the government *ought* to do something is itself a moral claim; it is not a neutral, nonmoral one. Regarding homosexual marriage, the government will either *support* the definition of a marriage as being a binding one-flesh union between a husband and a wife, or it will *not*. Regarding abortion, even if one is ignorant about the status of the pre-born, one cannot be neutral about the treatment of pre-born humans. To say abortion is permissible or up to individual choice because, after all, "we don't know the moral status of the fetus" is like a hunter shooting at something moving in the bushes before he finds out what's causing the movement.

The emptiness of the "right to choose" slogan. To say, "I believe in the freedom of choice between consenting adults" or "A woman has the right to choose" is a fairly empty and relative concept—like the phrase "to the right/ left of" something. The more fundamental question is, "Freedom to choose *what?*" Freedom to rape, murder, and torture babies for fun? No, choices can be immoral *or* moral. "Choice" is not morally neutral in itself.

When an abortion-rights interest group says that the government "shouldn't force its views on citizens," this raises the question: If the pre-born is a human being rather than just a blob of tissue, then permitting abortion-on-demand would result in the "forcing" of a view on an pre-born child—with lethal consequences. The "right to choose" is hardly neutral. It's often a matter of life and death.

Law and Morality

In answering the question about what should be encoded into law, there are dangers of overlegislation and underlegislation, and finding the balance is not always easy. Although I will try to cash out some of the specifics with regard to homosexuality later on, let me offer some general considerations here:

1. Where possible, we should try to discourage behaviors without criminalizing them. Laws, when possible, should be the second line of defense. Laws may, however, often reflect a lack of virtue within the state's citizenry. As the historian Tacitus (AD 55–120) wrote of Rome: "The more corrupt the Republic, the more numerous the laws."[3] At any rate, *we should be careful, rather than quick, to act through legislation;* forcing legislation through often produces a kind of legislative "victory" that tends to be short-lived. If a large portion of the population strongly opposes certain legislation, rather than ramming a piece of legislation through Congress, it would be wiser to *work incrementally toward a certain goal* (for example, banning late-term abortions isn't a full victory, but it has the virtue of saving more lives). After all, half a loaf is better than none. Christians should also engage in social involvement, the pursuit of justice, and public persuasion (for example, a wise use of the media to present factual information and the results of scientific studies about the effects of abortion on women) to make their case.

2. As citizens, we should engage in civil discussion or debate, seeking to persuade with public reasons aimed at the public good. Rather than simply asserting, "The Bible says…" or acting with a concern for a particular (Christian) interest group alone, we should offer public reasons for the position we believe should be adopted. This attempt at persuasion involves what theologians call "common grace," which allows Christians and non-Christians alike to pursue common goals for society.

Moreover, Christians should show concern for the *public* good. Part of this persuasion involves depending upon the Spirit of God and praying as we seek to change hearts and minds. And we should not ignore the redemptive role that the gospel plays in society ("special grace"), bringing about an accompanying transformation. Christians have often been guilty of depending upon government, political parties, and mere legislation to bring about social change and justice. Yet history has shown that Christians do not require political power to make a dramatic impact in society. In fact, power can often corrupt and betray us. The church needs to be the church, not a legislative body. That said, Spirit-filled Christians in a democratic society engage the public square, vote, run for office, and seek to serve the public good as part of their mandate to be salt and light. But in so doing, we must also keep in mind the limits of politics.

3. Citizens should remember three R's. I have appreciated the even-handed perspective of the Williamsburg Charter, which has sought to establish common ground with persons from different worldview perspectives in an attempt to advance civil discourse. As citizens, we should acknowledge the basic *rights* of our fellow-citizens without regard to their particular faith (or lack thereof). Rights entail certain *responsibilities* or duties to recognize the same rights for others. Finally, we should show *respect* for others through free, truly civil discourse, debate, and persuasion—rather than bullying, insulting, and distorting our opponents' position. We are to engage with tolerance, which implies putting up with perspectives with which we disagree. This will involve graciousness rather than deliberately trampling on what others consider their "holy ground."

Marriage, the Family, the Church, and the Government: Divinely-Given Institutions

Romans 13:4 states that government is to be a "servant of good" for those living within its borders. That is, it should administer justice, which involves punishing criminals (bearing the "sword"); the government has a divinely-given mandate to maintain order (1 Timothy 2:1-4 NIV—"that we may live peaceful and quiet lives"). Ideally, a good government will uphold the following:

- *A protection of basic individual human rights (life, property):* Each citizen should receive equal treatment under the law; this includes the pre-born and the elderly—and yes, homosexuals—and basic civil rights (not treating, say, racial or ethnic groups, women, or homosexuals as inferior).

- *A respect for privacy as much possible:* Sometimes certain legal encroachments on privacy may be required for one's personal safety (for example, random luggage searches at airports and other such inconveniences). On the other hand, not everything that takes place in the "privacy of one's home" should be left alone by the authorities (for example, child abuse, wife-beating, illegal drug usage). But government generally should avoid engaging in Big Brotherism as much as possible, all things being equal (for example, when not under warfare or terrorist conditions).

- *A respect for the religious rights of individuals and groups to worship (or not) according to the dictates of their conscience (freedom of religion):* The government should not favor or endorse one religion over or against others (a "sacred public square") or officially embrace a secular or "naked public square" (freedom *from* religion)—which also amounts to the government's endorsing one worldview or philosophy over or against another. Indeed, government can cooperate with religious groups (Christian, Jewish, Muslim, Buddhist) to help promote important goods for society at large.

- *An effort to preserve the integrity of important institutions that contribute to the well-being of society:* Historically, the family and religious structures have helped create social cohesiveness, community, stability, and reinforcement of values and virtue within society. So, for example, the government can encourage preservation of families by making divorce more difficult to obtain (as opposed to "no-fault divorce"); by helping to diminish abortion by insisting on the personhood of the pre-born; or by preserving a husband-wife marriage as normative rather than treating gay marriage or other marital configurations as legally equivalent.

Christian Political Involvement

Many at this point will recall the phrase "The Religious Right," a title generally reserved for Christians in general who have taken strong positions on public policy, and for well-known Christian leaders in particular who've influenced public policy, such as the late Jerry Falwell, Dr. James Dobson, or the Rev. Pat Robertson. On the positive side of the ledger, the Religious Right has had a zeal to change the culture rather than sit passively on the sidelines—something evangelicals in the more distant past had been guilty of. The Religious Right has recognized that political involvement (despite all of the baggage already mentioned) is a legitimate calling for the believer. Also, the Religious Right has made clear a desire to preserve certain important values such as monogamous marriage, the sanctity of human life, and religious freedom.

On the negative side, the Religious Right will often nostalgically appeal to "our Christian roots" or will press for "a return to Christian America." To outsiders in our pluralistic society, such language can appear quite threatening. (Keep in mind that Quakers, Baptists, and Catholics didn't exactly get equal treatment in America's early "Christian" days. In fact, far more Americans attend church today than they did during our nation's founding.) Indeed, this "call to arms" tends to play on the fears of many of the religious faithful who look at the culture around them and see noble traditions and common virtues slipping away. Besides *fear*, such appeals are directed toward retaining the reins of political *power*. Such grasping is wrongheaded. Although we are to be good citizens here on earth, our citizenship is ultimately in heaven (Philippians 3:20). We are first and foremost subjects of God's kingdom. Christians who put their trust in grasping or maintaining political power are engaging in idolatry. The Christian faith isn't some civil religion in which the state becomes a vehicle or instrument of the church.

Furthermore, the common perception by outsiders is that Christians are an interest group concerned about promoting their own welfare rather than the *public good*. They give the impression that adherents to minority religions or to no religion are second-class citizens and not participants in the nation's public life. Holding the controls of political power can easily corrupt, and church history reveals the damage and abuse springing from political power in the hands of church authorities.

Conservative Christians must be on guard against the temptation to trust in their *political activism*—achieving the desired results through legislation and having certain Supreme Court justices in place. In many ways, the church's role in society has been marginalized because of this fixation on political solutions to social injustices and societal decay. Rather than being change-agents in society, Christians have assumed that the way to bring about lasting change is to vote the right candidate into office. If we simply seek to promote our views into law without winning the hearts and minds of the broader culture, such victories will be short-lived.

Another problem among many conservatives is a kind of *moralism*—as some have said, "symbolism over substance." (This is often true of political liberalism as well.) This religious tokenism includes insistence on prayers in school, on the Pledge of Allegiance having "under God," on displaying Nativity crèches and using "Merry Christmas" (rather than "Happy Holidays") as a December greeting. I'm not necessarily against such things, but we must guard against preserving shadows of religion when the substance of religion no longer exists. How many politicians who advocate prayer in public schools truly engage in faithful prayer themselves? How many of them promote keeping "under God" in the Pledge of Allegiance live under the rule of God themselves?

The Prophetic Role of the Church

In 1934, theologians Karl Barth and Hans Asmussen drafted the Barmen Declaration in response to the increasing Nazification of Germany's churches and to the appeal of German nationalism:

> We reject the false doctrine that the Church could have permission to hand over the form of its message and of its order to whatever it itself might wish or to the vicissitudes of the prevailing ideological and political convictions of the day.[4]

Confessing churches must declare Jesus to be Lord over prevailing ideologies and secularly-motivated political commitments (whether this be the Green Party, the Peace Corps, or the Republican Party). While Christians should take seriously their responsibility as citizens, which may involve running for political office, we must inwardly detach ourselves from secular motivations and aspirations of any political movements that attempt to eradicate social ills and evils through political activism and legislation. Christians must take seriously the church's prophetic role in society, the power of prayer, and the role of God's Spirit in transforming hearts.

Many younger Evangelicals, it seems, are taking a somewhat different course by turning from a more compartmentalized way of thinking to something more holistic and integrated. Many hold the view that abortion and homosexuality are secondary issues (likely a reaction to the conservative politics of their elders), or at least as important as other issues such as racial injustice, poverty, and the environment. Many of these young Evangelicals believe that their religious predecessors have wrongly left social change in the hands of elected politicians or Supreme Court justices, and in so doing have abdicated their role as Spirit-inspired agents of social and moral change ("salt and light").

The solution, however, is not to treat crucial issues such as the God-given sanctity of life and the nature of marriage as *secondary*. Rather, we should robustly affirm these—along with other concerns—as important as well. Compartmentalization in the other direction isn't the solution!

Yet before listing any such public arguments or reasons about why this perspective is crucial and worthy of defense, I should emphasize that Christians should understand—and clearly communicate—that those engaging in homosexual acts are loved by God. Yet, as my pastor says, while God loves us as we are, He loves us too much to *leave* us as we are. This goes not only for homosexuals, but for every one of us prospective idolaters, who continually fall short of the glory of God. Christians shouldn't respond to homosexuality as though it is the worst of all possible sins or that Christians are superior because they don't engage in such acts. Christians also need to cultivate healthy marriages/family life before a watching world. Given the greater proportion of emotional pain found in the gay community (which other chapters in this volume address)—though I don't for a moment deny there are emotionally mature, well-adjusted homosexuals, we have an opportunity to embrace these fellow fall-damaged persons and point them to greater wholeness and hope in the gospel.

It's important that we avoid coming across as scolding ("You *ought* to see homosexuality as a problem"). In this spirit, perhaps it would be most instructive to raise key questions and challenge common assumptions to help highlight the importance of this monumental issue.[5]

1. The "No Big Deal" Legislation Question

Congressman Barney Frank (who is gay) asked: "What difference does it make to you if my partner and I get married? How does it change your life in any real way?" This is the perception many have, but the consequences are monumental.

Now if we're simply talking about same-sex "marriage," a lot of organizations perform "marriage" ceremonies that are not state-sanctioned—Episcopalians, Evangelical Lutheran Church in America, Metropolitan Community Church, Unitarian Universalists, Neo-Pagans (for example, Wiccan "handfasting"), and so on. The law doesn't prohibit such ceremonies from taking place, and gays can go on their way committed to each other for the rest of their lives. So in this sense, Barney Frank is right.

However, once the government actually sanctions and promotes same-sex unions as morally legitimate marriage—not merely *permitting* same-sex relationships in society (gay "domestic partnerships") as described above—then we are dealing with a different matter altogether. Contrary to Barney Frank's assertion, his idea would bring about *drastic* change. Consider how this would happen—in fact, is *already* happening.[6]

- As the law currently stands (as of this writing) employers, doctors, churches, insurance companies, and other institutions are free to recognize same-sex unions as morally legitimate or not (just as there are, say, doctors or hospitals that refuse to abort the pre-born out of similar moral convictions). A government sanctioning of gay marriage would apply pressure to require these institutions to impose the recognition of same-sex unions as morally legitimate marriages. *Adoption agencies* would be forced to allow same-sex couples to adopt children even though this goes against their moral convictions—or they would face the consequences of going out of business. Already, *companies* are forcing employees to sign statements, agreeing that gay marriage and same-sex relationships are just as legitimate as heterosexual marriage—on pain of termination.

- Should the majority of Americans (who do not believe that gay marriage is legitimate) be held hostage to minority opinion and activist judges (who typically *disregard* rather than uphold the definition of marriage as a union between husband and wife)? Should the majority be forced (under threat of various sanctions) to agree that homosexuality is legitimate? In Europe and in Canada, those vocal in their disagreement with homosexuality have been fined or (initially) imprisoned in the name of "hate crimes." In Canada, for instance, Catholic priest Fr. Alphonse de Valk was sued for articulating traditional Christian teaching on marriage, citing the Bible and the Catholic Catechism. Yet he's been accused of preaching "extreme hatred and contempt" against homosexuals.[7] Despite gay activists' ongoing appeals to "tolerance," their tolerance is only one-sided. They are doing their own politically correct version of "imposing morality."

- A landlord would be forced to rent an apartment to a gay couple even though he doesn't want his own children to be exposed to this lifestyle.

- Various Christian organizations taking a traditional, orthodox Christian view on homosexuality are being forced to allow gay leadership— or lose their tax-exempt status. Religious colleges that provide for traditional married student housing would be required to furnish housing for same-sex couples, even though it violates the institution's religious principles. In one instance, the InterVarsity Christian Fellowship group at Tufts University was "defunded" because it did not allow gays in leadership—although they were free to attend the group. (Can you imagine a GLBT group allowing a conservative evangelical to lead its group—or an atheist group allowing the same to lead its group?) Though the university later reversed its stance, the issue will certainly not go away.

- Certain denominations and ministries that have policies prohibiting gay marriages in their sanctuaries could be sued for discriminating against gays; these religious congregations would be required to change their policies and thus violate their conscience. Consider how Catholic Charities was forced out of adoption services because they were required by the government to permit adoption for gay and lesbian couples.[8] In 2007, a Methodist camp in Ocean Grove, New Jersey, lost its tax-exempt status because, out of religious convictions, it had refused to allow a lesbian couple to be "married" on its property.[9] In 2006, the *Seattle Times* describes a lawsuit against the YMCA (which the "Y" lost) by a lesbian couple for "sexual discrimination." The *Times* article underscores my point: "The [Washington] statewide measure would allow people, for the first time, to sue in state court, where damages could be more lucrative."[10]

- Public school students would be forced to receive sex education that condones homosexual relationships. On Chicago's North Shore (School District 113), students are required to hear *only* the pro-homosexual side of the debate in their curriculum—that homosexuality is biologically determined and morally legitimate. [11] In other places, students are not allowed to opt out of this kind of indoctrination, nor are parents notified about what is being taught. One couple in Massachusetts, Robb and Robin Wirthlin, fought against the school system that was teaching second grade public school children about gay marriage.

- A New Mexico photographer was sued for declining to take pictures at a lesbian wedding ceremony. A print shop was sued because its owners, out of moral conviction, declined publishing wedding invitations for a gay or lesbian couple.

- A doctor in California was sued for refusing to go against his moral convictions by refusing to offer "help" to an infertile lesbian couple. [12]

Again, these are not scare tactics. These changes are already taking place as this book is written. The future will undoubtedly bring about many more such cases of intolerance against those who hold to the traditional Christian teaching on homosexuality.

2. The Relativism Question

For many, marriage is just a matter of defining it according to what individuals want; it turns out to be just a social construction rather than a matter of human nature/design and how we best function and flourish in light of that design. The former approach assumes a relativistic perspective. This view is both self-refuting and undermining of civilization and order, and one wonders what nonarbitrary limits are to be set to prevent further innovative "marital" arrangements.

During the summer of 2004, I was listening to a radio talk show. A woman called in from Florida to express her own marriage preferences—to her dog! Why couldn't the state recognize *this* union as legal? Once we cast aside the time-tested male-female, one-flesh-union view of marriage in favor of marriage as individuals choose to define it, we have a grab bag of possibilities. Why not consider the following "marital arrangements" as having equal protections under the law?

- *Group marriage* (say, five men and three women or vice versa). Why define marriage as involving *two* persons "committed" to each other?

- *Incestuous marriage* (for example, a father and a daughter, a mother with a son, a brother and a sister).

- *Bestial marriage* (for example, a human with a dog, cat, or horse). Why think that humans can't marry nonhuman animals? This could be considered *speciesism*—inappropriately favoring your own species over others.

- *Pedophilia* (an older man marrying and having sex with a prepubescent child).

- *Polygamous* or *polyandrous marriage* (a man with multiple wives or a woman with multiple husbands).

- *Marriage to self.* A person may oppose "numbersism"—the prejudicial assumption that marriage must involve at least two persons.

- *Marriage with non-consenting adults.* Who says marriage has to involve consenting adults? Why not have a harem of sexual partners ("spouses") who are physically restrained from leaving?

- *Nonsexual marriage.* Why not call university fraternities or sororities or two brothers sharing an apartment a "marriage"?

- *Marriage to material objects.* Perhaps we can recognize a person for being married to his money, his job, and so on.

If the government doesn't recognize any of these categories to be considered "marriages," is that "unfair" and "discriminatory"? If marriage is just a socially constructed arrangement as a result of human choice and preference, it's hard to see how *any* marital arrangement can rightly be banned.[13] Why all the fuss about polygamy in some western states? The same kind of argument gays use to push revising the definition of marriage can be used to promote polygamy or any other marital configurations.

3. The "Loving Environment for Children" Question

We know that the husband-wife marital union has stood the test of time in terms of providing family stability. When the father is absent, for example, family problems are multiplied. Author of *Fatherless America,* David Blankenhorn, who himself doesn't have a moral agenda against gay marriage, has said in an interview that father absence is having a devastating impact on our children, creating "a whole range of social problems." He added that "if there is one thing in this life I know, it's that children need mothers and fathers." In this interview, he asserted:

> The first thing that would happen if we legalized same-sex marriage is that we would find ourselves talking about parents, not fathers and mothers. Even the term "parent" would be changed to something like "the person in the home caring for the child." That is not a definition in the long-term interest of children.[14]

Unquestionably, marriage is inherently geared toward reproduction (even if there are exceptions due to sterility or infertility) rather than needing to look outside for adding to one's family, which gay "marriage" necessarily requires. According to Linda Gunsberg's 1982 study, the husband-wife marital union, which has built into it male and female role modeling, shows that the inherently differing parenting styles of male and female are vital for a child's well-being and emotional stability.[15] It is well-known that single-parent homes are generally suboptimal (whether fatherless or motherless) and naturally deprive children of a stable environment, often resulting in social and psychological problems. By definition, children cannot be the natural product of homosexual unions, nor do they have naturally built into them complementary role models and parenting styles. Gay marriage would automatically deprive children of this role-model balance; it would idealize and institutionalize an inferior family structure. Yes, gays can be loving and caring, but that is a secondary consideration to what is in the best interests of children. As NARTH's amicus brief to the Hawaiian Supreme Court (1997) put it:

> It must be noted that if a move to create an entire class of permanently fatherless or motherless children were not attached to the issue of homosexual marriage, it is doubtful there would be a controversy, so overwhelming is the evidence of detrimental effect.[15]

Another significant factor that would undermine family stability is that gay "marriage" tends to be more promiscuous than heterosexual marital unions.

The most able defender of gay marriage, writer Andrew Sullivan, *presumes* that promiscuity and sex with more partners (that is, infidelity) can enhance the marriage connection between gays. The startling assumption is that openness to other partners is the norm. But one intuitively recognizes how damaging and destabilizing this is to a child's well-being. (Perhaps this point indicates that gay marriage is less concerned about the well-being of children than it is about sexual fulfillment and entitlements for the involved adults.)

Sullivan also mentions that the "openness of the contract makes [gay 'marriage'] more likely to survive than many heterosexual bonds." He claims that there is

> more likely to be a greater understanding of the need for extramarital outlets between two men than between a man and a woman... Something of the gay relationship's necessary honesty, its flexibility, and its equality could undoubtedly help strengthen and inform many heterosexual bonds.[16]

The potential damage to children is also acknowledged by Sullivan; he affirms that "the lack of children" gives "greater freedom" and flexibility to gay couples—that their "failures entail fewer consequences for others."[17]

Church considerations aside, as marriages and families go, so goes the culture. A society will be as healthy and strong as the family units that constitute it. If families are fragmented and dysfunctional, societies will be as well.

We must be careful about defining the ideal about marriage (or family) according to current cultural trends. Just because a third of all children in the United States are born out of wedlock, this is far from optimal. *Average* isn't *ideal* or *normal* (for example, the *average* temperature of patients in hospital beds may be well above *normal*). That said, we should give credit and support to abandoned (or widowed) single mothers who raise their children alone or to grandparents who raise their grandchildren without the help of (perhaps) deadbeat parents. Nevertheless, it is the traditional two-parent arrangement that helps provide an important balance that other arrangements (including gay marriage) don't offer.

Sociologist David Popenoe argues that fathers and mothers make complementary contributions to the lives of their children: "Children have dual needs that must be met [by the complementarity of male and female parenting styles]: one for independence and the other for relatedness, one for challenge and the other for support."[18] A child doesn't just need "parents"; she needs a mother and father, and must learn to relate to each in different ways. Maggie Gallagher argues in *The Case for Marriage* that cultures and communities die when the marriage idea dies out.[19]

Efforts by organizations such as NAMBLA (North American Man/Boy Love Association), which advocate pedophilia and lowering the legal age of sexual consent, should be resisted. Although NAMBLA condemns sexual abuse and coercion, it asserts: "We believe sexual feelings are a positive life force. We support the rights of youth as well as adults to choose the partners with whom they wish to share and enjoy their bodies."[20]

In a double issue of the *Journal of Homosexuality* (devoted to adult-child sex), one author approvingly refers to "social workers achieving miracles with apparently incorrigible young delinquents—not by preaching to them but by sleeping with them." This "did far more good than years in reformatories."[21] To make matters worse, the American Psychological Association (in its *Psychological Bulletin*) no longer views pedophilia as harmful.[22] There is even a (Dutch) journal, *Paedika: The Journal of Paedophilia,* whose premier issue began with the editorial acknowledgment: "The starting point of *Paedika* is necessarily our consciousness of ourselves as paedophiles."[23]

What is disturbing is the increased openness within the gay community about pedophilia and attempts to lower the age-of-consent laws. This, compounded by the much higher rate of sexual partnerships among gay men and the higher rate of pedophilia and child molestation by homosexuals, should raise warning flags about gay adoptions. Yes, many gays and lesbians can and do offer nurture and care to children, but this shouldn't be the basis for shaping public policy and revising our definitions of family and marriage.[24]

4. The "Scientific" Question

For those who appeal to "scientific backing" to support gay marriage, it should be pointed out that the very foundations used to promote the legitimacy of homosexuality have been the result of political power-playing rather than scientific research. What if it were known that the shift in attitude regarding homosexuality came as a result of strong political pressure rather than scientific research? Would this make *any* difference to our homosexual friend? Consider the 1973 reversal of the American Psychiatric Association's position on homosexuality: it had *nothing* to do with advances in scientific research to support the biology of homosexuality. In fact, prior to this time, the APA had listed homosexuality in its *Diagnostic and Statistical Manual of Mental Disorders*, believing that homosexuals needed treatment (often called "reparative therapy"). Its about-face was actually the result of strong political pressure from gay activists (the National Gay Task Force) to "legitimize" what was once considered a disorder. Even so, the APA vote was still far from unanimous. In fact, even in 1979, sex researchers Masters and Johnson said that homosexuals are "homosexually oriented by learned preferences," and, as late as 1985, declared the "genetic theory of homosexuality" to be "generally discarded today."[25]

We could point out the well-established point (though it is commonly ignored and even suppressed) that the "10 percent statistic" (based on Kinsey's flawed study) is false and that the gay population is more like 2 to 3 percent. We could ask: Does the corrective make a difference? If not, what if 2 to 3 percent, let alone 10 percent, of any given population, had a greater propensity for violence or alcoholism? What if they tended toward pedophilia?

The last question is not irrelevant. The same sort of unscientifically supported bullying has taken place more recently regarding the work of the secular organization NARTH (National Association of Research and Therapy of Homosexuality [www.NARTH.com]), which has effectively utilized reparative therapy to help persons deal with unwanted homosexual attraction—with numerous success stories in which many marry and have children. Yet activists within the APA therapy, as noted by NARTH founder Joseph Nicolosi (an APA member himself), have made scientifically unsupportable claims; such allegations include statements about the alleged "ineffectiveness of psychological care for those with unwanted homosexual attractions, that efforts to change sexual orientation are harmful and that the self-identified homosexual population has no greater rates of emotional disorders than the population in general."[26]

Despite the appeal that many gays make about science being "on their side," this isn't accurate.

5: The "'Born Gay' Sexual-Orientation Change" Question

This book will elsewhere note the evidence that people are not born gay and that same-sex attraction is not necessarily "fixed" for life if people are seeking change in the right way. There are well-documented cases (and I know a number of persons who have come out of a homosexual lifestyle) where homosexual orientation has been dramatically changed. This indicates that one is not necessarily "born that way."

We need to be clear that same-sex attraction—though not inborn—is also not a choice, but is deeply imbedded in the psyche. *Deeply*, but not necessarily *inextricably*. The work of NARTH, Exodus International, and similar organizations attest to the possibility of altering same-sex attraction to some degree and finding greater wholeness. Joe Dallas—an ex-gay, founder of Genesis Counseling, and co-editor of this volume—responds to the claim that even if gays change their behavior, they don't really change within. He compares this to saying, "A chain smoker may have stopped smoking cigarettes, but he still hasn't gotten rid of his cravings." Simply stopping certain activities may not go as far as one would like, but it is still a huge step forward. Furthermore, a person can move from saying, "I'm gay" to saying "I'm a struggler," which can itself bring significant healing. He can also make progress from seeing another male and having a strong sexual attraction ("whoa!") to a lesser reaction ("oh"); such steps are not insignificant. So it may be misleading to talk in terms radical and immediate "conversion" from homosexual attraction to heterosexual attraction—though we shouldn't rule this out—but rather a *decrease* of one desire and an *increase* of another.[27]

What some homosexual sympathizers call being "born gay" may be looking at things in reverse. Biology can be shaped by psychology! That is, our thoughts, choices, actions, and reactions—even if subconscious and established early in life—can shape the neurological patterns within the brain so that they become deeply embedded. Eventually this leads to a restructuring or transformation of the brain. These patterns help shape the direction of our lives, reinforcing thought patterns, habits, and desires.

Dr. Jeffrey Satinover of Harvard Medical School speaks of these bioneural processes that are shaped through habit formation:[28]

> The neocortex is the part of the brain that we might consider as the seat of the will…It is also the part of the brain whose connections between the neurons will be slowly modified over time, strengthening some connections, weakening others, and eliminating some entirely—all based on how experience shapes us. This ongoing process embeds the emerging pattern of our choices ever more firmly in actual tissue changes. *These changes make it that much more likely*

*for us to make the same choice with less direct effort the next time—and
that much more difficult to make a different choice.*[29]

Just because we're born a certain way doesn't mean that it ought to be affirmed—let alone that we're compelled to carry it out. We shouldn't make the mistake of moving automatically from "is" to "ought." What if people are "born with" a tendency toward aggression and criminal activity? What about those who claim their family has a tendency toward alcoholism? What if people have tendencies toward pedophilia, cannibalism, racism, rape, or substance abuse? Should we affirm this or seek to correct it?

Indeed, in December 2002, *The Archives of Sexual Behavior* questioned whether pedophilia is a mental disorder (why, it was asked, should the pedophile remain abstinent and deny himself at "significant emotional cost"?). *Tendencies* don't necessarily tell us how we *ought* to live. Presumed *explanations* for behaviors are not the same as *justifications* for those behaviors.[30] We know how we must regularly restrain our self-centered desires to do what is right; so if God has created us, we must live according to His intentions and designs for us—whether heterosexual or homosexual. Paul reminds the Corinthian believers that some of them had once practiced homosexuality: "such were some of you"; however, they were sanctified, justified, and washed, being enabled to live according to another, God-designed pattern (1 Corinthians 6:11).

We could add that the New Testament stresses the wrongness of homosexual *behavior.* Homosexual *attraction,* which goes beyond the direct control of a person, is not the issue. We reject the idea that homosexuality is a *status* issue, such as *race.* Homosexuality has historically been judged on the basis of behavior, not status (for example, "being gay").

Goals and Strategies of the Gay Rights Movement

The foregoing five points are some of the considerations that we should bring up to highlight the importance of the myriad of issues involved in the debate to normalize homosexual behavior. All of this brings us to the goals and strategies of the modern gay rights movement, and the challenge we have to respond to both in ways that are, above all else, Christlike.

While there are some homosexuals who struggle with their same-sex orientation and want to change, there are yet others who just want to be left alone and not stir things up politically—and there is also a vocal minority who make as their primary goal the overthrow of the "archaic institution" of heterosexual marriage or "radically reordering society's view of reality" or "transform[ing] the definition of family in American culture"—indeed, "the very fabric of society."[31] As the Ramsey Colloquium (a group of Jewish and Christian theologians, ethicists, philosophers, and scholars that meets periodically to consider questions of morality, religion, and public life) has put it, this movement "aggressively proposes radical changes in social behavior, religion, morality, and law."[32] This major goal is unsupportable.

One of the movement's key goals is to change the definition of marriage, departing from the understanding of marriage as a one-flesh union between husband and wife. *The standard definition of marriage should not be changed to include gay marriage. If, as noted earlier, we can tweak the definition of marriage as we like (based on feelings, being "born that way," and so forth), then why not include polygamy, bestiality, pedophilia, or group marriage?*

As mentioned earlier, such a redefinition will affect us all, including employers, religious institutions, medical doctors, and service providers who will be forced to either go against their religious convictions because of pressure from the gay community—or to close up shop.

Another issue is gays in the military (discussed in more detail in chapter 21). While I am not at all opposed to hiring hard-working, capable, respectful gays to work in a secular company, there may be situations where doing so may be a problem. One such matter is gays in the military. The assumption by pro-gay advocates is that "gays have just as much a right as anyone to fight in the military." However, as someone has put it, "The Marine Corps is not Burger King—you can't have it your way." The military isn't supposed to support a wide range of lifestyles as a kind of social experiment.

Rather, to be effective, it will have to weed out what will distract soldiers or naval officers. Surely it's a distraction if you sense your comrade has sexual feelings for you, and encouraging an open-door policy for gays to join the military would certainly affect recruitment. The military "discriminates" against those who are flat-footed, color-blind, and so forth. Not all Americans are fit for or have a right to serve in the military. As John Luddy argues,

> The clearest and strongest reason for the ban is to remove the influence of sexuality—not heterosexuality, not homosexuality, just

sexuality period—from an environment where the stakes are literally life and death.[33]

On the other hand, some goals of the gay rights movement are less ominous
and should be beyond the reach of government interference. Such issues include
legal sanctions or permissions for homosexual partners to have health-insurance
benefits for gay partners as well as hospital visitation (rather than "[biological]
family only" policies). While some may argue that there is a "slippery slope"
involved here, I believe such allowances do not change the definition of marriage
and yet allow the freedoms from government interference that both heterosexuals and homosexuals have a right to expect.

On a personal note, I have friends, relatives, acquaintances, and neighbors
who are homosexuals. All of these relationships can be described as mutually
warm, gracious, respectful, and so forth. I want homosexuals to know, first, that
they are loved and appreciated—not judged as inferiors or treated as outcasts.
Even though our stances may be dramatically different on this important issue,
I want to show them the love of Christ above all. I also recognize that many
homosexuals have experienced deep hurts; often it is written on their faces. If
we keep this in mind, we will be more effective at bridging the chasm that exists
between homosexuals and the church.

Speaking (and Living) the Truth in Love

The evangelical church that knows how to respond properly to homosexuality is more the exception than the rule. Typically, inquiring homosexuals seeking
a church home do not feel welcomed, and those struggling with same-sex attraction are not encouraged to confide in Christians because they do not feel safe.
Rather, they often feel singled out as the worst of sinners; indeed, they feel
condemned in an atmosphere in which jokes about homosexuals (for example,
in youth groups) are not uncommon. Religious groups like the Metropolitan
Community Church—despite their flawed handling of the biblical text—at
least get this right: They welcome homosexuals in hopes that they will experience the love of God. Evangelical churches should be doing this—warmly
welcoming all who come. They should be welcoming—and yet not affirming.
The impression that outsiders have about evangelical Christians is that they are
anti-homosexual—and the implicit message is that maybe God is too.

What would an ideal church community look like in light of the homosexual question? A few things come to mind. First, would be the cultivation of a welcoming atmosphere for all—homosexuals included—as we are all in dire need of God's love and grace. Second, a church should be a safe place for all sinners to come and investigate the claims of Christ and to find hope and healing. Those darkening the door of a church building should be aware that God loves them as they are—with their sin and doubts and fears—and that they do not need to clean up their act first for God to accept them. Third, the church leadership should set the example of modeling loving, pure relationships with homosexuals. Pastors should be preaching from the pulpit that homosexuality is not a worse sin than idolatry or adultery or greed (1 Corinthians 6:9-11), and those struggling with homosexuality—and any other sin—should feel confident that they can talk about this in a safe environment of love and friendship and accountability (for example, small groups, one-on-one counseling). Fourth, when Christians encounter homosexual activists, they should take the Dunkin' Donuts approach—breaking out coffee and pastries with kindness and grace—when there is anger and defiance. Rather than challenging gay activists in rallies, which often turn into emotional shouting matches, Christians should listen and love.

CHAPTER THREE

Homosexuality and Truth

○—Key Points—○

1. The gains of relativistic cultural philosophy have clouded a number of the issues surrounding homosexuality, the definition of the family, and the extent to which a biblical worldview ought to be promoted in the culture.

2. Relativism maintains that a belief can be true for one person (or culture) but not another.

3. Relativism must at some point become selective, as everyone believes there are some absolutes.

4. Regarding homosexuality and the law, we should try to discourage

behaviors without criminalizing them. Laws, when possible, should be the second line of defense.

5. As Christian citizens, when discussing homosexuality or other moral issues, we should engage in civil discussion or debate, seeking to persuade with public reasons aimed at the public good.

6. Christian citizens should remember the three R's: *rights, responsibilities,* and *respect.*

7. While it is correct to recognize America as a nation influenced by Christian principles, it should not be assumed that America is the church, nor that the legislation of moral codes can transform citizens into a moral people.

8. The normalization of homosexuality via the redefinition of the family will have long term, rather than immediate, repercussions on churches and families, and can be resisted using reasonable arguments promoting the public good.

9. Homosexuality need not be viewed as a secondary issue by Christians who place high importance on justice and poverty as well. It is possible and even mandatory to view all of these as critical issues worthy of attention and effort.

10. The church's role as a transforming agent cannot be overestimated, as the transformation of a human heart has more permanence and impact than legislation.

BOOK RESOURCES

When God Goes to Starbucks: A Guide to Everyday Apologetics by Paul Copan, Baker Books, 2008.

The Reason for God: Belief in an Age of Skepticism by Timothy Keller, Dutton, 2008.

Loving Homosexuals As Jesus Would by Chad Thompson, Brazos, 2004.

ONLINE APOLOGETICS RESOURCES

The Truth Project, www.thetruthproject.org. An online resource and seminar regarding basic Christian apologetics and the effective understanding and promotion of a biblical worldview.

"Reasonable Faith" by William Lane Craig, www.reasonablefaith.org.

NOTES

1. "Americans Are Most Likely to Base Truth on Feelings," 12 February 2002, www.barna.org/cgi-bin/PagePressRelease.asp?PressReleaseID=106&Reference=F.

2. John R. Searle, *Mind, Language and Society: Philosophy in the Real World* (New York: Basic, 1998), p. 17.

3. Or "Laws were most numerous when the Republic was most corrupt." Tacitus, *Annals* 3.27.

4. As quoted in Donald G. Bloesch, *The Church: Sacraments, Worship, Ministry, Mission* (Downers Grove, IL: InterVarsity Press, 2002), p. 275.

5. A few helpful resources on this question are Christopher Wolfe, ed., *Homosexuality and American Public Life* (Dallas: Spence, 1999); Robert P. George, *A Clash of Orthodoxies* (Wilmington, DE: ISI, 2001); see also "The Tyranny of the Minority: How the Forced Recognition of Same-Sex 'Marriage' Undermines a Free Society," *Salvo* 6 (Autumn 2008): 17-21; NARTH's Amicus Brief for Hawaii's Supreme Court (March 24, 1997), www.columbia.edu/cu/augustine/arch/narth.txt.

6. Unless otherwise mentioned, the examples given below are documented in Robert Gagnon's article, "Obama's Coming War on Historic Christianity over Homosexual Practice and Abortion," http://robgagnon.net/ObamaWarOnChristians.htm, accessed November 8, 2008.

7. Pete Vere, "Catholicism—A Hate Crime in Canada?" *Catholic Exchange,* June 4, 2008, http://catholicexchange.com/2008/06/04/112780/, accessed November 4, 2008.

8. Steve LeBlanc, "Catholic Charities to Halt Adoptions over Issues Involving Gays," *Boston.com* (March 10, 2006), www.boston.com/news/local/massachusetts/articles/2006/03/10/catholic_charities_to_halt_adoptions_over_issue_involving_gays/, accessed October 30, 2008.

9. "Ocean Grove Methodists Lose Tax-Exempt Status," *Lavender Newswire,* September 21, 2007, http://news.lavenderliberal.com/2007/09/21/ocean-grove-methodists-lose-tax-exempt-status/, accessed October 30, 2008.

10. Lornet Turnbull, "Sexual Orientation Bias Complaints Rare, Bias Difficult to Prove," *Seattle Times,* January 27, 2006, http://seattletimes.nwsource.com/html/nationworld/2002765036_gayrights27m.html, accessed October 30, 2008.

11. "Intolerant Progressive Educators," *Illinois Family Institute,* www.illinoisfamily.org/news/contentview.asp?c=34113, accessed November 8, 2008.

12. For examples of this activity, see Austin Nimocks, "Finally, 'Straight Talk' from the Gay Agenda," www.townhall.com.

13. But didn't the Bible permit polygamy? Did Jacob, David, Solomon, and others have more than one wife? In response, the spirit of Scripture seems to be that God *tolerates* such arrangements because of

human hard-heartedness. However, we are regularly pointed back to God's original design: "From the beginning it was not so," Jesus says (Matthew 19:8). Some of the points here are taken from Francis Beckwith, "Street Theatre in the Bay Area," *National Review Online,* February 26, 2004, www.nationalreview.com.

14. "Reasons for Marriage" (William Raspberry's interview with David Blankenhorn), *Institute for Marriage and Public Policy* website, www.marriagedebate.com/mdblog/2004_05_16_mdblog_archive. htm, accessed November 3, 2008.

15. As cited in the amicus curiae filed by the National Association for the Research and Treatment of Homosexuality (NARTH): see www.columbia.edu/cu/augustine/arch/narth.txt.

16. Andrew Sullivan, *Virtually Normal* (New York: Vintage, 1996), p. 202.

17. Sullivan, p. 202.

18. David Popenoe, *Life without Father* (New York: Free Press, 1996), p. 145, see especially ch. 5, "What Do Fathers Do?"

19. Maggie Gallagher, *The Case for Marriage: Why Married People Are Happier, Healthier, and Better Off Financially* (New York: Doubleday, 2000).

20. NAMBLA's "Welcome Page," http://216.220.97.17/welcome.htm, accessed October 16, 2006.

21. Edward Brongersma, "Boy-Lovers and Their Influence on Boys: Distorted Research and Anecdotal Observations," *Journal of Homosexuality* 20 (1990): 160.

22. NARTH, "The Problem with Pedophilia" 1998, www.narth.com/docs/pedophNEW.html, accessed October 18, 2006.

23. Cited in Jeffrey Satinover, "The 'Trojan Couch': How the Mental Health Associations Misrepresent Science," NARTH, www.narth.com/docs/TheTrojanCouchSatinover.pdf, accessed February 28, 2008.

24. See Gregory Rogers, "'Suffer the Children': What's Wrong with Gay Adoption," *Christian Research Journal* 28, no. 2 (2005), www.equip.org/free/JAH050.htm, accessed October 17, 2006. The failure of heterosexual couples to parent adequately isn't itself an argument for the superiority of homosexual adoption. Studies advocating the positive results of gay parenting tend to be biased, limited, anecdotal, and inadequate. Exceptions shouldn't be the basis for shaping public policy.

25. See Elizabeth Moberly, "Homosexuality and the Truth," *First Things* 71 (March 1997): 30-31.

26. "APA Leaders Respond with One Voice: Inclusion," September 5, 2008, www.narth.com/docs/apa leaders.html, accessed September 18, 2008.

27. These insights are taken from Joe Dallas's talk on homosexuality at Palm Beach Atlantic University (West Palm Beach, FL), January 24, 2008.

28. Jeffrey Satinover, *Homosexuality and the Politics of Truth* (Grand Rapids, MI: Baker, 2001), pp. 130-45.

29. Satinover, *Homosexuality,* pp. 135-36 (author's emphasis).

30. Thomas Schmidt, *Straight and Narrow?* (Downers Grove, IL: InterVarsity, 1995), p. 133.

31. Quotations taken from various sources. Citations (with documentation of sources) from *Americans for Truth About Homosexuality,* http://americansfortruth.com/issues/the-agenda-glbtq-activist -groups/pro-homosexual-media/andrew-sullivan, accessed October 8, 2008.

32. "The Homosexual Movement: A Response by the Ramsey Colloquium," *First Things,* March 1994, www.firstthings.com/ftissues/ft9403/articles/homo.html, accessed October 10, 2008.

33. From John Luddy, "Make War, Not Love: The Pentagon's Ban Is Wise and Just," *Policy Review* 64 (Spring 1993): 68-71; also, Gene Gomulka, "Homosexuality in Uniform: Is It Time?" *First Things* 30 (February 1993): 41-44.

A History of the Gay Rights Movement in America

by Joe Dallas

*You learn to like someone when you find out
what makes them laugh, but you can never truly love
someone until you find out what makes them cry.*

—Anonymous

E very conversation has *content* and *context.* The *content* is what we say; the subject we're conversing about. The *context* is not what we say, but under what terms we're saying it—the *nature* of our relationship with the person, the *history* of that relationship (short, long-term, good, tense), and the *broader social backdrop* against which we're having the conversation, all of which affect what we say and how it's received.

I see this plainly when I'm talking with my close friends. Over the years we've fallen into a pattern common to men. We express our affection for and comfort with each other through teasing and good-natured insults. So it's not unusual for me to meet up with a friend for breakfast and be greeted with, "Hey, you're looking brain-dead today. What trash bin did you get that sweatshirt out of?" And so the banter begins. Our years of friendship and ease with each other make it all fun, the context of our relationship allowing it.

But if I met a man socially or professionally for the first time and jumped right into that sort of familiarity, it would violate the context of the relationship (no history, no intimacy) and he'd be rightfully offended. Context matters.

Maybe that's what made the conversation between Jesus and a Samaritan woman, as recorded by John in the fourth chapter of his Gospel, so remarkable. The *content* of their conversation began with statements that seem, to the casual reader, insignificant. She's at a well; He approaches her and asks for some water. No big deal. But viewed in *context*, it's a very big deal indeed. Hebrews and Samaritans, especially male Hebrews and female Samaritans, didn't mix socially, a point she makes in verse 9.

Their personal and cultural histories came into play when they spoke, and that He would cross both cultural boundaries in order to engage her says a great deal, making the conversation a powerful one in both content and context.

That's the role the past often has in our present discussions. When we converse with a homosexual friend, co-worker, or loved one, the content of our dialogue matters, of course (and other chapters of this book will concentrate on what we should or shouldn't say). But the social backdrop of our discussion comes into play as well. This chapter, then, concerns itself with that by outlining a brief history of the gay rights movement in America, because to some extent (and often to a great extent) that history has already affected the thinking of the person you're conversing with, and whatever tensions, questions, or preconceived ideas he or she may have about you as a Christian. History influences attitudes, shaping or dismantling prejudices. So if our goal is to create and sustain an effective dialogue, it helps to know a bit of where our country has been regarding the subject, and how events and trends over the past decades have influenced the viewpoints of many homosexual people.

A Population, a Community, and a Movement

There has always been a *homosexual population*, made up of women and men who are primarily attracted to the same sex. At different times throughout history, that population has been visible but undefined, or visible and proud, or altogether unseen, depending on the country and the time. But the homosexual population has always existed and always will, whether it's recognized or ignored.

The *homosexual community*, usually referred to as the gay community, lesbian and gay community, or gay lesbian bisexual transsexual community (GLBT) is comprised of those within the homosexual population who choose to thus identify themselves, either to the public in general, or to a limited group, or only to each other. It is an identifiable group, though not necessarily to the population in general. Gay bars and clubs, for example, may exist in a community and be identifiable only to the gays and lesbians who patronize them, without the community at large realizing they are establishments that cater to gays. Or the community may have outlets for public identification, like gay pride parades, established pro-gay organizations, pro-gay churches, and so on. Often, however, many in the homosexual population choose not to identify themselves openly, so there are usually greater numbers of homosexuals in any given community than are visible.

The *gay rights movement* itself is made of both homosexual and heterosexual people who support the normalization of homosexuality in the culture and a variety of social and political goals toward that end. While its early participants were almost exclusively homosexual, over the years the movement has made alliances, generating support and participation from the general population at large. Whereas the homosexual community may be only partially visible and the homosexual population may at times be unseen, the gay rights movement is visible and self-identified. Indeed, visibility is crucial to the movement's success.

The three groups—population, community, and movement—may overlap, or they can be distinct from each other for several reasons.

For instance, many homosexuals choose not to be identified by their sexual attractions. Often called "closet cases" (someone who "stays in the closet" by refusing to acknowledge their homosexuality), they may be married, or fear the response of family and friends if they are more open, or they may view their homosexuality as a weakness or a sin to overcome. They may technically be part of the homosexual population, but won't engage with either the gay community or the gay rights movement. Likewise, some in the gay community may enjoy the social benefits of community without wanting involvement in the rigors of the gay rights movement, and many in the movement are heterosexual and thus cannot be part of the homosexual population or community.

What follows is a history of the third group, the gay rights movement, with secondary emphasis on the population and community, listing events that either helped define or advance it. (Some events listed will center on people or incidents that impacted the gay rights movement even if those involved weren't a part of it.)

To conceptualize the movement's goals at a given time, I've broken the timeline into three sections: *tolerance, normalization,* and *conformity.* I believe that while the general and unchanging goal of the movement has been to destigmatize homosexuality and secure certain rights and freedoms for homosexuals, there have been accompanying goals that have shifted with the times. So initially, the goal of securing *tolerance* for homosexual people through fair treatment and protection from violence and ostracizing was a goal. That evolved, in the mid to late 1960s, into efforts to see the culture not only tolerate but eventually *normalize* homosexuality. And that, in turn, segued into the demand for the culture to adopt a uniformly pro-gay viewpoint, and for different levels of discomfort or even retaliation to be meted out to those who don't conform.

Analyzing any movement's goals is speculative at best, since members of a movement have their own unique priorities and opinions. So if you ask 20 feminists what the goals of the women's movement are, you're likely to hear some common themes—gender equality, for example—with differing priorities. Some will say reproductive rights are their main concern; others will say equal pay and child care top the list. And so it is with the gay rights movement. Some of its members will cite same-sex marriage as their top priority; others will focus on a cure for AIDS; still others will insist antidiscrimination laws matter the most, so any attempt to say what a movement is about will fall short. Still, this brief overview will hopefully give the reader an improved understanding of the history, tactics, and success of the gay rights movement, and how each has played into both the thinking and experience of homosexual people.

1920–1970
A Call for Tolerance

In earlier times, to be homosexual meant to live with a secret that could easily destroy your life if it became known. Psychiatry said you were sick, the law said you were criminal, and if people said anything at all about you, it was often said in the hushed tones we use when describing the unspeakable. This was especially true up until the late '60s, and still largely the case even by 1970. So by any standards, life was hard for someone attracted to the same sex.

1948. *Sexual Behavior in the Human Male* is released by sexologist Alfred Kinsey, introducing the novel and, to some, very alarming idea that homosexuality was much more widely practiced, and homosexual people more common than most people realized. (The notion that 10 percent of the male population is homosexual was one of many conclusions drawn, erroneously, from Kinsey's work.) For decades his methodology and conclusions would come under fire, and to this day there's considerable disagreement as to how accurately he portrayed male sexuality.[1] (For more theories of the origin of homosexuality, see chapters 9 and 10 of this book.)

1951. The Mattachine Society is formed by Harry Hay, a man often referred to as the father of the gay rights movement. While the Society for Human Rights in Chicago came first, Mattachine was America's first *national* gay rights organization. Hay later described the choice of the organization's name:

> One masque group was known as the "Société Mattachine." These societies, lifelong secret fraternities of unmarried townsmen who never performed in public unmasked, were dedicated to going out into the countryside and conducting dances and rituals during the Feast of Fools, at the Vernal Equinox. Sometimes these dance rituals, or masques, were peasant protests against oppression—with the maskers, in the people's name, receiving the brunt of a given lord's vicious retaliation. So we took the name Mattachine because we felt that we 1950s Gays were also a masked people, unknown and anonymous, who might become engaged in morale building and helping ourselves and others, through struggle, to move toward total redress and change.[2]

1956. The Daughters of Bilitis, the nation's first lesbian activist group, is formed in San Francisco. The group joined forces with the male Mattachine Society to publish *ONE* magazine, the official standard-bearer of what was at that time called the "homophile movement." The group's name was taken from Pierre Louÿs's 1894 erotic poem cycle *Songs of Bilitis*.[3]

1967. In September, the first issue of *The Advocate*—a magazine targeted to homosexual readers—sells out all 300 12-page copies. Though initially having the feel of an underground paper because of its content and target audience, it will become the nation's leading pro-homosexual publication, eventually featuring interviews with the country's top celebrities and political/cultural leaders.[4] *The Advocate* is still in circulation today and has been mainstreamed into the culture, readily sold in large chain bookstores and other places where magazines are available.

1968. The Universal Fellowship of Metropolitan Community Churches holds its first meeting, establishing the first openly pro-gay denomination. On October 6, 1968, 12 people responded to an ad placed in *The Advocate* inviting them to worship in a newly formed church for homosexuals. The ad was placed by a 28-year-old former Pentecostal minister named Troy Perry. Nearly 40 years later, Reverend Perry is still one of the gay Christian movement's most influential leaders. As such, he is of interest to anyone hoping to understand pro-gay Christians.

The denomination Perry founded that October afternoon—the Universal Fellowship of Metropolitan Community Churches (UFMCC)—is, by his own claim, "the largest organization touching the lives of gays and lesbians in the world."

Nearly 300 UFMCC congregations exist worldwide, and with social and political action encouraged among its members, Perry's claim about UFMCC's influence is probably true.[5] (For more on pro-gay theology, see chapter 6 of this book.)

1969. The Stonewall Riots marked the official birth of a movement. In the early morning hours of June 28, nine plainclothes detectives entered a gay bar in New York's Greenwich Village called the Stonewall Inn. Intending to close the bar for selling liquor without a license, they ejected the nearly 200 patrons who were inside, then arrested the bartender, three transvestite customers, and a doorman. But when they escorted their charges outside, they found that an angry crowd had gathered on the sidewalk. Someone—exactly who and why are matters of discussion to this day—threw something at them, and within minutes the crowd, which eventually swelled to nearly 400, also began hurling rocks and bottles at the police. The officers retreated and barricaded themselves in the bar until backup enforcements arrived, and within 45 minutes the rioting stopped.

The scene repeated itself the next night when another crowd gathered outside the Stonewall, chanting "Legalize gay bars!" and "Gay is good!" Fires were started, and bottles were again thrown at police who battled with the demonstrators for two hours before they finally dispersed. Four nights later, yet another crowd—this one nearly 500 strong—took to the streets in Greenwich Village, marching and shouting slogans.

By then, many homosexuals saw themselves as a mistreated minority. Too often they were right. Assaulted for no other reason than the sheer prejudice of people who hated them, ignored at times in the legal process, and sometimes unreasonably harassed by police, they were, collectively, angry. The Stonewall riots gave public expression to their pent-up anger; the public expression, in turn, inspired a new defiance among gays.

Immediately after the rioting, homosexual activist groups began forming, first in New York, then nationwide. Plans for future demonstrations, political action, and cultural reform began to take shape. Within months, Gay Power (a term birthed shortly after Stonewall) took its place alongside its cousins of the '60s: Flower Power, Power to the People, and Black Power, and to this day, Stonewall is commemorated as the birth of the gay rights movement as we know it.[6]

How this period could affect the experience and attitude of a homosexual person today. Between 1920 and 1970 homosexual people were recognized in almost exclusively negative terms. Hiding, furtiveness, and public disdain were facts of life for most if not all, and the call for tolerance was often met with dismissal or violence, creating, in the minds of many homosexuals, an "us versus them" mentality that would prevail, in some cases, for decades. The pent-up anger unleashed during the Stonewall riots testifies to this, and to some extent continues to fuel the resentment you encounter when conversing with a gay man or lesbian woman.

1971–1985
A Push for Normalization

"Gay Pride" was a new and novel concept. Instead of asking for mere acceptance as fellow human beings, the movement, in the spirit of the other social movements of the time, was making demands rather than requests. The new tone was more defiant; less apologetic, as though gays and lesbians were collectively saying, "We've nothing to apologize for, we've suffered discrimination and ill treatment, and we're demanding that it stop." A refusal to accept classifications like "sick" or "sinful" would accompany this new tone.

1971. Colorado, Hawaii, Idaho, and Oregon repeal sodomy laws. Several states will follow suit; legal challenges from both pro- and anti-homosexual groups will follow, culminating in two landmark Supreme Court decisions: *Bowers v. Hardwick* in 1986, which will uphold a state's right to criminalize sodomy, and 2003's *Lawrence v. Texas*, in which the court will reverse itself by declaring antisodomy laws to be unconstitutional.

1971. In the spirit of Stonewall aggression, a new gay militant group called The Gay Raiders began campaigning against television networks to feature and discuss gay people on the air. They disrupted various programs including the *CBS Evening News*, a full decade before groups like ACT UP (AIDS Coalition to Unleash Power) or GLAAD (Gay & Lesbian Alliance Against Defamation) would come to prominence through similar widespread tactics.[7]

1972. In a made-for-TV movie titled *That Certain Summer*, an American housewife (Hope Lange) loses her husband (Hal Holbrook) to a young artist (Martin Sheen). While falling short of being an advocacy piece, it introduces what was at the time a hugely controversial, delicate subject. Eventually more made-for-TV movies were aired, including *A Question of Love*, starring Gena Rowlands and Jane Alexander; *An Early Frost*, starring Aidan Quinn; *And The Band Played On*, starring Richard Gere; *Tales of the City*, featuring Olympia Dukakis; and *Prayers for Bobby*, starring Sigourney Weaver. Major feature films followed, including: *Victor/Victoria*, starring Julie Andrews; *Making Love*, starring Harry Hamlin; *Longtime Companion*, starring Bruce Davison; *Philadelphia*, starring Tom Hanks; *The Hours*, starring Meryl Streep; *Milk*, starring Sean Penn. These movies provided powerful cinematic messages advocating the acceptance of homosexuality and criticizing the traditional view of sexuality as being outdated, ignorant, and dangerous. At times these films will be compared, in their ability to sway public opinion, to Sidney Poitier's *Guess Who's Coming to Dinner?*—a 1967 film poignantly decrying discrimination against a racially mixed couple.

1973. The American Psychiatric Association declassifies homosexuality as a disorder, thus declaring it no longer "abnormal." Prior to this, *The Diagnostic* *and Statistical Manual* (the APA's official list of disorders, originally compiled in 1952) had listed homosexuality as a sociopathic personality disturbance in its first version. The second version—DSM II—moved homosexuality from the category of personality disturbances to that of sexual deviations in 1968.

What had happened was that gay leaders began protesting the annual conventions of the American Psychiatric Association, demanding a reconsideration of homosexuality's diagnostic status, and further demanding that they be included in any future discussions within the APA on the subject. The APA consented; intense discussion and debate followed.

On December 15, 1973, the Board of Trustees of the APA, concluding months of negotiations with gay activists, voted to delete homosexuality altogether from the DSM. Opposition from several psychiatrists immediately followed. A referendum on the Board's decision was called, and in the spring of 1974, the entire membership of the APA was polled for their support or rejection of the Board's decision. Out of 10,000 voting members, nearly 40 percent opposed the Board's decision to normalize homosexuality. Though the 40 percent were clearly a minority, and the decision was upheld, it showed how deeply divided the APA was on the matter.

The American Psychiatric Association, like the American Psychological Association, has since aligned itself heavily with gay causes, furthering the impression among many that psychiatrists and psychologists in America generally view homosexuality as normal.[8] (For more on homosexuality and psychiatry, see chapter 8.)

1973. Parents of Gays, which will eventually become Parents and Friends of Lesbians and Gays (PFLAG) holds its first meeting in New York City at the Methodist church in Greenwich Village. Twenty people attend, and within decades the group will become one of the gay rights movement's most influential advocates for public policy changes.[9]

1976. During his campaign, presidential candidate Jimmy Carter commits to issuing executive orders banning discrimination against gays and lesbians in the military, housing, employment, and immigration. From his presidency on, gay rights will be a divisive forefront issue whenever a presidential candidate's intended domestic policies are discussed.[10]

1976. Exodus International, the largest network of Christian ministries addressing homosexuality from a traditional perspective, was birthed when a handful of small support-group ministries offering help to women and men conflicted about their homosexuality decide to meet for a time of mutual support and encouragement. The ministries formed a nonprofit corporation dedicated to equipping churches to minister to homosexuals, and to providing redemptive ministries to homosexuals and their families as well.

As of this writing, 234 member ministries exist around the world, the remainder of the network being comprised of professional counselors and local parachurch ministries, and for obvious reasons Exodus would find itself in varying degrees of clashes with the gay rights movement.[11] (For more on ministering to homosexuals, see chapters 11 and 12 of this book.)

1977. The Anita Bryant campaign in Dade County, Florida, had its origin when, in January 1977, the board of commissioners of that county approved an ordinance prohibiting discrimination based on sexual orientation. Local Christian leaders opposed the ordinance, seeing it as an official endorsement of homosexuality. One of them was Anita Bryant, a 37-year-old popular singer, author, and Miss America contestant. When asked to spearhead a campaign to repeal the Dade County ordinance, she accepted. She announced her intentions and began mobilizing support, and the press stepped up its coverage of her efforts, with good reason.

While Dade County's gay rights ordinance was not unique (similar laws were already on the books in other states), it was the first one officially opposed by a celebrity figure. Miss Bryant was interviewed and editorialized by newspapers, magazines, and network television.

Despite considerable pro-gay efforts, in June 1977 the voters in Dade County repealed the gay rights ordinance by a 69 percent to 30 percent margin. The battle over Dade County, though, was far from over. It simply transferred itself to cities across the nation, where similar gay rights ordinances were being considered, debated, and voted on. In a sense, the Anita Bryant campaign was a turning point for Christians and gays.

It marked a new awareness, among Christians, of homosexuality and the demands of the gay rights movement. Just as Bryant had, in her words, a "live and let live" attitude until the Dade County ordinance forced her to take a stand, so the church, in the aftermath of Dade County's battle, realized that a "great transformation" had taken place in the homosexual movement. As

Dr. Ronald Bayer, author of *Homosexuality and American Psychiatry*, commented years later:

> No longer content with mere tolerance, gay activist groups sought social acceptance, and the legitimization of homosexuality as an alternative sexual orientation.[12]

1978. Harvey Milk, an open homosexual, is assassinated by former San Francisco City Supervisor Dan White, who also kills Mayor George Moscone. One year earlier Milk had been elected to the San Francisco Board of Supervisors, where both he and Moscone had clashed with White on a number of issues. Milk had also played a high-profile role in defeating Sen. John Briggs's California Initiative Proposition 6, which would have prohibited public school teachers from any words or actions that could be construed as advocacy of homosexuality. Milk's death would largely be viewed as martyrdom for the gay rights movement.

Though White confessed to shooting both Milk and Moscone deliberately, a jury found him guilty of voluntary manslaughter instead of murder and sentenced him to seven years' imprisonment. This light sentencing would spark violent protests, and White himself, upon release in 1986, would commit suicide.[13]

1980. While Exodus International had formed as a network for primarily Protestant groups, there still remained the need for support among Catholics whose sexuality was at odds with their faith. By 1980, the late Terence Cardinal Cooke of New York decided to form a spiritual support system which would assist men and women with same-sex attractions in living chaste lives in fellowship, truth, and love. Fr. John Harvey was chosen to lead this new effort, named the Courage Apostolate at its first meeting in September 1980 at the Shrine of Mother Seton in South Ferry.[14]

1980. A U.S. district court judge orders the Army to reinstate Sergeant Leonard Matlovich, who was dishonorably discharged in the mid 1970s for disclosing his homosexuality to a superior officer. The resulting efforts of Matlovich to challenge the armed forces' ban on homosexuals serving are widely publicized and become part of a decades-long effort to overturn the military ban.[15] (For more on gays in the military, see chapter 21.)

1981. The first cases of AIDS are found in homosexual men in New York and Los Angeles. Referred to at the time as GRID (Gay Related Immune Deficiency), little is known of the condition that will soon decimate thousands and galvanize the gay rights movement as perhaps nothing in history to that point had done.[16] (For more on AIDS, see chapter 26.)

1984. The virus causing AIDS is identified, paving the way for testing and diagnosis. American researchers announce the discovery of HTLV-3 shortly after French scientists claim that AIDS is caused by LAV. The viruses turn out to be the same and are later called HIV.

1985. Movie star Rock Hudson dies from AIDS. When Hudson had his publicist announce his AIDS diagnosis, a public and deeply beloved face was put onto the issue. Many moviegoers of prior generations were shocked to learn of Hudson's homosexuality; most were saddened and sympathetic to his plight as a man grappling with the final stages of AIDS. The ripple effect on public awareness would be immeasurable.[17] (For more on AIDS, see chapter 26 of this book.)

How this period could affect the experience and attitude of a homosexual person today. From 1970 to 1986, much headway was made as the gay rights movement began to develop alliances with the media, the educational institution, and the entertainment industry. Many of the goals achieved during this period can and should be attributed to these alliances, which account for the strong bond forged between the gay community and these institutions—media, education, and entertainment—to this day. And the subsequent adversarial attitudes many conservative Christians sense from these institutions comes largely from their historical bonds and loyalties to the gay community, loyalties that make those who oppose homosexuality appear as adversaries to those institutions that so openly and enthusiastically support them. The conservative church came to be seen as the enemy of the gay rights movement and of gays themselves, an enmity creating tensions and preconceptions that commonly exist between gays and Christians when they interact.

1986–2008
A Demand for Conformity

As more of the country was shifting, however slowly, to a pro-homosexual position (that is, homosexuality is not immoral or unnatural; gays and lesbians should be protected from all forms of discrimination; churches should stop teaching homosexuality is a sin), the gay rights movement showed less tolerance for those who resisted the shift. At times comparisons between this movement and the French Revolution became hard to resist, as one remembers the initial goals of Liberty and Fraternity among the French, then the vindictive, unreasonable intolerance displayed for anyone questioning the Revolution's purity. It was no longer enough to adopt a live-and-let-live attitude. A uniformity in public opinion and expressions about homosexuality was more and more in demand, even as some major glitches were still being experienced.

1986. The U.S. Supreme Court rules antisodomy laws constitutional, allowing states to continue making homosexual behavior illegal. On June 30, the U.S. Supreme Court releases its 5-to-4 decision. The decision becomes a rallying point for gay rights, triggering renewed protests and activism in the movement.[18]

1986. The AIDS Coalition to Unleash Power (ACT UP) is birthed in New York City, giving "in your face" gay militancy a lean new look. Founded by playwright Larry Kramer, the group refers to itself as "a diverse, non-partisan group of individuals united in anger and committed to direct action to end the AIDS crisis." These "direct actions" constitute public confrontations and disruptions, setting ACT UP apart as notorious, courageous, or bullying, depending on the observer's views.

ACT UP events will come to include its premiere demonstration March 24 on Wall Street, to protest what it considers to be the profiteering of pharmaceutical companies (especially Burroughs Wellcome, manufacturer of AZT—a powerful drug taken by many AIDS sufferers). Seventeen people are arrested. Future demonstrations will include disruptions of mass at St. Patrick's Cathedral and massive street protests bringing traffic to a halt in New York City. Soon the organization will be synonymous with the saying "We're Here, We're Queer, Get Used to It!"[19]

1986. The American Psychiatric Association removes "ego-dystonic" homosexuality from their classification manual. When the APA reclassified homosexuality in 1973, it replaced "homosexuality" with "ego-dystonic homosexuality" as a diagnosable condition. "Ego-dystonic" meant that while homosexuality was not itself considered an illness, if it clashed with an individual's conscience or self-perception, it was ego-dystonic and treatable for that reason. But many psychologists and psychiatrists felt that by retaining this diagnostic classification, the APA was giving some credibility to those who still believed homosexuality was an unnatural, treatable condition, so in 1986, the diagnosis "ego-dystonic homosexuality" was removed entirely from the DSM.

The only vestige of ego-dystonic homosexuality in the revised DSM-III occurred under "Sexual disorders not otherwise specified," which included persistent and marked distress about one's sexual orientation.[20] (For more on homosexuality and psychiatry, see chapter 8.)

1988. October 11 marks the first national "Coming Out Day." Activists Dr. Robert Eichberg and Jean O'Leary establish the event in celebration of the Second National March on Washington for Lesbian and Gay Rights one year earlier, when 500,000 people had marched on Washington DC. The annual event will generate support and visibility, and from then on, each year October 11 becomes a day when families around the nation will hear a loved one declare to them "I'm gay."[21]

1993. The "Don't Ask, Don't Tell" policy is instituted in America's military after much dispute between newly elected President Bill Clinton and members of Congress and the Joint Chiefs of Staff. Clinton had originally committed himself to lifting the military ban on homosexuality but met with unanticipated levels of resistance. The "Don't Ask, Don't Tell" policy continued the ban with the provision that service members would no longer be questioned about their sexual orientation and, provided they kept it to themselves, they were free to serve. The decision was controversial and subjected to numerous challenges. (See chapter 21 of this book for more on gays in the military.)

1997. Ellen DeGeneres's character "Ellen Morgan" comes out as a lesbian on the popular sitcom *Ellen*, drawing 36 million viewers. Many more celebrities will soon "come out," hugely increasing public comfort and even sympathy for the gay rights movement: comedian Rosie O'Donnell, actors Richard Chamberlain and Tab Hunter, pop singer Clay Aiken, gospel singer Ray Boltz, rock star Michael Stipe, pop star George Michael, and actress Meredith Baxter, to name a few. But Ellen's disclosure will prove both landmark and galvanizing as she retains high visibility in television, films, and award shows. She'll soon become host of her own daytime talk show, and will become one of America's most influential lesbian and gay spokespersons.[22]

1998. Matthew Shepard is murdered. On October 7 of 1998, two motorcyclists in Laramie, Wyoming, passed what they thought was a scarecrow, oddly positioned on a fence in a near-freezing field. On closer inspection they realized they'd stumbled onto an unconscious male who'd been savagely beaten, lashed to the fence, and left to die. He was flown to the nearest hospital, where he remained in critical condition until he succumbed five days later, felled by an unusual level of cruelty.

He was a 22-year-old political science student named Matthew Shepard, and his killers' subsequent apprehension and trial would shed light on one of the most notorious crimes against a homosexual in American history. The night before he was found, he'd left a local bar with Aaron McKinney and Russell Henderson. These two young men drove Shepard to the remote field where he was found, robbed and beat him, then tied him to the fence.

Their motives are still being debated. Shepard's wallet was taken, suggesting robbery as a possibility, and McKinney and Henderson later claimed their use of amphetamines played into their violent behavior that night, leading to a drug-related mugging. But there was no avoiding the general belief that hatred for homosexuals inspired the killing. McKinney's defense attorney, in fact, initially laid out a "gay panic" strategy, claiming that Shepard had sexually propositioned the defendant, and McKinney's anti-homosexual reaction was uncontrollable.

The scenario most people have of the Shepard murder is that two heterosexuals lured a young man they knew to be gay into their car, possibly with the suggestion of a sexual encounter, but with an intent to overpower and assault him out of their hatred for homosexuals. This will remain one of the most infamous, well-publicized crimes of violence against a homosexual, and will spark renewed cries for hate-crime legislation and the silencing of voices opposing homosexuality for any reason.[23]

1999. The religious gay activist group Soulforce is formed by Rev. Mel White and his partner Gary Nixon, with the intention of recruiting and training volunteers to join in "confronting the antigay words and actions of fundamentalist Christians." White, a former pastor and professor at Fuller Theological Seminary, had ghostwritten books for some of America's foremost Christian leaders, including Billy Graham, Jerry Falwell, and Pat Robertson, and was recognized as an accomplished film producer and communicator. But in his autobiography *Stranger at the Gate* (Simon and Schuster, 1994) he describes what was not well-known about him: his private and lifelong struggle with homosexuality, a struggle he was aware of from his boyhood in the 1950s.

The coming decade would see the group's visibility and aggression expand. It would make itself known at annual denominational conventions, church trials for pastors charged with violating their denomination's standards regarding homosexuality, and Christian universities and churches, both national and worldwide. And with public support from allies such as Jay Bakker (son of PTL founders Jim and Tammy Faye Bakker), Arun Gandhi (grandson of Mohandas Gandhi), and Yolanda King (daughter of Martin Luther King Jr.), Soulforce would soon solidify its image as both a civil rights and progressive religious organization.

Asserting that teaching and preaching against homosexuality constitute "spiritual violence," White declares, "This spiritual violence must end. We love... the body of Christ too much to allow it to continue these policies that lead to suffering and death."

White also warns, "The toxic rhetoric flows unabated, primarily from sincere but misinformed religious leaders. It is poisoning the national discourse, dividing homes and churches, ruining families and wasting lives. We must do our best to stop that flow of poison at its source." But how? "What I suggest to all homosexuals and their supporters," White advises, "is to create tension between the church and the gay community." To that end, Soulforce soon becomes known as a group creating disruption and protest at churches, Christian universities, and Christian conferences around the country.[24]

2000. Vermont becomes the first state in the country to legally recognize civil unions between gay or lesbian couples. This marks a new turn in gay rights goals, as the question of whether or not same-sex relationships should be recognized by the government becomes one of the most prominent and divisive debates of the new decade. (For more on gay marriage, see chapter 20.)

2003. The U.S. Supreme Court rules in *Lawrence v. Texas* that laws prohibiting sodomy are unconstitutional, narrowly reversing its stance of seven years earlier in *Bowers v. Hardwick.* Newsweek soon runs a cover story posing the question, "Is Gay Marriage Next?"[25]

Gene Robinson, an openly gay man, is elected bishop-designate of New

Hampshire by the Episcopal General Convention during its meeting in Minneapolis. This election sparked outrage from conservative Anglican churches around the world and initiated a schism within the Episcopal Church as conservative member churches tried to distance themselves from a leadership they felt had descended into heresy. (For more on pro-gay theology, see chapter 6.)

2004. On May 17, same-sex marriages become legal in Massachusetts. The national debate over same-sex marriage thus gains steam, and will continue in various states as many of them consider, then pass, amendments to their state constitutions prohibiting the recognition of same-sex marriage. (For more on gay marriage, see chapter 20.)

2008. On May 15, the California State Supreme Court rules it unconstitutional to deny same-sex couples equal marriage rights, making California the second state to legalize same-sex marriage. Months later, in response to what many Californians view as the court's unwarranted judicial activism, Proposition 8, codifying the traditional man-woman definition of marriage into the state's constitution, is put on the ballot and, amidst predictable controversy, passes by a slim majority. Protests and court challenges soon follow. (For more on gay marriage, see chapter 20.)

Barack Obama is elected U.S. president, having promised the following to the gay community:

> As your President, I will use the bully pulpit to urge states to treat same sex couples with full equality in their family and adoption laws. I personally believe that civil unions represent the best way to secure that equal treatment.
>
> Just as important, I have been listening to what all Americans have to say. I will never compromise on my commitment to equal rights for all LGBT Americans. But neither will I close my ears to the voices of those who still need to be convinced. That is the work we must do to move forward together. It is difficult. It is challenging. And it is necessary.[26]

How this period could affect the experience and attitude of a homosexual person today. Trends established from the late 1980s to the present showed a shift from pluralism to conformity, as the gay rights movement began marginalizing and, at times, silencing those opposing the normalization of homosexuality. Many, both within and outside the gay community, now classify the conservative Christian who holds to the traditional view as being ignorant at best and, at worst, akin to a Nazi or member of the KKK. So the person holding the traditional view now finds himself not only to be outrageously politically incorrect, but, in many cases, called upon to defend and explain his "bigoted" belief that homosexuality is abnormal.

With a better understanding of where the gay rights movement has been, what it has achieved, and how it's affected the views and feelings of homosexuals we may interact with, let's now turn in chapter 5 from the subject of context to that of content—the right choice of words, and the avoidance of the wrong ones.

CHAPTER FOUR

A HISTORY OF THE GAY RIGHTS MOVEMENT IN AMERICA

○—KEY POINTS—○

1. *Content* and *context* play into every conversation, and context includes the historical backdrop of both parties involved. The history of gay rights in America will almost certainly, then, play into the context of any dialogue with a homosexual person.

2. The homosexual *population* has always existed, and is made up of those who are attracted primarily to the same sex. It is a population that may or may not be visible.

3. The homosexual *community* is made up of homosexual people who choose to interact with each other through shared social, philosophical, or political goals.

4. The gay rights movement is made up of both heterosexual and homosexual people who are committed to normalizing homosexuality in the culture and securing other pro-homosexual political or social goals.

5. Prior to the 1950s there was virtually no visible homosexual community or gay rights movement, although the first gay rights organization on record was formed in 1924.

6. From 1920 to 1970 the gay rights movement focused on attaining tolerance for homosexuals.

7. From 1970 to 1986, the gay rights movement focused more on seeing homosexuality *normalized* in the culture.

8. From 1986 to 2008, a growing demand for a uniform pro-homosexual viewpoint has arisen in the gay rights movement.

OTHER RESOURCES

About Time: Exploring the Gay Past by Martin Duberman, Gay Presses of New York, 1986.

"The American Gay Rights Movement: A Timeline," www.infoplease .com/ipa/A0761909.html.

NOTES

1. See Judith Reisman, *Kinsey, Sex and Fraud*, www.drjudithreisman.com/archives/2005/08/kinsey_sex_and.html.

2. Jonathan Katz, *Gay American History* (New York: Crowell Publishers, 1974).

3. See glbtq.com article on Daughters of Bilitis at www.glbtq.com/social-sciences/daughters_bilitis .html.

4. www.drakkar91.com/glbthistory/#1960-1969.

5. See Joe Dallas, *The Gay Gospel?: How Pro-Gay Advocates Misread the Bible* (Eugene, OR: Harvest House, 2007), pp. 67-68.

6. See Dallas, pp. 69-70.

7. See "American Gay Rights Movement: A Timeline."

8. See Ronald Bayer, *Homosexuality and American Psychiatry: The Politics of Diagnosis* (New York: Basic Books, 1981).

9. "The History of PFLAG," www.learntoquestion.com.

10. See ww.drakkar91.com/glbthistory/history2.html.

11. See Exodus International website at http://exodus.to.

12. See Dallas, pp. 76-78.

13. See Randy Shilts, *The Mayor of Castro Street: The Life and Times of Harvey Milk* (New York: St. Martin's Griffin, 2008).

14. See the Courage website at http://couragerc.net/TheCourageApostolate.html.

15. See "American Gay Rights Movement: A Timeline."

16. See "American Gay Rights Movement: A Timeline."

17. See "American Gay Rights Movement: A Timeline."

18. See "Sodomy Laws" www.sodomylaws.org.

19. See "ACT UP Capsule History," www.actupny.org/documents/capsule-home.html.

20. American Psychiatric Association, 1987; see Bayer, 1987, for an account of the events leading up to the 1973 and 1986 decisions.

21. See the Human Rights Campaign website, www.hrc.org/issues/10772.htm.

22. See "American Gay Rights Movement: A Timeline."

23. See Dallas, pp. 90-91.

24. See "Soulforce: A Brief History," www.soulforce.org/pdf/historybook.pdf.

25. *Lawrence v. Texas,* Cornell University Law School, www.law.cornell.edu.

26. See "Obama's Gay Promises," www.queerty.com/obamas-gay-promises-20080606/.

Terms, Definitions, and Concepts

by Joe Dallas

Let your speech always be with grace,
seasoned with salt, that you may
know how you ought to answer.

—Colossians 4:6

When Paul went to Athens hoping to evangelize, he was struck by the number of monuments to the different deities that he found on Mars Hill. As a Christian he was, of course, a monotheist, believing there to be only one God, and according to Luke's account, "his spirit was provoked within him when he saw the city was given over to idols" (Acts 17:16). But when communicating with the people he wanted to reach, Paul chose his words carefully, beginning with an emphasis on the common ground he shared with his listeners:

> Men of Athens, I perceive that in all things you are very religious, for as I was passing through and considering the objects of your worship, I even found an altar with this inscription: TO THE UNKNOWN GOD. Therefore. the One whom you worship without knowing, Him I proclaim to you (Acts 17:22-23).

He was direct but respectful, avoiding needless sarcasm about their idolatry, but also refusing to hedge the truth. His sermon on Mars Hill is a model of clarity, reason, and uncompromised speech. We could do much worse than to follow his lead.

On the subject of homosexuality we're challenged to use speech that is accurate, but not insulting; considerate but uncompromised. I call this adhering to our ABC's—that is, making sure our speech is *accurate*, *biblical*, and *considerate*.

The words or phrases we use when addressing the subject must be *accurate*. If I say homosexuality is a sin, that is accurate. But if I say that all homosexuals are promiscuous, child molesters, or political radicals, that's inaccurate, so it's also unacceptable. Accuracy is a mandate for anyone following the One who thought so little of lies that he referred to Satan as their father (John 8:44).

Our speech should also be *biblical*—doctrinally sound and scripturally balanced—and *considerate* as well. It may be accurate and biblical to say homosexuality is a perversion of what God intended, yet needlessly inconsiderate to call a homosexual a pervert. I can just as easily say a person is committing a sin without resorting to overtly offensive terms. At times truth will, by its nature, offend, and there will always be those who will accuse us of inconsideration no matter how carefully we choose our words. But when possible, we should strive to be not only accurate and doctrinally sound, but as considerate as we can be without sacrificing truth. And in most cases, all three elements—accuracy, biblical fidelity, and considerateness—can and should be evident in our speech.

To that end, let's review and define some terms likely to come up in the coming chapters and, indeed, in any conversations about homosexuality.

Sexual Orientation

The nature of a person's sexual attractions (toward the opposite sex, or the same sex, or both) define her or his sexual orientation. Sexual attraction is identified and measured by sexual arousal, evidenced in physical (including genital) response, and an awareness of what "turns us on" based on the history of our sexual behavior, thoughts, and feelings.

If a person's primary sexual attractions are toward the opposite sex, the person's orientation is heterosexual. *Hetero* is taken from the Greek term *heteros* meaning "different," so a heterosexual is attracted to the different, opposite, sex.

If a person's primary sexual attractions are toward the same sex, the person's orientation is homosexual. *Homo* is taken from the Greek term *homos* meaning "same," so a homosexual is attracted to the "same."

If a person's sexual attractions are toward both sexes, the person's orientation is bisexual.

The Bible does not use the term *orientation*, though it does mention heterosexual and homosexual feelings, and heterosexual or homosexual behavior. Heterosexual feelings are biblically described in either positive or negative terms, depending on the circumstances. So if, for example, a man is sexually attracted to another man's wife, Scripture would refer to the attraction as lust (Matthew 5:27-28), but if he feels passion for his own wife, Scripture recognizes the attraction in positive terms (1 Corinthians 7:2-4). There are proper and improper ways, then, of expressing a heterosexual orientation.

In contrast, there are no proper ways of expressing a homosexual orientation to be found in the Bible. Homosexual feelings are only mentioned once in Scripture (Romans 1:27) in negative terms (men "burning in lust" for each other), and homosexual behavior is only referred to in negative terms in both Old and New Testaments (Leviticus 18:22; 20:13; Romans 1:26-27; 1 Corinthians 6:9-10; 1 Timothy 1:9-10).

Bisexuality is a concept not found in Scripture, since there are no biblical references to men or women engaging sexually with both sexes. This does not mean the Bible denies the existence of bisexuality; rather, it simply doesn't mention it. But the prohibitions against same-sex genital contact found in the Scriptures mentioned above would apply, regardless of the orientation of the person practicing them.

The Bible does not condemn homosexual or bisexual orientation as a deliberate sin, but any deliberate expression of homosexuality, through actions, sexual fantasy, or lust, is biblically prohibited. And while some still view sexual orientation as a choice, research and experience show it to be an involuntary condition, not chosen but discovered, and deeply ingrained. (For more on this see chapters 9 and 10, "Theories of Origin," parts 1 and 2.) It's a mistake and, to many homosexuals, an insult to say, "You chose to *be* homosexual." Homosexual *actions*, like heterosexual ones, are certainly chosen, and the decision to embrace or celebrate the homosexual orientation by "coming out" and declaring "I'm gay" is a choice as well. But the orientation itself is an involuntary condition the homosexual person neither chose nor requested.

Terms Referring to Homosexual People

Homosexual. *Homosexual* is a word first coined in 1869 by German author Karl-Maria Kertbeny in reference to men who were sexually attracted to other men. It is still used as a morally neutral term to describe attractions or behavior, and can be used interchangeably with the word "condition," though some would take offense at their orientation being referred to in that way. There is still some controversy over the very concept of a homosexual, as some would argue that we are all heterosexuals by God's design, even those of us with homosexual inclinations, and that using such a label is a compromise with the goals and lingo of the gay rights movement. [1] But most would agree that using the term "homosexual" to describe a person, an attraction, or a behavior does not suggest approval; only description.

Gay. Traditionally meaning "happy" or "lighthearted," the term has become a common and broadly accepted reference to homosexuality, particularly to homosexual men. According to historian John Boswell, it was a code word in the early twentieth century for homosexuals, and is used by Cary Grant in a notable scene from the 1939 film called *Bringing Up Baby* in which, dressed in a woman's robe, Grant declares "I've suddenly gone gay!"

While *gay* may have been used as a code among homosexuals in earlier times, in the 1970s many pushed for its use as a replacement for the word *homosexual*, since *gay* had a more positive connotation. To this day it is generally used in a positive sense, so when someone says "I'm gay," they usually mean "I'm homosexual and I'm proud of it." *Gay*, then, is a term that implies approval more than the term *homosexual* when it's used in self-reference. When used by a third party it may or may not indicate approval. For example, a person who does not approve of homosexuality may still refer to a "gay bar," gay parade," or "gay man" if referring to a man who identifies himself that way.

Likewise, if a Christian man who holds traditional views on sexuality were to have homosexual temptations or inclinations, he'd be unlikely to refer to himself as "gay," since that would indicate approval of those inclinations. He'd be more likely to say "I struggle with homosexual temptations." Conversely, a homosexual who's accepting of his homosexuality would not say "I struggle with homosexuality," since his sexual feelings are not something he struggles against. Nor would he be likely to use the term *homosexual* in reference to himself, preferring instead the more positive, self-affirming term *gay*.

Lesbian. The word comes from Lesbos, a Greek island of the East Aegean Sea where the ancient Greek lyric poet Sappho lived in the sixth century BC. Many of her poems are about her passion for her students, which some say was specifically sexual and others claim to have been platonic. Regardless, her writing is known for its celebration of love between females, and her name is often invoked as a less direct reference to lesbianism than the word *lesbian* itself. (As in, "There was a Sappho-like quality to their relationship.")

While the term *gay* was often used to refer to both homosexual men and women in the early days of the gay rights movement, lesbian activists pushed for use of the term *lesbian and gay* to refer to homosexual people, giving lesbian women a more specific reference.

Just as *gay* indicates approval of homosexuality, so *lesbian* indicates approval and acceptance as well. So a Christian woman holding the traditional view on sexuality would probably not, if she felt attracted to the same sex, say, "I'm a lesbian." She'd be more likely to refer to herself as someone "struggling with same-sex attractions."

Bisexual. A person who is sexually attracted to both sexes is bisexual. A bisexual person is not necessarily as attracted to one sex as the other, but his or her attractions to both sexes are strong enough to constitute erotic and romantic responses to both. Some bisexuals will say, "I'm more turned on by women than men, but I am very attracted to men as well," or vice versa.

GLBT. *Gay, lesbian, bisexual, and transgender* (GLBT) is a term used to describe the modern gay rights movement or the homosexual community. GLBT is an inclusive term, bringing under one umbrella the most prominent "sexual minorities" (homosexual men and women, bisexuals, and transgenders). But the term is not meant to imply that all four groups are homosexual. As mentioned above, bisexuals are attracted to both sexes as opposed to homosexuals, who are primarily attracted only to the same sex.

Transgender is generally used in reference to transsexuals—women or men who feel they are literally one sex trapped inside the body of another, often dressing and living in the role of the opposite sex, and at times undergoing sex-change surgery to resolve their conflict.[2]

Common Slang or Pejorative Terms

The following terms are generally considered insults or vulgarities, and have no place in an intelligent, respectful discussion. On some occasions homosexual men or women themselves may use them, either in self-mockery or for shock effect. While some homosexuals may use these terms in self-reference, it would be needlessly offensive for anyone else to use them:

- *Faggot* or *fag.* Slang referring to a homosexual man.
- *Dyke.* Slang referring to a lesbian. The term *bull dyke* is often used to describe a noticeably masculine or mannish lesbian woman.
- *Fairy.* Slang usually referring to a noticeably effeminate homosexual man, though sometimes it's used to describe any male homosexual.
- *Queer.* Slang historically used to describe all homosexuals, especially homosexual men. Though normally seen as an insult similar to *faggot*, in recent years some homosexuals have reclaimed the word to describe themselves or their ideology (such as "queer theory" or "queer politics.") When used in that way it normally describes homosexuals who are aggressively open about their sexuality. A common saying used by some gay activists in the 1990s, for example, was "We're Here, We're Queer, Get Used to It!"
- *Queen.* Slang for an effeminate homosexual man, often referring to one who is flamboyant or imperious, hence the title suggesting royalty.
- *Fag hag.* Slang for a heterosexual woman who is attracted to homosexual men, or who enjoys socializing with homosexual men in lieu of heterosexual ones.

Commonly Used Terms or Phrases We Don't Recommend

"Love the sinner, hate the sin." This is a well-intentioned saying that has become a cliché. To say we "love the sinner" when referring to homosexuals often sounds as though we view them as "the sinner" while seeing others, ourselves included, as the "non-sinners." Likewise, when we say we "hate the sin," it implies we consider homosexuality a worse sin than others, which is a viewpoint not founded in the Bible. The phrase falls short of being considerate and, possibly, of being biblical as well.

Suggested alternatives:

- "I love you but I disagree with you."
- "I love you and yes, I think homosexuality is a sin. The one doesn't cancel out the other."
- "Loving you doesn't mean approving of everything you do. I certainly don't expect you to approve of everything about me, but I'm not about to say you don't love me if you don't approve of me!"

"Struggling with homosexuality." This phrase is only appropriate when referring to someone who is in conflict over their homosexuality and who views it as a sinful tendency to resist. They are, then, "struggling" with their homosexuality. But people who accept their homosexuality are not struggling with it. In those cases, the phrase falls short of being accurate.

Suggested alternatives:

- "A person who is homosexual."
- "A person who's attracted to the same sex."
- "A person who identifies as gay or lesbian."

"The gay lifestyle." The phrase implies there is one lifestyle observed by all homosexuals, which is untrue. Many homosexual men are promiscuous; many are not sexually active at all; many fall somewhere in between. Many lesbian women frequent bars or dance clubs; many live very sedate, conservative lifestyles. There is, in short, no such thing as a typical homosexual person. The phrase falls short of being accurate or considerate.

Suggested alternatives:

- "The way some homosexuals live."
- "The lifestyle of some homosexuals."

"The gay agenda." The phrase implies a uniform social or political agenda shared by all homosexuals. It also implies there is something inherently wrong in having an agenda. Both points are untrue. There is diversity among homosexuals, including political and social diversity. For that reason no one agenda could be shared by all homosexuals, although it is fair to say there are some goals—same-sex marriage, acceptance of gays in the military, and so on—that are common to the political gay rights *movement*, even if they're not shared by all homosexual people. Additionally, there's no wrong in having an agenda, since all people have political, personal, and social preferences or goals they'd like to see achieved. The phrase falls short of being accurate or considerate.

Suggested alternatives:

- "Common gay rights goals"
- "The gay rights agenda"

Commonly Used Clinical Terms and References

These are terms likely to arise in discussions about the psychological aspects of homosexuality, or therapeutic approaches to it.

Gender identity is a person's sense of identity as male or female, usually including their comfort with their own masculinity or femininity, or their level of comfort with the role their culture expects them to live out as a male or female. So a person with a healthy gender identity will not be plagued with doubts or confusion as in, "Am I manly enough?" or "Am I feminine enough?" Many theorists presume that problems with gender identity often accompany homosexuality, while others assert that many homosexual men are traditionally masculine and secure with their manhood, and many lesbian women display no uncertainties about their womanhood. Gender identity, then, should be seen as an issue separate from, but sometimes connected to, homosexuality itself.

Reparative therapy is a phrase referring to counseling, psychotherapy, or other forms of psychological treatment for homosexuals who are in conflict over their sexuality. It first became prominent with the 1991 publication of Dr. Joseph Nicolosi's book *Reparative Therapy for Male Homosexuality* and soon became a common term of reference. It derives from a theory (shared by Dr. Nicolosi with others) that homosexuality represents unmet emotional needs or conflicts that need repairing, in which cases therapy should attempt to repair the damage or deficits the person experiences. It is a controversial term, sometimes used as a pejorative by those who oppose attempts to modify sexual orientation. It is also used in a more neutral or even respectful tone by those who condone it, and practitioners of it often refer to themselves as "reparative therapists."[3]

"Reparative therapy" should not be used as an umbrella term covering every treatment approach for women and men with unwanted homosexual desires. Other forms of counseling or therapy may be designed to help such people, but without subscribing to all the tenets of reparative therapy. Some counselors, for example, may support their client's goal to abstain from homosexual behavior, yet they may not believe male homosexuality always springs from deficiencies in the father/son relationship, or that gender-identity issues always contribute to homosexuality. Likewise, not everyone who offers treatment for people in distress over their homosexuality should be referred to as a "reparative therapist." The term is properly used when referencing treatment approaches and practitioners subscribing to the theories and approaches cited above.

Gay-affirmative therapy. The opposite of *reparative therapy*, which views homosexuality as an unhealthy and treatable condition, *gay-affirmative therapy* views homosexuality as a normal variation of human sexuality. When someone experiences a conflict over their homosexuality, a gay-affirmative therapist would view the *conflict* as the problem, not the homosexuality. The term itself was first coined by Alan Malyon (past president of the American Psychiatric Association's Division 44 Society for the Psychological Study of Lesbian, Gay, and Transgendered People) as a reference to psychotherapeutic techniques that did not stigmatize homosexual people. In a broader sense, it can apply to any form of counseling or therapy that views homosexuality as being normal and seeks to enhance a homosexual person's comfort with his/her sexuality.

Ego-dystonic homosexuality. When the American Psychiatric Association changed the diagnostic status of homosexuality in 1973, they removed it from their list of diagnosable disorders (*The Diagnostic and Statistical Manual of Mental Disorders*, or the DSM) and replaced it with the term *ego-dystonic homosexuality*. The term refers to someone whose homosexuality is at odds with their worldview, or personal desires, and is therefore in conflict with their sense of themselves (ego-*dys*tonic as opposed to ego-*syn*tonic). By replacing "homosexuality" with "ego-dystonic homosexuality," the APA declared that homosexuality in and of itself was not a disorder, while still making treatment available for those to whom it was unacceptable. After considerable debate and controversy, ego-dystonic homosexuality was also removed from the DSM in 1986. As of this writing, the only diagnosis that can refer to a person's conflict over their homosexuality would be "Sexual Disorders Not Otherwise Classified."[4]

Hermaphrodite. Though this term technically applies to animals, organisms, or humans who have both male and female reproductive organs, it is most often used in references to people born with both male and female genitals. The condition is not a sexual orientation, but a physical abnormality, yet it often arises in discussions about homosexuality and ethics, when people ask, "Well, what about the hermaphrodite? What does the Bible say about them?" There are, in fact, no direct biblical references to the condition. It should not be viewed as a subject related to homosexuality, because it is a physical abnormality rather than a sexual orientation, and is best viewed as a complex medical condition requiring prolonged, thoughtful treatment and decision making.[5]

AIDS-Related Terms

The following terms will often come up in discussions about AIDS.

AIDS. The letters stand for *Acquired Immune Deficiency Syndrome.* It is a syndrome (a set of problems making up a disease) that can be acquired through sexual contact with a person infected with the AIDS virus (HIV) or a shared intravenous needle from an infected person, or through birth, if the mother was infected with the AIDS virus. It's referred to as an immune deficiency because the person with AIDS suffers from a weakness in the body's immune system, which fights off diseases. It is the disease, in turn, that may kill the individual, not the AIDS itself.

HIV stands for *Human Immunodeficiency Virus,* which is the virus that can lead to AIDS in the person infected with it. A person can be infected with HIV and never develop AIDS. There is testing widely available privately and through public health organizations to determine whether or not a person has become infected. There is, as of this writing, no vaccine for the virus, but there are several treatments available for people infected with it, and for people who have AIDS as well.

HIV positive, HIV negative. Both terms refer to a person's status relative to HIV, which can cause AIDS. If a person is *HIV positive,* they are infected with the virus. If someone is *HIV negative,* she or he is not infected. [6] (See chapter 26 in this book, "HIV and AIDS.")

Other Commonly Used Terms

Same-sex attractions. A term often used in lieu of *homosexuality*, especially among people who are uncomfortable applying the term *homosexual* to themselves. They view *same-sex attraction* as more of a description of their feelings, whereas *homosexual*, seems to describe them as people. Thus many prefer identifying their feelings by this term rather than referring to themselves using the more comprehensive term *homosexual*. To them, saying, "I have same-sex attractions" is more accurate and acceptable than saying "I am a homosexual," a label they may not consider applicable to themselves.

Ex-gay. A term used by many who identify themselves as having either overcome homosexuality (they no longer feel attracted to the same sex), or as having stopped homosexual behavior, or as having rejected the label/identity "gay." In a broader sense it may be used to describe ministries that serve people in conflict over their homosexuality ("ex-gay ministries") or counselors/ministry leaders involved in such groups ("ex-gay counselors" or "ex-gay leaders"). It can be a neutral or pejorative description, depending on the user's intent—and there has been considerable debate and disagreement over the use, meaning, and appropriateness of the term. (See chapter 13, "Change, Growth, and the 'Post-Gay' Concept.")

Homophobia. This word was coined in 1972 by psychologist George Weinberg, a gay activist who used it in his book *Society and the Healthy Homosexual* (St. Martin's Press). Though originally referring to an unreasonable dread, fear, or hatred of homosexuals, *homophobia* has broadened in meaning, and is now used to describe negative attitudes toward homosexuality and, at times, any objections to homosexuality no matter what their basis may be.

It is hoped that by better understanding terms that are useful, and avoiding those that aren't, our understanding of homosexuality from a Christian perspective will be enhanced. That, in turn, cannot help but improve our ability to communicate biblical truths clearly, respectfully, and effectively.

CHAPTER FIVE

TERMS, DEFINITIONS, AND CONCEPTS

○──KEY POINTS──○

1. The ABC's of respectful dialogue are *accurate*, *biblical*, and *considerate*.

2. Terms used in reference to homosexual people should match the person they are meant to describe. A person who is openly homosexual and comfortable with it should not be referred to as someone who "struggles with homosexuality"; neither should a person who is homosexually attracted but who believes homosexuality to be a sin be called "gay." Attempts should be made to use terms appropriate to the person or situation.

3. Pejorative terms (*faggot, dyke, queer*) have no place in a Christian's vocabulary, even if they are occasionally used by homosexuals themselves.

4. Groups at times change the terms they want to be identified by, and their wishes should be respected when it is possible to do so without compromising biblical truth. If a homosexual woman wants to be referred to as a lesbian, there's no compromise of truth involved. If a homosexual insists that a moral objection to homosexuality is "homophobia," it would be a compromise of truth to agree and therefore his wish should not be complied with.

5. Phrases or terms we commonly use should be reviewed at regular intervals to ensure they meet the criteria for sound, biblical speech.

ADDITIONAL RESOURCES

The Apologetics Study Bible: Understand Why You Believe, Charles Colson, gen. ed., Holman Bible Publishers, 2007.

When God Goes to Starbucks: A Guide to Everyday Apologetics by Paul Copan, Baker Books, 2008.

"Dialogue with a Homosexual" by Jason Dulle, www.apostolic.net/biblicalstudies/homosexualuc2.htm.

NOTES

1. See, for example, R. V. Young, "The Gay Invention: Homosexuality Is a Linguistic as Well as a Moral Error" for a detailed argument against the use of the word, www.touchstonemag.com/archives /article.php?id=18-10-036-f.

2. For a further discussion of transsexuals see Joe Dallas, "The Transsexual Dilemma," *Christian Research Journal*, 2008 (vol. 31, no. 01).

3. See, for example, the website for the National Association for Research and Therapy for Homosexuality at www.narth.com.

4. See "Homosexuality and the DSM-I," www.healthieryou.com/mhexpert/exp1052101c.html.

5. For more information see www.hermaphroditism.info/.

6. For more information on AIDS and HIV, see Aids Infonet.org, www.aidsinfonet.org/fact_sheets/ view/101.

PART TWO

CHAPTER SIX

Understanding Pro-Gay Theology

by Joe Dallas

Biblical authority is not tyranny. We read, reflect and reconcile ourselves with Scripture, but we never simply remake it or reject it if we affirm its authority.

—Marion Soards, *Scripture and Homosexuality*

When the culture debates the normality versus abnormality of homosexuality in primarily secular terms, pro-gay advocates rely heavily on secular arguments drawn from secular disciplines. Psychology, philosophy, and sociology (along with, at times, the physical sciences) are all invoked to bolster pro-gay claims that homosexuality is essentially normal and morally neutral. But when attempting to convince the Christian population of the normality of homosexuality, another form of advocacy is needed; one that recognizes the authority of the Bible and, rather than ignoring its references to homosexuality, meets those references head on and claims, in effect, that yes, the Bible is authoritative; but no, it does not condemn homosexuality.

To support this claim requires what I often refer to as a *revision* of the scriptures relative to homosexuality. For that reason, pro-gay theology can be seen as a revisionist approach, and advocates of pro-gay theology are themselves *revisionists*. Those holding the traditional view—that homosexuality as a condition is one of many manifestations of fallen nature, and that homosexual acts are condemned in both the Old and New Testaments without qualification or contingency—are, in contrast, *traditionalists*. Likewise, theologians who develop or promote pro-gay theology can properly be called pro-gay theologians.

The promotion and widespread acceptance of the revisionist view can be seen in the controversies mainline Protestant denominations are experiencing, as they debate what the Bible does or does not say about homosexuality. As of this writing (2008) the Episcopal Church, United Methodist Church, Evangelical Lutheran Church of America, and the Presbyterian Church USA are all embroiled in ongoing discussions and, in some cases, denominational splits over the ordination of openly homosexual clergy, and the affirmation of the revisionist approach.

Churches that eventually adopt the revisionist view are often referred to as *gay friendly* or *open and affirming* churches or denominations, and Christians who identify themselves as homosexual, bisexual, lesbian, or transgender often refer to themselves as *gay Christians*, or *gay and lesbian Christians*.

It should be mentioned that the revisionist viewpoint is not entirely new. Writings supporting it can be found as early as the 1950s, and in the 1970s and 1980s it experienced a rapid expansion, especially in 1981 with the release of Dr. John Boswell's book *Christianity, Social Tolerance and Homosexuality*, a popular and groundbreaking explanation and defense of the revisionist view. And while many who hold the pro-gay theological position could also be called "liberal" in their theology (taking a critical view of Scripture and eschewing the belief that the Bible is divinely inspired) there are also pro-gay theologians who hold very conservative views regarding the authority and role of the Bible. An essential belief shared by both groups, though, is the belief that the verses traditionally understood to condemn homosexuality have been *mistranslated, misinterpreted,* or *misunderstood*.

In the interest of better understanding how pro-gay advocates interpret the Bible verses that refer to homosexuality, let me offer an accounting of those verses from both Old and New Testaments, then offer the traditional interpretation of those verses, then the revisionist interpretation, and then a response/rebuttal to the revisionist view. This material is taken from my book *The Gay Gospel?: How Pro-Gay Advocates Misread the Bible* (Harvest House, 2007), which should be referred to for a fuller treatment of the subject. For a more in-depth study of the original languages behind scriptural references to homosexuality, see Robert Gagnon's *The Bible and Homosexual Practices: Texts and Hermeneutics* (Abingdon Press, 2002).

Genesis 2:18-24
Created Intent

> So God created man in his own image, in the image of God created he him; male and female created he them. And God blessed them, and God said unto them, Be fruitful, and multiply, and replenish the earth...And the LORD God said, It is not good that the man should be alone; I will make him an help meet for him. ...And Adam said, This is now bone of my bones, and flesh of my flesh: she shall be called Woman, because she was taken out of Man. Therefore shall a man leave his father and his mother, and shall cleave unto his wife: and they shall be one flesh (Genesis 1:27-28; 2:18,23-24 KJV)

Traditional View

God's intention for human sexual relationships is limited to heterosexual union between man and woman in marriage.

Revisionist Argument:
"The creation account is irrelevant"

The Genesis account does not forbid homosexuality; it simply doesn't refer to it, for obvious reasons. A gay couple could hardly begin the population process. But these verses cannot be seen as a model for all couples. Many heterosexual couples are childless, or unable to have sexual relations. Are they in sin because they do not conform to the Genesis account?

Response one. While it is true that this passage does not "forbid" homosexual relations, it does provide the primary model for sexuality by which other forms of sexual expression must be judged. Thomas Schmidt puts it well:

> [Genesis] provides a basis for biblical commands and for subsequent

reflection on the part of those who wish to construct a sexual ethic to meet changing situations…It is appropriate for us to explore the relevance of biblical commands about marriage and to evaluate modern homosexuality in light of Genesis.[1]

Stanton Jones, in regard to creation as a model for sexuality, adds:

The heart of Christian morality is this: God made sexual union for a purpose—the uniting of husband and wife into one flesh in marriage. God uses sexual intercourse, full sexual intimacy, to weld two people together.[2]

Response two. The male-female union, introduced in Genesis, is the only model of sexual behavior consistently praised in both Old and New Testaments. While other forms of behavior—polygamy and the use of concubines, for example—are introduced and even allowed in the Old Testament, a monogamous relation between husband and wife is the standard upheld in Scripture as the ideal. While the often-used phrase "God created Adam and Eve, not Adam and Steve" seems flippant, it is a fair assessment of created intent: whereas heterosexuality is commended throughout the Bible, not once is a homosexual relationship mentioned in anything but negative terms.

Genesis 19:4-9
The Destruction of Sodom

Before they [the angels visiting Lot to judge the wickedness of Sodom and determine whether or not to spare it] lay down, the men of the city, even the men of Sodom, compassed the house round, both old and young, all the people from every quarter: And they called unto Lot, and said unto him, Where are the men which came in to thee this night? bring them out unto us, that we may know them. And Lot went out at the door…and said, I pray you, brethren, do not so wickedly. Behold now, I have two daughters which have not known man…do ye to them as is good in your eyes: only unto these men do nothing. …And they said, …now we will deal worse with thee, than with them (Genesis 19:4-9 KJV, insert added).

Traditional Position

The men of Sodom were attempting homosexual contact with Lot's visitors. Sodom was subsequently destroyed for its great wickedness.

Revisionist Argument One:
"Inhospitality was the sin of Sodom"

Sodom was destroyed because of the inhospitality of its citizens, not because of homosexuality. Both John Boswell and Derrick Bailey support this view, basing it on two assumptions: Lot was violating Sodom's custom by entertaining guests without the permission of the city's elders,[3] thus prompting the demand to bring the men out "so we may know them"; and the words "to know" do not necessarily have a sexual connotation.

The Hebrew word *yada* means "to know," and is used here when the men said they wanted to know Lot's guests, Since *yada* appears 943 times in the Old Testament, but only carries a sexual meaning in perhaps 10 of those 943 times, the argument, then, is that the men of Sodom had no sexual intentions toward Lot's visitors.

Response. This argument makes little sense in light of Lot's responses to the men. His first response—"Do not so wickedly, my brethren"—could hardly apply to a simple request to "get to know" his guests. His second response is especially telling: He answered their demands by offering his two virgin daughters, another senseless gesture if the men wanted only a social knowledge of his guests. And why, if these men had innocent intentions, was the city destroyed for inhospitality? Whose rudeness was being judged—Lot's, or Sodom's citizens?

This theory raises more questions than it answers. While Boswell and Bailey are correct in pointing out the seriousness of inhospitality in biblical times, inhospitality alone cannot account for the severity of Lot's response to the men, or for the judgment that soon followed.

Revisionist Argument Two:
"Rape, not homosexuality, was the sin of Sodom"

This argument, proposed by Virginia Mollenkott, Troy Perry, and others, is more common and far more plausible than the "inhospitality" theory. "Violence—forcing sexual activity upon another—is the real point of this story," Mollenkott asserts.[4] Accordingly, homosexuality had nothing to do with Sodom's destruction. Had the attempted rape been heterosexual in nature, judgment would have fallen just the same. Violence, not homosexuality, was being punished when Sodom fell.

Response. This argument is partially true; the men of Sodom certainly were proposing rape. But for such an event to include "all the men of the city, both young and old," homosexuality must have been commonly practiced. Mollenkott makes a persuasive case for the event being much like a prison rape, or the kind of assault conquering armies would commit against vanquished enemies.[5] But her argument is weakened by Thomas Schmidt's cited evidence in early literature connecting Sodom with more general homosexual practices:

> The second century BC Testament of the Twelve Patriarchs labels the Sodomites "sexually promiscuous" (Testimony of Benjamin 9:1) and refers to "Sodom, which departed from the order of nature" (Testament of Naphtali 3:4). From the same time period, Jubilees specifies that the Sodomites were "polluting themselves and fornicating in their flesh" (16:5, compare 20:56). Both Philo and Josephus plainly name same-sex relations as the characteristic view of Sodom.[6]

Revisionist Argument Three:
"General wickedness, not homosexuality, was the sin of Sodom"

The real sins of Sodom, according to Ezekiel 16:49, were "pride, fullness of bread, and abundance of idleness...neither did she strengthen the hand of the poor and needy" (KJV). These sins have nothing to do with homosexuality.

Response. Again, this argument is partially true. When Sodom was destroyed, homosexuality was only a part—or symptom—of its wickedness. Romans 1 gives a similar illustration, describing the generally corrupt condition of humanity, while citing homosexuality as a symptom of that corruption. But Ezekiel also says of the Sodomites, "And they were haughty, and committed abomination before me." The sexual nature of these "abominations" is suggested in 2 Peter 2:6-7: "And turning the cities of Sodom and Gomorrah into ashes, condemned them to destruction...And delivered righteous Lot, who was oppressed by the filthy conduct of the wicked."

In Jude 7 we similarly read, "Likewise, Sodom and Gomorrah and the surrounding cities, which, in the same manner as they, indulged in sexual immorality and pursued unnatural lust, serve as an example by undergoing a punishment" (NRSV).

Dr. Bruce Metzger of Princeton Theological Seminary mentions other references to Sodom's sexual immorality. In 3 Maccabees 2:5 we read of "the people of Sodom who acted arrogantly" and "who were notorious for their vices." Reference is also made in Jubilees 16:6 to "the uncleanness of the Sodomites."[7]

The pro-gay interpretation of Sodom's destruction has merit. Homosexual rape was attempted, and the Sodomites were certainly guilty of sins other than homosexuality. But in light of the number of men willing to join in the rape, and the many other references—both biblical and extrabiblical—to Sodom's sexual sins, it is likely that homosexuality was widely practiced among the Sodomites. It is also likely that the sin for which they are named was one, but only one, of the many reasons judgment finally fell on them.

Moses and Homosexuality

> Thou shalt not lie with mankind, as with womankind: it is abomination (Leviticus 18:22 KJV).

> If a man also lie with mankind, as he lieth with a woman, both of them have committed an abomination: they shall surely be put to death (Leviticus 20:13 KJV).

Traditional Position

Under Levitical law, homosexuality was one of many abominable practices punishable by death.

Revisionist Argument One:
"Idolatrous homosexuality is the problem"

The practices mentioned in these chapters of Leviticus have to do with idolatry, not homosexuality. The Hebrew word for "abomination," according to Boswell, has less to do with something intrinsically evil and more to do with ritual uncleanness. The Metropolitan Community Church's pamphlet, "Homosexuality: Not a Sin, Not a Sickness," makes the same point: The Hebrew word for abomination found in Leviticus "is usually associated with idolatry."[8]

Roger Biery agrees, associating the type of homosexuality forbidden in Leviticus with idolatrous practices. Pro-gay authors refer to the heathen rituals of the Canaanites—rituals including both homosexual and heterosexual prostitution—as reasons God prohibited homosexuality among His people.

They contend that homosexuality itself was not the problem, but its association with idolatry and, at times, the way it was practiced as a part of idol worship. In other words, God was not prohibiting the kind of homosexuality we see today; He forbade the sort that incorporated idolatry.

Response one. The prohibitions against homosexuality in Leviticus 18 and 20 appear alongside other sexual sins—adultery and incest, for example—which are forbidden in both the Old and New Testaments, completely apart from the Levitical codes. Scriptural references to these sexual practices, both before and after Leviticus, show God's displeasure with them whether or not any ceremony or idolatry is involved.

Response two. Despite the UFMCC's contention that the word for "abomination" (*toevah*) is usually associated with idolatry, it in fact appears in Proverbs 6:16-19 in connection with sins having nothing to do with idolatry or pagan ceremony:

> These six things doth the LORD hate: yea, seven are an abomination [*toevah*] unto him: A proud look, a lying tongue, and hands that shed innocent blood, an heart that deviseth wicked imaginations, feet that be swift in running to mischief, a false witness that speaketh lies, and he that soweth discord among brethren (KJV).

Idolatry plays no part in these scriptures; clearly, then, *toevah* is not limited to idolatrous practices.

Response three. You can't have it both ways—if the practices in these chapters are condemned *only* because of their association with idolatry, then it logically follows that they would be permissible if they were committed apart from idolatry.

But that would also mean incest, adultery, bestiality, and child sacrifice (all of which are listed in these chapters) are also only condemned when associated with idolatry; otherwise, they are allowable. No serious reader of these passages could accept such a premise.

Revisionist Argument Two:
"You're picking and choosing!"

Revisionists often ask, "Even if these Scriptures do condemn homosexuality, what's that got to do with us today? Paul clearly said that we, as Christians, are not under the law."

That being the case, some assume that even if these verses *do* condemn homosexuality, that condemnation is not relevant to us today. So unless you want to start living under *all* the prohibitions and commandments of the Law, you can't apply these verses to homosexuals. You can't just pick and choose which parts of the Law you want to abide by—it's all or nothing.

Response. A proper reading of the Bible in its entirety shows us the relationship Christians have with the Law. A few points on this need to be made:

1. *The Law is good.* While it is true that we as believers are not under the Law, and that, in fact, we cannot keep the Law no matter how hard we try, the Law itself is good, and the New Testament in no way dismisses it. Paul described the Law as "holy and good" (Romans 7:12) and as a "schoolmaster" that makes us aware of our need for salvation (Galatians 3:24 KJV). Jesus Himself said that He did not come to destroy the Law, but to fulfill it (Matthew 5:17). So whatever role we assign the Law, we must begin with the premise that it is perfect, just, and good.

2. *The New Testament clarifies portions of the Law that are no longer binding upon the Christian.* When portions of the Law are specifically mentioned in the New Testament as no longer binding, then we are not obliged to keep them. Far from "picking and choosing," this is simply a matter of taking the Bible as a whole. So for example, when Hebrews chapter 11 tells us that we are not bound to sacrifice animals to atone for sin, since Christ's sacrifice is sufficient, we are not ignoring the Law's earlier commandments to make sacrifice. We're simply recognizing that the final sacrifice

has been made, so the verses commanding sacrifice are no longer binding.

The same can be said of dietary and ceremonial laws, which were binding to Israel but not to modern Christian believers according to Galatians 3:10-13.

3. *Some commandments are* contained *in the Law; some also* transcend *the Law.* In Leviticus 18 and 20, incest, bestiality, adultery, and homosexuality are prohibited. And these prohibitions are repeated in the New Testament as well, making them not only a part of the Law, but the broader biblical ethic as well. In fact, according to Leviticus 18:27, all the abominations practiced and prohibited in this chapter (adultery, homosexuality, incest, and bestiality) defiled the land when they were committed by the land's inhabitants. God also stated He "abhorred" the people who inhabited the land before Israel did, because they practiced these behaviors (Leviticus 20:23). Clearly these practices offended God no matter who practiced them, or in what context.

In other words, there are some commandments *contained* in the Law that are not binding upon believers; others are both *contained* in the Law and also *transcend* the Law.

The commandment to love God, for example, is spelled out in the Law, but repeated throughout both Testaments as well. The same is true of the commandments to love one's neighbor, speak the truth, and deal justly with all people. Although these rules are contained in the Law, they're also stressed in the Gospels, epistles, and books of wisdom and poetry.

If the commandment to abstain from any form of homosexual behavior was a minor technicality only applicable to Israel during a specified point in history, then it would hardly be worth our attention today. But when a commandment is contained within the Law, then repeated and reiterated throughout Scripture, then it is not only binding today; it is also binding to all.

Jesus and Homosexuality

Revisionist Argument One:
"Jesus said nothing about homosexuality."

This one is a favorite at gay parades. Invariably, when the gay Christian movement is represented, someone in their group will hold up a sign saying:

HERE'S WHAT
JESUS SAID ABOUT
HOMOSEXUALITY:

The idea, of course, is that if Jesus did not specifically forbid a behavior, then the behavior must not have been important to Him. Stretching the point further, this argument assumes that if Jesus was not manifestly concerned about something, we shouldn't be, either.

Troy Perry is typical of gay Christian leaders in making much of this argument based on silence:

> As for the question "What did Jesus say about homosexuality?" the answer is simple. Jesus said nothing. Not one thing. Nothing! Jesus was more interested in love.[9]

So, according to the argument of silence, if Jesus didn't talk about it, neither should we.

Response. This argument is misleading and illogical for four reasons. First, the argument assumes that the Gospels are more authoritative than the rest of the books in the Bible. The idea of a subject being unimportant just because it was not mentioned by Jesus is foreign to the Gospel writers themselves. At no point did Matthew, Mark, Luke, or John say their books should be elevated above the Torah or, for that matter, any writings yet to come. In other words, the Gospels—and the teachings they contain—are not more important than the rest of the Bible. *All* Scripture is given by inspiration of God (2 Timothy 3:16). The same Spirit that inspired the authors of the Gospels also inspired the men who wrote the rest of the Bible.

Second, the argument assumes that the Gospels are more comprehensive than they really are. Not only are the Gospels no more authoritative than the rest of Scripture, they're not comprehensive either. That is, they do not provide all we need to know by way of doctrine and practical instruction.

Some of the Bible's most important teaching, in fact, does not appear in the Gospels. The doctrine of man's old and new nature, outlined by Paul in Romans 6; the future of Israel and the mystery of the Gentiles, hinted at by Christ but explained more fully in Romans 9 through 11; the explanation and management of the spiritual gifts detailed in 1 Corinthians 12 and 14; the priesthood of Christ illustrated in Hebrews—all of these appear after the Gospel accounts of Christ's life, death, and resurrection. (And we're not even mentioning the entire Old Testament!) Would anyone say these doctrines are unimportant simply because they weren't mentioned by Jesus?

Or, put another way, are we really to believe that Jesus didn't care about wife-beating or incest just because He said nothing about them? Aren't the prohibitions against incest in Leviticus and 1 Corinthians, as well as Paul's admonition to husbands to love their wives, enough to instruct us in these matters without being mentioned in the Gospels? There are any number of evil behaviors Jesus did not mention by name; surely we don't condone them for that reason alone!

Likewise, Christ's silence on homosexuality in no way negates the very specific prohibitions against it, which appear elsewhere in both the Old and New Testaments.

Third, this argument is inaccurate in that it presumes to know all of what Jesus said. The Gospels do not profess to be complete accounts of Jesus' life and teachings. Whole sections of His early years are omitted; much of what He did and said remains unknown.

Luke wrote his Gospel so Theophilus would "know the certainty of those things, wherein thou hast been instructed" (Luke 1:4 KJV). John's motives are broader: "These are written that you may believe that Jesus is the Christ, the Son of God, and that believing you may have life in his name" (John 20:31). But none of these authors suggested they were recording *all* of Christ's words.

John, in fact, said that would have been an impossibility: "And there are also many other things which Jesus did, the which, if they should be written every one, I suppose that even the world itself could not contain the books that should be written" (John 21:25 KJV).

If that's the case, how can we be certain He said nothing about homosexuality? No one can say. But we know there are other equally important subjects left undiscussed in the Gospels, but mentioned in detail in other books of the Bible. Homosexuality, while absent from Matthew, Mark, Luke, and John, is conspicuously present in both Testaments. And, just as conspicuously, it is forbidden.

Fourth, this argument wrongly assumes that because Jesus said nothing specifically about homosexuality, He said nothing about heterosexuality as a standard. In Mark 10:5-9, Jesus spoke in the most specific terms about God's created intent for human sexuality:

> From the beginning of the creation God made them male and female. For this cause shall a man leave his father and mother, and cleave to his wife; and they twain shall be one flesh...What therefore God hath joined together, let not man put asunder (KJV).

In this passage, Jesus had been presented with a hypothetical question: Was divorce lawful? Instead of giving a simple "yes" or "no," He referred to the Genesis account and, more specifically, to *created intent* as the standard by which to judge sexual matters. By citing Genesis, He emphasized several key elements of the created intent for marriage and sexual relating: Independence was one—a man was to leave his own home to establish his own family with his wife; a "one flesh" sexual union (between male and female, man and wife) was another; and, of course, monogamy.

Revisionist Argument Two:
"Jesus mentioned homosexuals favorably when referring to 'eunuchs.'"

In his book *Jonathan Loved David*, Episcopal priest Tom Horner suggests that Jesus was referring to homosexuals when He said the following in Matthew 19:10-12:

> There are eunuchs who were born thus from their mother's womb, and there are eunuchs who were made eunuchs by men, and there are eunuchs who have made themselves eunuchs for the kingdom of heaven's sake. He who is able to accept it, let him accept it.

Horner stretches the definition of the term *eunuch*—which is traditionally understood to mean castrated, or without reproductive organs—to also include homosexuals, thus bringing homosexual men not only under the umbrella of this passage, but also under the blessings pronounced in Isaiah, when God promises:

> To the eunuchs...I will give them an everlasting name that shall not be cut off (Isaiah 56:4-8).

With this new understanding of *eunuch*, we could assume that eunuchs were and are a special class of individuals, some of who were born homosexual and suffered outcast status, but are favored by God, much as the meek and the downtrodden, who Jesus described as blessed in the Sermon on the Mount. And, of course, we would conclude that Jesus singled them out and recognized that at least some of them were homosexual, implying that, to Him, homosexuality was a non-issue.

Response. This argument is misleading and inaccurate, as it distorts the meaning of the term *eunuch*.

The most glaring contradiction to Horner's use of the term and his application of it to homosexuals lies in the word itself. The Hebrew word used in each Old Testament reference to eunuchs is *cariyc*, taken from a root word meaning "to castrate." Eunuchs were, as Jesus said and as is commonly understood, either castrated deliberately to be put into service guarding women without the threat of sexual interaction, or they were born without testicles. In the New Testament, the term *eunouchos*—"a castrated person, or an impotent man"—is used in both Jesus' and Luke's references to eunuchs (Acts 8:26-40). Either way, the unambiguous meaning of the term had nothing to do with sexual preference and everything to do with sexual function.

Eunuchs were often seen as pitiable, outcast, or second-rate because of their inability to reproduce and, as always, God expressed a special tenderness toward the outcast. Thus the special promises and comfort offered eunuchs in Isaiah's promise. But an unbiased look at the scriptural references to eunuchs would never have yielded Horner's conclusion that homosexuals were included in their ranks.

This is not to say that homosexual eunuchs—that is, men who were sexually attracted to the same sex but were unable to perform sexually—did not exist. It is only to say that homosexuality, or any sexual orientation for that matter, cannot be read into the meaning and concept of eunuch.

Revisionist Argument Three:
"Jesus healed a centurion's male lover, thus offering
tacit approval of their homosexual relationship."

In Matthew 8:5-13, we see a Roman centurion approach Jesus in distress over his servant, who he clearly loved and who was seriously ill:

> When Jesus had entered Capernaum, a centurion came to Him, pleading with Him, saying, "Lord, my servant is lying at home paralyzed, dreadfully tormented." And Jesus said, "I will come and heal him." The centurion answered and said, "Lord, I am not worthy that You should come under my roof. But only speak a word, and my servant will be healed. For I also am a man under authority, having soldiers under me. And I say to this one, 'Go,' and he goes; and to another, 'Come,' and he comes; and to my servant, 'Do this,' and he does it." When Jesus heard this, He marveled, and said to those who followed, "Assuredly, I say to you, I have not found such great faith, not even in Israel!"…And his servant was healed that same hour.

Clearly Jesus was pleased with the faith of this centurion and, true to form, He was moved with compassion and healed his servant from a distance. That much we can all agree on.

But a pro-gay slant to this story has gained popularity. Promoted by Horner and frequently cited on website postings (such as the Cathedral of Hope Metropolitan Community Church website at www.cathedralofhope.com), this interpretation of Christ healing the centurion's servant suggests that the servant and his master had a sexual relationship, the centurion's concern for the servant was born not of brotherly but romantic love, and that Jesus was fully aware they had a same-sex relationship so, by healing the servant, He offered an endorsement of their love.

The sexualizing of the centurion/servant relationship comes from the Greek *pais*, the word Matthew used when referring to the servant and which, according to Horner, was often a term used to describe the younger partner in a male homosexual union.

Response. This argument is misleading for two primary reasons. First, while the centurion's love for his *pais* was unquestionable, the knee-jerk conclusion that their love was sexual is very questionable. Other words for a homosexual lover were available at the time Matthew recorded this event, words that would have made a sexual relationship between men much clearer. And while it is true that *at times* there were sexual relations between servants and masters, as there are today between employers and employees, the leap from *at times* to *all the time* is too large. We can no more assume that a slave/master relationship in Christ's time *had* to be sexual just because *some* slave/master relationships were, any more than we can assume an employer/employee relationship today *has* to be sexual, just because *some* employer/employee relationships are.

More important to this discussion, though, is the implication that if Jesus healed someone, He approved of their life in general. This requires a broader leap in logic than the assumption that the centurion/servant relationship was sexual, because it requires that we accept Christ's endorsement of the sexual and moral behavior of every person He healed. And that's too much to require.

It's too much because it first presumes healing to be a reward for merit, rather than an act of grace, yet nothing in any Gospel, historical, or epistle account of healing implies this. In fact, when Christ healed, it was out of compassion, not obligation.

It's also too much to assume because we know Christ healed hundreds, perhaps thousands, of individuals in the Gospel accounts in crowdlike settings (Matthew 4:23-24; 8:16), curing all who were present. Are we really to assume that every sick individual who came to Jesus for healing was living a righteous life, making His touch into a stamp of approval? The pro-gay interpretation of this story requires that we do, because it's strength rests not only on the assumption that the centurion and his servant were lovers (a possibility, though unprovable) but also on the assumption that Christ's healing indicated Christ's approval. And that's an assumption nowhere to be found in Scripture or common sense.

But what about the centurion's faith? Jesus declared He'd never seen anything like it, making the pro-gay argument more compelling if indeed the centurion and his servant had a sexual relationship, a possibility, however remote, that we have to allow. Suppose they were lovers. Would that not make Jesus' remarks on this man's faith an endorsement of him and, by extension, his homosexual relationship?

We'd have to concede to Horner and other revisionists if that were the case. But even if we stretch this story to make it one in which Jesus heals a man's male lover while commending the man's faith, we're still left without a confident foundation for the "Jesus approved of homosexuality approach." A person's faith, while laudable, doesn't legitimize his behavior.

Rahab the harlot and her role in Israel's conquest of Jericho, illustrates this. When Joshua's spies needed a place to hide while surveying Jericho, she provided it, striking a bargain with them that they would spare her life, and her family's, when they took the city. She feared them and their God, and in honor of that, she not only was spared when Jericho fell, but her name appears in Hebrew's "roster of faith" (see Hebrews 11:31).

And she was a harlot. Is anyone really going to suggest that, because she prostituted herself at the time God spared her and honored her faith, that He somehow approved of her behavior? Clearly, her sin didn't nullify her faith, but neither did her faith legitimize her sin. And if indeed the centurion in question was involved in homosexuality when Jesus healed his servant, we would say the same of him as well.

We are left, then, with some general conclusions about the Gospels and pro-gay theology. Homosexuality may not have been mentioned by Jesus; many other sexual sins weren't, either. But He couldn't have spelled out the standard for sexual expression more clearly: male to female, joined as God intended them to be. He can't be assumed to have approved of anything less. He reiterated the place eunuchs, and indeed all outcasts, have in God's heart, but to read "homosexual" into "eunuch" is akin to reading "sexual orientation" into the word "castration." The two are simply worlds apart. And while there's a remote though unlikely possibility Jesus was healing a man's homosexual lover when He healed a centurion's servant, "healing" and "approval" are two very different things as well. Likewise, a commendation of a man's faith can't be construed into a blessing on a man's behavior.

Paul and Homosexuality:
Romans 1:26-27
"Natural" vs. "Unnatural"

> For this cause God gave them up unto vile affections: for even their women did change the natural use into that which is against nature: And likewise also the men, leaving the natural use of the woman, burned in their lust one toward another; men with men working that which is unseemly, and receiving in themselves that recompense of their error which was meet (KJV).

Traditional Position

Paul begins Romans describing humanity in its unredeemed, rebellious state. His goal is not to pick out any particular sin and rail against it, but rather, to prove all people—whether Gentile or Jewish—are lost until redeemed by Christ. He starts with the human race in general, stating all people have a consciousness of God but, in their fallen state, deliberately ignore both it and Him and live as they please (Romans 1:18-21). This is not a limited, select group of people Paul's describing here; he's providing a wholesale view of all people born in sin. Accordingly, their hearts and minds became "darkened" (verses 21-22) and idolatrous (verse 23). He then cites homosexuality as a symptom of the problem, describing it as unnatural and unseemly, then cites several other sins in this chapter that, along with homosexuality, are common. (Though of all sins listed here, only sexual relations between members of the same sex are described as "unnatural.")

Chapter 1 ends with a summation that anyone practicing these sins is worthy of death, thus placing all Gentiles under a death sentence. Paul doesn't assume everyone is guilty of committing *all* the sins he names, but he does assume they're commonly practiced, and that no reader could review this chapter without seeing a few of his own transgressions on the list.

Then he turns to his Jewish readers and tells them, essentially, not to assure themselves they're not under a death sentence as well, since sinful practices are found among all people, Jewish and non-Jewish. In short, Paul opens Romans with a sweeping condemnation of everyone, and an appeal to trust in Christ's atonement, not themselves, or their own righteousness.

Revisionist Argument One:
"In these verses, Paul is not describing true homosexuals,
but heterosexuals who practice homosexuality, thus
'changing their nature,' which is something God abhors."

The real sin here, according to this argument, is in changing what is natural to the *individual*. Boswell takes this argument up when he states:

> The persons Paul condemns are manifestly not homosexual: what he derogates are homosexual acts committed by apparently heterosexual persons. The whole point of Romans 1, in fact, is to stigmatize persons who have rejected their calling, gotten off the true path they were once on.[10]

Scanzoni and Mollenkott agree, saying,

> What Paul seems to be emphasizing here is that persons who are heterosexual by nature have not only exchanged the true God for a false one but have also exchanged their ability to relate to the opposite sex by indulging in homosexual behavior that is not natural *to them*.[11]

In short, Paul in Romans 1 describes *heterosexuals* who have deliberately committed *homosexual* acts, thus violating their true nature. This has nothing to do with lesbians and gays who are in loving, committed relationships, and to whom these relationships come naturally. Homosexuality, if committed by true homosexuals, is therefore not a sin, and is not referenced here.

Response. Paul is not speaking nearly so subjectively in this passage as this argument would suggest. There is nothing in his wording to imply he even recognized such a thing as a "true" homosexual versus a "false" one. He simply describes homosexual *behavior* as unnatural, no matter *who* it is committed by.

His wording, in fact, is unusually specific. When he refers to "men" and "women" in these verses, he chooses the Greek words that most emphasize biology: *arsenes* and *theleias*. Both words are rarely used in the New Testament; when they do appear, they appear in verses meant to emphasize the sex of the subject, as in a *male* child (*arsenes*). In this context, Paul is very pointedly saying that the homosexual behavior committed by these people was unnatural to them as males and females (*arsenes* and *theleias*); he is not considering any such thing as sexual orientation. He is saying, in other words, that homosexuality is biologically unnatural—not just unnatural to heterosexuals, but unnatural to *anyone*.

Additionally, the fact that these men were "burning in lust" for each other makes it highly unlikely that they were heterosexuals experimenting with homosexuality. Their behavior was born of an intense inner desire. Suggesting, as Boswell and Mollenkott do, that these men were heterosexuals indulging in homosexual behavior requires mental gymnastics.

Besides, if verses 26 and 27 condemn homosexual actions committed by people to whom they did not come naturally, but don't apply to people to whom those actions do come naturally, then doesn't consistency compel us to apply the same logic to all the practices mentioned in this chapter? Such consistency would require us to say that not only homosexuality, if practiced by someone to whom it comes naturally, and in the context of a loving relationship, is not condemned in these verses. It would require us to say *all* of these behaviors, if practiced by someone to whom they come naturally, and in the context of a loving relationship, are not condemned in these verses.

Read Romans chapter 1 again, and you'll notice between verses 20 and 31, Paul names 23 sins:

1. homosexuality
2. unrighteousness
3. sexual immorality
4. wickedness
5. covetousness
6. maliciousness
7. envy
8. murder, strife
9. deceit
10. evil-mindedness
11. whispering
12. backbiting
13. hating God
14. violence
15. pride

16. boasting

17. inventing evil things

18. disobedience to parents

19. lack of discernment

20. untrustworthiness

21. lack of love

22. lack of forgiveness

23. lack of mercy

Boswell, Mollenkott, and others suggest that sin number 1—homosexuality—is a sin only if it doesn't come naturally to you. But I doubt any pro-gay apologist would apply the same contingency to sins 2 through 23. But why? Since they're all lumped together in the same passage, wouldn't logic require it? Bishop Bennett Sims points this out in an interview with *Christianity Today* magazine, referring to this line of thought about Romans 1:

> The logical effect of the exemption argument is to suggest that, given the proper motivation, there are loving ways to be "full of envy, murder, strife, malignity"…this is moral absurdity.[12]

To which I would add, as in the case of the prohibitions against homosexuality in Leviticus and the pro-gay contingencies applied to them, you simply cannot have it both ways.

Revisionist Argument Two:
*"These verses only apply to people given over to idolatry,
not gay Christians who worship the true God."*

Noting that verse 23 describes the people in Romans 1 as having "changed the glory of the incorruptible God into an image like corruptible man—and birds and four footed animals and creeping things," some pro-gay apologists argue this chapter can only be applied to people who blatantly worship idols or false gods. Troy Perry, for example, states:

> The homosexual practices cited in Romans 1:24-27 were believed to result from idolatry and are associated with some very serious

offenses as noted in Romans 1. Taken in this larger context, it should be obvious that such acts are significantly different than loving, responsible lesbian and gay relationships seen today.[13]

Response. Idolatry certainly plays a major role in Romans 1. Paul begins his writing by describing humanity's rebellion and decision to worship creation rather than the Creator. The pro-gay theorist seizes on this concept to prove that Paul's condemnation of homosexuality does not apply to him—he does not worship idols; he is a Christian.

Thomas Schmidt cautions against this line of thought:

> Paul is not suggesting that a person worships an idol and decides therefore to engage in same-sex relations. Rather, he is suggesting that the general rebellion created the environment for the specific rebellion. A person need not bow before a golden calf to participate in the general human denial of God or to express that denial through specific behaviors.[14]

A commonsense look at the entire chapter bears this out. Consider again the 23 sins listed in this chapter. Will this interpretation, applied to homosexuality, also apply to numbers 2 through 23 on this list? In other words, are they, too, only sinful if practiced in the context of idolatry, but legitimate if practiced, as Perry argues, in a "loving, responsible" way?

This, of course, is ridiculous. Like homosexuality, these sins are not just born of idol worship; they are symptomatic of a fallen state. If we are to say homosexuality is legitimate, so long as it's not a result of idol worship, then we also have to say these other sins are legitimate as well, so long as they, too, are not practiced as a result of idolatry.

Revisionist Argument Four:
"Paul is describing excessive, irresponsible sexual behavior based on lust and promiscuity. This has nothing to do with responsible, committed, loving homosexual relationships."

Though none of the major pro-gay theorists mention this in their writings, I've heard it often enough to feel it warrants inclusion here. Often, when my gay friends and I would have candid conversations about the Bible, we'd get stuck on Romans 1 and begin wondering if there was any way to get around it. That's when someone in the group would say, "Well, I don't go around 'burning in lust' for people, or jump in bed with anyone. So I really don't see myself in Romans 1." And that, at first glance, seemed good enough to quiet our doubts.

Response. The people practicing homosexuality in this chapter were, according to Paul's wording, lusting after members of the same sex and engaging in same-sex erotic acts. Nothing in his phrasing or choice of words states, or even implies, they were doing it with many people of the same sex, or that they were doing it frequently or randomly. In other words, Paul condemns the thing itself, without qualifying the condemnation to only apply to the homosexuality when it's practiced "irresponsibly" or with many partners. Like adultery or fornication, it's no less a sin if it's committed once in a lifetime with one partner; no more a sin if it's committed daily with several partners. The condemnation here is of the thing itself, not the way it's practiced.

1 Corinthians 6:9-10 and 1 Timothy 1:9-10
Paul's Use of the Terms *Malakos* and *Arsenokoite*

> Know ye not that the unrighteous shall not inherit the kingdom of God? Be not deceived: neither fornicators, nor idolaters, nor adulterers, nor effeminate [Greek, *malakos*], nor abusers of themselves with mankind [Greek, *arsenokoite*], nor thieves, nor covetous, nor drunkards, nor revilers, nor extortioners, shall inherit the kingdom of God (1 Corinthians 6:9-10 KJV).

> The law is not made for a righteous man, but for the lawless and disobedient, for the ungodly and for sinners, for the unholy and profane, for murderers of fathers and murderers of mothers, for manslayers, for whoremongers, for them that defile themselves with mankind [Greek, *arsenokoite*], for menstealers, for liars, for perjured persons, and if there be any other thing that is contrary to sound doctrine; according to the glorious gospel of the blessed God, which was committed to my trust (1 Timothy 1:9-11 KJV).

Traditional Position

By referring to *arsenokoite*, meaning "homosexual," and *malakos*, meaning "homosexual prostitution" or possibly "pederasty" (sex between adult men and younger boys), Paul is saying that homosexuality, homosexual prostitution, and pederasty are vices excluding their practitioners from the kingdom of God, or which are soundly condemned in the Law.

Revisionist Argument One:

"Paul was referring to prostitution only, or immoral behavior in general, when he mentioned arsenokoite. *And* malakos *doesn't refer to gay men, but rather to men who prostitute themselves, probably dressed as females or at least assuming a feminine sexual role."*

Boswell argues this the most cogently, though it's a point raised by virtually every pro-gay apologist. *Arsenokoite*, they claim, is a word coined by Paul. It never appeared in Greek literature before he used it in these Scriptures, though there were, at the time, other words for "homosexual" available in Greek. Had he meant to refer to homosexuality, he would have used one of the words already in existence. This he sees as one of his strongest selling points for pro-gay theology, one in which he comes into sharp contrast with traditionalists.

On the proper use of *malakos* he may find less resistance. It appears not only in these passages, but also in Matthew 11:8 and Luke 7:25, when Jesus describes those who are "gorgeously appareled and live in luxury." Whether in these verses He's referencing rather weak, indolent men, or those who literally service kings as cross-dressed prostitutes, is unclear. What *is* clear is that such men, while obviously spoken critically of by Jesus and Paul, were not necessarily homosexuals. Whether homo- or heterosexual in their desires, they were, most likely, men who engaged in homosexual sex for pay or reward, and thus were never representative of most homosexuals. On this point, we agree with Boswell et al: *malakos* is not a term condemning all forms of homosexuality.

But when traditionalists argue that *arsenokoite* does offer such a sweeping condemnation, Boswell points out the word is peculiar to Paul, suggesting he didn't have homosexuality in mind when he used it.[15] Prostitution is Boswell's first choice:

> *Arsenokoite*, then, means "male sexual agents," i.e. active male

prostitutes, who were common throughout the Hellenistic world in the time of Paul…male prostitutes capable of the active role with either men or women.[16]

And if male prostitutes weren't the specific source of Paul's criticism, Boswell suggests he was condemning general immorality in lieu of homosexuality per se.[17] At any rate, the term, according to this argument, refers to some sort of immoral man, but not to a homosexual.

Response. Paul's coining of a new term isn't out of character, as he coined 179 terms in the New Testament. Coined terms do not, simply because they are original to the "coiner," significantly change the context of the verses they appear in.

It's especially unremarkable that he would have coined this one, considering the Greek words it employs, and the source he seems to have drawn the phrase from.

Arsenokoite is a combination of the words *arsane* and *koite*, both of which appear infrequently in the New Testament. *Arsane* was mentioned earlier in this chapter as to its appearance in Romans 1. It refers to a male or males with an emphasis on their gender. *Koite* appears only twice in the New Testament, and means "bed" or "couch," used in a sexual connotation:

- "Let us walk honestly…not in chambering [*koite*]" (Romans 13:13 KJV).
- "Marriage is honorable…and the bed [*koite*] undefiled" (Hebrews 13:4).

The first striking point about Paul's use of these two words when creating the term *arsenokoite* is that there's nothing in the words *male* or *bed* implying trade, buying, or selling, making Boswell's guess that they referred to prostitution an unlikely one. The two words combined, as Paul used them, put "male" and "bed" together in a sexual sense, with no hint of prostitution involved. This is not to say that later writers could not use the word to mean something more general, such as a "base" or "lewd" man. They could, but in so doing, even if their intent was clear, it would be a technical misuse of the word.

For example, in modern English, the word *whore*, which technically means "prostitute," is often used to describe a woman who is morally loose and promiscuous, though not really one who sells herself for sex and not, therefore, a true prostitute. Likewise, some may refer to a cruel, thoughtless man as a "bastard," a term literally referring to someone born out of wedlock, but figuratively used to malign someone's general character. In both cases, we may know the speaker's intent, while recognizing he's technically, linguistically in error.

The same may be said for *arsenokoite*. While Boswell correctly points out other authors' later uses of it when referring to men who commit immorality, but not necessarily with other men, they, too, miss Paul's original, technical meaning.

Arsenokoite ("males" combined with "bed" or "couch") is, as Dailey points out, the Greek counterpart to the Hebrew phrase *mishkab zakur*.[18] *Mishkab* is Hebrew for "bed" or "couch" with a sexual connotation; *zakur* in Hebrew means "male" or "males." The phrase *mishkab zakur* is found in Leviticus 18:22 and Leviticus 20:13, where sex between men is expressly forbidden. This makes it impossible to accept Boswell's suggestion that Paul meant anything other than homosexuality when using the term *arsenokoite*, considering that it's derived directly from the Hebrew prohibitions of that very thing!

Indeed, the Septuagint, which is the Greek translation of the Old Testament, uses the terms *arsane* and *koite* when translating prohibitions against homosexuality in these same Levitical passages:

- "Thou shalt not lie with a man as with a woman" (Leviticus 18:22). "...*meta* **arsenos** *ou koimethese* **koiten** *gyniakos*"

- "If a man lies with a man as with a woman, they have committed an abomination..." (Leviticus 20:13). "...*hos an koimethe meta* **arsenos koiten** *gynaikos*"

When Paul adopted the term *arsenokoite*, he took it directly from the Greek translation of Leviticus's prohibitions against homosexual behavior, and his intent couldn't be clearer. Though *arsenokoite* is unique to Paul, it refers specifically and unambiguously to sex between men.

More needs to be considered, though, before moving on from Paul's teachings. While his specific condemnations of homosexuality are evidence enough against the revisionist view, his statements about human nature in general should be considered as well, especially in response to common pro-gay arguments about the cause and nature of homosexuality.

According to Paul, we as believers contain, and are deeply affected by, both an old and a new nature. Our old nature, often referred to as "the flesh," was inherited from our father Adam, and no one has escaped it or, for that matter, the struggles and consequences it brings, (Romans 5:12-21). Because of these two natures, Paul describes an internal war we experience on a regular basis; a relentless tug of war between the desires of our flesh, which are invariably ungodly, and those of our new spiritual nature, which tend toward life and righteousness (Romans 7:15-25; Galatians 5:17). Nowhere does he suggest this struggle will end in this life. On the contrary, he virtually promises it will continue, sometimes ferociously, sometimes mildly. Because of this, he encourages us to mortify desires that may seem natural to us (Romans 6:12-14) and yield our bodies daily to God's will and service (Romans 12:1). If, in the process of doing this, we find our carnal desires diminishing, so much the better. But it's obedience, not absence of temptation, that God requires.

In this light we can sympathize with the deeply ingrained nature of homosexuality, no matter what its origins, as we realize our own deeply ingrained sinful desires. And since we didn't choose our inherited Adamic nature, we can concur that homosexuals, by and large, have not chosen their orientation. But we can and must declare that if they claim to belong to Christ, then they, like us, are required to put aside what seems natural, deeply ingrained, and even unchangeable within, then submit themselves as living sacrifices to God, yielding to His purposes instead of their own passions. Only then can they, or any of us, find true peace.

CHAPTER SIX

UNDERSTANDING PRO-GAY THEOLOGY

○—KEY POINTS—○

1. Pro-gay theology is a revision of the Bible verses that have traditionally been understood to refer to, and condemn, homosexual behavior.

2. The term "pro-gay theologian" refers to theologians who have developed or promote pro-gay theology.

3. While pro-gay theologians vary in the way they interpret the Bible,

they generally agree that it does not condemn homosexual behavior, and that the traditional Christian viewpoint on homosexuality is wrong.

4. Churches and denominations that accept and promote pro-gay theology are often called "Gay friendly churches"; "Open and Affirming churches"; or "GLBT (Gay, Lesbian, Bisexual, Transgender) friendly churches."

5. Christians who are homosexual, bisexual, or transsexual and who affirm pro-gay theology often refer to themselves as "Gay Christians"; "Gay and Lesbian Christians"; "GLBT Christians"; or "Queer Christians."

6. Those who believe in and promote pro-gay theology could be referred to as revisionists; those who oppose it are traditionalists.

7. Pro-gay theology appears in writings as early as the 1950s, but it's most notable promotion came in the 1970s and 1980s. John Boswell's *Christianity, Social Tolerance, and Homosexuality* (1980), Letha Scanzoni and Virginia Mollenkott's *Is the Homosexual My Neighbor?* (1978), and Peter Gomes's *The Good Book: Reading the Bible with Mind and Heart* (2002) are among the most well-known works promoting pro-gay theology.

8. Some pro-gay theologians come from a theologically liberal position and take a "low view" of biblical authority. Others claim a theologically conservative position and take a high view of Scripture, stating they believe the Bible is the ultimate authority and is the inspired Word of God. Believers in pro-gay theology are likewise diverse in their opinion of the Bible's inspiration and authority.

9. Pro-gay theology teaches that scriptural references to homosexuality have been mistranslated, misinterpreted, or misunderstood.

10. Revisionists often refer to historical errors of biblical misinterpretation committed by some Christians (the justification of slavery or the subjugation of women, for example) and claim that traditionalists are repeating this error today.

BOOKS WRITTEN FROM A REVISIONIST PERSPECTIVE

Christianity, Social Tolerance, and Homosexuality: Gay People in Western Europe from the Beginning of Christianity to the 14th Century by John Boswell, Chicago University Press, 1980.

Jesus, the Bible, and Homosexuality: Explode the Myths, Heal the Church by Jack Rogers, Westminster John Knox Press, 2006.

The Children Are Free: Re-Examining the Biblical Evidence on Same-Sex Relationships by Jeff Miner and John Tyler, Jesus Metropolitan Community Church, 2002.

Online Resources from a Revisionist Perspective

"The Bible and Homosexuality," *Whosoever: An Online Magazine for Gay, Lesbian, Bisexual, and Transgendered Christians,* http://whoso ever.org/index.shtml.

"The Bible Is an Empty Closet," Evangelicals Concerned, www.ecinc .org/Scriptures/clbrpg.htm.

Notes

1. Thomas Schmidt, *Straight and Narrow?* (Downers Grove, IL: InterVarsity, 1995), p. 41.
2. Stanton Jones, "The Loving Opposition," *Christianity Today*, 19 July 1993, p. 22.
3. John Boswell, *Christianity, Social Tolerance, and Homosexuality* (Chicago: University of Chicago Press, 1980), pp. 93-94; Derrick Bailey, *Homosexuality and the Western Christian Tradition* (Hambden, CT: Shoe String Books, 1975).
4. Letha Scanzoni and Virginia Mollenkott, *Is the Homosexual My Neighbor?* (New York: Harper and Row, 1978), pp. 57-58.
5. Scanzoni and Mollenkott.
6. Schmidt, pp. 88-89.
7. Bruce Metzger, "What Does the Bible Have to Say About Homosexuality?" *Presbyterians for Renewal* magazine, May 1993, p. 7.
8. Boswell, p. 100; Troy Perry, *Don't Be Afraid Anymore* (New York: St. Martin's Press, 1990), p. 341.
9. Perry, p. 341.
10. Boswell, p. 109.
11. Scanzoni and Mollenkott, pp. 65-66, emphasis added.
12. Bennett Sims, "Sex and Homosexuality," *Christianity Today*, 24 February 1978, p. 25.
13. Perry, p. 342.
14. Schmidt, pp. 78-79.

15. Boswell, pp. 341, 344.

16. Boswell, p. 342.

17. Boswell, p. 342.

18. Timothy Dailey, *The Bible, Church and Homosexuality* (Washington, DC: Family Research Council, 2004), p. 11.

REBUTTING
PRO-GAY THEOLOGY

by Joe Dallas

*But if I were a Christian homosexual this one
question would bother me most: Am I interpreting
Scripture in the light of my proclivity, or should I be
interpreting my proclivity in the light of Scripture?*

—AUTHOR PAUL MORRIS, FROM *SHADOW OF SODOM*

In chapter 6 I've attempted to review the most common pro-homosexual arguments used when interpreting scriptures, and set of arguments that make up what's known as pro-gay theology, or revisionist theology. But one of the most common concerns I hear among believers holding the traditional view on the Scriptures and homosexuality, is the problem of articulation. Many believers have a strong hold on the Bible and are well versed in its standards, but when conversing with those holding a revisionist view, they often feel inept while trying to articulate the traditional position. In the interest of providing a model for conversation, then, this chapter will consist of a running dialogue between a believer holding the traditional view, and a homosexual holding the revisionist viewpoint. This is offered with the hope it will enable the reader to better discuss and, when necessary, debate the merits of the traditional view, and the weaknesses of the revisionist one.

On the Deeply Ingrained Nature of Homosexuality

Pro-gay argument: "How can you say it's wrong to be gay when it's been proven that gays are born that way? Do you think God made a mistake when He made me gay?"

Response: "Of course God didn't make a mistake when He made you, but why assume He made you gay?"

Pro-gay argument: "Well, I sure didn't choose these feelings!"

Response: "Maybe not, but we *all* have feelings we don't choose. We all feel angry sometimes, or jealous, or we feel like lying, or having a sexual relationship with someone outside of marriage. Those feelings aren't a choice, but we do choose whether or not to act on them."

Pro-gay argument: "But these aren't just minor temptations like the ones you just named. I've had them all my life. I was born with them, in fact!"

Response: "I beg to differ. I really don't believe homosexuality is inborn, but even if it is, that doesn't mean God intended it."

Pro-gay argument: "You're saying my deepest feelings are wrong!"

Response: "I'm saying we all have feelings—deep ones, at that—which aren't necessarily right, and which we shouldn't give in to."

On the Origins of Homosexuality

Pro-gay argument: "But I read a study that said my sexual feelings come from some variation in the hypothalamus. I can't do much about that, can I?"

Response: "I read that study too, but no one's sure if it's accurate."

Pro-gay argument: "Why do you say that?"

Response: "First, the study has never been replicated. And second, the researcher wasn't really sure which of his subjects were gay and which ones weren't, and he admits he doesn't know if the differences he found in brain sizes were the cause of homosexuality, or if they were caused by homosexuality. The scientific community isn't at all convinced he's proven anything."

Pro-gay argument: "But there's another study on twins that seems to prove gays are born that way."

Response: "That one isn't too conclusive, either. Nearly half the identical twins studied didn't have the same sexual preference. Don't you think the percentage should have been higher? And none of those twins were raised apart, so who can tell what made them gay? Besides, none of the twin studies have been replicated, either. In fact, other twin studies have had completely different results."

Pro-gay argument: "Well, I've felt gay all my life, so I must have been born this way!"

Response: "Maybe, or maybe it started so early you can't even remember it. Anyway, who says that 'inborn' means 'ideal'?"

Pro-gay argument: "So you think God might have given me these feelings and then expected me to resist them?"

Response: "Just because we've got feelings, it doesn't mean God gave them to us. I've got feelings, too, that I have to resist. And I feel like I've had them all my life. It's not easy for me, either. "

On Homosexuality and Psychology

Pro-gay argument: "Well, maybe you can do something about those feelings, but homosexuality can't be changed. All the psychologists agree on that."

Response: "Actually, they don't. Did you know there have always been, and still are, plenty of psychologists who think homosexuality can be changed, if the patient really wants that sort of change?"

Pro-gay argument: "But I don't! Besides, even if I did, the only people who would do a thing like that would be right-wing fanatics."

Response: "There are plenty of credible therapists, non-Christian as well as Christian, who would help you if you wanted it."

Pro-gay argument: "But I'm not sick, am I? Didn't the American Psychiatric Association say homosexuality is normal some 20 years ago?"

Response: "That's not exactly what they said. They *did* decide homosexuality wasn't a disorder, but they didn't quite say it was normal, either. Truthfully, politics played more into that decision than anyone realizes."

Pro-gay argument: "Maybe so, but 10 percent of the population couldn't possibly be mentally ill!"

Response: "I never said you're mentally ill. The Bible says homosexuality isn't natural; it doesn't say homosexuals are crazy. But if you're saying 10 percent of the population is gay, I'm afraid that's way off. Every study done on the gay population, both here and abroad, shows it's much smaller than 10 percent."

Pro-gay argument: "Well, I don't believe God wants me to deny something

I've had all my life—something I've tried to change, and something so many other people have too. That just doesn't sound like God to me!"

Response: "That's funny. It sounds *exactly* like God to me. And it sounds like He requires of you the same things He requires of all of us. He asks us to deny something we've had all our lives—our *selves*—and take up our crosses daily to follow Him. He knows we've tried to change ourselves, and He knows we can't! But Jesus never said we had to change ourselves. He told us to follow Him, and to live obediently. The inward change is up to Him, but the obedience is up to us. Plenty of other people have 'selves' too, by the way. They may choose to indulge their selves, but as Christians, we're called to something different. We're not here to satisfy our selves. We're here to lose them! In the long run, that's the only way to really find ourselves, anyway."

Pro-gay argument: "Yes, but when you say homosexuality is wrong, you're really expressing the same old problem: homophobia."

Response: "What exactly is *homophobia*?"

Pro-gay argument: "Homophobia is the unreasonable fear or hatred of gays, and it's everywhere. Our whole society is saturated with it."

Response: "That sounds horrible. And if people have hated or feared you, I'm sorry to hear it. No one should be treated that way. But tell me, exactly how have *I* done that to you?"

On the Use of the Bible and Homophobia

Pro-gay argument: "By using the Bible verses to condemn me whenever you talk about homosexuality!"

Response: "But I believe the Bible. You say, as a gay Christian, that you believe it too. Doesn't that mean we both take our moral guidance from Scripture?"

Pro-gay argument: "Yes."

Response: "Then what's wrong with quoting it when I explain why I believe homosexuality is wrong?"

Pro-gay argument: "Because most people who quote the Bible to gays are homophobic, and they're using the Bible as an excuse to hate us."

Response: "That's a strong accusation. Am I acting like I hate you? I believe homosexuality's wrong, sure. But that's a belief, not a phobia. If I was homophobic, could I be sitting here talking to you? After all, if I had a phobia about gays, I'd be afraid to be anywhere near you!"

Pro-gay argument: "But you think homosexuality's a big sin or something."

Response: "I think it's a sin, no worse or better than some of my own sins. But thinking something is a sin, and having a phobia about it, are two very different things."

Pro-gay argument: "But don't you know how many lesbians and gays get beaten up because people like you go around saying it's a sin?"

Response: "I'm against anyone getting hurt, and I'll speak out against gay bashing as much as I'll speak out against gay practices. But nobody gets beat up just because I, or any other Christian, says homosexuality is a sin."

Pro-gay argument: "Oh, yes they do! Studies show that gay bashers come from religious homes, just like yours."

Response: "Some do, but it's their own craziness, not religion, that makes them do those terrible things. Some murderers and rapists also come from Christian homes, but that doesn't mean their religious upbringing made them commit their crimes. Thinking homosexuality is wrong doesn't make you beat homosexuals up. I think it's wrong, and I'm not beating you up, am I?"

Pro-gay argument: "No, but it does happen!"

Response: "Yes, and we should work together to prevent it. But silencing the Christian view of homosexuality isn't the way to do it. The fact is, you and I have completely different views of homosexuality. I can live with that. But I would ask, with all due respect, that you not accuse me of things I've never done—things like hurting gays, or spreading prejudice. Because when you do that, you're guilty of the very thing you say conservative Christians do to you. You're spreading myths and stereotypes. We may not agree on homosexuality, but I'm sure we both agree on the need to be truthful, even when we disagree."

On the "I'm Gay and Christian" Position

Pro-gay argument: "If you think homosexuality is wrong, how do you explain *me*? I'm born again and I'm gay, and I take my Christian life just as seriously as you do!"

Response: "Are you saying whatever a Christian does is okay because he's a Christian?"

Pro-gay argument: "Of course not, but I know God loves me just as I am."

Response: "Sure He does. But that doesn't mean He approves of every part of your life."

Pro-gay argument: "He hasn't told me that!"

Response: "What's to tell? We've got His Word in writing. And no matter how much He loves and accepts you, if His Word says your behavior is wrong, then He's already told you what He thinks of it."

Pro-gay argument: "But if He thinks badly of it, why do I feel His presence every week at my church? Our whole congregation is gay, and He knows it. So why is He blessing us?"

Response: "I'm not sure that He is. We can sometimes think we're feeling God's blessings, when in fact we're having an emotional, or even a demonic, experience. But just for the sake of argument, let's say you're right—God's presence is in your church. God's presence isn't quite the same as His approval. I can think of lots of ministers who had God's blessing on their lives, but who weren't living right."

Pro-gay argument: "If you're talking about my being gay, there's no reason He wouldn't condone what I do. I'm in a long-term relationship. My lover and I care very much about each other. God doesn't have any problem with that."

Response: "Because you love each other? That's a shaky foundation. The Bible doesn't say any kind of relationship is okay if there's love in it. What about adultery? Or fornication? Are those okay, too, as long as both people involved love each other?"

Pro-gay argument: "You don't understand. People involved in adultery have a choice. I don't! I've been gay ever since I can remember, and I've tried to change more times than I can count. So I've finally accepted who I am, and I'm sure it's okay with Him."

Response: "Because it's okay with you?"

Pro-gay argument: "Not just me. Plenty of other gay Christians too! We tried to change because people like you tell us we're sinners, but we don't have a choice over our sexual orientation. I've known so many people who tried to go straight, and all of them are back in the gay community now."

Response: "That doesn't make it right. I know it's hard to change. I know some Christians who have to resist homosexual temptations nearly every day. But then, doesn't every Christian have to resist temptations every day? That's what sanctification is all about—growing daily to become more like Him! When we're born again, our sinful feelings don't just vanish. Some of them, in fact, stay with us our whole lives.

"And I know, in your case, those feelings are very deeply ingrained. It would probably be harder for you to resist them than people in the church realize. But God isn't going to change His standards to accommodate ours. Please, don't decide something is right just because it's hard to get over. That's tampering with the Word of God. I think you'll find it's better, in the long run, to obey God's Word than to try to change it."

On the Authority and Inspiration of the Bible

Pro-gay argument: "Whatever reasons you have for objecting to homosexuality, you won't find any of them in the Bible. It's been badly mistranslated; the fact is, it doesn't condemn gays and lesbians the way you think it does."

Response: "I never said it condemns gays and lesbians, any more than it condemns anyone else. The Bible says we've all sinned, and we're all in need of redemption."

Pro-gay argument: "Fine, but I mean it also doesn't condemn loving sexual relationships between men or between women. Those men who wrote the Bible didn't even know what homosexuality was. It's only in the last century that we have come to understand what sexual orientation is. Biblical writers didn't know anything about people who felt they were gay from the time they were young, and who are in lasting, responsible lesbian and gay relationships."

Response: "But there's no contingency in the Bible about homosexuality. It doesn't say, 'Thou shalt not lie with man as with woman, unless that's your orientation.' The biblical authors probably weren't concerned about what caused certain behaviors—they were concerned with the behaviors themselves. By the way, it's quite an insult to God and His Word to ignore what the Bible says about homosexuality just because its authors never heard of 'sexual orientation.' They may never have heard about alcoholism either, but don't you think they knew what they were talking about when they prohibited drunkenness? Orientation, in itself, doesn't justify behavior."

Pro-gay argument: "But the Bible has always been used to back prejudice—haven't you noticed that? The KKK does it, the Nazis did it, and now the Religious Right's doing it to gays and lesbians!"

Response: "So many people use the term 'the Religious Right' nowadays that I'm not even sure what it is. But if you mean conservative Christians, then you're wrong. Sure, bigots have twisted the Bible in the past, but the fact that some Christians were wrong in the past doesn't automatically mean they're wrong in the present. It only means we should be careful before we take a stand on something, and believe me, I am."

Pro-gay argument: "Don't you think Christians of colonial times said the same thing while they bought and sold their slaves?"

Response: "That's a bad comparison. Gays have never been bought and sold in America; you've never been denied the right to vote; there are no gay and straight classrooms or drinking fountains; and you've always had the right to hold property and participate in the political process. In fact, you've always had the same rights all Americans have had. The same sure can't be said about African-Americans."

Pro-gay argument: "But bigotry is bigotry, no matter who it's directed against."

Response: "You're right about that. But is taking a biblical stand a form of bigotry? I'm saying homosexuality is wrong. I'm not saying homosexuals are less than human and should be treated as such. It's unfair and inaccurate when you confuse a moral position with bigotry."

Pro-gay argument: "But you're way too sure of yourself. You're not a language expert, so how can you be so sure the Bible really does condemn homosexuality? It's written in ancient languages."

Response: "But it's been translated by experts who know more about language than either one of us. Check the credentials of these guys before you write their translations off. They knew what they were doing."

Pro-gay argument: "Maybe so, but you fundamentalists sure do pick and choose what Scriptures you want to believe in. You yank out the passages on gays and say how terrible we all are, but you don't seem half as concerned about other Bible verses."

Response: "That's true, to a point. Sometimes Christians do get more excited about homosexuality than other sins. But they also preach against sins they're guilty of. Face it, if I wanted to pick and choose which Bible verses to take seriously, I'd only choose the ones that applied to your sins, and never mention the ones that apply to mine. But I don't do that; I admit I've got struggles too. Most other fundamentalists do the same."

Pro-gay argument: "But when you quote verses on homosexuality, you clobber us with them!"

Response: "I've heard you quote Scriptures; you don't seem to think you're hitting someone with them just because you're quoting them. When I quote Scriptures on homosexuality, I'm only doing so to back my belief that homosexuality is a sin. That's not clobbering. It's talking."

On Homosexuality and the Book of Genesis

Pro-gay argument: "So exactly which Scriptures do you think condemn homosexuality?"

Response: "Well, Genesis, for example, makes God's intent for sexual relationships pretty clear when it describes the first couple."

Pro-gay argument: "There's nothing about gays in those verses!"

Response: "My point exactly. The story of Adam and Eve doesn't say anything about homosexuality, only heterosexuality. It gives a very clear picture—a standard—of God's intention for men and women. It's the only standard upheld throughout the Bible."

Pro-gay argument: "So you're saying all of us should, like Adam and Eve, be married, and have kids? And that those who don't perfectly fit that model are in sin?"

Response: "Not at all. People have different callings and situations in life. Some are single; some married. Some are widowed; some celibate. All are valid. But the only standard for sexual expression that you'll find consistently praised in both Testaments in that of heterosexual monogamy."

Pro-gay argument: "Then I'd say a lot of Christians are doing a lousy job keeping that standard!"

Response: "And I'd agree with you. But when people aren't living up to a standard, the solution is to change the behavior of the people, not the standard itself. Besides, it's not just the creation account that comes to mind when I think of the Bible and homosexuality. There's the story of Sodom, later in Genesis, which makes a very strong statement."

Pro-gay argument: "But not against homosexuality. The men in Sodom were condemned for trying to rape Lot and his visitors."

Response: "That, among other things. But you've got to admit that homosexuality must have been practiced pretty commonly in Sodom, or all the men of the city wouldn't have tried to participate in the rape. Besides, several other scriptures refer to Sodom's sins as being sexual, as well as idolatrous and prideful."

Pro-gay argument: "Then you admit Sodom wasn't destroyed because of gays?"

Response: "Sodom was destroyed because of wickedness, period. You know, lots of modern cities around the world are full of people practicing all sorts of sin, sexual sins as well as nonsexual. If judgment were to fall on any of them, I'd never say it was because of the sexual sins alone. It would no doubt be because of the cumulative effect of the many sins. And that, to my thinking, is what happened in Sodom. Besides, thank God, we don't have to figure out who's getting judged or for what reason. That's in God's hands. Our responsibility is to determine what He wants from us, and, to the best of our ability, mold our lives to His will. On that point, I hope we agree."

On Homosexuality and Leviticus

Pro-gay argument: "The Holiness Code in Leviticus had to do with Israel, not us. It was necessary for them to procreate to keep their race alive, so of course homosexuality would be looked down on. Besides, we're not under the Law, so why even mention it?"

Response: "You're right about the Law, thank God. We're not under it, and I, for one, am glad, because I'd never be able to keep it. But the chapters that the Levitical prohibitions against homosexuality appear in also contain other sexual sins—adultery and incest, for example—that are condemned in the New Testament as well."

Pro-gay argument: "But homosexuality was associated with idol worship back then. That's why God condemned it."

Response: "Not necessarily. Sure, there were rituals that heathen nations practiced including all sorts of sexual orgies, homosexual or heterosexual or both. But it's quite a stretch to assume that's the only form of homosexuality practiced at the time. More important, though, is the contingency you seem to be putting into these chapters. Are you saying that if the other sins in those chapters—incest, adultery, and bestiality—weren't associated with idol worship, then they'd be okay too?"

Pro-gay argument: "Of course not!"

Response: "Then you can't have it both ways. Either all the sins in those chapters were condemned because of their association with idolatry, or none of them were."

Pro-gay argument: "So you're saying you believe what Leviticus says about homosexuality being a sin? And that you think homosexuality is wrong?"

Response: "I do."

Pro-gay argument: "Then to be consistent, you also have to believe I should be stoned to death, because that, as you know, is the penalty those verses in Leviticus call for if someone commits a homosexual act."

Response: "Interesting point. Do you believe these chapters also condemn adultery? And do you believe adultery is wrong?"

Pro-gay argument: "Obviously they condemn it, and yes, I believe it's wrong."

Response: "Then to be consistent, you also have to believe that Bill Clinton, Rev. Jim Bakker, and Franklin D. Roosevelt should have been stoned to death, because they all committed that sin. And, as you know, stoning is the penalty those verses in Leviticus call for if someone commits adultery."

Pro-gay argument: "Nonsense! Just because I think adultery's wrong doesn't mean I think people who commit it should be put to death! If Bill Clinton, Rev. Jim Bakker, or Franklin D. Roosevelt had lived in Israel's camp at that time, death would have been their punishment. That's what those verses mean. Adultery's wrong, sure, but in the New Testament, we're certainly not told that adulterers have to be put to death."

Response: "Thank you. I couldn't have said it better myself. If a homosexual was found guilty of that behavior in Old Testament times, death would have been his punishment, as it would have been for the adulterer. But though both are still sins, neither one warrants the death penalty today. That doesn't legitimize them, though. It's possible, as you just said so well, to believe something's wrong without believing the person doing the wrong needs to be penalized in a significant way. And that, to my thinking, is a proper approach to the Old Testament's position on homosexuality."

On Jesus and Homosexuality

Pro-gay argument: "How come you're so against homosexuality? Jesus didn't say a word against it."

Response: "I'm no more against homosexuality than any other sin. And, frankly, whether or not Jesus mentioned it is a secondary point. It's plainly condemned in other scriptures."

Pro-gay argument: "But His teachings are the foundation of the faith!"

Response: "Not exclusively. Paul said *all* Scripture—that means the whole Bible—is profitable for instruction in righteousness. Christ's teachings are very important, sure. But they're not meant to be our only source of guidance. If that were the case, we wouldn't need a 66-book Bible; we'd just use the four Gospels. But there's plenty of important doctrinal and historical information in the other books, as well. They carry as much weight as the Gospels."

Pro-gay argument: "Still, if Jesus thought homosexuality was important, don't you think it's strange He said nothing about it?"

Response: "Who is to say He didn't? He might have said quite a bit on the subject and it never got recorded. But even if He didn't, that's no proof it wasn't important to Him. He didn't explicitly say anything in the Gospels about wife-beating or child abuse either, but I'm sure they were important to Him."

Pro-gay argument: "Wrong! He held up a standard of love for children and respect for women, so it's obvious He did not approve of abusing them."

Response: "Exactly. He also held up a standard for sexual relationships when He referred to the marriage of a man and woman as being God's intention. So even if He didn't say anything about homosexuality, it's obvious He didn't approve of it, just as He didn't approve of anything short of God's intention for the sexual experience, which, He clearly said, was marriage."

Pro-gay argument: "That's an argument from silence."

Response: "So is yours. You see? You can't prove Jesus condoned something just because He didn't mention it. I can't prove what He said or didn't say about it, either. But I do know what He upheld as a standard, and it certainly wasn't homosexuality."

Pro-gay argument: "Yet He taught that eunuchs have a place in the kingdom, and that would include gays."

Response: "A eunuch was a man who'd either been castrated, or who'd been born without reproductive organs. Surely you don't think that's the definition of the average homosexual."

Pro-gay argument: "Eunuchs were outcasts. So are gays and lesbians. And it looks like, in some cases, eunuchs were gay."

Response: "Perhaps, but what made them eunuchs wasn't their orientation, but the fact they were unable to reproduce. Lesbian women and gay men can, by and large, reproduce, and in most cases their organs are intact. So the word *eunuch* really doesn't apply to them."

Pro-gay argument: "But if Jesus Himself approved of a gay relationship, you'd have to concede He approves of homosexuality, wouldn't you?"

Response: "I suppose. What relationship are you referring to?"

Pro-gay argument: "The relationship between a centurion and his servant, who Jesus healed. The gospel says he loved his servant, and in those days, centurions often had sexual relationships with their servants. And not only did Jesus heal this man's lover, but He openly commended the man's faith! How could that be, if He disapproved of their relationship?"

Response: "Your question makes several assumptions, so let me answer each of them. First, we don't know that these two had a sexual relationship. Yes, at times, centurions had relations with their slaves. That doesn't mean every centurion did. Bosses sometimes have affairs with their secretaries too, but we don't assume every boss and secretary are involved. So right off the bat, your argument unravels, because you've no way of knowing the relationship between servant and centurion was sexual.

"Second, even if they *did* have a sexual relationship, do you really think Jesus approved of the lifestyle of every person He healed? Healing is an act of grace, not a stamp of approval, and nothing in Scripture indicates He granted it as a reward.

"Finally, if in fact they were homosexual, Jesus could well recognize someone's faith and even commend it, without necessarily condoning their behavior. Does Rahab the harlot come to mind? She was clearly a woman of faith, but there were parts of her life that sure didn't square with God's will."

Pro-gay argument: "But God is love, and that, after all is what Jesus taught: that we're to love each other. That's what He was all about."

Response: "Not quite. Yes, He taught us to love one another, and we sure could do a better job of it. But He also taught obedience, repentance, and the need to conform our lives to God's will, not ours. So when you say 'All He taught is love,' you oversimplify both Him and His teachings. And that's something none of us, I'm sure, wants to do."

On Homosexuality and Romans Chapter 1

Pro-gay argument: "I know you think the New Testament has a lot to say against homosexuality, but actually, if you study its original language and intent, you'll see that it doesn't."

Response: "That's certainly not true of the first chapter of Romans. Paul lists quite a few sins there—homosexuality included. Of course, homosexuality is not the major sin of Romans 1, anymore than it's the main sin in Leviticus. But it's definitely there, condemned and forbidden."

Pro-gay argument: "But the people Paul described in Romans 1 weren't really gay. That's why it was a sin! God didn't want them changing their nature. They were heterosexuals indulging in homosexuality. What made it wrong was the fact that it wasn't natural to them. Otherwise, it would have been fine."

Response: "And what about the gossips, adulterers, and backbiters in Romans 1? Were they, also, people who weren't 'really' gossips, adulterers, or backbiters? It didn't come naturally to them—*that* was the problem? I don't think so. Nothing in Scripture says a certain sexual behavior is a sin unless it somehow comes naturally to you but not the rest of us."

Pro-gay argument: "But I don't think Paul had any idea what it was like to be truly gay."

Response: "Probably not, but he knew what it was like to wrestle with sin, and he said so plainly. Anyway, I don't think it would have mattered one bit whether or not he personally struggled with sexual sin. It's the behavior he condemned, without even considering what factors might have led someone to that behavior in the first place."

Pro-gay argument: "But Paul lived in a time when they knew nothing about homosexuality as we know it today. At that time, it mainly meant sex between adults and minors—pederasty—or prostitution, maybe. That's what Paul condemned, not homosexuality as we know it today."

Response: "Actually, you're both misrepresenting the times and underestimating Paul. The idea of adult, mutually consented upon homosexuality wasn't so foreign at that time. Gay historian John Boswell himself claims that the idea people were born gay was prevalent in Hellenistic times and that Aristotle himself both understood and approved of the homosexual orientation. And to suggest Paul was unaware of these prominent figures is as much of a stretch as suggesting that modern preachers would be unaware of Sigmund Freud. Besides which, don't you believe the Bible was divinely inspired?"

Pro-gay argument: "Of course!"

Response: "Then if the Holy Spirit, who is God, inspired its writers, surely God Himself was aware of everything we now know about homosexuality, and then some! By the way, it's not only in Romans that Paul mentions homosexuality. Later in the New Testament, in 1 Corinthians and 1 Timothy, he lists homosexuality as one of many other sins keeping people away from God."

On Paul and the Term *Arsenokoite*

Pro-gay argument: "But the word he uses for 'homosexuals' in those Scriptures really means 'male prostitutes.'"

Response: "Where did you get that idea?"

Pro-gay argument: "I've read it time and again. Theologians have done careful word studies on Paul, and that's what they found. The word Paul used—the one we usually think of as meaning 'homosexual'—didn't mean homosexual at all."

Response: "Well, it certainly didn't mean 'prostitute.' The word you're talking about is *arsenokoite*. It's a Greek term Paul took directly from the Greek translation of the Old Testament. In fact, it's from the Greek translation of the Leviticus verses that specifically refer to homosexuality, not prostitution. So there's no way Paul could have meant it as anything but a reference to homosexuality. Besides, if you look at the word itself—a compound of the Greek words *arsane*, meaning "male," and *koite*, meaning "bed" or "couch," you'll see there's nothing in the word even suggesting prostitution. It's sex between men, not sex for money, that Paul is writing against."

Pro-gay argument: "Well, I still believe the Bible doesn't say anything against my sexuality. God loves me as I am, and I stand on that."

Response: "And you have every right to. But at some point you've got to ask yourself: Do I believe the pro-gay theology because I really think it's true, or because, despite the majority opinion of Bible scholars as well as a common-sense reading of the Scriptures, I want to believe it? Is it *conviction* we're talking about here, or convenience? Only you can answer that."

CHAPTER SEVEN

REBUTTING PRO-GAY THEOLOGY

○—KEY POINTS—○

1. To practice *exegesis* ("leading or drawing forth") means to draw the meaning of a document from the document itself, as opposed to *eisegesis,* in which the reader imposes a meaning onto the document. Traditionalists generally believe pro-gay theology is a systematic form of eisegesis, and that the traditional view is reached by practicing exegesis.

2. A high view of Scripture acknowledges that God the Holy Spirit, who inspired the authors of the Bible, fully understood homosexuality, not only as it was known in ancient times but also as we know it today, when He inspired the references to it in both Testaments.

3. Homosexuality is not cited in Scripture as the main cause of Sodom's destruction in Genesis chapter 19. (See Ezekiel 16:49.) But the number of men who gathered there to participate in a homosexual rape (Genesis 19:4) and references to Sodom's sexual sin elsewhere in Scripture (2 Peter 2:6-7 and Jude 7) indicate homosexuality was one of many sins practiced there, leading to its judgment.

4. While some regulations in Leviticus are clearly not binding today, many (such as commands against adultery, bestiality, and incest) have universal application. Prohibitions against homosexuality appear in the same chapters as these (Leviticus 18:22 and 20:13) and is condemned in the New Testament as well, making the Levitical prohibition against homosexuality applicable today.

5. The fact that Jesus did not condemn homosexuality in the Gospels is not proof He approved of it, since there are a number of other behaviors—incest and bestiality, for example—that are clearly wrong though not mentioned by Christ. The Gospels do not claim to be exhaustive, or of higher authority than the rest of Scripture.

6. The centurion's love for his servant who Jesus healed (Matthew 8:5-13) shouldn't be assumed to have been sexual, just as any employer's love for an employee should not automatically be interpreted as romantic love. Since nothing in Matthew's account implies a sexual relationship, such an interpretation has to be imposed on this account, rather than drawn from it.

7. When Jesus referred to eunuchs as having a special place in the kingdom (Matthew 19:12) he was referring to a group usually recognized as castrated men. At times, the term might also include men who, for reasons other than castration or birth defect, were unable

to reproduce. Yet even if this reference could be stretched to include males with homosexual orientation, it says nothing indicating permission for such men to engage sexually with other men.

8. Twenty-four behaviors or character failings (including homosexuality) are described by Paul in the first chapter of Romans (Romans 1:26-32). If a contingency can be applied to his condemnation of homosexuality in this chapter, then it can also be applied to the other behaviors mentioned in this chapter as well, murder and deceit included. So either all the sins listed here are objectively wrong without exception or contingency, or none of them are.

9. The Greek term *arsenokoite*, which is used twice in the New Testament by Paul when referring to homosexuality (1 Corinthians 6:9; 1 Timothy 1:10) is derived from the Greek translation of Leviticus 18:20 and 20:13, both of which condemn male homosexuality.

10. While specific instruction and guidance are given to heterosexual couples throughout Scripture, not one verse in Scripture recognizes or offers guidance to a same-sex couple as such.

Books Written in Rebuttal to the Revisionist Perspective

The Bible and Homosexual Practices: Texts and Hermeneutics by Robert Gagnon, Abingdon Press, 2002.

The Gay Gospel?: How Pro-Gay Advocates Misread the Bible by Joe Dallas, Harvest House Publishers, 2007.

Straight and Narrow? Compassion and Clarity in the Homosexual Debate by Thomas Schmidt, InterVarsity Press, 1995.

Online Resources

"What Does the Bible Say About Homosexuality?" by Robert Gagnon, www.robgagnon.net/ArticlesOnline.htm.

"Our Position" from Focus on the Family website, www.focusonthe family.com/socialissues/sexual_identity/progay_revisionist_theology /our_position.aspx.

PART THREE

HOMOSEXUALITY AND AMERICAN PSYCHIATRY

Where We've Been and Why It Matters

by Joe Dallas

We are in a new era in which diagnosis has such social and political implications that one is constantly on the front lines fighting on issues our forebears were spared.

—PSYCHIATRIST ROBERT STOLLER

Any understanding of the evolution of cultural views on homosexuality must include a brief understanding of the psychiatric profession's historical and current approaches to it. To the clinician this is doubly important, since current psychological views on homosexuality don't exist in a vacuum and, in fact, have developed in the context of significant research, upheaval, and revisions. To the general reader, the history of homosexuality and American psychiatry is also crucial, as it gives us broader understanding of the influence psychology wields in public opinion and policy. For that reason, we'll begin this chapter in the late 1800s, and will from there chronicle significant events relative to the subject.

1869–1956:
Classification

These years were marked by attempts to understand the phenomenon often referred to as inversion. Some theorists considered it an inborn abnormality; others a form of mental illness. Since psychiatry itself was in its early years, numerous approaches to the art of diagnosis were taken, and, in fact, the *Diagnostic and Statistical Manual for Mental and Emotional Disorders* did not come into being until the end of this period, a period in which homosexuality was viewed as both an abnormality to be cured and a mystery to be solved.

1869. Carl Westphal, a professor of psychiatry in Berlin, publishes a case history of a "female homosexual," referring to her condition as "contrary sexual feeling." He considers her lesbianism to be congenital, not acquired, and through his work he comes to be credited as the first to place the study of homosexuality in the clinical arena.[1]

1886. Richard von Krafft-Ebing produces *Psychopathia Sexualis*, one of the most influential works on homosexuality to date, in which he approached the condition as both environmental and inherited.[2]

1935. Sigmund Freud states in his "Letter to an American Mother" that "homosexuality is assuredly no advantage, but it is nothing to be ashamed of, no vice, no degradation; it cannot be classified as an illness." This letter, in which Freud plainly states his belief that homosexuality represents a deficit in sexual development, would come to be referred to and quoted extensively by pro-gay and traditionalist parties.[3]

1940. Newdigate Owensby promotes pharmacological shock therapy for the treatment of homosexuality, a form of treatment that would later come to be known as "aversion therapy." Aversion therapy, practiced well into the 1970s, would become the horror story in the backgrounds of many homosexual patients, some of whom endured forced electroshock therapy, the specter of which would be raised during future discussions of treatment for homosexuality.[4]

1948. *Sexual Behavior in the Human Male*, Alfred Kinsey's groundbreaking work, is released, which listed his findings after taking the sexual histories of 5300 American men. The findings, especially on homosexuality, shocked

American sensibilities: 37 percent of the subjects admitted at least one homosexual experience since their adolescence, and 10 percent claimed to have been homosexual for at least three years.[5]

Kinsey's wording was plain but would for decades be frequently misinterpreted by those claiming he had proven 10 percent of the population to be gay. However, rather than claiming 10 percent of the male population was homosexual, he stated that 10 percent of the males surveyed *claimed to have been homosexual for at least three years.* They had not necessarily been homosexual all their lives, nor would they necessarily be homosexual in the future.

Subsequent studies have, in fact, challenged the 10 percent claim. *USA Today* reported on April 15, 1993, a new survey of 3321 American men indicating that 2.3 percent of them had engaged in homosexual behavior within the previous ten years; only 1.1 percent reported being exclusively homosexual. In 1989 a U.S. survey estimated that no more than 6 percent of adults had any same-sex contacts and only 1 percent were exclusively homosexual. A similar survey in France found that 4 percent of men and 3 percent of women had ever engaged in homosexual contacts, while only 1.4 percent of the men and 0.4 percent of the women had done so within the past five years.[6] A Christian journalist concluded, not surprisingly, that the 10 percent statistic proposed by Kinsey was "dying under the weight of new studies."[7]

1952. The first edition of the *Diagnostic and Statistical Manual of Mental Disorders* (DSM) groups the "sexual deviations" (including homosexuality) under the category of "sociopathic personality disorders."

Why it matters. Two issues were raised during this period that are especially relevant to us today: The power of classification and statistics to influence public opinion, and the myriad of professional opinions regarding the origin and nature of homosexuality.

Kinsey's work proved the former: By simply describing the number of American men who'd reported some form of homosexual experience, he both shocked the nation and, to an extent, desensitized the public by making it aware of how common homosexuality was. And while cultural acceptance of it was still far off, Kinsey's book served as an important early step removing some of the shock element that often accompanied the mention of homosexuality. And the variety of positions already being taken on the origins and nature of homosexuality—inborn or acquired; pathological or normal—served as forerunners to the ongoing debates we continue to be embroiled in.

1956–1973:
Challenge

Up to this point very few of the professional voices addressing homosexuality considered it to be anything but abnormal, no matter what its origins. But the "abnormal" position was now to be called into question by sympathetic doctors, zealously committed homosexual activists, and the growing influence of a burgeoning gay rights movement.

1956. Psychologist Evelyn Hooker begins publishing research on homosexuals she interviewed outside of the clinical environment. Having befriended a number of homosexuals, she became convinced they had not been adequately represented in research thus far, most of which had been done in clinical or institutional settings. So with a grant from the National Institute of Mental Health, Hooker began her interviews in 1954, eventually concluding that homosexuals were essentially as well adjusted as heterosexuals. Obviously groundbreaking and controversial, her research laid the foundation for a massive challenge to traditional thought.[8] It should be noted that Hooker's work has been subject to challenges as well.[9]

1962. *Homosexuality: A Psychoanalytic Study* by Irving Bieber is released, offering a broad overview of the treatment of homosexual men and the introduction of the Family Triad—Distant Father; Close Binding Mother—that would come to be commonly associated with male homosexuality. (See chapters 9 and 10, "Theories of Origin," parts 1 and 2.)

1972. The term "homophobia" is coined by psychologist George Weinberg, referring to the "dread of being in close quarters with homosexuals."[10] Its meaning would expand to include, according to Dr. Joseph Nicolosi, "any belief system that values heterosexuality as superior to and/or more natural than homosexuality,"[11] and the word itself would come to be invoked frequently and generously to refer to even the most modest objections to homosexuality.

Years later, Andrew Sullivan, the well-known gay journalist would make some surprising comments on the word:

Perhaps the most depressing and fruitless feature of the current debate about homosexuality is to treat all versions of this [conservative Christian] argument as the equivalent of bigotry. They are not. At its most serious, it [the Christian prohibition against homosexuality] is not a phobia; it is an argument.[12]

Why it matters. Psychiatrists and psychologists holding the traditional view on homosexuality were by now having to interact with research challenging their claims. The fact that Hooker's work allegedly showed that homosexuals were as mentally healthy as heterosexuals (a point still under debate by some, see NARTH reference above) forces the question we still have to consider: Is homosexuality primarily a moral issue or a clinical one? And is it possible for someone having what is biblically referred to as unnatural tendencies to still be essentially healthy, mentally and emotionally? The same questions posed to traditionalists in the 1950s are worth considering today.

1972–1979:
Confrontation

The Stonewall riots of 1969 had marked the beginning of the gay rights movement in America, a movement marked by the defiance and aggression seen in other social movements of the time. No wonder, then, the same tone and tactics seen in movements confronting conventional wisdom would now be seen in earnest as homosexuals began demanding affirmation, not just tolerance, a demand that would now extend itself to the institution that bestowed the label of "healthy" or "sick" on millions of citizens: The American Psychiatric Association.

1972: APA annual meeting sponsors a panel—"Psychiatry: Friend or Foe to Homosexuals: A Dialogue"—that includes gay activists, gay sympathetic psychiatrists, and a disguised gay psychiatrist, Dr. H Anonymous (John Fryer, MD).

1973. The Board of Trustees of the APA approves the deletion of homosexuality from the DSM-II and substitutes a diagnosis of "sexual orientation disturbance." Events leading to this decision constitute one of the most fascinating and telling chapters in gay rights history.

Gay leaders began protesting the annual conventions of the American Psychiatric Association, demanding a reconsideration of homosexuality's diagnostic status, and further demanding that they be included in any future discussions within the APA on the subject.[13] The APA consented; intense discussion and debate followed.

On December 15, 1973, the Board of Trustees of the APA, concluding months of negotiations with gay activists, voted to delete homosexuality altogether from the DSM. Opposition from several psychiatrists immediately followed. A referendum on the Board's decision was called, and in the spring of 1974, the entire membership of the APA was polled for their support or rejection of the Board's decision.

The results are noteworthy. Out of 10,000 voting members, nearly 40 percent opposed the Board's decision to normalize homosexuality. Though the 40 percent were clearly a minority, and the decision was upheld, it showed how deeply divided the APA was on the matter.

Recounting the events, Dr. Ronald Bayer, the author of the most comprehensive book on the subject, comments:

> The entire process, from the first confrontation organized by gay demonstrators to the referendum demanded by orthodox psychiatrists, seemed to violate the most basic expectations about how questions of science should be resolved. Instead of being engaged in sober discussion of data, psychiatrists were swept up in a political controversy. The result was not a conclusion based on an approximation of the scientific truth as dictated by reason, but was instead an action demanded by the ideological temper of the times.[14]

Yet the APA decision did not necessarily reflect the views of American psychiatrists. A survey conducted by the journal *Medical Aspects of Homosexuality* in 1979 (six years after the APA decision) asked 10,000 psychiatrists if they felt homosexuality "usually represented a pathological adaptation." Sixty-nine percent of the respondents said "yes," and 60 percent said homosexual men were less capable of "mature, loving relationships" than heterosexual men.[15] Obviously, there remained a huge discrepancy between the American Psychiatric Association's official position and the views of many of its members.

Why it matters. The APA landmark decision of 1973 is often cited as proof that the issue is settled: The members voted; the decision was made; homosexuality is normal. Yet the facts say otherwise: The decision was hardly unanimous, as the subsequent 1979 poll showed. But to the Christian believer, larger issues than that are at play. Even if all members of the APA *had* agreed from the beginning that homosexuality was normal, and if all psychiatrists currently in practice viewed it as healthy, that has no bearing on the Christian position on the subject. The Bible speaks of homosexuality (as well as other sexual sins) in moral, not psychological, terms. In developing a sense of ethics, the Christian cannot take his cues from the mental health profession. What is deemed mentally sound by man may not be morally viable to God.

1980 to the Present:
Confirmation

Now that homosexuality had been normalized, the ensuing decades would show ongoing, committed efforts on the part of pro-gay leadership within the American Psychiatric Association and American Psychological Association to see that the homosexual-affirming position was confirmed, in policy and practice, and in all areas of each organization. Yet a new trend was also developing within both associations: As both became more insistent, in their official literature and ethical standards, that the only acceptable viewpoint for mental health professionals to hold regarding homosexuality was a gay-affirmative view, both were met with vigorous resistance.

Pro-gay advocacy groups within both associations worked to convince their organizations to officially support gay causes (same-sex marriage, antidiscrimination laws, and so on) and to officially condemn reparative therapy and consider making it unethical for licensed therapists to offer it. Traditionalists within both groups became more vocal in pointing out the heavy-handedness of such tactics, forming more alliances with each other and generating support from unexpected sources, including former APA presidents who held to a pro-gay position but also recognized the rights of patients who didn't share that view to seek treatment compatible with their perspective. The clash between the two groups continues to grow and perpetuate itself as of this writing.

1980. DSM-III creates a new class, the "psychosexual disorders," including psychosexual dysfunction, paraphilia (fetishism), gender-identity disorder (transsexualism), and *ego-dystonic homosexuality*, a classification referring to those who were homosexual but did not want to be, making them suitable for treatment.

1982. The APA establishes the Caucus of Homosexual-Identified Psychiatrists, which later becomes the Caucus of Lesbian, Gay, and Bisexual Psychiatrists.[16]

1985. The Association of Gay and Lesbian Psychiatrists is established.[17]

1987. The DSM-III-Revised deletes the diagnosis of homosexuality entirely, leaving the paraphilias and sexual dysfunctions as the two main classes of "sexual disorders." Now anyone seeking treatment for unwanted homosexuality would be classified accordingly, and all direct mention of homosexuality was now completely expunged from the manual.

1991. The book *Reparative Therapy of Male Homosexuality* by Joseph Nicolosi is released amid considerable controversy and celebration, from gays and conservatives respectively. This would mark a new wave of books addressing social and religious conservatives who had never accepted the APA's 1973 position change, and still considered homosexuality a condition to be resisted and, if possible, prevented. Nicolosi's work would also draw high levels of opposition from pro-gay advocates within the APA, who saw him as a reactionary trying to undo the gains they'd made within the association, while drawing praise from those who felt the APA had moved from a neutral position on homosexuality to one of pro-gay advocacy.

1992. The National Association for the Research and Therapy of Homosexuality is founded by Drs. Joseph Nicolosi, Benjamin Kaufman, and the late Charles Socarides. Established as an alternative for people seeking treatment for unwanted homosexuality, its statement of purpose declares:

> We respect the right of all individuals to choose their own destiny. NARTH is a professional, scientific organization that offers hope to those who struggle with unwanted homosexuality. As an organization, we disseminate educational information, conduct and collect scientific research, promote effective therapeutic treatment, and provide referrals to those who seek our assistance. NARTH upholds the rights of individuals with unwanted homosexual attraction to receive effective psychological care and the right of professionals to

offer that care. We welcome the participation of all individuals who will join us in the pursuit of these goals.[18]

2000. The American Psychiatric Association issues two position statements, one in support of same-sex civil unions and the other expressing reservations about "reparative therapies." This marked the shift in discussions on homosexuality from "Is it normal?" to "Is it ethical to treat it as an unwanted condition?" The statement reads in part:

> Therapies Focused on Attempts to Change Sexual Orientation (Reparative or Conversion Therapies)
>
> POSITION STATEMENT
>
> Approved by the Board of Trustees, March 2000
> Approved by the Assembly, May 2000
>
> The political and moral debates surrounding this issue have obscured the scientific data by calling into question the motives and even the character of individuals on both sides of the issue. The validity, efficacy and ethics of clinical attempts to change an individual's sexual orientation have been challenged. To date, there are no scientifically rigorous outcome studies to determine either the actual efficacy or harm of "reparative" treatments. The literature consists of anecdotal reports of individuals who have claimed to change, people who claim that attempts to change were harmful to them, and others who claimed to have changed and then later recanted those claims.[19]

Thus the APA expressed tacit official disapproval of reparative therapy without outright stating it is unethical or harmful. (Note the wording: "There are no scientifically rigorous outcome studies to determine either the actual efficacy or harm of 'reparative' treatments.")

2001. Columbia University's Dr. Robert L. Spitzer released the evidence for his conclusions that "homosexuals can change" in a historic panel discussion. He had interviewed 200 subjects (143 men and 57 women) who were willing to describe sexual and emotional histories, including their self-reported shift from homosexual to heterosexual.

Dr. Spitzer was currently Chief of Biometrics Research and Professor of Psychiatry at Columbia University. But he is better known for his scientific role in 1973—when he was *the* instrumental figure in the American Psychiatric Association's decision to remove homosexuality from its diagnostic manual of mental disorders, making his work all the more poignant and controversial.[20]

2004. Dr. Robert Perloff, former president of the APA, addresses a NARTH convention, emphasizing "The Importance of Client Self-Determination." Citing self-determination as the right of every patient seeking treatment, Dr. Perloff stated,

> I am here as the champion of one's right to choose...It is my fervent belief that freedom of choice should govern one's sexual orientation...If homosexuals choose to transform their sexuality into heterosexuality, that resolve and decision is theirs and theirs alone, and should not be tampered with by any special interest group—including the gay community. The right to seek therapy to change one's sexual adaptation is considered self-evident and inalienable.[21]

2005. Another APA former president addressed the NARTH convention. In November 2005, psychologists Nicholas Cummings, PhD, and Rogers Wright, PhD, charged "intellectual arrogance and zealotry" within the APA, which they claimed was now dominated by social-activist groups. Their remarks expressed what numerous members of the APA had long felt but were afraid to express.

Dr. Cummings said he was dismayed to see activists exploit the stature of the parent body to further their own social aims—pushing the APA to take positions in areas where they had no conclusive evidence.

"When APA does conduct research," Dr. Cummings said, "they only do so when they know what the outcome is going to be...only research with predictably favorable outcomes is permissible."[22]

When writing their book *Destructive Trends in Mental Health*, Wright and Cummings had invited the participation of a number of fellow psychologists, who flatly turned them down—fearing loss of tenure, loss of promotion, and other forms of professional retaliation. "We were bombarded by horror stories," Dr. Cummings said. "Their greatest fear was of the gay lobby, which is very strong in the APA."

"Homophobia as intimidation" is one of the most pervasive techniques used to silence anyone who would disagree with the gay activist agenda. Sadly, I have seen militant gay men and lesbians—who I am certain do not represent all homosexuals, and who themselves have been the object of derision and oppression—once gaining freedom and power, then becoming oppressors themselves.[23]

Why it matters. To Christian professional counselors, concerned apologists, and those seeking treatment for unwanted homosexual attractions, the current controversies within the APA hold long-term, major ramifications. As of this writing, the American Psychiatric and American Psychological Association have released official statements questioning the effectiveness of reparative therapy, warning of its possible harmful effects, and condemning any form of therapy based on theories viewing homosexuality as essentially unhealthy. Unquestionably these official positions have a chilling effect, but not chilling enough to prevent groups like NARTH from thriving, nor to prevent patients from seeking out treatment addressing their homosexuality from a traditional perspective. Meanwhile, the ongoing debates seem to focus on the following questions:

1. Do therapists who offer the traditional approach (often called "reparative therapists") make it clear to prospective patients what they can reasonably expect if they seek to change their sexual orientation? What exactly does "change" mean, and do all or even most patients experience the same form and levels of change?

2. Are pro-gay advocates being accurate when they charge that "reparative therapy" actually harms many or most of the patients who seek it? Other than anecdotal evidence, what proof exists that a patient's voluntary attempts to change can be harmful?

3. Is it fair to say that people seeking to change their orientation do so because of "internalized homophobia"? (A claim many opponents of reparative therapy make.) What about the patient's religious or philosophical worldview, which may prohibit homosexual relations? Is that not a legitimate motivating factor, and should it not be respected?

4. Is it really the place of either the American Psychiatric or Psychological Associations to dictate to its practitioners what their

position on homosexuality should be, or to make similar dictates to the patient population at large?

These are the questions challenging today's Christian counselor, psychologist, or therapist, and they remind all of us why these controversies and conflicts do, indeed, matter.

CHAPTER EIGHT

HOMOSEXUALITY AND AMERICAN PSYCHIATRY

○—KEY POINTS—○

1. If we want to discuss homosexuality with any credibility, we need to be clear about theories of origins.
2. If we want to offer hope, we need to be clear about prospects of change.
3. If we are to counsel others, we need to have informed consent.
4. We need to re-evaluate treating minors.
5. We need to be clear about diagnostic status.
6. We need to remember that psychology tells us what is, not what should be.

ADDITIONAL RESOURCES

Crompton, Louis, *Homosexuality and Civilization* by Louis Crompton, Belknap Press, 2003.

Male Homosexuality: A Contemporary Psychoanalytic Perspective by Richard Friedman, Yale University Press, 1988.

Homosexuality and American Psychiatry: The Politics of Diagnosis by Ronald Bayer, Basic Books, 1981.

"The History of Psychiatry and Homosexuality," www.aglp.org/gap/1_history/.

NOTES

1. Ronald Bayer, *Homosexuality and American Psychiatry: The Politics of Diagnosis* (New York: Basic Books, 1981), p. 19.

2. "The History of Psychiatry and Homosexuality," www.aglp.org/gap/1_history.

3. Kenneth Lewes, *The Psychoanalytic Theory of Male Homosexuality* (New York: Simon and Schuster, 1988), pp. 33-34.

4. "The History of Psychiatry and Homosexuality."

5. Alfred Kinsey, *Sexual Behavior in the Human Male* (Philadelphia: Saunders Press, 1948), pp. 625, 638.

6. "Homosexual Urban Legends," www.traditionalvalues.org/urban/two.php.

7. "What Causes Homosexuality? Pt. 3," www.johnankerberg.org/Articles/_PDFArchives/streams-of-life/SL1W0903.pdf.

8. Bayer, pp. 49-53.

9. "Normal or Abnormal?" review of Stanton Jones and Mark Yarhouse, *Ex-Gays?: A Longitudinal Study of Religiously Mediated Change in Sexual Orientation* (Downers Grove, IL: IVP Academic, 2007), at www.narth.com/docs/mentaldisorder.html.

10. Richard Isay, *Being Homosexual* (New York: Farrar, Strauss, Giroux, 1989), p. 145.

11. Joseph Nicolosi, *Reparative Therapy of Male Homosexuality: A New Clinical Approach* (New York: Jason Aronson, Inc., 1991), p. 138.

12. Andrew Sullivan, *Virtually Normal* (New York: Alfred Knopf, 1995), p. 212.

13. Bayer, pp. 99-126.

14. Bayer, p. 34.

15. Bayer, p. 167.

16. "The History of Psychiatry and Homosexuality."

17. "The History of Psychiatry and Homosexuality."

18. NARTH mission statement, www.narth.com/menus/mission.html.

19. See APA official statement at www.psych.org/Departments/EDU/Library/APAOfficialDocuments andRelated/PositionStatements/200001.aspx.

20. "Prominent Psychiatrist Announces New Study Results: 'Some Gays Can Change,'" www.narth.com/docs/spitzer2.html.

21. "Former APA President Supports NARTH's Mission Statement, Assails APA's Intolerance of Differing Views," *NARTH Bulletin*, vol. 13, no. 3 (December 2004).

22. "'Psychology Losing Scientific Credibility,' Say APA Insiders," www.narth.com/docs/insiders.html.

23. "Psychology Losing Scientific Credibility."

THEORIES OF ORIGIN, PART 1
Inborn Theories
by Joe Dallas

We can no longer simply consider ideas according to rules of logic and evidence, but must now take into account the political and polemical forces that surrounded them and gave them form. Henceforth, the history of ideas about homosexuality is at least as much the history of opinion as it is of ideas.

—KENNETH LEWES, PhD, *THE PSYCHOANALYTIC THEORY OF MALE HOMOSEXUALITY*

The question "What causes homosexuality?" is of real interest to pastors, Christian counselors, parents, apologists, and, of course, homosexuals themselves. The pastor ministering to a homosexual parishioner needs to know if he's addressing someone with an incurable condition or a chosen sin; the Christian counselor likewise wonders if his treatment approach should include attempts to change his homosexual clients' feelings, or teach his client to live with them. Parents of gay children wonder if they're to blame, Christian apologists want to understand and answer the "born gay" arguments they're sure to encounter, and homosexuals themselves understandably ask, "Why me?" All of which leads us to now consider theories of the origins of homosexuality.

Theories of origin should be examined through the lenses of three questions:

1. What are the theory's *claims*, and are they accurate?
2. What is the *worldview* of the theorist?
3. Is the theory *confirmed in, compatible with,* or *contradicted by* the Bible?

The *claims* of a theory obviously need to be understood if the theory is to be of any use. The *worldview* of the theorist needs to be considered because, as Dr. Lewes claimed in the above quote, preconceived ideas about homosexuality—whether it's normal or abnormal, for example—cannot help but influence a person's conclusions about its origins. So a pro-gay theorist isn't likely to accept research indicating homosexuality springs from developmental disorders or unhealthy family dynamics, since his preconceived position is that homosexuality is normal, and something normal can't be birthed by abnormal or unhealthy influences. A theorist whose worldview is traditionally Judeo-Christian will also be skeptical of studies claiming homosexuality is a normal, inborn variant. Our *presumptions,* born largely of worldview and experience, are likely to color our *conclusions.* To accept this fact doesn't require a rejection of assumptions or conclusions, but it encourages us to re-examine them when necessary, and admit their influence on our approach to theories of origin.

Most important, though, is an examination of theories in light of Scripture. If the Bible *confirms* a theory, we can solidly support it. If the theory itself is not found in Scripture, yet doesn't *contradict* Scripture, we can consider it. If it's clearly *contradicted* by Scripture, we reject it.

So a theorist proposing homosexuality is a symptom of fallen nature is taking a position the Bible confirms, warranting support. Theories claiming it springs from family dynamics are suggesting something the Bible neither confirms nor denies, so we can at least consider them. And theories insisting homosexuality is normal and to be accepted because it's observable in nature, are to be rejected on the basis of equating the morality of mankind with that of the animal kingdom. The Bible is clear in its distinction between human beings and animals. As always, the authority of Scripture determines a theory's relevance to the believer. And as the following pages will show, most theories on homosexuality's origins are neither confirmed nor contradicted by Scripture, so they can at least be considered. Where the Bible is adamant, we should be as well. Where it is silent on a subject, such as the specific causes of homosexuality, we have leeway to subscribe to a number of theories, provided we hold them loosely enough to respect both their strengths and possible flaws, and our incomplete understanding of such a complex subject.

From that perspective, we'll consider four general categories of the most commonly held theories on causation in part 3 of this book: *inborn, developmental, spiritual/demonic,* and *interactive.* This is not to say there are no other categories of theories, historical or current, but these are the ones that seem to be most widely accepted, making them the ones we're most likely to interact with. In this chapter, we'll focus on the inborn theories of the origins of homosexuality.

Inborn Theories: An Overview

As a category, *inborn theories* refers to those claiming homosexuality is something one is born with, and that alone accounts for it. It may view homosexuality as something genetic (determined by a gene or set of genes) or biological (caused by prenatal influences other than genes).

Historically, proposing homosexuality was inborn didn't necessarily mean viewing it as normal. Some saw it as an inborn abnormality, like a birth defect, while others argued it was an inherited condition as natural as skin color. Today, though, the "normalcy" position is the standard one among inborn proponents, so this theory is usually, if not always, accompanied by the belief that inborn sexual preferences are natural and healthy variants, rather than problems or defects.

According to Ronald Bayer's history of homosexuality and psychiatry, the contrast between the inborn and developmental camps showed itself in the nineteenth century, when scientific study of homosexuality began in earnest. There was division even in the inborn camp as to whether it was an inborn abnormality or one of many normal traits. Nineteenth-century French neurologist Jean-Martin Charcot, for example, concluded homosexuality to be inborn when he found he couldn't reverse it through his preferred treatment of hypnosis, suggesting he at least initially considered it to be abnormal. Karl Ulrichs, though a prominent nineteenth-century defender of homosexuals, nonetheless claimed their brains had not developed "along expected lines," suggesting male homosexuals were female souls "lodged in a male's body." Havelock Ellis took a more benign view in *Sexual Inversion*, stating that homosexuality was both inborn and normal, and Magnus Hirschfeld, a renowned defender of homosexual rights in Germany, found it to be a nonpathological condition determined by glandular secretions.[1]

Freud himself considered the possibility of a biological component when he wrote, "It is not for psychoanalysis to solve the problem of homosexuality. It must rest content with discovering the psychical mechanisms that resulted in the determination of the object choice. There its work ends, and it leaves the rest to biological research."[2]

Whether or not they took their cues from Freud, scientists and sex researchers in the ensuing decades, up to and including recent history, have certainly tried to discover a biological or genetic cause for homosexuality. From the late nineteenth century to the present, numerous studies, recounted in works such as Bayer's, Kenneth Lewes's *The Psychoanalytic Theory of Male Homosexuality*, and *My Genes Made Me Do It* by Neil E. and Briar Whitehead,[3] have attempted to show a link between genes or biology with sexual preference.

Some have researched the sexual histories of siblings to determine such a link, as did F.J. Kallman in 1952, who proposed a genetic base for homosexuality through his studies of twins.[4] Others, such as Dr. John Money and associates at Johns Hopkins University, looked to prenatal hormonalization of the brain to explain gender identity and homosexuality. Citing the "Adam/Eve Principle" as a possible explanation for the effects of hormonal imbalance on the pre-born child's brain, Money's comments fell in the inborn but abnormal camp.[5] Other theorists of the late twentieth century followed suit, including Dr. James Weinrich[6] and Günter Dörner,[7] who proposed that male homosexuals may have developed a "feminine sexual brain" caused by androgen deficiency, a conclusion he based on a study of "effeminate" homosexual men. But while researchers labored to isolate genetic or biological causation, detailing their results in numerous reports,[8] the notion of inborn homosexuality continued to raise eyebrows, both among traditionalist and pro-gay researchers, well into the 1990s.

Dr. John Money, a known advocate for pro-gay causes, criticized (in spite of his own research described above) the inborn theory when he declared in the 1970s: "The child's psychosexual identity is not written, unlearned, in the genetic code, the hormonal system or the nervous system at birth."[9] Masters and Johnson were similarly adamant in 1984 when they wrote, "The genetic theory of homosexuality has been generally discarded today...No serious scientist suggests that a simple cause-effect relationship applies." [10] And openly gay psychologist Dr. John DeCecco, editor of the *Journal of Homosexuality*, said, "The idea that people are born into one type of sexual behavior is foolish." [11]

It can be safely said, then, that while the inborn theory has always enjoyed supporters, it was far from the dominant view. Even among homosexuals, the "born gay" notion wasn't historically a popular one. In the 1940s, when sexologist Alfred Kinsey asked homosexuals how they "got that way," only 9 percent claimed to have been born gay. [12] In 1970, nearly the same percentage of 979 gays in San Francisco answered the same way. [13] But all of that was to change in 1991, when two studies thrust the inborn theory into the public's consciousness, where it would remain both popular and solidly intact.

LeVay, Pillard, and Bailey: A New Era

In 1991 Dr. Simon LeVay, a neuroscientist at the Salk Institute of La Jolla, California, examined the brains of 41 cadavers—19 allegedly homosexual men, 16 allegedly heterosexual men, and six allegedly heterosexual women.

His study focused on a group of neurons in the hypothalamus structure called the interstitial nuclei of the anterior hypothalamus, or the INAH3.

He reported this region of the brain to be larger in heterosexual men than in homosexuals; likewise, he found it to be larger in heterosexual men than in the women he studied. For that reason, he postulated homosexuality to be inborn, the result of size variations in the INAH3, and his findings were published in *Science* magazine in August 1991. [14]

Though his research was trumpeted and LeVay himself became, for a season, a chief spokesman for the inborn theory, he had his detractors, and his study had its flaws. First, *his results were not uniformly consistent.* On the surface it appears that *all* of LeVay's homosexual subjects had smaller INAH3s than his heterosexual ones; in fact, three of the homosexual subjects actually had *larger* INAH3s than the heterosexuals. Additionally, three of the heterosexual subjects had *smaller* INAH3s than the average homosexual subject. Thus, as Dr. John Ankerberg of the Ankerberg Theological Research Institute notes, six of LeVay's 35 male subjects—17 percent of his total study group—contradicted his own theory. [15]

Second, *LeVay did not necessarily measure the INAH3 properly.* The area LeVay measured was quite small—smaller than snowflakes, according to scientists interviewed when his study was released. His peers in the neuroscientific community cannot agree on whether the INAH3 should be measured by its size and volume or by its number of neurons.[16]

Third, *it is unclear whether brain structure affects behavior or behavior affects brain structure.* Dr. Kenneth Klivington, also of the Salk Institute, points out that neurons can change in response to experience. "You could postulate," he says, "that brain change occurs throughout life, as a consequence of experience."[17] In other words, even if there is a significant difference between the brain structures of heterosexual and homosexual men, it is unclear whether the brain structure caused homosexuality, or if homosexuality affected brain structure.

In fact, one year after LeVay's study was released, Dr. Lewis Baxter of UCLA obtained evidence that behavioral therapy can produce changes in brain circuitry, reinforcing the idea that behavior can and does affect brain structure.[18] So even if differences do exist between the INAH3s of homosexual and heterosexual men, it is possible that the diminished size of the homosexual's is caused by his behavior, rather than his behavior being caused by the INAH3's size.

Fourth, *LeVay was not certain which of his subjects were homosexual and which were heterosexual.* He admits this represents a "distinct shortcoming" in his study. Having only case histories on his subjects to go by (which were by no means guaranteed to provide accurate information about the patient's sexual orientation), he could only assume that, if a patient's records did not indicate he was gay, he must have been heterosexual.

Yet 6 of the 16 reportedly heterosexual men studied had died of AIDS, increasing the chances that their sexual histories may have been incompletely recorded.[19] If it is uncertain which of LeVay's subjects were heterosexual and which were homosexual, how useful can his conclusions about "differences" between them really be?

Fifth, *LeVay did not approach the subject objectively.* Openly homosexual himself, he told *Newsweek* magazine that, after the death of his lover, he was determined to find a genetic cause for homosexuality or he would abandon science altogether. Furthermore, he admitted that he hoped to educate society about homosexuality, affecting legal and religious attitudes toward it.[20] None of this diminishes his credentials as a neuroscientist. But his research can hardly be said to have been unbiased.

And the scientific community did not by any means unanimously accept

LeVay's study. Comments from other scientists in response to LeVay's work are noteworthy. Dr. Richard Nakamura of the National Institute of Mental Health said it would take a "larger effort to be convinced there is a link between this structure and homosexuality."[21] Dr. Anne Fausto-Sterling of Brown University was less gentle in her response: "My freshman biology students know enough to sink this study."[22]

Dr. Rochelle Klinger, a psychiatrist at Medical College of Virginia, doubts we will "ever find a single cause of homosexuality."[23] *Scientific American* summed up the reason many professionals approach the INAH3 theory with caution: "LeVay's study has yet to be fully replicated by another researcher."[24]

Pillard and Bailey's Twin Study

Another study frequently cited from the same period—the fall of 1991—is the twin study released around the same time as LeVay's. Psychologist Michael Bailey of Northwestern University (a gay rights advocate) and psychiatrist Richard Pillard of Boston University School of Medicine (who is openly homosexual) compared sets of identical male twins to fraternal twins (whose genetic ties are less close). In each set, at least one twin was homosexual. They found that, among the identical twins, 52 percent were both homosexual, as opposed to the fraternal twins, among whom only 22 percent shared a homosexual orientation.[25] Pillard and Bailey suggested that the higher incidence of shared homosexuality among identical twins meant that homosexuality was genetic in origin. But this suggestion, like LeVay's, had its problems.

Pillard and Bailey's findings actually indicate that something besides genes must account for homosexuality. If 48 percent of identical twins, who are closely linked genetically, do *not* share the same sexual orientation, then genetics alone *cannot* account for homosexuality. Bailey admitted as much by stating, "There must be something in the environment to yield the discordant twins."[26]

Also, each set of twins Pillard and Bailey studied was raised in the same household. If the sets of twins in which both brothers were homosexual had been raised in *separate* homes, it might be easier to believe that genes played a role in their sexual development. But since they were all raised in the same households, it is impossible to know what effect environment played, and what effect, if any, genes played. Dr. Fausto-Sterling commented that "in order for such a study to be at all meaningful, you'd have to look at twins raised apart."[27]

And Drs. Pillard and Bailey, like Dr. LeVay, did not approach their subject objectively. Their personal feelings about homosexuality, like LeVay's, certainly do not disqualify them from doing good research on the subject. But their feelings must be, at the very least, considered. Pillard said, in fact, "A genetic component in sexual orientation says, 'This is not a fault,'" and both he and Bailey stated that they hoped their work would "disprove homophobic claims."[28]

It should also be noted that a later study on twins yielded results different from Pillard and Bailey's. In March 1992 the *British Journal of Psychiatry* published a report on homosexuals who are twins (both fraternal and identical) and found that only 20 percent of the homosexual twins had a gay co-twin, leading the researchers to conclude that "genetic factors are insufficient explanation of the development of sexual orientation."[29]

Despite these criticisms, media coverage of the studies was generous and largely favorable, and it soon became clear that a broader acceptance of the inborn theory inevitably led to broader public acceptance of homosexuality. William Cheshire, the editorial page editor for the *Arizona Republic*, was a good example. "My feelings about gays and lesbians were dominated by religious beliefs," he said in a 1993 interview with *U.S. News and World Report*. But after reviewing certain studies purporting to prove that homosexuals were born that way, he "did a complete reversal in [his] attitude toward gays and lesbians," and he began actively promoting, through his paper, antidiscrimination laws for gays.[30]

Gays themselves reported finding comfort in the studies, because, as one gay man enthused, "I felt in my heart that this [homosexuality] is something I was born with." The "born gay" studies, he added, "made me feel good about myself. They made me feel less a sinner."[31] Small wonder, then, that many (though not all) pro-gay apologists advocate the inborn theories.

Other Studies

Since the release of the findings of LeVay, Pillard, and Bailey, numerous other researchers have suggested their findings indicate the genesis of homosexuality can be found in biology, brain structure, or genes, and while the earlier work of LeVay, Pillard, and Bailey was widely and (according to some) easily criticized, a number of recent and more sophisticated studies are compelling and shouldn't be dismissed. Some of the most notable (as of this writing in 2009) have been classified by the organization Religious Tolerance, which describes them in detail.[32] They include:

1. **Studies based on fingertip ridges**
   J.A.Y. Hall and D. Kimura at the University of Western Ontario at London, Ontario, Canada found in 1999, that 30 percent of the homosexuals tested had a surplus of ridges on their left hand, whereas only 14 percent of the heterosexuals did.[33]

2. **Studies based on finger lengths**
   Psychologist Marc Breedlove in 1999 reported that among 720 volunteers he studied, lesbians were found to have shorter index fingers than heterosexual women; gay males tended to have shorter index fingers than heterosexual males.[34]

3. **Studies based on birth order**
   Researcher Ray Blanchard studied families with a male homosexual child and found that the probability that a male child will grow up as a homosexual increases by about 33 percent for each brother born before he was. Blanchard suggests that this effect may be caused by an immune response within the mother during pregnancy.[35]

4. **Study of genes**
   Dean Hamer of the National Cancer Institute surveyed the families of 114 gay men, seeking to find which other family members might also be homosexual. They concluded that "there were increased rates of gay people among family members genetically related to each other even when raised apart in different households."[36]

5. **Study of eye blinking inhibition**
   Researchers at University of East London at King's College reported that groups of homosexual and heterosexual men and women showed significant differences when responding to bursts of loud noises. "The reaction of the lesbian test subjects was closer to that which would be expected among straight men. And, gay men reacted closer that of women, although to a lesser extent."[37]

6. Hearing sensitivity study

Researchers at University of Texas reported structural differences in the inner ears between lesbians and heterosexual women. They found that lesbians had inner ear characteristics that were more like those of men. These findings indicate that sexual orientation is at least partly decided before birth—perhaps at conception.[38]

7. Studies of ear emissions

University of Texas at Austin researchers observed that as a group, homosexual and bisexual women's emissions were slightly more like that of men, and less frequent and weaker than those of the heterosexual women.[39]

8. Homosexual males' responses to pheromones

Researchers at Karolinska Institute in Stockholm, Sweden studied 12 heterosexual men, 12 heterosexual women, and 12 homosexual men to compare their responses to odors while PET scans were taken of their brain activity. When gay men and heterosexual woman were exposed to the smell of testosterone, the part of their brain that deals with sexual response was activated. Heterosexual men did not show this reaction. When heterosexual men were exposed to testosterone, there was no sexual response in the brain. When heterosexual men were exposed to estrogen, there was a sexual response. The study was published in the *Proceedings of the National Academy of Sciences* on May 10, 2005.[40]

9. Lesbian responses to pheromones

Researchers at Karolinska Institute in Stockholm, Sweden repeated the above study on lesbian subjects. They found that lesbians' brains react differently to sex hormones than those of heterosexual women.[41]

10. Brain-scan testing on homosexuals and heterosexuals

Swedish researchers at the Stockholm Brain Institute at Karolinska Institute furthered their work by using neural magnetic resonance imaging (MRI) on a group composed of both heterosexual and homosexual men and women. They found key similarities between the brains of homosexual males and heterosexual females vs. those of lesbians and heterosexual males. Their findings were published in the *Proceedings of the National Academy of Sciences* on June 16, 2008.[42]

A Biblical Response

When analyzing research purporting to show homosexuality is inborn, some Christians react in a knee-jerk fashion, leaping to discredit the research at any cost. This mistake is based, I believe, on the notion that if homosexuality is ever proven to be inborn, the Christian position will then be debunked. Yet nothing in a truly biblical approach to the matter denies the possibility that attractions to the same sex may have physical roots. Granted, a *traditional* position among Christians may be threatened, if that position insists homosexuality is chosen or acquired after birth. But history and common sense remind us of the difference between a traditional position and a truly biblical one.

A *traditional* position, held by many believers, reads something like this:

1. Homosexual orientation is either chosen or caused by faulty parenting, sinful choices, trauma, or a combination of all three.

2. Attempts to prove homosexuality is inborn are engineered to justify homosexuality and advance gay rights, and should thus be dismissed.

3. When someone truly repents of homosexuality they lose all homosexual desires, which further proves it cannot be an inborn trait.

4. To recognize the legitimacy of any "born gay" studies is to make ungodly concessions to the pro-homosexual view.

However earnest or well intended, there are flaws in this position, which a *biblical* one will consider, drawing some markedly different conclusions:

1. Homosexual orientation, like a number of other tendencies, *may* be influenced by faulty parenting, or sinful choices, or trauma, or a combination of all three. It could also be influenced, or even created by, inborn characteristics, since the Fall of man has affected all of us physically, psychologically, and spiritually. "Behold, I was brought forth in iniquity, and in sin did my mother conceive me" (Psalm 51:5).

2. Attempts to prove homosexuality is inborn may *at times* be

engineered to legitimize the behavior, but it's inaccurate and unfair to presume *all* such research is so tainted it can't be considered. "He who answers a matter before he hears it, it is folly and shame to him" (Proverbs 18:13).

3. Repenting of a sinful behavior by no means guarantees losing all temptations toward that behavior, as many who've repented of homosexuality will attest. Inborn or not, it tends to be deeply ingrained, so the desire for it may remain long after repentance. And the need for it to be resisted may last for many years—or for a lifetime. That's a reality of life in this fallen world. "The flesh lusts against the Spirit, and the Spirit against the flesh; and these are contrary to one another, so that you do not do the things that you wish" (Galatians 5:17).

4. No concession is made to a pro-gay viewpoint by acknowledging that homosexuality *could be* inborn. Acknowledging possible inborn tendencies toward a sin is a far cry from legitimizing the sin itself. "Do not let sin reign in your mortal body, that you should obey it in its lusts" (Romans 6:12).

A biblical response, then, will consider the inborn theory by posing the questions advised earlier in this chapter:

1. What are the theory's *claims*, and are they accurate?
2. What is the *worldview* of the theorist?
3. Is the theory *confirmed in, compatible with,* or *contradicted by* the Bible?

Accuracy of Claims and Worldview of Theorists

In answer to the first, the theory's claims are self evident: Homosexuality is partially or completely caused by inborn factors. As to their accuracy, the jury is still out. Some of the studies mentioned above seem credible; even unassailable. Others are less so.

The eye-blinking study, for example, drew criticism from Professor Warren Throckmorton for highlighting similarities in blink responses between lesbian women and heterosexual men, but showing less marked similarities between homosexual men and heterosexual women. He also pointed out the effect smoking has on blink responses, a factor the study should have considered.[43]

Then there are the pheromone/scent studies, purporting brain differences between homosexual and heterosexual subjects based on their responses to smells. A written exchange between Dr. Throckmorton and Dr. Ivana Savic of the Karolinska Institute in Stockholm regarding the research into homosexuals' responses to pheromones includes a clear acknowledgement by Dr. Savic that she recognizes such responses could be learned, not necessarily inborn.[44] Additionally, Dr. Jeffrey Satinover, an author and lecturer in Civil Liberties and Constitutional Law at Princeton University, points out that such studies often neglect a consideration of the "chicken or egg" question: Is the difference in brain structures between homosexuals and heterosexuals the *cause for*, or *caused by*, homosexual leanings? Reviewing an interview with one of the study's authors, he remarks:

> The key statement in the *New York Times* interview with one of the authors of the article is this: "We cannot tell if the different pattern is cause or effect."
>
> The same discussion arose after LeVay's study and he finally conceded—years later—that repetition of homosexual activity can change the brain to produce the effects he discovered—likewise here as the researchers state directly.[45]

And in a response to this and other inborn theories, the National Association for the Research and Therapy of Homosexuality makes a serious point regarding any studies of the brain by emphasizing the capacity of brain structures to change in response to experience, making it all the more difficult to determine cause and effect:

> The widely-held and erroneous presumption that brain structures are fixed and unresponsive to experience generates a second presumption, also tacit: That if a brain structure or function can be correlated to a behavioral trait then the trait must be both unchangeable and innate.
>
> Unaddressed and left non-explicit, this two-step sequence of tacit presumptions attached to explicit, high quality scientific data but of only a correlative kind, almost invariably generates in the mind of the scientifically unsophisticated something akin to a "belief."

Every single study that has emerged since the original LeVay study that falls into the above class—looking for or finding bimodal statistical physiological correlates (nervous system or otherwise) to homosexual versus heterosexual populations, in both males and females, however defined—comes with the same essential caveat: That cause and effect cannot be distinguished by the study.[46]

All things considered, we may answer our first question about the accuracy of these studies with a definite "maybe." They may, in fact, accurately point us to inborn sources of sexual orientation, though pointing and concluding aren't nearly the same.

The second question, regarding the worldview of the theorists, isn't easily answered, though many of their comments regarding their work indicate a strong bias toward gay rights. Still, bias needn't invalidate results, so questioning their ability to conduct objective research seems unwarranted.

Theories in Light of Scripture

As to the third question—Is the theory *confirmed in, compatible with,* or *contradicted by* the Bible?—we can allow that the inborn theory itself needn't be seen as contradictory. If we are a fallen race, then the possibility of inborn sinful tendencies has to be considered.

Scripture teaches that we inherited a corrupt sin nature that affects us physically and spiritually (Psalm 51:5; Romans 5:12). We were born spiritually dead (John 3:56) and physically imperfect (1 Corinthians 15:50-54). We cannot assume, then, that because something is inborn, it is also God-ordained. There are mental, psychological, physical, and sexual aspects of our beings that God never intended us to have. Inborn, in short, does not mean "divinely sanctioned," as the possible link between genes and other unhealthy behaviors indicates. Albert Mohler, president of the Southern Baptist Theological Seminary in Louisville, Kentucky, and a well-known Christian apologist, acknowledges this when he urges believers not to shy away from examining the validity of some inborn research:

> Given the consequences of the Fall and the effects of human sin, we should not be surprised that such a causation or link is found. After all, the human genetic structure, along with every other aspect of

creation, shows the pernicious effects of the Fall and of God's judgment.[47]

In 1983, for example, the former director of the National Council on Alcoholism reported on a number of chemical events that can produce alcoholism.[48] In 1991, the City of Hope Medical Center found a certain gene present in 77 percent of their alcoholic patients.[49] Obesity and violent behavior are now thought to be genetically influenced.[50] Even infidelity, according to research reported in *Time* magazine, may be in our genes![51]

Surely we are not going to say that obesity, violence, alcoholism, and adultery are legitimate because they were inherited. So it is with homosexuality. Whether inborn or acquired, it is still, like all sexual contact apart from marriage, biblically condemned, and what is biblically condemned cannot be legitimized by a quick baptism in the gene pool. Or, as conservative columnist Selwyn Duke more succinctly puts it, "Biology doesn't determine morality."[52]

None of this negates the importance of the research cited above; rather, this clarifies it. The discovery of a single gene responsible for homosexuality is unlikely, as is the possibility that same-sex attractions arise exclusively from inborn factors. Still, if homosexuality is minimally, partially, or completely generated by inborn elements, we need to know. Knowing would inform our approach to homosexuals with deeper respect for the depth of their orientation, and the enormous struggles faced by those dealing with what is often an unwanted orientation that could be inborn as well as ingrained. And for the sake of responsible ministry, apologetics, and participation in public-policy debates, shouldn't we, of all people, be informed?

Christian leaders and conservative voices are recognizing the need to scrutinize, but not necessarily discount, inborn theories. Selwyn Duke points out the wrongness of an unduly defensive Christian posture by reminding us:

> That homosexuality may have a basis in biology is rejected by many on the right for the same reason it is embraced by homosexuals. The reasoning is that if such feelings are biologically-induced, then homosexual behavior is neither sinful nor a choice. The truth is, however, that both sides have fallen victim to a misconception... If biology determined morality, then any tendency attributable to nature would have to be thought moral.[53]

John Derbyshire, columnist for the conservative *National Review*, recognizes the validity of inborn research but challenges its attempt to normalize homosexuality when he writes:

> I don't think that the fact of a predilection's being inborn should necessarily lead us to a morally neutral view of the acts it prompts.[54]

And Albert Mohler, responding to those who insist that inborn theories prove the legitimacy of homosexuality, exhorts all of us to hold informed, accurate positions without compromising higher biblical truth:

> Christians must be very careful not to claim that science can never prove a biological basis for sexual orientation. This does not alter God's moral verdict on homosexual sin (or heterosexual sin, for that matter), but it does hold some promise that a deeper knowledge of homosexuality and its cause will allow for more effective ministries to those who struggle with this particular pattern of temptation. If such knowledge should ever be discovered, we should embrace it and use it for the greater good of humanity and for the greater glory of God.[55]

CHAPTER NINE

THEORIES OF ORIGIN, PART 1

○—KEY POINTS—○

1. Theories on the origins of homosexuality should be considered by how they are confirmed by, compatible with, or contradicted by Scripture.

2. The inborn theory claims homosexuality is primarily or exclusively caused by inborn elements (genes, biological influences, and so on) rather than postnatal elements.

3. Historically, inborn theorists have been divided as to whether or not homosexuality constitutes an inborn abnormality or a normal variant of human sexuality.

4. As the gay rights movement gained visibility and influence, the notion of homosexuality being a civil rights issue was buttressed by arguments

for the inborn nature of the orientation, making inborn theories both a political and psychological issue.

5. In 1991, studies released by Simon LeVay and Drs. Pillard and Bailey broke new ground for the inborn theory, and it has grown in acceptance and influence since then.

6. Subsequent studies have added weight to the evidence that homosexuality may have some inborn elements, but to date, there is not verifiable proof that this is an inborn condition.

7. It is possible to accept the possibility that inborn elements contribute to homosexuality without legitimizing homosexuality itself.

8. An informed Christian approach to ministry, apologetics, and social action will give a fair hearing to current research while recognizing that "inborn" does not necessarily mean "normal" or "God-ordained."

RESOURCES

Homosexuality and the Politics of Truth by Jeffrey Satinover, Baker Books, 1996.

My Genes Made Me Do It! by Neil and Briar Whitehead, Huntington House Publishers, 1999.

NOTES

1. Ronald Bayer, *Homosexuality and American Psychiatry: The Politics of Diagnosis* (New York: Basic Books, 1981), pp. 17-19, 21.

2. Sigmund Freud, "Über die Psychogenese eines Falles von weiblicher Homosexualität" ["The psychogenesis of a case of female homosexuality"], *Internationale Zeitschrift für Psychoanalyse* VI, 1920, pp. 1-24, in *Collected Works* XII, pp. 271-302.

3. Respectively: New York: Simon and Schuster 1988; Lafayette, LA: Huntington House Publishers, 1999.

4. F.J. Kallman, "Comparative twin study of the genetic aspects of male homosexuality," *Journal of Nervous and Mental Disease*, 1952, 115:288-98.

5. See Joe Dallas, *Desires in Conflict*, rev. ed. (Eugene, OR: Harvest House Publishers, 2003), p. 96.

6. James D. Weinrich, *Sexual Landscapes* (New York: Scribner's Sons, 1987).

7. G. Dörner, W. Rohde, F. Stahl, et al., "A neuroendocrine predisposition for homosexuality in men," *Archives of Sexual Behavior*, 4:1 (1975).

8. For a concise review of hormonal, genetic, and neuro-anatomic research over the past three decades, see Tahir Ijaz, M.D., *Homosexuality—An Analysis of Biological Theories of Causation*, www.flyfish ingdevon.co.uk/salmon/year2/hormones/tahir.htm#genstudies.

9. John Money, *Perspectives in Human Sexuality* (New York: Behavioral Publications, 1974), p. 67.

10. William Masters, Virginia Johnson, and Robert Kolodny, *Human Sexuality* (Boston: Little, Brown and Co., 1984), pp. 319-20.

11. John DeCecco, editor of the *Journal of Homosexuality*, quoted in *USA Today*, March 1, 1989, p. 4D.

12. Paul Gebhard, *The Kinsey Data* (Philadelphia: Saunders Press, 1979), p. 23.

13. Alan Bell and Martin Weinberg, *Homosexualities: A Study of Diversities Among Men and Women* (New York: Simon and Schuster, 1978).

14. Simon LeVay, "A Difference in Hypothalamic Structure Between Heterosexual and Homosexual Men," *Science*, 30 August 1991, pp. 1034-37.

15. John Ankerberg, "The Myth that Homosexuality Is Due to Biological or Genetic Causes" (research paper), Ankerberg Theological Research Institute, P.O. Box 8977, Chattanooga, TN 37411.

16. "Is This Child Gay?" *Newsweek*, 9 September 1991, p. 52.

17. "Is This Child Gay?".

18. *Los Angeles Times*, 16 September 1992, p. 1; cited in *NARTH Newsletter*, December 1992, p. 1.

19. "Sexual Disorientation: Faulty Research in the Homosexual Debate," *Family* (a publication of the Family Research Council, 700 13th St. NW, Ste. 500, Washington, DC 20005), June 1992, p. 4.

20. "Is This Child Gay?" p. 52.

21. Quoted in *Los Angeles Times*, 30 August 1991, sec. A, p. 1.

22. Quoted in *Time*, 9 September 1991, p. 61.

23. Quoted in "Is This Child Gay?" p. 52.

24. "Gay Genes Revisited," *Scientific American*, November 1995, p. 26.

25. Michael Bailey and Richard Pillard, "A Genetic Study of Male Sexual Orientation," *Archives of General Psychiatry*, 1991, no. 48, pp. 1089-96.

26. David Gelman, "Born or Bred?" *Newsweek*, 24 February 1992, p. 46.

27. Quoted in Gelman.

28. Quoted in Gelman.

29. Michael King and Elizabeth McDonald, "Homosexuals Who Are Twins," *The British Journal of Psychiatry*, March 1992, vol. 160, p. 409.

30. "Rethinking the Origins of Sin," *Los Angeles Times*, 15 May 1993, sec. A, p. 31.

31. Joseph Shapiro, "Straight Talk About Gays," *US News and World Report*, 15 July, 1993, p. 48.

32. "Studies on the Causes of Sexual Orientation," Essays 1-4, www.religioustolerance.org/hom_caus4 .htm.

33. Caleb Crain, "Did a germ make you gay?" *Out* magazine, August 1999, pp. 46-49, cited in "Studies on the Causes."

34. "Male hormone levels in womb may affect sexual orientation, study says," CNN.com Health, March 29, 2000, www.cnn.com/2000/HEALTH/03/29/, cited in "Studies on the Causes."

35. R. Blanchard, "Fraternal birth order and the maternal immune hypothesis of male homosexuality," *Hormones & Behavior*, 2001, 40, pp. 105-114, cited in "Studies on the Causes."

36. Dean Hamer and Peter Copeland, *The Science of Desire: The Search for the Gay Gene and the Biology of Behavior* (New York: Simon & Schuster, 1994), cited in "Studies on the Causes."

37. "Sexual orientation 'hard-wired' before birth—startling new evidence revealed in the blink of an eye," University of East London, October 2, 2003, www.uel.ac.uk/ cited in "Studies on the Causes."

38. "Lesbian Ears," *The Globe and Mail*, Toronto, ON, March 19, 1998, cited in "Studies on the Causes."

39. "Sexuality and Ear Emissions," *Washington Post*, April 5, 1999, p. A07, http://equake.geol.vt.edu/, cited in "Studies on the Causes."

40. "Gay Men Respond Differently to Pheromones," Associated Press, May 9, 2005, http://start.earthlink.net/, cited in "Studies on the Causes."

41. Randolph E. Schmid, "Sexuality may be in the genes—Study. Lesbians react similarly to men. Researchers test brain differences," Associated Press, May 9, 2006, cited in "Studies on the Causes."

42. Ivana Savic and Per Lindström, "PET and MRI show differences in cerebral asymmetry and functional connectivity between homo- and heterosexual subjects," *Proceedings of the National Academy of Sciences* USA, cited in "Studies on the Causes."

43. Warren Throckmorton, "Homosexuality and Genes: Déjà vu All Over Again?" October 30, 2003, www.narth.com/docs/dejavu.html.

44. See "Associated Press Corrects Story on Olfactory Responses and Sexual Orientation," www.narth.com/docs/smell.html.

45. "Latest Gay Brain Study Scrutinized," www.narth.com/docs/scrutinized.html.

46. "Latest Gay Brain Study."

47. "Is Your Baby Gay? What If You Could Know? What If You Could Do Something About It?" www.albertmohler.com/blog_read.php?id=891.

48. Frank Seixas, former director of the National Council on Alcoholism; quoted in Dannemeyer, William, *Shadow in the Land*, SanFrancisco: St. Ignatius Press, 1989, p. 55.

49. Joe Dallas, "Born Gay?" *Christianity Today*, 22 June 1992, p. 22; *Chronicle of Higher Education*, 5 February 1992, p. A7.

50. "Rethinking the Origins of Sin."

51. Robert Wright, "Our Cheating Hearts," *Time*, 15 August 1994, pp. 44-52.

52. Selwyn Duke, "What If Homosexuality Is Inborn? www.inplainsite.org/html/if_homosexuality_were_biologic.html.

53. Duke.

54. John Derbyshire, "Metaphysics, Science, Homosexuality: Are we talking biology or choice?" *National Review Online*, February 16, 2005, www.nationalreview.com/derbyshire/derbyshire200502160748.asp.

55. Mohler.

THEORIES OF ORIGIN, PART 2

Developmental, Spiritual, and Interactive Theories

by Joe Dallas

> *Man is a stately castle, intricately and masterfully constructed. The castle, however, was given a life of its own. When man took it on himself to be God, he ruined everything—the decay became so extensive that only one with the eyes of a craftsman could see the structural beauty that remained underneath. Man is an amalgamation of dignity and depravity, a glorious ruin.*
>
> —FROM *THE WOUNDED HEART* BY DAN ALLENDER

Years ago my pastor gave an illustrated sermon explaining what happened when humanity went from good to defiled. He stepped up to the pulpit and read from Genesis chapter 1, then expounded on creation and the unmistakable love for the created that went into it. As he did so, a painter entered and sat down on a stool next to him where a large easel had been placed, and began painting a lovely, spacious meadow scene in oils.

The artist was unusually skilled, so we could barely concentrate on what our pastor was saying as trees, lake, midday sun, tall grass, and blue/red sky sprang up in front of us.

Then, just as the painter put his finishing touches on the canvas, our pastor pulled a pan of black paint out from under the pulpit, dipped both hands into it, then turned to the easel and smeared the paint over the freshly created scene.

The congregation's reaction was almost violent. We booed, gasped, and shouted, "How could you!" outraged as we saw ugly black smears defacing what had been so carefully and tenderly created. Much of what had been beautiful still was, of course, but some of it was completely blotted out, most of it was marred, and none of it could ever be the same. The ruin was complete.

Never had I seen the concept of the Fall so well expressed. Through Adam's disobedience and Eve's deception, there went the human family, still beautiful but defaced; still existing but marred, never in this life to be all it was meant to be.

Theories on the origins of homosexuality must take this tragedy into account when explaining how and why we experience desires God never meant us to have. Whatever else may have gone wrong—family dynamics, early trauma, genes, hormones, spiritual interference, or poor choices—at the root of it all lies the ugly mystery of fallen nature. We are all created by God, but clearly, we are not all God created us to be.

In chapter 9 we examined inborn theories claiming homosexuality may have a genetic or biological base. To summarize:

1. A number of studies—some credible; some suspect—suggest homosexuality may be influenced by inborn elements. While inconclusive, they warrant attention and analysis, and should be taken into consideration in any discussion on the origins of sexual orientation.

2. "Inborn" need not mean "normal," so if homosexuality is proven to be inborn, such proof would not diminish or contradict the biblical position.

3. When approaching a theory we should ask what the theory's claims are and if they're accurate; what the worldview of the theorist is; and whether the theory is confirmed in, compatible with, or contradicted by the Bible.

In this chapter, we'll continue reviewing prevalent theories of origin by examining the *developmental, spiritual,* and *interactive* theories.

Developmental Theories of Origin

While scientists and physicians were no doubt theorizing on homosexuality's development prior to his time, this discussion will begin with Sigmund Freud, who took a position on the subject more benign than many conservatives, yet more traditional than pro-homosexual apologists would have wished. When writing to the mother of a homosexual, who'd contacted him in hopes of helping her son, Freud responded accordingly:

> Homosexuality is assuredly no advantage, but it is nothing to be ashamed of, no vice, no degradation, it cannot be classified as an illness; we consider it to be a variation of the sexual function produced by a certain arrest of sexual development.[1]

In early psychoanalytic thought, then, homosexuality was described by Freud himself as a developmental issue—that is, an issue springing from something that had gone wrong, something preventing normal sexual development. While stopping far short of describing homosexuals as mentally ill, and in fact challenging the use of the word *illness* to describe homosexuality itself, he nonetheless considered it a symptom of developmental arrest, a concept that continues to this day to influence and guide the thinking of many clinicians, ministers, and laity associated with the issue.

Kenneth Lewes, who examined psychoanalytic thought and its relation to homosexuality in his book *The Psychoanalytic Theory of Male Homosexuality*,[2] and Ronald Bayer, who chronicled the history of homosexuality's relation to American psychiatry,[3] describe the developmental theory as the dominant view among psychiatrists and analysts for decades following Freud's remarks. At times a "profound fear or resentment" was indicted as the blocker of normal development; at other times, a phobic response to the opposite sex; a narcissistic object choice; or an "inverted Oedipus complex" were some of the many factors attributed to male and female homosexuality, which Freud described as "an inhibition in development."[4] But whatever the specifics causing the developmental stunting, the general consensus was that heterosexual response was the end result of mature and normal development, so homosexual response, by its nature, indicated that the homosexual had not achieved full sexual development.[5]

Bieber and the Homosexual Triad

By 1962, the Freudian approach may have lost some of its dominance, as new schools of thought like the behavioral and the humanist were finding their adherents. But in most circles, however diverse, homosexuality was still largely viewed in a negative light, both culturally and clinically. It was commonly explained as something falling short of normal development, an approach solidified and expounded on when Irving Bieber released his book *Homosexuality: A Psychoanalytic Study of Male Homosexuals.* This work described a project begun in the 1950s involving 77 psychiatrists who treated, and reported on, 106 homosexual patients and 100 heterosexual ones to serve as controls. Family histories were gleaned from the patients, and from these histories Bieber described a dynamic that seemed common to the backgrounds of homosexual men, soon to be known as the *triangular system.*

Sixty-nine percent of the homosexual patients reported "restrictive and binding" maternal behavior on the part of their mothers, as opposed to 32 percent of the heterosexual patients.[6] The majority of homosexual patients likewise described their relationships with their fathers as marked by "profound interpersonal disturbance," as opposed to the majority of heterosexual patients, whose father-son relations were generally "far more wholesome."[7] It is this family portrait—too close to Mom; too far from Dad—that would be, and continues to be, painted by countless homosexual men describing their history.

Bieber's prominence existed alongside that of Charles Socarides, a New York–based psychoanalyst who, with Bieber, became two of the country's most vocal and committed opponents to homosexuality's declassification by the American Psychiatric Association in 1973 (see chapter 8). Believing homosexuality represented "massive childhood fears" stunting normal development,[8] Socarides saw it as a pre-oedipal condition creating (among male homosexuals) a dread of intimacy with women.

The developmental theory in general, by this time, presumed male and female homosexuals had not properly bonded with their parent of the same sex, or had experienced some level of too-close bonding with the parent of the opposite sex, or endured some form of trauma relative to the parent of the opposite sex or, perhaps, another significant opposite-sex figure. And while this theory was secular in origin, Christian mental-health practitioners would soon adopt it, modifying it into a more spiritual-friendly form and integrating it into Christian thought.

Moberly, Nicolosi, and Reparative Therapy

Christian Psychologist Elizabeth Moberly, in her 1986 book *Homosexuality: A New Christian Ethic*, proposed that the family dynamic described by Bieber, and so often found among homosexuals, left them longing for deep yet denied intimacy with the parent of the same sex and, accordingly, with unmet yearnings for same-sex intimacy in general. This, she proposed, accounted for the homosexual drive, which she described as an attempted solution to the problem of unmet need:

> From amidst a welter of details, one constant underlying principle suggests itself: that the homosexual—whether man or woman—has suffered from some deficit in the relationship with the parent of the same sex; and that there is a corresponding drive to make good this deficit—through the medium of same-sex, or "homosexual" relationships.[9]

Though she shared the traditional Christian viewpoint of homosexuality as being a biblically prohibited sin, Moberly advocated for ministry to homosexuals featuring more than a call to repentance from homosexual acts. Healthy same-sex intimacy, she insisted, was the answer to the homosexual drive, an intimacy to be sought through therapeutic, social, or ministry-oriented relationships.

It should be noted that Moberly's work emerged in the mid-1980s, not long after the American Psychiatric Association deleted homosexuality from its list of disorders. The Christian population by and large disagreed with the APA decision and would be receptive to a therapeutic approach offering compassion, without legitimization, to the homosexual. Concurrently, ministries such as Exodus International (a national referral network of ministries to homosexuals) and Homosexuals Anonymous (a Christian 12-step approach to homosexuality founded on the principles of Alcoholics Anonymous) were growing in visibility and influence. Largely headed by laypeople, these groups welcomed a clinician who shared their views and contributed much-needed expertise to their work. So Dr. Moberly's ideas and approaches were quickly embraced, expanded on, and absorbed by people involved in any form of Christian ministry addressing homosexuality.

This was especially true of Dr. Joseph Nicolosi, a California-based psychologist who felt the population of women and men who were homosexual in their orientation, but traditional in their sexual mores, were done an injustice by the psychiatric community. Describing such people as "non-gay homosexuals," he pointed out the need for clients dissatisfied with their homosexuality to have therapeutic services offered to them; services that would not contradict their worldview by insisting their only option was to embrace the homosexuality they were resisting.[10] Accordingly, he founded the National Association for the Research and Therapy of Homosexuality (NARTH), an organization advocating within the psychiatric community for the rights of patients to pursue treatment for homosexuality, if they so choose. It was Nicolosi's approach to both the origins and treatment of homosexuality that would come to be known as *reparative therapy.*

The term *reparative* applies to both the treatment of homosexuality, and the homosexual drive itself, as attempts to repair either a damaged sense of self, or a deficit experienced when same-sex intimacy (usually with the parent of the same sex) has gone wrong in early childhood. According to Nicolosi, "*reparative* refers to the concept of homosexuality as a reparative drive."[11] (Interestingly enough, in 1962 Dr. Sandor Rado used a similar phrase, claiming homosexuality represented "a reparative attempt on the part of human beings to achieve sexual pleasure when the normal heterosexual outlet proved too threatening."[12])

Though Nicolosi's work primarily concerned men, the reparative approach to developmentally induced homosexuality found niches in treatment of women as well. Psychologist Elaine Siegel, for example, describes encountering this same-sex drive when treating lesbian women:

> The women dealt with this basic lack of attunement to their infantile needs with great adaptive strengths and an amazing variety of creative maneuvers that nonetheless express: Mother didn't teach me who I am. Therefore, another like myself must show me that I have a sexual self. But the mirroring they received from their female lovers was as distorted as their primary maternal experience had been, locking them into the never-ending cycle of the repetition compulsion.[13]

Therapist Mary Beth Patton makes a similar point:

> A woman dealing with same-sex attraction is longing for a con-
> nection with the feminine in herself that was denied in her own
> development because of an inadequate identification and attune-
> ment in relating to mother.[14]

And therapist Janelle Hallman uses the phrase *defensive detachment* (a term common to reparative therapists) to describe the mother-daughter dynamics she often sees in her clients, a detachment due to "the daughter's perceptions, sensitivities, or negative conclusions and beliefs about her mother and the nature of their relationship."[15]

Sexualization

It could logically be argued that many heterosexuals had difficulty bonding with their parent of the same sex, yet never experienced homosexual desire. And that is where, according to developmental theorists, the mystery of *sexualization* arises.

Sexualization, in this context, occurs when an emotional need is converted, involuntarily and unconsciously, into a sexual desire. Dr. Julie Harren Hamilton describes a boy's sexualization of same-sex needs as follows:

> To this child, it feels very natural that he longs for male love. In fact,
> he typically thinks that he was born that way, having craved male
> love for as long as he can remember. Indeed, he has craved this love
> most of his life. However, initially it was not a sexual craving. Instead,
> it was an emotional craving, a legitimate need for non-sexual love,
> an emotional need that has become sexualized.[16]

Therapist Mary Beth Patton acknowledges something similar when addressing female homosexuality:

> This longing often transforms into emotional dependency with
> another woman and is generally the defining feature of female homo-
> sexuality. Rather than finding the feminine in herself, she looks to
> another female to give her the identification and connection she is
> missing.[17]

And Dr. Judd Marmor, writing in the *Harvard Mental Health Letter*, aptly describes both a typical genesis of emotional need for same-sex bonding, and its subsequent sexualization, when he notes:

> A little boy whose behavior is effeminate, who does not like competitive athletics, and who prefers music and art, may be disappointing to a macho father, who tends to reject the boy and distance himself from him. The mother may respond by overprotecting her son. Such reactions disturb the boy's capacity to identify positively with his father and cause him to over-identify with his mother. He may ultimately develop homosexual erotic responses which are reinforced by later experiences.[18]

Summary

The developmental theory, then, could be broken down into three very general points:

1. The pre-homosexual boy or girl experiences an unsatisfactory relationship with his/her parent of the same sex. The parent-child problem could be as benign as an ongoing misinterpretation on the child's part (as in, "Dad was always gone to work, so I assumed he didn't want to be with me") or as severe as overt abuse or rejection.

2. The child is thus left with a deep emotional need for same-sex bonding and identification that remains unmet.

3. At a critical point in the child's development, the emotional need for same-sex bonding becomes involuntarily sexualized, thus the homosexual response represents a sexual desire born of a legitimate, but unmet, emotional need. As Nicolosi puts it: "The [homosexual] person is attempting to 'repair' unmet same-sex affective needs (attention, affection and approval) as well as gender-identification deficits through homoerotic behavior."[19]

Accurate and Biblical?

The foregoing are the claims of the developmental theorists, and they resonate with many women and men. So to answer the first question we pose when considering a theory—*What are its claims and are they accurate?*—we should be impressed on the one hand by the number of qualified practitioners who specialize in this field and vouch confidently for the developmental approach, while recognizing on the other hand that this theory, no matter how popular, is difficult to prove.

A casual review of the literature cited in this chapter, as well as the number of books and articles written by professionals who've practiced this approach and people who've received help through it, shows an overwhelming number saying "yes" to the accuracy of the developmental theory. This cannot be dismissed.

But neither can its detractors, who criticize its subjective nature, challenge its assumptions, and question its application to all homosexuals. These criticisms deserve to be heard, even by those who still subscribe, in part or in whole, to the developmental approach.

It is subjective, no doubt, in that it relies on retrospective analysis on the patient's part (that is, "This is what my childhood was like; this is what did or did not happen") which by its nature requires speculation and interpretation. Reviewing one's life in counseling is a highly subjective experience; a meaningful one, to be sure, and many benefit hugely from it. But its potential for inaccuracy can't be denied. In other words, if we conclude a man's homosexuality springs from a poor father-son bond, and if that bond is concluded to have been poor based on the adult's recollections of it, we should admit that our conclusions, however strongly held, are based on data that's largely or completely unverifiable.

Then again, most of us know what our childhood was like. We know what we experienced with both parents; in counseling, we may analyze how those experiences shaped our ways of relating and being. And that analysis is, in many cases, valid and even life-changing. Verifiable or not—indeed, fully accurate or not—a patient's memories, from which he draws conclusions relevant to the developmental approach, help him better understand *why* he feels *what* he feels, an understanding that can produce profound relief.

The assumptions about parent-child relations that the developmental approach relies on also draw fire, especially if they are too rigidly held and applied to all homosexuals. It is one thing to say, "Many women and men report unsatisfactory relations with their parent of the same sex, and a yearning for same-sex love, which seems to have taken on a sexual component." It's quite another to insist, "All homosexuals had unsatisfactory relations with their same-sex parent; therefore homosexuality always springs from unhealthy family dynamics." We don't, after all, know all homosexual people, much less their family histories. And to presume that because *X* number of homosexuals who we've seen in treatment had a certain family experience, then therefore *all* homosexuals share that experience, is presumptuous and smacks of arrogance.

Finally, there is the question of the sexualization of same-sex desires. Why does it happen to some and not to others? After all, countless heterosexuals experienced unsatisfactory relations with parents and peers of the same sex, yet never experienced homoeroticism. Here we should hold our theories loosely enough to admit there's much about them, and about the subject in general, that we don't know. A few points to consider regarding sexualization:

1. The sexualization of same-sex desires is a plausible concept, but it shouldn't be assumed to apply to all homosexuals. Many lesbian women and gay men report excellent relations with both their parents; many heterosexuals report poor relations with theirs. So when it comes to theories of causation, one size does *not* fit all.

2. There is a difference between *traits* and *causes*. A historically unsatisfactory relationship with a same-sex parent may be a *trait* shared by many homosexuals that did not necessarily *cause* their homosexuality, or it may indeed be causative in some or many cases, yet not in others. "Case by case" should be the standard when applying theories to individuals.

3. There may or may not be a genetic or inborn cause of homosexuality, but there may be inborn *characteristics* that make some people more susceptible to the sexualization of unmet need than others. That could explain why some people with unhealthy parent-child dynamics experience this involuntary sexualization, and others don't.

Responding to the threefold query regarding the claims and accuracy of a theory, the worldview of its proponents, and its compatibility with Scripture, we may answer that the developmental theory seems to hold true for many; perhaps not for all. But it is one that often proves effective, and has precedence, history, and widespread support in its favor. Whether or not it's accurate in all cases is another matter, one on which the jury is, and will no doubt remain, out.

The worldview of its proponents varies, but tends to be conservative, largely influenced by Judeo-Christian values. And while Scripture by no means states homosexuality springs from developmental factors (nor does it indict parents of homosexuals, or suggest any one cause of homosexuality, for that matter) the theory does not contradict biblical teaching, and for that reason is at least compatible with Scripture.

The Spiritual Theory of Origin

The belief that homosexuality is caused by demonic forces deserves mention. Although it has few well-known advocates, and because books and seminars adhering to this approach do not tend to be mainstream (nor do they receive widespread coverage and discussion), a significant number of people do seem to subscribe to it. So significant, in fact, that *National Review*'s John Derbyshire commented thus:

> The least scientific of current theories, this one is probably the most widely believed, taking the world at large. Most devout Muslims, for example, believe it, and so do many Christians.[20]

If large numbers of people throughout the world believe homosexuality is spiritually induced, the exact ways and means of that induction are unclear. But proponents of the spiritual theory generally agree that Satan, who hates humanity and seeks its destruction, attempts to influence people through suggestion, seduction, or possession to do things contrary to what is right and decent.

The spiritual theory is more likely to have its followers among people predisposed to believe in an immediate, dynamic approach toward sins and/or life problems through deliverance prayer, exorcism, the laying on of hands for healing, or the binding and rebuking of dark spiritual forces. This almost certainly limits its adherents to Charismatic or Pentecostal believers (or those of other religions who believe in Satan and demons, such as Muslims) although non-Charismatics certainly believe in Satan as well, and might in rare instances hold this view.

Accordingly, to the spiritual theorists, homosexuality is a manifestation of demonic activity in a person's life, an activity the individual may well have opened himself up to, as described by proponent Bryon Smith:

Mild to moderate sexual alterations happen to everyone during their lives. When a person begins to crave same-sex relationships something serious has been affected within them on a spiritual and mental level. The next thing that begins to suffer is the body.[21]

In some cases, proponents of the spiritual theory see homosexuality as a *route* to demonic possession rather than a *symptom* of it:

"Promiscuity, as well as homosexuality and pornography," says 73-year-old Fr. Jeremy Davies, "is a form of sexual perversion and can lead to demonic possession. Offering what may be an explanation for the explosion of homosexuality in recent years, Fr. Davies said, "Among the causes of homosexuality is a contagious demonic factor."[22]

Exactly how someone becomes demon possessed is rarely explained, possibly because there's no scriptural formula citing the step-by-step process through which a person is invaded. To be sure, the Bible attests to the reality of demon possession, citing numerous examples in the Gospels and the book of Acts.* But these citations offer descriptions of people already possessed, without explaining how the possession came to be. So a number of questions arise when approaching the subject:

- Did the individual make a choice to give himself to Satan?
- Did an ongoing sin set the person up for possession?
- Is involvement in the occult a prerequisite for this?
- Exactly how is demonic possession recognized? By the severity of a particular sin, a supernatural manifestation, discernment on another's part, or all three?

These remain largely unanswered in the Bible, leaving many to speculatively form their own conclusions. The website www.Bible.com offers its take on the correlation between demonic activity and homosexuality by saying the individual gives himself to the sin, with possession following:

People become homosexuals because they yield to abnormal acts or lust. It is through some source that they have received a demonic spirit that drives them to their lust. Viewing evil videos or pornographic

---

* See, for example, Matthew 4:24; 8:16,33; 9:32; 12:22; Luke 8:36; Acts 8:7; 16:16.

books is a way of opening the door for Satan to give one an evil, perverse spirit.[23]

Benny Hinn refers to the "Spirit of Homosexuality" and the "Spirit of Perversion" as being synonymous;[24] and John Eckhardt affirms his belief that homosexuality, like many other sexual sins, indicates possession:

> Being in deliverance, we understand that if you are engaged in any sexual immorality, whether it's fornication or adultery, homosexuality or lesbianism, there are demons in your life. There is no way that you can practice sin and not open the doors for demons to come into your life. We believe in the power of deliverance and that every person who has lived a lifestyle of homosexuality or lesbianism does need deliverance.[25]

Finally, the Christianity and Homosexuality website offers this testimonial from a young man who claims deliverance was the answer to his struggle with homosexuality:

> The next time I went to the weekly evangelical meetings I said to Ed, "I believe that homosexuality is a sin and I want to fight the devil and not be a homosexual anymore." Ed replied, "When the homosexual demon is out of you, you will be as repulsed by homosexuality as you currently are by heterosexuality." I can now testify that when the demon is 100 percent gone this is true.[26]

Demonic Origins: An Accurate and Biblical Approach?

Knee-jerk pros and cons are common to discussions involving demonic activity. Adherents to the spiritual theory might say the issue is settled: Demons are real, many human problems can and should be ascribed to them, and those who refuse to agree are spiritually unenlightened. Critics can be just as adamant, insisting that "the devil made me do it" is an age-old cop-out, and deliverance attempts and rituals are unbiblical, unnecessary, and downright silly. Somewhere in between lies a more nuanced, reasonable approach.

First, what are the claims of the spiritual theorists? The claims themselves seem vague, and even contradictory, at times:

- "Homosexuality *causes* demon possession"; "Homosexuality is *caused by* demon possession."
- "Demons *possess* the homosexual from *within*"; "Demons *oppress* the homosexual from *without.*"
- "Deliverance *alone* is the answer"; "Deliverance needs to be followed up with counseling."

This vagueness no doubt stems in part from the intuitive, subjective process by which deliverance ministers discern demonic activity. Nonetheless, the claims of the spiritual approach seem to be that, in general, homosexuality is a demonic manifestation requiring some form of specialized release. Which raises the question, Are the claims accurate?

While respecting the sincerity of those holding to the spiritual view, and recognizing fully the contributions many holding such views have made to the church and culture at large, it would still seem that of all the positions cited so far, this one runs the most counter to Scripture.

Neither the inborn theory nor the developmental theory is specifically spelled out, or *commended by*, the Bible, but neither do they *contradict* the Word. But the spiritual approach, with its insistence that homosexuality represents demonic activity, appears to contradict what both the Old and New Testaments tell us about sin. A few points are in order here:

1. In both the Old and New Testaments sexual sin is mentioned, sometimes graphically; sometimes in passing. But not one Bible verse referencing sexual sin refers to it as a manifestation of demon possession or oppression.

2. Jesus addressed adultery (Matthew 5:31; John 8:1-11), fornication (Matthew 15:19), and lust (Matthew 5:28) in the Gospels without once calling them demonic, and without once advising exorcism or spiritual deliverance as the solution to them. Rather, He advised repentance ("Go and sin no more"—John 8:11) and watchful caution ("If your...eye causes you to sin pluck it out"—Matthew 5:29) as means of remedying and preventing sexual sin.

3. Jesus referred to sexual sin not as being demonic in origin, but as being human in origin, springing from the heart, when He said, "Out of the heart proceed evil thoughts, murders, adulteries, fornications..." (Matthew 15:19).

4. Paul also described sexual sin as a manifestation of the flesh rather than a demonic problem when he told the Galatians, "The works of the flesh are evident, which are: adultery, fornication, uncleanness, lewdness..." (Galatians 5:19).

5. While we do see numerous examples of demonic possession in the Gospels and Acts, none of the manifestations of possession were of a sexual nature. One demon-possessed individual threw himself into fire (Mark 9:22); another exhibited superhuman strength (Mark 5:3); one was mute (Matthew 9:32); another practiced divination (Acts 16:16). But none displayed sexual sin in any noticeable form, which is significant, if in fact sexual sin indicates demon possession.

6. Nowhere in the Gospels, the book of Acts, or the epistles do we see Jesus, Paul, or any of the apostles recommending exorcism or deliverance for or to a person who has been practicing sexual sin.

For these reasons it seems the spiritual theory lacks biblical backing and, in fact, contradicts Scripture when it insists that homosexuality is a manifestation of demonic activity requiring deliverance or exorcism. This is not to say, however, that such approaches are always wrong. No one taking the Bible seriously will deny its references to Satan and demons, and we are in fact called to recognize his strategies (2 Corinthians 2:11), resist him (James 4:7), and be prepared to do spiritual battle when necessary (Ephesians 6:10-13).

But while women and men advocating the spiritual theory usually do so from a specifically Christian worldview, we nevertheless take issue with this approach, finding it to be in conflict with important biblical principles of personal responsibility and repentance.

The Interactive Theory

It seems we are on the most solid theoretical ground when we resist holding to any one theory on the development of homosexuality as being always true in all cases, and instead hold to an interactive approach stating, in essence, that homosexuality is probably caused by a constellation of factors, some known and some unknown, including physical and emotional ones. The interactive theory considers both the inborn and developmental theories as having merit, with each of them contributing to the formation of attractions to the same sex.

This approach is hardly new. In the late nineteenth century, Richard von Kraft-Ebbing, author of the renowned *Psychopathia Sexualis*, adhered to it when he explained homosexuality as being both environmental and hereditary in nature.[27] Today, a number of experts would agree with him. Consider what Dr. Dennis McFadden, neuroscientist at the University of Texas, has to say in light of his research:

> Any human behavior is going to be the result of complex intermingling of genetics and environment. It would be astonishing if it were not true for homosexuality.[28]

Likewise, Dr. J. Michael Bailey of Northwestern University and his associates, admit that "although both male and female sexual orientation appear to be at least somewhat heritable, environment also must be of considerable importance in their origins."[29]

And after reviewing all major biological explanations and studies on homosexuality, authors and researchers Byne and Parsons proposed

> an interactional model in which genes or hormones do not specify sexual orientation per se, but instead bias particular personality traits and thereby influence the manner in which an individual and his or her environment interact as sexual orientation and other personality characteristics unfold developmentally.[30]

This approach takes into account the fact that we are physical and emotional, just as Scripture affirms. Each part of ourselves no doubt affects our development; each plays into our responses and behaviors. So the interactive theory gives a nod to inborn theorists claiming genes or biology influence us. It resists the conclusion that inborn influences are the *only* ones causing homosexuality, but will instead recognize they may cause an individual to be more susceptible to it later in life. *Fridae* online magazine indicates this when referring to the interactionist model:

> One school of thought, the so-called "interactionist" model, suggest that our genes predispose certain personality traits (rather than sexual orientation directly), which influences the way we interact with the environment as sexual orientation develops.[31]

It may simply be the case that a person is probably not born homosexual (though we must remain open to the possibility, and to further research on the subject) but is perhaps born with a set of traits that makes him/her more susceptible to homosexuality later in life, given certain developmental variables. If that's the case, then homosexuality itself may not be inborn, but the traits that make it more likely for one person to be attracted to the same sex than another are, in fact, inborn. So the inborn and developmental elements may be working in concert, producing sexual orientation together, rather than as single agents.

This could help explain why one woman raised by a mother she felt disconnected from becomes a lesbian while another, experiencing the same mother-daughter problems, does not. Both have a similar story, but one may be born with elements making her more inclined toward a sexualization of emotional needs than the other. These elements, be they genetic or biological, get the ball rolling, but need to be combined with environmental factors in order to produce homosexual orientation.

Conversely, suppose there are certain genes that make one more inclined toward homosexuality if other factors come into play, but suppose those factors—family dynamics, early trauma, whatever—never do come into play. That could again account for one person's sexual attractions going to the same sex, while another's lean toward the opposite one. The interactive model proposes that a combination of elements are necessary for homosexuality to develop. Take one or more away, and the orientation may never appear.

Ultimately, though, we're left admitting there's much we don't understand about the origins of same-sex attraction. We may hold primarily to an inborn, developmental, or interactive theory, while admitting none of them fully explain this phenomenon. So thankfully, complete understanding is not required of us when we approach an issue. In fact, we can freely admit what we do not know while holding fast to what we do.

And from that position—holding to and obeying truth as it's been revealed in Scripture; considering new information as it arises; considering new data in light of biblical absolutes; and maintaining due humility and teachableness—we can continue to approach this subject intelligently, responsibly, and redemptively.

CHAPTER TEN

THEORIES OF ORIGIN, PART 2

○—KEY POINTS—○

1. The developmental theory claims homosexuality is an acquired condition created by elements that have disrupted normal sexual development.

2. Historically, developmental theorists held the dominant view until the 1970s, when the pathology of homosexuality was called into question by the American Psychiatric Association and alternative explanations, such as the inborn theory, arose to explain what was now considered a normal variation.

3. Two key elements of the developmental view are unmet need and sexualization. Unmet needs are viewed as arising from early family relations that left the child unsatisfied and longing for same-sex bonds. Sexualization occurs when the emotional need becomes a sexual desire through an unconscious involuntary process.

4. The most well known current proponents of the developmental view would be Dr. Joseph Nicolosi and his organization NARTH (National Association of the Research and Therapy of Homosexuality).

5. The spiritual theory attributes homosexuality to demonic possession or oppression, seeing it as something requiring a form of exorcism or deliverance ministry.

6. The interactive theory holds that both inborn and early childhood elements work in concert to create homosexuality. The orientation is thus seen as something caused by a constellation of factors, rather than a single one.

RESOURCES

Handbook of Therapy for Unwanted Homosexual Attractions by Julie Harren Hamilton and Philip J. Henry, eds., Xulon Press, 2009.

Homosexuality: A Psychoanalytic Study of Male Homosexuals by Irving Bieber, Basic Books, 1962.

Homosexuality by Charles Socarides, Jason Aronson, Inc., 1978.

Homosexuality: A New Christian Ethic by Elizabeth Moberly, Attic Press, 1983.

On the Origins and Treatment of Homosexuality: A Psychoanalytic Rein-terpretation by Gerard van den Aardweg, Praeger, 1986.

Reparative Therapy of Male Homosexuality: A New Clinical Approach by Joseph Nicolosi, Jason Aronson, Inc., 1991.

The Heart of Female Same-sex Attraction by Janelle Hallman, InterVarsity Press, 2008.

Sexual Identity: A Guide to Living in the Time Between the Times by Mark Yarhouse and Lori Burkett, University Press of America, 2003.

NOTES

1. Cited in Ronald Bayer, *Homosexuality and American Psychiatry: The Politics of Diagnosis* (New York: Basic Books, 1981), p. 27.

2. Kenneth Lewes, *The Psychoanalytic Theory of Male Homosexuality* (New York: Simon and Schuster, 1988).

3. See Bayer, pp. 21-40.

4. Bayer, p. 29; Lewes, pp. 64-65.

5. Some disagreed, most notably Thomas Szasz, well known for his published criticisms of modern psychiatry as a somewhat power-hungry institution in his book *The Myth of Mental Illness* (New York: Harper and Row, 1974). As early as 1965 he challenged the notion of heterosexuality representing optimum health as being a biological issue touted as a social one (Bayer, p. 57). Still, the traditional view held sway well into the 1960s.

6. Irving Bieber, *Homosexuality: A Psychoanalytic Study of Male Homosexuals* (New York: Basic Books, 1962), pp. 60-84.

7. Bieber, pp. 114-115.

8. Bayer, p. 35.

9. Elizabeth Moberly, *Homosexuality: A New Christian Ethic* (Greenwood, SC: Attic Press, 1983), p. 57.

10. Joseph Nicolosi, *Reparative Therapy of Male Homosexuality: A New Clinical Approach* (New York: Jason Aronson, Inc., 1991), pp. 3-4.

11. NARTH website "So You Want to Be a Reparative Therapist," www.narth.com/docs/soyouwant .html.

12. Bayer, p. 29.

13. E. Siegel, *Female Homosexuality: Choice without Volition* (Hillsdale, NJ: The Analytic Press, 1988).

14. M.B. Patton, "Enmeshment and women dealing with same-sex attraction," Collected Papers from the NARTH Annual Conference, NARTH, Encino, CA.

15. Janelle Hallman, *The Heart of Female Same-sex Attraction* (Downers Grove, IL: InterVarsity Press, 2008), p. 58.

16. "Homosexuality 101: What Every Therapist, Parent, And Homosexual Should Know," www.narth.com/docs/hom101.html.

17. Patton.

18. Judd Marmor, "Homosexuality: Nature vs. Nurture," *The Harvard Mental Health Letter*, Oct. 1985, p. 6.

19. "The Meaning of Same-sex Attraction," www.narth.com/docs/niconew.html.

20. "Metaphysics, Science, Homosexuality: Are we talking biology or choice?" *National Review Online*, February 16, 2005, www.nationalreview.com/derbyshire/derbyshire200502160748.asp.

21. Bryon Smith, "Spiritual Things," www.dream-link.org/spiritualthings/homosexual.html.

22. "Westminster Exorcist Says Promiscuity Can Lead to Demonic Possession," LifeSite News.com, August 15, 2008, www.lifesitenews.com/ldn/2008/aug/08081506.html.

23. "What Does the Bible Say About Homosexuality?" www.bible.com/bibleanswers_result.php?id=246.

24. Benny Hinn video, www.youtube.com/watch?v=HcstbB1J_f8.

25. John Eckhardt, "The Truth about Homosexuality, Part 2," www.impactnetwork.net/pdf/homosexuality2.pdf.

26. Cited at www.christianityandhomosexuality.com/index.htm.

27. Bayer, p. 30.

28. D. McFadden, "Scientists challenge notion that homosexuality's a matter of choice," *The Charlotte* (North Carolina) *Observer*, August 9, 1998.

29. J. Bailey, R. Pillard, M. Neale, Y. Agyei, "Heritable factors influence sexual orientation in women," *Archive of General Psychiatry*, 1993, pp. 50, 217-223, 222.

30. W. Byne and B. Parsons, "Human sexual orientation: The biologic theories reappraised," *Archives of General Psychiatry*, 1993, pp. 50, 236-237.

31. "The Interactionist Model," *Fridae* online magazine; "Demystifying Homosexuality" *Fridae* online magazine March 1, 2004.

PART FOUR

Counseling Men Who Struggle with Homosexuality

by Joe Dallas

The battles that count aren't the ones for gold medals. The struggles within yourself—the invisible, inevitable battles inside all of us—that's where it's at.

—Olympic gold medalist Jesse Owens

In 1984 I stepped into a professional counselor's office for the first time, frightened at the prospect of discussing things I'd never spoken to anyone about, and vulnerable beyond words. I was twenty-nine-years old, and had just made a decision so momentous it required me to relocate to another county, release most of my friendships, abandon my social network, and find a new job, church, and identity.

I had just said *yes* to following Christ, which required saying *no* to homosexuality. What had been a primary form of self-identification for the past six years would now be called sin, and what had been a natural way of expressing myself sexually would now be deemed unnatural and wrong. No part of my life was exempt from reform—social life, thought life, sex life—and I was essentially being transplanted from one world to another.

Repenting of homosexual behavior did not, of course, erase my homosexual desires, which was just one of the many conflicts landing me on the counselor's couch. I was also depressed, ashamed, angry at everyone, terrified of intimacy, and without any clear sense of direction other than a conviction that I needed to be grounded in the faith and in fellowship, pay my bills, live responsibly, and somehow deal with my soul and my sexual self.

With all that on my plate, you'd think I'd have a lot to say when the counselor opened our session by asking, "So what brings you here?" But no. Despite the emotional tornado in my gut, I sat dumbfounded, scrambling for the right words to form my questions and describe my pain. So while I stared at him mutely, he leaned back in his chair, nodding and indicating with a shrug that he'd wait, along with me, for the words to come.

"I'm a Christian," I finally bleated, "and I've been into homosexuality for years. And I know I was wrong, so I'm starting over."

"And what," he asked quietly, "does *starting over* mean?"

Hearing my own answer left me desolate. "I…don't…have…any…idea!"

Then I wept, long and hard, while he listened. And that's how my counseling began.

For the next 13 months I came for weekly sessions, investing in a process that steered me through one of the most trying and exhilarating seasons of my life. Having become a pastoral counselor myself years later, I've experienced the view from the couch and the counselor's chair, and I hope never to lose my respect for the courage, stamina, and gut-level honesty a counselee displays by walking through my door.

I respect, in fact, all aspects of the counseling relationship. It's an invigorating experience, not necessary for all but so vital to many, including Christians in conflict over deeply ingrained tendencies they want to understand, resist, and overcome.

So in this chapter I'd like to discuss what goes into counseling a man who struggles with homosexuality (counseling women who struggle with lesbianism will be dealt with in chapter 12), a discussion that will include principles and practices, general points to consider, and a five-task model of counseling I've used over the years and found to be effective.

A note about the term "counseling." "Counselor" and "therapist" have become generic terms for anyone offering guidance, since anytime one person instructs another he is technically offering "counsel." But this chapter is written specifically for those who offer counseling as a calling or a profession: licensed psychologists, marriage and family therapists, social workers, or pastoral counselors, all of whom meet for regularly scheduled sessions with their coun-selees for a period of time, and all of whom have a level of education and training qualifying them to counsel.

This is not to suggest that others can't also offer useful advice and support to men struggling with their sexuality. Ministers, spiritual mentors, or commit-ted friends can all be a vital part of a man's growth. But this chapter will focus exclusively on the relationship between professional counselor and counselee.

Here, then, are some principles for professional Christian counselors and therapists to consider when addressing homosexuality.

Principle One: The Christian Counselor Must Be Informed

To ensure competent service and to protect your professional integrity, you should stay abreast of your governing organization's ethical standards and guidelines. That means knowing where your governing organization stands on homosexuality and related issues, and on treatment approaches. Mishandling of a patient or client and malpractice lawsuits can be avoided by simply staying current. Know your state's requirements for operating as a professional coun-selor, which may include a master's degree, supervised training, and a written or oral exam. If you're qualified to counsel, you already have a good professional and theoretical foundation to work from when dealing with people, provided you always work within the scope of your credentials and experience. But in addition to your general training, it would be helpful to read what's been writ-ten from a Christian perspective on the issue, and to consult with those already involved in this work. I would especially recommend reading and studying three books on the subject written for counselors:[1]

- *Reparative Therapy of Male Homosexuality: A New Clinical Approach* by Joseph Nicolosi
- *Handbook of Therapy for Unwanted Attractions*, edited by Julie Har-ren Hamilton and Philip Henry
- *Ex-Gays?: A Longitudinal Study of Religiously Mediated Change in Sexual Orientation* by Stanton Jones and Mark Yarhouse

These books walk the reader through approaches, techniques, and the challenges of counseling more thoroughly than this one chapter can. Addi-tionally, they provide case studies and suggested interventions invaluable to any counselor taking this type of work seriously, so please invest your time and effort into reading them.

A thorough working knowledge of biblical references to human nature, the struggle between flesh and spirit, and sanctification is also crucial, so be sure to brush up on Romans, 1 and 2 Corinthians, and Galatians. I'd also strongly advise consulting with the National Association for the Research and Therapy of Homosexuality (www.narth.com) to see what training they currently offer for counselors and therapists, and with Exodus International (a network of Christian ministries and counselors addressing homosexuality) to review their materials and consider joining their network for ongoing support and education (www.exodus-international.org).

APA Positions

Be sure you also know the American Psychiatric Association's *current* positions on diagnosis, treatment guidelines, and ethical concerns. As of this writing (2009) the following points are relevant to your work as a professional counselor treating men who struggle with homosexuality:

1. Homosexuality is *not* a diagnosable condition found in the *Diagnostic and Statistical Manual of Mental and Emotional Disorders.* Neither is *ego-dystonic homosexuality* (a classification that used to appear in the DSM indicating a person was in distress over her/his homosexuality—see chapter 8, "Homosexuality and American Psychiatry"). The APA does not consider homosexuality to be a disorder of any kind, sexual or otherwise. Both you and the men who come to you should know that while homosexuality may be a moral or spiritual issue, it is not, according to the APA, a psychological one. You can discuss to what extent you agree or disagree with the APA's position, but you should protect yourself and your client by letting him know what that position is.

2. The DSM (as of this writing in 2009) *does* classify "distress over one's sexual orientation" under DSM section 302.9, which is an appropriate diagnostic code to use when treating unwanted same-sex attractions.

3. Other DSM codes can be used as well if the man you're working with presents other, more clearly diagnosable conditions. When

in doubt over the appropriate way to diagnose, whether for treatment, recordkeeping, or insurance purposes, always consult with a colleague or supervisor.

4. As of this writing, the American Psychiatric Association and American Psychological Association do not *endorse* treatment for homosexuality (often referred to as reparative therapy), nor do they specifically *prohibit* or *condemn* it. Both have issued cautionary statements, expressing reservations about the possibility of changing sexual orientation and about theories of origin indicating homosexuality is unhealthy. (See chapter 8, "Homosexuality and American Psychiatry.") Robert Epstein, editor in chief of *Psychology Today* magazine, clarified these positions well:

> The APA has never condemned sexual conversion therapy but has merely issued cautionary statements, one of which reminds psychologists of their obligation to "respect the rights of others to hold values, attitudes and opinions that differ from [their] own"...Although homosexuality was removed from the DSM...as a mental disorder in 1973, all editions of the DSM have always listed a disorder characterized by "distress" over one's sexual orientation (DSM section 302.9). Both gays and straights have a right to seek treatment when they're unhappy with their sexual orientation, and some choose to try to change that orientation.[2]

5. Refer regularly to the APA official website for updates on professional ethics.[3] Also refer to the NARTH (National Association of Research and Therapy for Homosexuality) website at www.narth.com for updates on controversies on clinical issues concerning the Christian professional. Make sure you also know the organizations you answer to professionally, and that you have regular access to their current standards.

Further Considerations

It's often asked, What mode of counseling is best: psychoanalytic, behavioral, rational emotive, nouthetic, cognitive?

I'd say there is no one counseling mode that's proven to be more effective than others for men struggling with homosexuality. Counselors taking an analytic, behavioral, cognitive, or nouthetic approach can help people deal with any number of life problems, this one being no exception. What matters is that your approach is biblically sound, clinically viable, and one that you're well versed in.

Some counselors wonder if they need to have personally struggled with homosexuality in order to be an effective counselor to other men who struggle. The answer is no. Just as you don't need to have personally dealt with the many other issues you address as a counselor, neither must you have experienced same-sex attractions. Your ability to empathize, interpret, and offer guidance isn't limited by which problems you've personally had, and many counselors with no first-hand knowledge of homosexuality have proven to be effective, compassionate helpers to those who struggle.

And regarding the question of whether women should counsel men who struggle, or whether only male counselors do this sort of work, I generally recommend men working with men; women with women. A number of subjects and details come up in the counseling relationship that may, by their sexual nature, be difficult for a man to discuss with a woman. Additionally, those operating from an analytic perspective place high emphasis on the transference issues inherent in counseling, issues often having to do with unresolved father-son or peer-to-peer problems. Dealing with a counselor of the same sex can, they advise, help bring these conflicts to light.

Principle Two: The Christian Counselor Holds a Biblical Worldview While Respecting Those with Other Perspectives

Since this chapter is titled "Counseling Men Who Struggle with Homosexuality," the operative word is "struggle." We're concerning ourselves with men who are to some degree, whether partially, primarily, or exclusively, attracted to the same sex, and who are in conflict over their attractions. Their homosexuality, then, is *ego-dystonic*, in contrast to men who are attracted to the same sex and feel no conflict over these attractions, making them *ego-syntonic*. (See chapter 8 for a discussion of ego-dystonic and ego-syntonic homosexuality.)

Sometimes, though, a man may come for counseling, but not for his sexuality. This brings up the question of motivation, and the different approaches determined by a counselee's reasons for seeking help. While most same-sex-attracted men coming for Christian counseling will be ego-dystonic, some will not. So before exploring counseling approaches for men who struggle (which will make up the bulk of this chapter) let's look at some of the situations in which an ego-syntonic presents himself for counsel.

One example is an adult male who may be comfortable with his own homosexuality, but may also be financially reliant on his parents, who learn about his sexuality and demand he "get help" or be cut off financially. Or he may come from a family holding traditional views on sexuality, and though he doesn't share their views, he feels the need to appease them by trying to change, or by at least going through the motions of counseling. In some cases, the counseling is quid pro quo—a man "comes out" to his family, and they say, "If you'll see a Christian counselor for at least one session to hear our side, then we'll go to a pro-gay counselor to hear your side." In each of these cases, the man has no *internal* conflict over his homosexuality, but feels acute *external* pressure to address it in counseling.

Another example may be a teenager who has either disclosed his homosexuality to his parents, or they've discovered it against his will. He may have already adopted a pro-homosexual position, but they demand he get help, whether he wants it or not.

A third example may be an adult male who presents himself as undecided, stating he's not sure where he stands on homosexuality but wants to better understand the biblical position, clarify his options, then make a decision. Or a man might claim to be solidly pro-gay and confident, but wants to work on other relational or emotional problems.

In all these cases, the counselee is ego-syntonic or at least undecided, presenting the Christian counselor with the challenge of meeting the counselee's needs by respecting his right to determine his goals, while also being honest about his own beliefs and positions. And, I believe, this challenge can be met.

When describing her work with lesbian clients, Christian family therapist Mary Beth Patton recalls that a number of lesbians came to her, having no problem with their lesbianism but wanting to work on other emotional or relational problems. I think her approach was commendable:

> So, I worked with them just as they came. I did not bring up the issues of changing or even questioning their sexual orientation. To me, it would have been disrespectful and inappropriate. My stance as a

> therapist is that my client has the right to self-determination. As an
> adult I respect her ability to make decisions for herself.[4]

As a Christian, she knew where she stood and did not compromise her stand, but as a therapist, she also knew she did not have the right to impose it. Instead, she met her clients where they were and offered whatever help she could.

So, as Dr. Epstein said earlier in this chapter, the APA expects clinicians to "respect the rights of others to hold values, attitudes and opinions that differ from [their] own," so if a homosexual man comes to you for professional care, giving you no reason to believe he's in distress over his homosexuality, then he is ego-syntonic ("syntonic" meaning "compatible") as opposed to ego-dystonic ("dystonic" meaning "incompatible or unacceptable") and his views on that should not be challenged.

Still, your work with him can do a lot of good, even if it never addresses his homosexuality directly, by helping him achieve more emotional health and strength.

I am not suggesting the Christian clinician needs to avoid stating his position, and, in fact, if you market yourself as a Christian therapist (much less as one who treats homosexuality), then anyone coming to you will probably know where you stand. But the client's goals and views need to be respected, and you can offer that respect without compromising your own position.

Avoiding Compromise

Good counseling requires intrinsic rather than extrinsic motivation, so it seems wrong for the Christian counselor to be aligned with goals that are forced on the counselee. Not only are the goals unlikely to be attained, but the counseling relationship itself will be founded on coercion, creating an unworkable and unacceptable situation.

So it helps to ask the counselee how he himself feels about his sexuality, what goals he'd like to pursue in counseling, and then decide whether they are goals you can help him attain. In most cases you can align yourself with his goals (which may include decreased anxiety, improved family relations, better communication skills, and so on) without compromising your values as a Christian.

When dealing with minors this is especially delicate. In some matters, parents are (and should be) able to demand their children see a counselor. For instance, if the child or teen is suicidal, openly self-destructive, severely depressed, or suffering acute emotional or mental disturbances, then intervention is called for, regardless of the minor's own wishes.

But homosexuality doesn't seem to fall into any of these categories. It is unquestionably not an orientation God intended; it's decidedly a sin when it's practiced. And parents surely have the right to at least require their children to remain sexually inactive, no matter what their orientation. But the question of whether or not a teenager claiming "I'm gay" warrants forced counseling is another matter entirely.

When parents call asking me to meet with their minor son, I require a meeting with the parents first to hear more about the situation, and to make sure they understand that if their son is clearly in conflict over his sexuality, then counseling may be very effective. But if he is *not* in conflict over it, or is undecided, then I cannot force him to accept my viewpoint.

Likewise, I can't help a counselee achieve goals I myself find immoral. So if a teen says, "Help me persuade my parents that homosexuality is normal," I'd have to decline, asking if instead I could help him and his parents maintain a strong bond despite their different views, and work with the family to develop acceptable boundaries and policies in the home. Sometimes that's an acceptable approach to the teen; other times, he'll refuse, which is his prerogative.

That's why when parents ask me to try to persuade their son to adopt my position, I refuse, reminding them that I'm a counselor, not an evangelist, and that such a coercive approach to counseling will not only *not* work, but will probably drive a wedge between them and their child that may never close.

This isn't to say the Christian counselor is neutral on the subject; rather, he is respectful of his counselee's views. I do find it both fair and prudent to let an ego-syntonic counselee know my position on homosexuality. It would be damaging for us to begin working together with him assuming I approved of it, only to find midway through our work that I did not. (There are several ways this could happen, from him simply asking me at some point where I stood, or from visiting my website, or learning I attend a conservative Bible-believing church.) He'd rightfully feel deceived, and the resulting mistrust would damage, and perhaps end, our relationship. But if he is comfortable working with me despite our different views, with the understanding that I will not impose my position on him but will instead help him to achieve his stated goals, then we can establish a productive counseling alliance.

Christian professionals face this situation regularly. A Christian doctor may see a patient who's living with his girlfriend, and on moral principle wishes he would either marry her or move out. But he didn't come looking for help in that area, and he'd be wrong to impose his views when the patient didn't ask for them. Christian dentists, accountants, or personal trainers are often in the same position. We know God's standards; we wish all people would live by them. But as a counselor, remember, you're there to help the counselee achieve his goals, and he alone has the right to set those goals.

Principle Three: The Christian Counselor Is Clear About Prognosis and Approach

Despite what I just said about treating men who are ego-syntonic, the fact is, most of the ones coming to you as a Christian counselor will probably be ego-dystonic, in which case they'll probably share your worldview. They're attracted to men, but they don't want to be. Maybe they've been involved in a relationship they've repented of, or maybe their struggle is completely internal. Either way, they'll have two questions for you: *Can I change? If so, how?*

Browse the web and you'll find testimonials from people who used to hold the traditional view on homosexuality and were themselves homosexual. So they sought professional help in hopes of changing their orientation. Now, years later, they've changed their position to a pro-gay one and have decided the help they sought to overcome their attractions was no help at all. One of their main complaints is that their therapist made promises of change that weren't realized, or was unclear as to what "change" meant, or took an approach that was unhelpful at least—and harmful at worst. We can disagree strongly with their pro-gay position while still weighing the importance of their complaints. If we offer help, after all, we should clarify what that help will be and what results it will bring.

Some counselors or ministers say that if someone repents of homosexuality and then follows the right steps, they can and should change completely. No temptations; no homosexual desires at all, ever.[5] Others say behavior can change but feelings never will; still others say in some cases people's feelings can change, but probably not completely, and that change is dependent on how exclusive or nonexclusive their homosexuality has been.[6]

I'm not here to tell you what your definition of "change" should be (although I will offer a sample definition in this chapter; also, see chapter 13 for an examination of the change issue), but I'd encourage you to be sure it's clear, and that you have biblical and clinical backing for it.

The same goes for your general and specific treatment approach. Your *general* approach to counseling or therapy may be psychoanalytic, behavioral, cognitive, humanist, or eclectic. Your *specific* treatment approach to homosexuality may be to analyze family history and identify past hurts needing attention, or it may be to concentrate on the sexual desires themselves and learn new ways to manage them, or it may be to enhance gender-identity confidence. Whatever your general and specific approaches are, state them clearly from the outset of counseling, while also making it clear to your client what sort of changes he can expect, and how you and he will attempt to see those changes happen. Clarify your ideas on the prognosis and treatment approach in writing, and be sure your client signs and keeps a copy.

The confusion I expressed when my counselor asked me what "starting over" meant was borne largely from lack of experience with counseling in particular and recovery in general. Many people seeking professional counseling don't know what to expect, how counseling operates, or what's required of them as counselees. Clarifying these points early in the counseling relationship can only enhance its effectiveness.

Principle Four: The Christian Counselor Provides a Place of Safety, Education, and Exploration

Though it's an office, your counseling room should also be a sanctuary; a place of safety. The man coming there needs to feel safe to express and explore what he feels, and to be respectfully educated, drawing on your expertise as it regards his sexuality, relationships, pains, and aspirations. As a result of working with you, he should achieve and maintain sexual purity, but that's not all. He should also have a greater self-knowledge, a clearer sense of direction, the relief of having been able to speak about things he hasn't addressed before, healthier relating skills, reduced anxiety born of putting things into perspective with you, and an improved ability to manage temptations and desires. Your office is the greenhouse—the place of safety and nurturing—where all this growth can occur.

In her "Essentials of Therapy," Mary Beth Patton outlines elements that should always exist in therapy, and that help create a genuine place of safety.

I'm passing them on to you because they're invaluable, as is her work in the *Handbook of Therapy for Unwanted Homosexual Attractions*, which I highly recommend. They are:

1. The therapist must establish a good working relationship and help the client develop a strong sense of trust in the therapeutic relationship.

2. The therapist must help the client to identify and grieve the past losses or abuse in [his] family of origin and in any other relationship or situation.

3. The therapist must provide an environment where feelings can be explored, validated, and understood.

4. The therapist encourages the client to establish positive role models and friendships with both sexes. The client has to make a definite attempt to seek healthy, balanced, and caring people that have respectful boundaries.

5. [Men] need to be in touch with their own "wanting" or passion in life.[7]

As a man who's been on both the giving and receiving end of counsel, I'll vouch for these elements, and I encourage you to adopt them as well.

The Man Who Struggles:
Who He Is, What He's Facing, What He Needs to Hear

So who is the Christian man who struggles with homosexuality and comes to you for help?

Perhaps he's a married man whose wife just found a history of gay porn use on his computer; or maybe he's a single man who's attracted to men but is dating a woman, and isn't sure to what extent he can consummate a marriage relationship. Or he could be a pastor who's been caught in an affair with a male parishioner; or he's a single youth minister who falls deeply and silently in love with other men in his church. Maybe he used to be openly gay, but recently came to Christ and is still working out his sanctification; or perhaps he's a middle-aged man who was just arrested for an indecent act in a park or public restroom. He may routinely hook up with other men over the Internet and meet for anonymous encounters, or he could be a celibate single who doesn't use porn and is sexually inactive, but knows he's attracted to men nonetheless, or he could be sexually inactive but addicted to porn, using it several times a week. He may be HIV-positive and afraid; perhaps he's openly effeminate with glaring gender-identity issues; maybe he's burly and rough.

Just as there's no such thing as a typical homosexual, there's also no such thing as a typical ego-dystonic. Despite the variety of profiles listed above, though, you should know that Christian men struggling with homosexuality tend to have three things in common.

- They've had a genuine born-again experience, and they hold to a traditional biblical view, which largely accounts for their coming to you.

- They feel angry or bewildered that God hasn't removed their homosexuality, considering the number of years they've prayerfully begged Him to.

- They usually don't call themselves "gay," because they view that word as a positive way of describing something they don't feel positive about. Instead, they identify themselves primarily as Christians, but they feel largely misunderstood by the church, which (they feel) sees them as either the worst or the weirdest of sinners.

So in light of the common experiences and situations listed above, I find it helpful during the initial session to make sure the counselee understands some general points:

- *The role of sanctification in counseling, and the role of counseling in sanctification.* As a believer in Christ, the counselee is being sanctified (1 Thessalonians 4:3-4), and correction is part of the sanctification process (Hebrews 12:8; Revelation 3:19). Counseling, then, is a part of this season of his correction and sanctification.

- *The difference between orientation and behavior.* The homosexual orientation is an involuntary condition that he is not morally responsible for; homosexual behavior is a voluntary act with moral consequences. God calls him to repent of behavior, and to manage orientation.

- *Theories of origin are useful but inconclusive.* We can consider explanations for homosexuality's origins and see how they may fit the client's own experience, but there's still much about the orientation that we don't understand, so we won't shove the client into a predetermined box by presuming to already know why he's attracted to men.

- *The how is more important than the why.* Obedience is a primary call to all Christians, so we'll emphasize *how* you can help the counselee live obediently more than *why* he's been tempted to do the opposite.

- *Prognosis for change.* While respecting the different views on the "change" issue, my experience has been that if a man has been primarily attracted to men, he will continue, to a greater or lesser degree, to be homosexually attracted. (If he has been classically "bisexual," he may experience complete absence of homosexual attractions.) This is not to say change doesn't happen. I believe it does in four primary ways:

  1. change in behavior
  2. change in perspective
  3. change in frequency of homosexual attractions
  4. change in intensity of homosexual attractions

To what extent each type of change is experienced, and the extent to which heterosexual attractions will likewise develop, varies from person to person. There is no way to accurately predict these changes, though past sexual responses are good indicators of future potential. Counseling, then, will help him manage existing homosexual attractions, and explore his potential for heterosexual ones as well. The outcome isn't likely to be a *conversion* of the one into the other; but rather a *decrease* of the one and an *increase* of the other.

- *Counseling goals.* Since he's presenting unwanted homosexuality as a primary issue, counseling goals will probably include:
  - developing tools for permanent abstinence from homosexual behavior, whether the viewing of porn or acting out sexually with another man
  - management of homosexual desires
  - enhancing of heterosexual response when and where appropriate

- addressing damage done to primary relationships (if applicable)
- correcting unhealthy relational patterns (if applicable)
- attaining or maintaining of healthy relationships
- enhanced intimacy with God
- other specific goals unique to the counselee and his situation

These goals should be fully explored and explained in the initial session(s), written out, and referred to throughout the counseling relationship.

The ROUTE™ Model

With these principles and general points in mind, let me offer a model for the counseling experience that involves five general tasks: **R**epentance, **O**rder, **U**nderstanding, **T**raining, and **E**ndurance. This model is compatible with various counseling and therapy approaches because it addresses different seasons the counseling is likely to take, rather than a prescription for a form of counseling (psychodynamic, behavioral, and so on). This is offered, then, as a description of tasks a man struggling with homosexuality is likely to face in his counseling experience, along with suggested points to consider and make during each task phase.

It goes without saying that these are not the only tasks a counselee faces. Individuals bring along their unique challenges and situations, all of which have to be considered by the counselor, who partners with the man to determine which issues will be the focus of their work. But the tasks cited in the ROUTE™ model do seem to be the most common and general ones faced by men who struggle with homosexuality. The time each task phase takes—weeks for some, months for others—varies from man to man, and depends largely on the challenges faced during each. What matters is that each is completed, hopefully before moving on to the next one.

First Task: Repentance

General goal:	Turning away from behavior that's become unacceptable.

Internal goals:

1. Clarified direction ("*Why* am I seeking counseling, and *where* am I headed in my personal growth?")

2. Increased hunger for righteousness ("I want what's right, but God help me to want it *more.*")

3. Increased hatred of sin; appropriate brokenness and humility ("God increase my hatred of sin and my sensitivity to You.")

4. Increased confidence in God's grace ("I believe You love and forgive me, Lord, but help my unbelief! Don't let me drown in shame or condemnation.")

External goal: Reject unacceptable behaviors by separating (as much as possible) from them (Matthew 6:29-30). This can include getting filtering services for the computer, cutting off unhealthy relational ties, or committing to avoid places and circumstances likely to enhance a relapse.

By this time: The counselee has had a crisis of truth that has drawn his attention to the problem. Whether through internal conviction or an external situation, he's now motivated to seek your help, and to distance himself from a form of behavior or internal fantasy or lust that's no longer acceptable to him. Now he needs to take action.

Points to consider and make:

1. All true change begins with repentance, and repentance is about *action*, not just confession or acknowledgment.

2. God initiated the man's repentance and recovery process through His foreknowledge (Ephesians 1:4)

so we can be confident that what God has initiated, He will also sustain (Psalm 138:8) and complete (Philippians 1:6).

3. To repent is to turn from what's unacceptable, but it's also to turn *toward* what is healthy and right. So the counselee is not just called to turn away from homosexuality, but to turn toward holiness and emotional and sexual health.

Be sure to:

1. Address any immediate urgent concerns. These can include the need for legal counsel if a criminal act is involved, a family attorney if a separation or divorce is looming, medical testing (HIV, STDs), psychological testing if significant emotional or mental problems are evident, screening for anxiety or depression, or reporting if abuse or molestation of a minor is evident. In most cases, none of these will apply, but if they do, start by addressing them due to their urgency.

2. Stress a practical approach to repentance. A good question to pose at this point is, What sexual behaviors have you been prone to, and what practical steps should we take to ensure you don't repeat them?

3. Remind the counselee that he's repenting because God is correcting him. And when God corrects, He does so because He has *purposes* and a *future* in mind for the man He corrects. Otherwise, why would He bother?

On a personal note:

Saul of Tarsus's first words after his crisis of truth on Damascus were "Lord, what would you have me to do?" Counselees often ask God the same when they begin, and it helps them prioritize when they're told that obedience comes first, and that if they're wanting to make progress, they need to start by removing, as much as possible, access to the behaviors they're turning from. Learning and healing come more freely when sin has been acknowledged and abandoned.

Second Task: Order

General goal:	Establishing a structure of disciplines and alliances to enhance direction and motivation.
Internal goals:	1. Deeper intimacy with God, resulting in deeper holiness and spiritual fruit (John 15:4).
	2. Stronger and more consistent motivation.
	3. Deeper awareness of counselee's belonging to, and responsibility to, his primary relations (wife, family, close friends, and community) and the body of Christ in general.
External goals:	1. Establishment of devotional life of prayer, study of Scripture, and personal reflection.
	2. Establishment of weekly accountability if needed.
	3. Making confession and restitution if needed.
By this time:	The counselee should have taken steps to distance himself from sexual behaviors that are contrary to his goals, and he should have addressed any urgent concerns as exampled above. He's made a new start, whether through a lifestyle change or a simple renunciation of sinful behavior patterns and a recommitment to his sanctification. So he's likely to be grieving over sin, hopeful (perhaps even idealistic) about the new start he's making, and still experiencing acute pain if he's in a crisis situation such as a divorce, loss of ministry position, or exposure of hidden sexual behavior to his wife or family. He'll continue to need reassurance and comfort, and now he also needs a daily and weekly structure to incorporate and follow, to help keep him on track.

Points to consider and make:	1. Life changes of any sort require establishing personal checks and balances to sustain direction and motivation. That's the value of establishing order and structure at this point.

2. What the heart has rejected the brain has nonetheless recorded. No matter how fervently we renounce a deeply ingrained behavior pattern, its memory has been recorded, and at some point of stress or discomfort, the memory will beckon. Disciplines and accountability enhance our motivation to resist at such times, and strengthen our resolve to stay the course (Hebrews 3:13).

3. If a man's ongoing secret sin has been confessed or exposed, it's impacted the people he's closest to, who may be deeply hurt or enraged by his behavior. In that case, he needs to acknowledge to them his awareness of the hurt he's caused, express remorse over it, and explain what specific steps he'll be taking to prevent such actions in the future (Matthew 3:8).

Be sure to:	1. Encourage the client to immediately develop the daily habit of prayer and Bible study. Remind him that ultimately his love for God will sustain him and inspire him to obedience, and he cannot love a God who he's not intimate with. Intimacy comes through communication; communication with God comes through daily disciplines.

2. Help the client locate proper accountability if he's had a pattern of regular acting out. A local men's accountability group, an accountability partner, or an established sexual purity group such as Celebrate Recovery or Sexaholics Anonymous can all be helpful. Remind him that everyone attempting to resist an ongoing, life-dominating behavior needs the auxiliary

strength of others encouraging him and holding him accountable on a regular basis, because left to his own devices, he's likely to abandon his direction and relapse to old, familiar patterns. (See chapter 15, "Sexual Addiction.")

3. Help the client whose marriage is in crisis over recent behaviors realize his wife needs time to rebuild trust and intimacy with him, and may be on her own emotional roller coaster. Joint sessions with the two of them may be helpful at this point, to help her better understand his process and to hear her questions and concerns as well. His willingness to express to her his pain over his behavior, listen to her pain as well, and explain to her the steps he's taken to prevent future relapses, will all help stabilize the marriage. (See "The Spouse's Dilemma," chapter 17.)

On a personal note:	I often refer to structure as the counselee's "meds" (slang for "medication") because through discipline and accountability, it ensures regular motivation and clarification. Just as a personal trainer hopes his clients will observe healthy dietary and lifestyle habits between his workout sessions with them, so I hope my clients stay on their "meds" during the week. When they do, the results are concrete and obvious.

Third Task: Understanding

General goal:	A working knowledge of sexual and emotional patterns.
Internal goal:	The "Aha!" experience. (As in, "Aha! Now I see why I feel that way, or experience this pain, or have these temptations.")

External goals:	1. Become better educated on root causes of sexual and emotional conflicts.
	2. Analyze family dynamics and personal history to better understand patterns, tendencies, and weaknesses to be aware of.
By this time:	The counselee should have incorporated regular prayer, Scripture reading, and reflection into his daily routine, and accountability via a group or individual on a weekly basis, if he's had a history of "acting out" with porn or with partners. If married, he should also have made clear to his wife his remorse over any betrayal of her through the use of porn, or any adulterous behavior, and shown zeal to regain her confidence through consistency, humility, and personal growth. By now he may be saying, "Okay, I've cleaned my act up and have things in order. Now what?" So now he needs to better understand his long-term issues so he can better manage his emotional and sexual self.
Points to consider:	1. Understanding what causes sexual sin may not banish sexual temptation or emotional pain, but it helps us better manage it.
	2. Behind sexual sin there are, more often than not, legitimate emotional needs the counselee may have been trying to meet through illegitimate sexual behavior. We can and must repent of sinful behavior; we cannot repent of a legitimate need. So now's the time to recognize the need and learn healthier ways of meeting that need (Isaiah 55:2).
	3. Examining early history (including family dynamics) is not an attempt to blame. Rather, it helps us better understand why we relate and respond the way we do, where we've made the wrong decisions, where we've been *wrong*, and where we've been *wronged*.

4. When we understand why we relate and respond the way we do, we're better able to correct our patterns, because the better we understand our system, the better we can manage it.

5. When we better understand where we've been *wrong*, we can take responsibility to confess and correct our wrongs. When we better understand where we've been *wronged*, we can take responsibility to confront when necessary, and forgive.

Be sure to:

1. Spend time examining the counselee's family history and empathically listen, grieving alongside him when appropriate; probing for clarification when needed. This may well be the first time he's reviewed this information with anyone, and that alone can be a profound source of relief and enlightenment.

2. Try not to "lead" the counselee into whatever theories you may have on homosexuality's origins by asking questions like, "What went wrong between you and your father?" or "What sort of rejection did you experience from peers?" Let him tell his own story by asking open-ended questions, such as, "What sort of words would you use to describe your early home life?"; "What was your relationship with your parents like?"; "How would you describe yourself as a child?" You will frequently hear information confirming standard developmental theories of male homosexuality; other times, you'll hear very different histories. What matters is what the counselee experienced and how it shaped him.

3. Explore with the counselee how he learned to view men, women, and himself. Look for relationships and experiences that helped shape these views.

4. Explore with the counselee the relationships that have affected him the most deeply, for good or for bad, up to this point.

5. Have the counselee describe his earliest awareness of same-sex attractions, how he felt about them, how he has expressed them over the years, and any significant emotional or passionate experiences he's had with men.

6. Try to determine what relational needs stand out in the counselee's history, and help him determine the best way to meet them in the here and now.

On a personal note:

My counselor told me it was going to be far easier to abandon my sexual sin than it would be to unlearn the unhealthy relational patterns I'd developed out of fear of intimacy and unresolved anger. How right he was!

For that reason, this task tends to be the longest, sometimes taking several months, as counselor and counselee walk through the counselee's memories, triumphs, and pains. This strengthens the therapeutic bond, clears up misconceptions the counselee may have held about himself, inspires him to forgive himself for what he's not responsible for, take responsibility as needed, and forgive and let go of long-term hurts. Understanding, then, brings invaluable relief and clarity.

Fourth Task: Training

General goal: Maintain sexual integrity.

Internal goals: Higher tolerance for discomfort, frustration, or "cravings," and adaption of a soldier or athlete mind-set when addressing internal conflicts (2 Timothy 2:3-5).

External goals:	1. Maintain consistency.
	2. Manage temptations when they arise.
	3. Attain, strengthen, or correct primary relationships.

By this time: The counselee should have a deeper understanding of his sexual and emotional makeup, equipping him to better manage both. His last task phase should have strengthened his bond with you, and whereas your empathic posture during the understanding phase might be deemed maternal, in this training phase your posture becomes more paternal, challenging him and coaching him along, in contrast to the last phase's emphasis on listening and empathizing.

Points to consider: 1. Temptation is guaranteed and is no indication the counselee is doing anything wrong. The goal, then, is not to reach a point of freedom from temptations, but rather to successfully and consistently respond to them when they arise (James 1:12).

2. Resistance of sin is an act of worship; a sacred thing in and of itself (Romans 6:12-14).

3. Relationship health is critical. The counselee needs to examine his primary relationships to determine whether he needs to attain social and peer relationships, which may entail overcoming his shyness or social timidity (Proverbs 18:24). Or he may need to correct existing relationships in which he has committed wrong acts, which may entail overcoming pride (Matthew 5:24). Or he may need to confront primary relationships in which he is being consistently wronged, which may entail overcoming passivity (Matthew 18:15-17; Proverbs 17:10).

Be sure to: 1. Help the counselee examine the best methods for dealing with sexual temptations as they arise.

2. Stress the healing nature of relationships; close peer and social relationships in particular. His need for same-sex bonding is critical and can be met through close, consistent friendships. Help him to build them.

3. Examine his primary relationships to see where and how they may need correcting or confronting (a family member he has wronged whom he needs to apologize to; a dominating wife whom he's allowed to demean him, whom he needs to confront; and so on). If he is allowing unhealthy relational patterns to continue, he's frustrating his own progress.

On a personal note:

In this fallen world, where sexual idolatry is evident and glaring, maintaining sexual purity is one of life's greatest challenges. For years I assumed there was something foundationally wrong with me because I was so frequently tempted. Real freedom came for me when my counselor helped me understand that God wasn't requiring me to be temptation-free; rather, He was calling me to be faithful when tempted.

Fifth Task: Endurance

General goal: Finishing the course (2 Timothy 4:7).

Internal goal: Contentment and awareness of passion and calling.

External goals: Relapse prevention.

By this time: The counselee should have experienced internal and external changes. His behavior should be more noticeably consistent with his beliefs; his understanding of himself should be enhanced; his sexual attractions toward men will likely be *present* to some degree but not *powerful*, in that he knows how to deal with them, and their frequency and intensity may well have diminished by now. His social and accountability alliances should be in place; and his mind-set should be one of a steward who manages property (his own body) that belongs to God, and who will someday answer for how he's managed that property (1 Corinthians 6:19-20). By this point his season with you is coming to a close.

Points to consider: 1. In this life we don't arrive, so he should stay watchful and aware of his ability to return to the behaviors he's worked so hard to overcome (1 Corinthians 10:12).

2. This is a good time to examine his passion and calling in life, by determining his gifts, his passion, and the opportunities to utilize both. He wasn't called to repentance just to remain sexually pure, important as that is. There have also been long-term goals God's set for him, goals he couldn't achieve while morally compromised. Now's the time to examine what those goals might be.

3. Stewardship of our bodies and passions is a life-long challenge, calling for different efforts at different times. So while this was a significant season of change and reform for him, it won't be his last. There may be a number of other life issues he'll need to face, so he should take the lessons he's learned in this season of reform and apply them to the next.

Be sure to: Remind him that in the future he may want to reconnect with you to discuss his progress, new challenges he's facing, and new lessons he's presented with. It's not necessary, I'm sure, to encourage you to say that your door will be open.

On a personal note:

By the time my work with my counselor was finished, I may not have been a new man, but I was surely an improved one. I wasn't free of sexual temptations, but they had far less hold on me and I knew what to do with them when they arose. I was more integrated socially than I'd ever been; more at peace with my past than I'd dared hope; more aware of my tendencies (both good and bad) and far more equipped to deal with them. The time, money, and effort I put into counseling proved to be one of the best investments I'd ever made, and I'm more convinced than ever that, when done carefully and biblically, the counseling experience can be life-changing for both counselor and counselee. God grant that you find this to be true in your work, now and always.

CHAPTER ELEVEN

COUNSELING MEN WHO STRUGGLE WITH HOMOSEXUALITY

◦——KEY POINTS——◦

1. The Christian counselor has a responsibility to be informed, hold a biblically based worldview while respecting the views of his counselees, be clear regarding the prognosis and treatment approach, and provide a place of safety for his counselees.

2. Just as there is no such thing as a typical homosexual, so there's also no such thing as a typical ego-dystonic homosexual. Each man who struggles with homosexuality is unique in his experience, behavior, and needs.

3. Some men coming for counseling may be ego-syntonic in their homosexuality, and in such cases the Christian counselor will try to find goals compatible with the counselee's needs and the counselor's ethical and moral stance. In most cases this is possible and advisable.

4. Most men coming for counseling who deal with homosexuality will be ego-dystonic, holding a biblical and traditional viewpoint on homosexuality.

5. The ROUTE™ model (Repentance, Order, Understanding, Training, Endurance) provides an overview of critical tasks the counselee is likely to face during his counseling experience.

RESOURCES

Reparative Therapy of Male Homosexuality: A New Clinical Approach by Joseph Nicolosi, PhD, Jason Aronson, Inc., 1991.

Handbook of Therapy for Unwanted Attractions, edited by Julie Harren Hamilton and Philip Henry, Xulon Press, 2009.

Ex-Gays?: A Longitudinal Study of Religiously Mediated Change in Sexual Orientation by Stanton Jones and Mark Yarhouse, IVP Academic, 2007.

NOTES

1. Published, respectively, by Jason Aronson, Inc., 1991; Xulon Press, 2009; IVP Academic, 2007.
2. Robert Epstein, "Am I Anti-Gay? You Be the Judge," *Psychology Today*, January/February 2003.
3. www.psych.org/MainMenu/PsychiatricPractice/Ethics/ResourcesStandards.aspx.
4. Mary Beth Patton, "Working with Lesbian and Bi-Sexual Women," *Handbook of Therapy for Unwanted Homosexual Attractions*, Julie Harren Hamilton and Philip Henry, gen. eds. (Longwood, FL: Xulon Press, 2009).
5. Stephen Bennett, "The Cry of a Parent's Broken Heart: A Child's Homosexuality and Tears That Go Unseen," *AFA Online Journal*, November 20, 2002, www.afa.net/homosexual_agenda/GetArticle .asp?id=61.
6. See, for example, Joe Dallas, *Desires in Conflict*, rev. ed. (Eugene, OR: Harvest House Publishers, 2003).
7. Mary Beth Patton, "Essentials of Therapy," Hamilton and Henry, gen. eds., pp. 92-94.

COUNSELING WOMEN WHO STRUGGLE WITH LESBIANISM

by Melissa Fryrear, M.Div.

> *Emotional healing is almost always a process.*
> *Our heavenly Father is not only wanting to free us from*
> *the pain of past wounds, he is also desirous of bringing*
> *us into maturity, both spiritually and emotionally. He*
> *loves us enough to take the months and years necessary to*
> *not only heal our wounds, but also build our character.*
> *Without growth of character we will get wounded again.*
>
> —FLOYD McCLUNG

Almost 20 years ago I was sitting in a living room with a number of lesbian friends talking about the continuum of sexuality, including the variances between heterosexuality, bisexuality, homosexuality, and transsexuality. At one point in the conversation, I quickly stood up and boldly proclaimed, "I don't know about anyone else in the room, but I'm 99.9 percent gay and that's all there is to it!"

Ninety-nine-point-nine percent gay. The scales were greatly tipped, weren't they?

That was then—another time, a different world. A time when I identified myself as a lesbian, which placed me in solidarity with a world of like-minded women, gave me a long-term relationship, and offered a clear sense of self and purpose.

But this is now, and who'd have thought? Who in that living room would have guessed this bold young woman, so sure of her sexual identity, would someday attend a church with her partner, respond to the gospel, be lovingly discipled, walk away from lesbianism, grow in grace, and finally exchange her proclamation of "I'm 99.9 percent gay" to "I'm 100 percent His!" That's the power of the good news, and a testament to godly counsel.

That's also why I feel so strongly about ministry to women dealing with lesbianism. Twenty years ago I benefited from it, and now, by God's grace, I'm part of it.

I wanted to begin this chapter with this "I'm 99.9 percent gay!" story because I want to ask you to keep in your mind this picture of a scale and the cause and effect relationship that one side can have over the other...all related to the degree of weight or influence. (By the way, I'm going to share about the remaining tenth of a percent later.) Keep this scale in mind as we discuss lesbianism, and how you can counsel the woman who struggles with it. In this chapter, I'd like to look at three parts of that woman's life: where she's *been*, where she *is*, and what she *needs*.

Where She's Been: Emotional Roots

We've learned from countless testimonials, and from literature on the subject, that there's no one single factor that causes same-sex attraction. Rather, it is a combination, and an accumulation, of a number of possible influencing factors. That's true of male homosexuality and lesbianism as well. But just as there are different factors contributing to a person's sexual orientation, there are also unique factors that can contribute to lesbianism; factors that may be different than those contributing to male homosexuality.

So let me begin with this important observation: Female homosexuality is a complex condition...maybe because women are complex. (I'm a woman so I can say that!)

I'll also say this—over the past 15 years I've met hundreds of women desiring to overcome lesbianism, and while each woman's experience is unique, it's interesting to note a number of common influencing factors in many of their lives.

As a Christian who believes in the biblical worldview, I do not believe people are born "gay." Instead, I would like to offer for your consideration what

I've have found to be five of the most common influencing factors for many women who struggle with same-sex attraction.

Family Dynamics

As is the case with male homosexuality, the relational dynamics within the home—either real or perceived—may play an influencing role.

First, I want to point out that if you are the parent of a son or daughter living homosexually, you are not to blame for his or her same-sex struggle. As Christians who hold to the biblical worldview, we know from the beginning chapters of Genesis that there is no such thing as a perfect family—there is no such thing as a perfect parent-child relationship.

And, as we know, every child is unique and every child perceives his or her world differently. Much to parents' dismay, one of the things they cannot control is a child's perception, and we have found that oftentimes, much of the homosexual struggle is based on the child's perception and his or her interpretation of life events.

So please understand that in discussing family relationships I am not implying that a mother and father do not love their daughter. What I am saying is that sometimes what *literally* happened in a family is damaging; at other times, what was *perceived* to have happened (whether or not it actually did) is what causes the pain. Some daughters have been ignored, mishandled, or abused. Others have been truly loved and cared for, but for whatever reason, they haven't accurately *perceived* their parents' love. So my goal in this chapter is not to blame, but to explain. With that qualification made, let's examine three family elements that I feel do often shape a girl's future sexual orientation.

Element One: The Mother-Daughter Relationship

An infant girl's first two years of life are ideally spent developing a deep and secure bond with her primary caregiver—her mother. This leads, then, to a healthy sense of personal identity.[1]

Psychologist Erik Erikson calls this the development of "Basic Trust,"[2] while Christian author and teacher Leanne Payne refers to this process as "coming into a sense of being."[3] With a solid sense of identity formed, a little girl then has a good foundation in place for continued emotional growth and development.

If, however, this foundation is not solidly laid, a little girl may fail to come into this sense of personal identity and may subsequently be vulnerable to an inner sense of emptiness and longing. And that inner sense of emptiness and longing may emerge later in her life into an overwhelming drive to connect with, and find her identity in, another woman.[4]

Remember, now, the picture of the scale and the idea of multiple, influencing factors, because there are so many that could play into this sort of mother-daughter scenario.

In her book *Out of Egypt: One Woman's Journey out of Lesbianism*, Jeanette Howard offers several examples of long-term fractured mother-daughter relationships. Howard describes relational patterns that emerged as she interviewed hundreds of women overcoming lesbianism.[5]

One example is the *Doormat* relationship. This describes a situation in which the mother may embody true qualities of Christ in that she is kind, ever-giving, and self-sacrificing. Her daughter, however, may perceive her as downtrodden and weak...someone who is always subject to the whims of others or subject to the whims of men in particular. In this case, the problem wasn't the mother's behavior, but her daughter's perception of it, leading her to reject female identity because of its perceived weakness.

This type of rejection is seen in Anne Paulk's interviews of women dealing with same-sex attraction (as recorded in her book *Restoring Sexual Identity*), when she asked, "Did you want to be like your mother when you were growing up?" Eighty-four percent of the women responded "No." Anne also asked them, "Growing up, which gender seemed to have more desirable characteristics to be like?" Seventy-five percent of the women responded that men were more desirable role models. Why? Their perception was that men are

- strong and in control,
- not easily pushed around,
- less likely to be victimized,
- respected and valued more than women.[6]

Another example Howard offers is the *My Best Friend* relationship, in which the mother—out of her own state of emotional unhealthiness—is unable to meet the emotional needs of her daughter, and there is a reversal of need. As the women described it, the daughter felt like *she* was the parent in the relationship, rather than her mother.[7] And if the daughter has become the mother, then who's going to mother her? Obviously, she'll long for some form of nurturing female connection to compensate for the mothering she's missed.

At other times the daughter may simply feel a lack of connection with her mother. Sometimes a mother may really have been emotionally absent, distracted by other things she felt were more important than her child. In those cases, a woman neglecting her daughter for her career, her boyfriends, or her social life left the girl feeling unloved and hurting. Hurting so badly, in fact, that the only way she can cope with the pain of feeling unwanted by the mother she wants is to stop wanting the mother. This is what counselors and therapists refer to as *defensive detachment*—that is, a decision to emotionally detach from the source of pain.

Eleanor, a woman overcoming lesbianism said, "As I grew up, I remember spending much of my time observing my mother rather than connecting with her emotionally. I knew I was meant to feel something about this woman, but I did not."[8]

Allison, another woman, likewise commented, "I withdrew from any affection my mom tried to show me because I feared subsequent rejection."[9]

Examples of this can be found in descriptions given by mental health professionals. Elaine Siegel, a psychoanalyst who's treated many lesbian women, describes the enmeshment some her patients had with their mothers:

> They were expected to fulfill their mothers' needs, not their own. From the very beginning, they received in one way or another the message that it was unacceptable, even dangerous, to become like their mothers. "Mother didn't teach me who I am. Therefore, another like myself must show me that I have a sexual self." But the mirroring they received from their female lovers was as distorted as their primary maternal experience had been, locking them into the never-ending cycle of the repetition compulsion.[10]

Therapist Mary Beth Patton describes the *disidentification* she's seen some of her clients experience in relation to their mothers when she writes:

> Women who deal with same-sex attraction, often possess a history of disidentification with their mothers, and therefore with their femininity. This leads to a longing for connection with the feminine

that becomes sexualized in adolescence or adulthood. Women dealing with same-sex attraction are longing for a connection with the feminine in themselves that was denied to them in their own development because of an inadequate identification in relating to their mothers. Rather than finding the feminine in themselves, they look to another female to give them the identification and connection they are missing.[11]

Family therapist and author Janelle Hallman makes a similar point:

A disruption in attachment means that many women with same-sex attraction most likely lacked consistent moments of caring attunement. They may have missed significant ongoing experiences of being the object of another's undivided, engaged, and regulating attention.[12]

One of Hallman's own clients describes how, for her, this led to detachment from her mom:

I remember when I was five or so my parents had gotten into a fight. My mother got into the car and just drove off. [I] was crying, asking, "Where is she going? What's going on?" My dad seemed helpless. [I] think that was when I checked out with Mom. I was devastated and I remember the feeling was just unbearable. So I checked out.[13]

Singer Melissa Etheridge, openly and proudly lesbian, is surprisingly candid about the effect her relationship with her mother had on her own development. When asked during an interview with *The Advocate* (a well known pro-gay publication) what she thought caused her lesbianism, she replied:

My relationship with my mother. It was strained as a child, and I think that adds to my attraction to women. It's about what I didn't get as a child: that female energy I crave.[14]

Of course, a mother may have really loved and valued her daughter, but has been unable to either be with her or bond with her as fully as the child wanted and needed her to. Long work hours, physical limitations, situations that can't be prevented—these can all be misread by the child, who might see them as a rejection and, in response, emotionally detach. Either way, if a little girl does not form a close relationship with her mother, she may be vulnerable to a future sexual identity struggle.

Element Two: The Father-Daughter Relationship

While mothers play a significant role in their child's life, fathers play an equally significant role. And while for some, homosexuality at its core may involve a real or perceived breakdown in the relationship with one's same sex parent, for others the relationship with one's opposite sex parent may also play an influencing role.

There are four things in particular that are ideal for a father to convey to his daughter. These include

- protection
- attention
- adoration
- support

When a father is physically present and emotionally available to his daughter, and able to convey these to her, it does three important things:

1. It helps to instill within her a sense of worth as a person.
2. It helps to instill within her a sense of value specifically as a female.
3. It helps her learn how to relate to the opposite gender in a healthy way.

If, on the other hand, the father is unavailable, or the daughter perceives he is absent from her life, the converse may occur.

She may be insecure in her sense of worth as a person; devalue who she is as a female; and be unable to relate in a healthy way with the opposite sex.

For example, a real or perceived "unprotecting father" may fail to foster for his daughter a sense of security and safekeeping. Or a father can inadvertently hurt his daughter if he fails to reflect back to her worth, value, and honor as a female. She doesn't learn, for example, that being a girl is special and wonderful.[15]

Janelle Hallman sees this as critical to female development:

> To gain this sense of autonomy or differentiation…a girl is utterly
> dependent on the involvement of an attuned father who will notice,

validate, affirm and support the delineation of her personhood and healthy individuation.[16]

When mother and daughter bond, and dad in turn validates, all's well. But his power to validate is a two-edged sword, as Susan found out.

She shared a story about the first time she went to a school dance. Although she usually wore just blue jeans and a T-shirt, she decided to dress up for this dance. Not owning any makeup herself, she borrowed her mother's. "The application process was difficult," she said, adding, "how on earth do women manage to do this every day?"

Timidly she proceeded down the stairs. "Dad," she asked, "how do I look?" Her father casually glanced up from his evening newspaper, briefly examined her appearance, and then smirked, "Who hit you in the eyes?"

Her dad may have been teasing but his words hurt her feelings—and her budding femininity was wounded.

Running back to the bathroom with tears streaming down her cheeks, she scrubbed her face until it was raw and vowed, "I will never, ever, ever do that again."

And guess what? Fifteen years later when she told this story, she still had never worn any makeup or put on a dress.[17]

Early problems with a father can create negative ideas about men in general. Anne Paulk reports that 46 percent of the lesbian women surveyed described their fathers as "detached."[18] Concerning their perception of men, some of the comments the women made were: "Men care only about themselves"; "All men want is sex"; "Men cannot be trusted"; "Men are womanizers"; and, "A man can never love me like a woman can."

Now that may be true of some men, but it's certainly not true of all men.

But again, remember that a girl's perception, regardless of whether it's true, can become her reality.

Element Three: The Parents' Marital Relationship

The relationship between a girl's father and mother may also play an influencing role in her identity development as a female and in her perception of what it might mean to be a wife and a mother one day.

Women, on average, tend to be more relationally perceptive than men and, as such, a daughter may be keenly aware of how her mom and dad relate to and treat each other.

One woman described her parents as an "indifferent couple," explaining that when they were together they failed to show love, affection, and appreciation for each other. Other women commented that their mother's critical comments about their father negatively affected their view of men and their roles as husband and father. Still other women felt that because their father was minimizing of their mother, her roles in the family were subsequently devalued.[19]

Hallman refers to this when she cites the Bell, Weinberg, and Hammersmith studies of 1981 as indicating that "in general, homosexual women did not observe as much meaningful affection between their parents as did non-homosexual women."[20]

Megan, for example, shared, "I wanted to know the strength, joy, and beauty of my parents' love for one another but I never saw that. As such, I did not desire marriage; I did not aspire to become a wife or a mother."

So the family dynamics I've often seen in the background of lesbian women include:

- mother-daughter relationships in which the mother appeared to be weak, causing the daughter to reject the perceived weakness of womanhood.

- mother-daughter relationships in which the mother tried to be more of a friend than a nurturer, leaving the daughter still longing for maternal love.

- mother-daughter relations in which the daughter felt abandoned, ignored, or unaccepted, leading to an eventual emotional detachment from the mother.

- father-daughter relationships in which the father was, or seemed, emotionally unavailable or unaffirming.

- marriages that were or seemed unhealthy, causing the daughter to reject the concept of wife and mother.

In each case, the developing child experiences a combination of pain over what she is not receiving, and the longing to receive it, if not from the mother, than from another female source.

Sexual Abuse

Many women were sexually abused yet never became lesbian; many women were never abused yet *did* become lesbian. So it's not accurate to say that all women engaging in same-sex behavior have been abused, nor to assert that sexual abuse in all cases causes lesbianism. It's true, however, that the occurrence of sexual abuse among lesbian-identified women is disproportionately high when compared to national estimates of sexual abuse against women in general. Christian counselors and clinicians who've dealt with lesbian women have said as much.

In the interviews Anne Paulk conducted for *Restoring Sexual Identity: Hope for Women with Same-Sex Attraction*, 66 percent of the women struggling with same-sex attraction interviewed experienced sexual abuse.[21] Dr. Stanton Jones, provost of Wheaton College and author of the book *Homosexuality: The Use of Scientific Research in the Church's Moral Debate*, adds, "Experience of sexual abuse as a child...more than tripled the likelihood of later reporting homosexual orientation."[22] And drawing from my own experience, I'll say that in the decade I was on staff with one of Exodus International's largest ministries, I never met one woman struggling with lesbianism who had not been sexually threatened or violated.

In the 15 years I've served in this area of ministry, it comes as no surprise to me that as a result of being sexually violated by a man, many women have rejected their identity as a woman (because it's perceived to be a liability), shunned relationships with men, and turned exclusively to other women for affection and love. Additional studies have confirmed the prevalence of sexual abuse in the histories of lesbian women, as Janelle Hallman found when she compiled a number of such histories:

- Matthews, Hughes, Johnson, Razzano, and Cassidy found in 2002 that 16 percent of the 279 heterosexual women they surveyed had suffered childhood abuse, in contrast to 30 percent of 550 lesbians surveyed.[23]

- Balsam, Rothblum, and Beauchaine found in 2005 that 30 percent of the 348 heterosexual women studied were abused as children, compared to 44 percent of the 332 lesbians in the same study.[24]

- Hughes, Haas, Razzano, Cassidy, and Matthews (2000) found

that 24 percent of their 279 heterosexual female subjects reported childhood abuse, compared to 41 percent of the 550 homosexual ones.[25]

- Hughes, Johnson, Wilsnack found in 2001 that 27 percent of the 57 heterosexual women they surveyed had been abused as children, compared to 42 percent of the 63 homosexual women also surveyed.[26]

- Tjaden, Thoennes, and Allison (1999) stated that "same-sex cohabitating women were nearly twice as likely as [the] opposite sex to report forcible rape as a minor."[27]

- National Lesbians Health Care Survey reported that 19 percent of the 1779 lesbians interviewed had been involved in incestuous relationships growing up, while of them 41 percent reported rape or sexual attacks or abuse.[28]

Consider, too, some public comments from celebrity lesbians about their own violations. Rosie O'Donnell, who's outspoken about her lesbianism, wrote in her book *Find Me*:

> I was an abused kid. I thought I had dealt with the fallout in therapy. How naïve I was. Abuse is often an ongoing saga for everyone who has lived through it. It may start and stop in real time, but in mind time it goes on forever.[29]

Ellen DeGeneres, in the April 2005 edition of *Allure* magazine, talked about the sexual abuse she suffered at the hands of her stepfather,[30] and singer Melissa Etheridge recalls early abuse at the hands of her own sister.[31]

I need to re-emphasize that these studies and quotes don't maintain that sexual abuse by itself *causes* homosexuality, and it's certainly not in the background of every lesbian-identified woman. But it's in the background of many, making it impossible for counselors to ignore it as a potential link in the chain of influences shaping a woman's identity and desire.

Gender Nonconformity

Gender nonconformity in a woman means appearance, behaviors, and preferences that are typically considered masculine. Columbia University's Gordon and Meyer describe it:

> Gender expression (or outward appearance) [that] does not follow traditional gender roles: "feminine boys," "masculine girls," and (people) who are androgynous, for example. It can also include (people) who look the way boys and girls are expected to look but participate in activities that are gender nonconforming, like a boy who does ballet.[32]

According to Dr. George Rekers, professor of neuropsychiatry at the University of South Carolina School of Medicine, "gender nonconformity in childhood may be the single most common observable factor associated with homosexuality," as well as "the retrospective sense of having been different from other children."[33] Zucker and Bradley found that "a substantial proportion of homosexual men and women recall greater rates of childhood cross-gender behavior than those of their heterosexual counterparts,"[34] and Hallman, citing several studies for support, goes so far as to say:

> In fact, gender non-conformity in childhood is considered to be one of the strongest correlating factors with later adult homosexuality. This does not mean that gender nonconformity directly causes homosexuality, but it may still have a substantial developmental influence.[35]

I've known many lesbian-identified women who conform to our culture's standards of femininity, while other heterosexual women may be nonconforming in mannerisms and behavior, yet they're not lesbian. Still, the nonconformity itself often seems to be an indicator of future lesbianism. It may be caused by prenatal hormonal influences or influenced by peer or sibling relationships,[36] in which case the girl will feel like a "tomboy" from early in life.

At other times, gender nonconformity may be freely chosen as a defense mechanism, which I can attest to. I tried to look like a man when I lived homosexually in an effort to keep myself safe—a type of protection to keep me from being hurt and violated.

But whether it's hormonal, acquired, or even chosen, this "tomboy" way of being, which is often called "butch," shows up when a woman looks and behaves in a mannish way. Some people argue that the whole idea of masculine or feminine is a "social construct" meant to keep people in little boxes, but I disagree. I believe there really is such a thing as God-given femininity, and embracing it myself has been one of life's greatest blessings.

Peer Pressure

Whether intentional or unintentional, peers exert a tremendous amount of influence over us during our formative years through either acceptance or rejection. And for many women, those formative years were marked by an ongoing, overwhelming sense of feeling "different." This can be especially true of the girl whose nonconformity makes her "stand out," but it can also be true of the girl whose conflicts are invisible and internal, but no less real.

When a girl with lesbian tendencies compares herself to peers of the same sex, she may not, in her own estimation, measure up. And like other girls experiencing confusion while blossoming into womanhood, she can feel trapped in a "third sex" mentality. She knows she's not a man, but she doesn't feel like a woman, either.[37]

She may then withdraw from others and isolate herself, which can fuel an already existing inner sense of rejection. This then further alienates and separates her from the very ones with whom she legitimately needs to spend her time to support and affirm her womanhood.

Judgments and Inner Vows

A final common influencer in many women's lives is what we might call *judgments and inner vows.*

As a result of life events happening to her and around her as she is growing up, a girl may unconsciously make important conclusions, or judgments, about people or things: herself, women, men, the roles of mothers and fathers, marriage, and sexuality.

As a result of being sexually violated, for example, many women made judgments about being a woman and about men, such as, "Being a woman is bad"; "Women are weak"; "Men only want sex"; or "Men cannot be trusted."

Diane Mattingly, in her online *Christianity Today* article, "My Path to Lesbianism," wrote:

> Girls disconnected from their mothers often begin to hate their emotions and all the other things that make them women. I don't necessarily mean those things that make us look feminine on the outside, but those internal characteristics that actually make us feminine beings. For example, I was always comfortable wearing dresses, getting

my nails done, and wearing lots of jewelry, so I didn't see those as contemptible qualities in my mother. But when I saw her let herself be a victim of my father's verbal assaults, I vowed that I would never be like my mother. I'd never be under the control of a man, never be dependent on a man, never be weak or admit my vulnerability.[38]

Janelle Hallman's client, who earlier described detaching from her mother after seeing her drive away following a fight with her father, describes her thinking at the time:

"Mom will leave me and I don't matter. It doesn't matter. She will leave me." *So it was sort of my way of making a resolve,* "Yes, Mother will leave—she's gone, she didn't want you—now get over it." I had to detach to stop that feeling of abandonment.[39]

Similar to judgments, inner vows are inflexible determinations that restrict a girl to thinking, feeling, and acting only in agreement with the vow. These are also made as a result of life events happening to her and around her—again, unconsciously. It's as though the judgments are the verdict ("I the jury find women to be weak") and the inner vows are the sentencing ("Because women have been found guilty of weakness, it is the sentence of this court that I will reject the traditional feminine identity").

And the sentences—"I will never trust a man"; "I will never let a man touch me"; "I will never get married"—may be for life.

Emotional Needs

Family dynamics, sexual abuse, gender nonconformity, peer pressure, and inner vows are all specific problems that can combine to create one large, general problem: a strong but unmet need for intimacy with the same sex, or *homoemotionality*, that develops into homosexuality when the emotional evolves into the sexual. For some, seeking out lesbian relationships could be understood as an unconscious attempt to restore what was missing in the relationship between a daughter and her mother.[40] For others, a breakdown in the affirmation process between father and his daughter may negatively affect a girl's view of herself and men, leaving her with a genuine need for love that is safe, combined with a belief that "safety" and "men" don't go together.

Therapist Julie Harren Hamilton asserts that homo-emotional needs play largely into this part of orientation development:

> Initially it was not a sexual craving. Instead, it was an emotional craving, a legitimate need for non-sexual love, an emotional need that has become sexualized.[41]

That's why many believe that at its core, lesbianism is not about sex. It is primarily about connecting, or more specifically, about connecting emotionally, with another woman. And it's this need to connect emotionally that can later develop into a sexual expression through a process often called *sexualization*.

Sexualization

Social psychologist and author Daryl Bem, in an effort to understand sexual desire, has put forth the *EBE Theory*, or the Exotic Becomes Erotic Theory. His ideas can apply to women, and offer a good place to start in understanding the development of sexual desire. Bem's theory states that what is exotic, foreign, or different to us becomes erotic. He explains that that which is us, is identified with; and that which is not us, is sexualized.[42]

The word "sexualize" can refer to a deliberate act of eroticizing, or "lusting after," an individual (as in, "Television ads often *sexualize* young women"). But it can also refer to an involuntary process by which an individual's *emotional* desire, through no conscious effort or decision on her part, becomes a *sexual* desire.

Ask a lesbian woman or male homosexual when and how their desire for the same sex became erotic, and there's no way they can pinpoint the date and time. It's usually a gradual, subtle process, just like what heterosexuals experience when they become aware of their desires. There's a mystery to this, and we don't have all the answers when it comes to sexualization. Why, for example, do some women feel deep unmet emotional needs for same-sex bonding yet never experience a sexualization of those needs, while others do? At this point no one seems to know, just as we don't fully know *how* this process happens, though we know it *does* happen. And once it happens, a strong sexual and emotional response has been born.

That, in brief, is where the woman struggling with lesbianism *has been*.

WHERE SHE IS

When the woman who's sexually attracted to women comes to a Christian pastor, counselor, or mentor, she brings with her any number of unmet needs.

Many of them have been identified and elaborated on earlier in this chapter and are elements commonly found in the background of lesbian-identified women. They may not be the stories of *all* lesbian women, but they're the stories of *many* such women, including women you, if you're a counselor or pastor, are likely to meet.

So the woman coming to you may not only be dealing with lesbianism, but with these relational, identity-oriented issues as well.

She may very well bring disidentification and the rejection that often comes with it; or early abuse and the shame, confusion, and relational difficulties that come with that. She may bring old hurts from her family life that keep her from integrating well with others, or she may bring mistrust of men, or women, or both. Read again the root emotional issues I've described, and be reminded that if these happen to be root issues for the woman who comes to you for help, then even if she's repented of lesbian behavior, those issues are going to remain, and they'll need to be dealt with.

I should also point out that when a woman says "I'm lesbian," it doesn't necessarily mean "I'm exclusively lesbian." Sometimes, a woman's sexual orientation is fluid—an important consideration in counseling women.

Dr. Lisa Diamond of the University of Utah conducted a study, later published in the magazine *Developmental Psychology*, that found many women are not exclusive in their attractions. Rather, there can be a broad fluctuation of sexual identities and behaviors among non-heterosexual women throughout the course of their lives.

In a follow-up report, for example, she found that half of the women interviewed had changed their sexual identity more than once in the two-year time since the original study. She commented, "Western culture expects sexuality to come in one neat package when often that is not the case."[43] We also need to mention the variations of same-sex behavior, four in particular. And each can vary with regard to the level of involvement.

The first we'll call *same-sex experimentation.* This describes a woman who has experimented in a same-sex experience but who has not embraced lesbianism as an identity.

The second is *emotional enmeshment*. This describes a woman who would never act out sexually with another woman, but often because she has no sense of who she is as a person, she has relied on another woman to gain an identity for herself and a sense of well-being.

The third could be labeled *Generation Y* or *The Millennial Generation*. This describes a younger woman who is heterosexual but who has engaged in same-sex behavior for a variety of reasons:

1. She is actually trying to draw the attention of a young man in whom she is interested. There have been popular reality dating shows, like *ElimiDate* and *The 5th Wheel*, that promote same-sex behavior between women because that is what the men are aroused by.

2. She lacks personal sexual boundaries and so when confronted with a situation—regardless of whether it involves a young man or a young woman—she sees no reason to refuse.

3. She considers bisexuality in vogue or chic.[44]

In the work we do we're seeing a dramatic increase in the number of younger women who are crossing over sexual boundaries and engaging in often casual same-sex behavior.

In the fall of 2006, CBS News cited a Centers for Disease Control report which stated, "More American women—particularly those in their late teens and 20s—are experimenting with bisexuality or at least feel more comfortable reporting same-sex encounters."[45] Some sexuality experts say it's even more likely that many young women simply see same-sex experimentation as a "rite of passage." The trend among college women has prompted some sexual behavior experts to use the term "LUG": "Lesbian Until Graduation" or "BUG": "Bisexual Until Graduation."

It's important to point out, though, that a woman in one of these three categories would probably not consider herself a true lesbian and often sees her involvement with another woman as only temporary.

The final variation is what I would describe as the classic form of lesbianism. This includes women who strive to fulfill emotional needs and sexual desires solely in relationships with other women. They fully embrace the lesbian identity. For her, entering into lesbianism and the lesbian culture brings a sense of freedom, relief, pleasure, power, sisterhood, and intimacy.[46] And women in this category often have very little attraction to men, or none whatsoever.

That's where the woman you may counsel has been and that's where she now is, which brings us to the important question of how she should be counseled.

WHAT SHE NEEDS

As Joe Dallas did in the previous chapter on counseling the male homosexual, I'd like to approach the question of "what she needs" by offering five brief points and suggestions to counselors. (Joe and I collaborated on these points, which is why some of them appear in his chapter as well as this chapter.) I've tried to put into words what I've seen and learned over the years while dealing with women, and I'm hoping these principles and practices will help strengthen your own abilities to counsel women who struggle with lesbianism.

If you're a Christian and a licensed professional, such as a psychologist, clinical social worker, or marriage and family therapist, you have the dual obligation to obey the standards and practices your profession calls for and the authority of the Bible. There's usually no conflict between these two—and if there is, I'm sure you realize you're a Christian first and foremost. Still, it's usually not an either/or matter. Jesus' advice to "render unto Caesar what is Caesar's, and render unto God what is God's" applies pretty well to the Christian professional. You should know and respect your profession's regulations, always making sure your work also honors God. So with that as our goal, let me offer these following principles and practices for your consideration.

Principle One: The Christian Clinician Must Be Informed

To ensure competent service and to protect your professional integrity, you should stay abreast of your governing organization's ethical standards and guidelines. That means knowing where your governing organization stands on homosexuality and related issues, and on treatment approaches. Mishandling of a patient or client and malpractice lawsuits can be avoided by simply staying current.

Practice: Stay Informed and Responsible

Be sure you know the American Psychiatric Association's *current* positions on diagnosis, treatment guidelines, and ethical concerns. As of this writing (2009) the following points are relevant to your work:

1. Homosexuality is *not* a diagnosable condition found in the *Diagnostic and Statistical Manual of Mental and Emotional Disorders.* Neither is *ego-dystonic homosexuality* (a classification that used to appear in the DSM indicating a person was in distress over their homosexuality—see chapter 8, "Homosexuality and American Psychiatry"). The APA does not consider homosexuality to be a disorder of any kind, sexual or otherwise. Both you and the women who come to you should know that while homosexuality may be a moral or spiritual issue, it is not, according to the APA, a psychological one. You can discuss to what extent you agree or disagree with the APA's position, but you should protect yourself and your client by letting her know what that position is.

2. The DSM (as of this writing in 2009) *does* classify "distress over one's sexual orientation" under DSM section 302.9, which is an appropriate diagnostic code to use when treating unwanted same-sex attractions.

3. Other DSM codes can be used as well if the woman you're working with presents other, more clearly diagnosable conditions. When in doubt over the appropriate way to diagnose, whether for treatment, recordkeeping, or insurance purposes, always consult with a colleague or supervisor.

4. As of this writing, the American Psychiatric Association and American Psychological Association do not *endorse* treatment for homosexuality (often referred to as *reparative therapy*), nor do they specifically *prohibit* or *condemn* it. Both have issued cautionary statements, expressing reservations about the possibility of changing sexual orientation and about theories of origin indicating homosexuality is unhealthy. (See chapter 8, "Homosexuality and American Psychiatry.") Robert Epstein, editor in chief of *Psychology Today* magazine, clarified these positions well:

   > The APA has never condemned sexual conversion therapy but has merely issued cautionary statements, one of which reminds psychologists of their obligation to "respect the rights of others to hold values, attitudes and opinions that differ

from [their] own."...Although homosexuality was removed from the DSM...as a mental disorder in 1973, all editions of the DSM have always listed a disorder characterized by "distress" over one's sexual orientation (DSM section 302.9). Both gays and straights have a right to seek treatment when they're unhappy with their sexual orientation, and some choose to try to change that orientation.[47]

5. Refer regularly to the APA official website for updates on professional ethics.[48]

Also refer to the NARTH (National Association of Research and Therapy for Homosexuality) website at www.narth.com for updates on controversies on clinical issues concerning the Christian professional. Make sure you also know the organizations you answer to professionally, and that you have regular access to their current standards.

Principle Two: The Christian Clinician Holds a Biblical Worldview While Respecting Those with Other Perspectives

Sometimes, a lesbian woman may come for counseling, but not for her sexuality. When describing her work with lesbian clients, Christian family therapist Mary Beth Patton recalls that a number of lesbians came to her, having no problem with their lesbianism but wanting to work on other emotional or relational problems. I think her approach was commendable:

> So, I worked with them just as they came. I did not bring up the issues of changing or even questioning their sexual orientation. To me, it would have been disrespectful and inappropriate. My stance as a therapist is that my client has the right to self-determination. As an adult I respect her ability to make decisions for herself.[49]

As a Christian, she knew where she stood and did not compromise her stand, but as a therapist, she also knew she did not have the right to impose it. Instead, she met her clients where they were and offered whatever help she could.

Practice: Respect the Client's Goals and Beliefs

As Dr. Epstein said earlier in this chapter, the APA expects clinicians to "respect the rights of others to hold values, attitudes and opinions that differ from [their] own," so if a lesbian-identified woman comes to you for professional care, giving you no reason to believe she's in distress over her lesbianism, then she is ego-syntonic with her sexuality ("syntonic" meaning "compatible") as opposed to ego-dystonic ("dystonic" meaning "incompatible or unacceptable") and her views on that should not be challenged.

Still, your work with her can do a lot of good, even if it never addresses her lesbianism directly, by helping her achieve more emotional health and strength. Patton found this to be true in her own work with lesbians:

> I became aware of a significant amount of enmeshment in their intimate relationships and in their friendships. As I worked with them to establish a greater sense of individuality, I saw these relationships improve and change.[50]

And in at least one case, her work with an ego-syntonic woman actually helped the client move on toward heterosexual relating, even though they never directly addressed the rightness or wrongness or lesbianism during their sessions!

> One client decided, on her own, that she was done with women and wanted to find a good man. She had been in the gay lifestyle for over twenty years, but had been married in her early twenties, so I assumed she was more bisexual than she had originally presented.[51]

I am not suggesting the Christian clinician needs to avoid stating his or her position, and, in fact, if you market yourself as a Christian therapist (not to mention one who treats homosexuality!) then anyone coming to you will probably know where you stand. But the client's goals and views need to be respected, and you can offer that respect without compromising your own position.

Christian professionals face this situation regularly. A Christian doctor may see a patient who's living with her boyfriend, and on moral principle wishes she would either marry the man or move out. But she didn't come to him looking for help in that area, and he'd be wrong to impose his views on her when she didn't ask for them. Christian dentists, accountants, or personal trainers are often in the same position. We know God's standards; we wish all people would live by them. But as a clinician, remember, you're there to help. Your client will tell you the sort of help she wants.

Principle Three: The Christian Clinician Is Clear About Prognosis and Approach

Despite the discussion about treating women who are ego-syntonic, the fact is, many or most of the ones coming to you as a Christian counselor or pastor will be ego-dystonic, in which case they'll probably share your worldview. They're attracted to women, and they don't want to be. Maybe they've been involved in a lesbian relationship they've repented of, or maybe their struggle is completely internal. Either way, they'll have two questions for you: Can I change? If so, how?

Browse the web and you'll find testimonials from people who used to hold the traditional view on homosexuality, and who were themselves homosexual. So they sought professional help in hopes of changing their orientation. Now, years later, they've changed their position to a pro-gay one, and have decided the help they sought to overcome their attractions was no help at all. One of their main complaints is that their therapist made promises of change that weren't realized, or was unclear as to what "change" meant, or took an approach that was unhelpful at least, harmful at worst. We can disagree strongly with their pro-gay position, while still weighing the importance of their complaints. If we offer help, after all, we should clarify what it will be, and what results it will bring.

Practice: Clarify Your Beliefs Regarding Sexual Orientation Change and Treatment Approach

Some counselors or ministers say that if someone repents of homosexuality and then follows the right steps, they can and should change completely. No temptations; no homosexual desires at all, ever. Others say behavior can change but feelings never will; still others say in some cases people's feelings can change, but probably not completely, and that change is dependent on how exclusive or nonexclusive their homosexuality has been.[52]

I'm not here to tell you what your definition of "change" should be (see chapter 13 for an examination of the change issue), but I'd encourage you to be sure it's clear, and that you have biblical and clinical backing for it. The same goes for your general and specific treatment approach. Your *general* approach to counseling or therapy may be psychoanalytic, behavioral, cognitive, humanist, or eclectic. Your *specific* treatment approach to homosexuality may be to analyze family history and identify past hurts needing attention, or it may be to concentrate on the sexual desires themselves and learn new ways to manage them, or it may be to enhance confidence or a combination of all of these.

What matters here is that you make it clear to your client what sort of changes she can expect, and how you and she will attempt to see those changes happen. Clarify your ideas on the prognosis and treatment approach in writing, and be sure your client signs and keeps a copy.

Principle Four: The Christian Clinician Provides a Place of Safety, Education, and Exploration

Though it's an office, your counseling room should also be a sanctuary, as in a place of safety. The woman coming there needs to feel safe to express and explore what she feels, and to be respectfully educated, drawing on your expertise with regard to her sexuality, her relationships, her pains, and her aspirations. As a result of working with you, she should have a greater self-knowledge, a clearer sense of direction, the relief of having been able to speak about things she hasn't addressed before, healthier relating skills, reduced anxiety born of putting things into perspective with you, and an improved ability to manage temptations and desires. Your office is the greenhouse—the place of safety and nurturing—where all this growth can occur.

Practice

In her "Essentials of Therapy," Mary Beth Patton outlines five elements that should always exist in therapy.[53] They are:

1. The therapist must establish a good working relationship and help the client develop a strong sense of trust in the therapeutic relationship.

2. The therapist must help the client to identify and grieve the past losses or abuse in her family of origin and in any other relationship or situation.

3. The therapist must provide an environment where feelings can be explored, validated, and understood.

4. The therapist encourages the client to establish positive role models and friendships with both sexes. The client has to make a definite attempt to seek healthy, balanced, and caring people that have respectful boundaries.

5. Women need to be in touch with their own "wanting" or passion in life.

As a woman who's been on both the giving and receiving end of counsel, I'll vouch for these practices, and I encourage you to adopt them as well.

Principle Five: The Christian Clinician Considers the Uniqueness of the Client and Attempts to Address Her Individual Needs

The general problem of lesbianism will present in the women you'll counsel, but the specific problems associated with it will certainly vary from woman to woman.

Remember, Jesus responded to people according to need. To a Samaritan outcast He offered respect and a clear gospel invitation (John 4:7-26); to an inquiring religious leader He offered instruction (John 3:3-21); to a trembling, condemned adulteress He offered grace (John 8:11); and to self-righteous Pharisees He offered a swift kick (Matthew 23:13-36). In each case, sin was the general problem, but the needs of the individual were unique and needed to be addressed as well. The Christian clinician should, as Christ said, "go and do likewise."

Walk with me again through some of the emotional and relational problems I described earlier in this chapter, problems that so often go along with lesbianism. Let me look at them again with you and offer some ideas on how to respond to each when you're working with women who struggle.

Family dysfunction. If her family of origin is a source of longstanding pain, she'll need to safely express her rage and her deep sadness over what was lost, or never had. Going over her family history in chronological order can be helpful. Listen empathically, letting her know you're with her while she explores what went wrong, expresses her pain over it, and examines how it's affected her decisions and abilities to relate. Then, as she seems more able to move ahead, look with her at new options and possibilities. Some of her family relations may be corrected or strengthened; some may need to be confronted, or let go. Together you can determine her approach to family members, with proper boundaries and expectations in place.

Emotional detachment. Since emotional detachment is an involuntary response to pain, she can't simply "decide" to stop detaching. Getting past this will take safety and respect on your part, as you validate the reasons for the detachment (as in, "You were in such pain, no wonder you detached!") while you also talk with her about her fears of intimacy, abandonment, or humiliation. She should also be encouraged to take small "baby step" risks with people by being in their presence more, volunteering more comments when in a group setting, and seeing that the payoff for detaching no longer outweighs the liabilities.

Gender nonconformity. If your client is stereotypically masculine, don't try to re-make her. She's probably spent a lifetime dealing with either the shame of feeling "not woman enough," or anger over the arrogance of other people who've tried to mold her into their concept of what a woman should be. Let her know, by your tone and content, that you accept her as she is, and encourage her to integrate more, and feel more aligned, with other women. During counseling, explore how she views women and men, and get an agreement that as part of your work, she will let you gently challenge those views. Then let her decide to what extent, if any, she wants to explore new ways of expressing herself.

Sexual abuse. Review the history of her abuse, and listen empathetically. That alone can be healing. Look not just at what happened, but at the impact it had. After allowing time to explore and grieve the abuse, help her decide how (if at all) to deal with the abuser. Confront? Withdraw? Let go? At some point there must be a time to forgive as well, and you'll need to gently guide her toward that. Be sure not to rush her when she's processing pain, but don't leave her feeling that her pain is the end of her story either.

Sexual fluidity. Examine her sexual history to see what her responses have been like, which can help determine her potential for heterosexual responses. Assure her she can't decide how to respond; she can only deal with the responses themselves. Assure her that if there is a change, it will come as a result of moving ahead, not trying to change. So encourage her to move ahead in her love for God, healthy intimacy with friends and loved ones, mental and relational achievements, and pursuing whatever her passion in life may be. Her life is, after all, so much more than this struggle, and her view of herself should be as a woman belonging to God and set, by Him, on an indescribably rich, hopeful journey.

I should know. I was given truth, shown respect, and patiently guided by believers who took me in and made me strong. For me, and for so many women like me, that made all the difference. Today I can hardly look over these past 20 years without returning, again and again, to Charles Wesley's magnificent description of grace:

> *Long my imprisoned spirit lay, fast bound in sin and nature's night;*
> *Thine eye diffused a quickening ray—I woke, the dungeon flamed with light;*
> *My chains fell off, my heart was free, I rose, went forth, and followed Thee.*
> *Amazing love! How can it be*
> *That Thou, my God, shouldst die for me?*
> —FROM THE HYMN "AND CAN IT BE?"

May the end result of your work with the women who come to you be their ability to join me, strong and loud, in singing these treasured words.

CHAPTER TWELVE

COUNSELING WOMEN WHO STRUGGLE WITH HOMOSEXUALITY

○—KEY POINTS—○

1. Factors contributing to lesbianism can include family dynamics, sexual abuse, gender nonconformity, peer pressure, and inner vows.

2. Family dynamics often reported by women struggling with lesbianism include disidentification from their mother; enmeshment ("My Best Friend") with their mother; invalidation from father; or rejection of the image of marriage they perceived in their home.

3. A child may actually experience an event or series of events, or may perceive the event(s) whether or not they occurred as she saw them. Either way, she will respond emotionally to what she perceives, be it accurate or inaccurate.

4. Gender nonconformity is one of the most common predictors of adult homosexuality.

5. Early unmet emotional needs may eventually become sexualized, a process by which the emotional becomes the erotic.

6. Sexual orientation in women tends to be more fluid than with men, causing many women who at one point identify themselves as lesbians to, at a later point, identify as heterosexual or bisexual.

7. An effective ministry approach to a woman struggling with lesbianism will include counseling, pastoring, mentoring, and social alliances.

RESOURCES

The Heart of Female Same-sex Attraction by Janelle Hallman, InterVarsity Press, 2008.

Restoring Sexual Identity: Hope for Women Who Struggle with Same-sex Attraction by Anne Paulk, Harvest House Publishers, 2003.

"Working with Lesbian and Bi-Sexual Women" by Mary Beth Patton, from *Handbook of Therapy for Unwanted Homosexual Attractions: A Guide to Treatment*, edited by Julie Harren Hamilton and Philip J. Henry, Xulon Press, 2009.

NOTES

1. Bob Davies and Lori Rentzel, *Coming Out of Homosexuality* (Downers Grove, IL: InterVarsity, 1993), p. 44.

2. See Arlene F. Harder, "The Developmental Stages of Erik Erikson," www.learningplaceonline.com/stages/organize/Erikson.htm.

3. Leanne Payne, *The Broken Image* (Grand Rapids, MI: Baker Books, 1995).

4. Davies and Rentzel, p. 45.

5. Jeanette Howard, *Out of Egypt: One Woman's Journey out of Lesbianism* (Grand Rapids, MI: Monatch Books, 2001).

6. Anne Paulk, *Restoring Sexual Identity: Hope for Women Who Struggle with Same-sex Attraction* (Eugene, OR: Harvest House Publishers, 2003), p. 244.

7. Howard, pp. 83-86.

8. Howard, p. 77.

9. Howard, p. 87.

10. Elaine Siegel, *Female Homosexuality: Choice Without Volition* (Hillsdale, NJ: The Analytic Press, 1988), p. 22.

11. Mary Beth Patton, "Working with Lesbian and Bi-Sexual Women," *Handbook of Therapy for Unwanted Homosexual Attractions: A Guide to Treatment*, ed. Julie Harren Hamilton and Philip J. Henry (Longwood, FL: Xulon Press, 2009), pp.101-102.

12. See Janelle Hallman, supplemental website material for *The Heart of Female Same-sex Attraction*, http://ivpress.com/title/ata/3429-supplement.pdf.

13. Janelle Hallman, *The Heart of Female Same-sex Attraction* (Downers Grove, IL: InterVarsity Press, 2008), p. 66.

14. The *Advocate* magazine, July 26, 1994, p. 46.

15. Howard, pp. 105-110.

16. Hallman, *The Heart of Female*, pp. 69-70.

17. Howard, p. 107.

18. Paulk, p. 24.

19. Howard, p. 111.

20. Hallman, *The Heart of Female*, p. 71.

21. Paulk, p. 25.

22. Stanton L. Jones and Mark A. Yarhouse, *Homosexuality: The Use of Scientific Research in the Church's Moral Debate* (Downers Grove, IL: InterVarsity Press, 2000), p. 57; referring to Edward O. Laumann, John H. Gagnon, Robert T. Michael, and Stuart Michaels, *The Social Organization of Sexuality: Sexual Practices in the United States* (Chicago: University of Chicago Press, 1994), p. 344, table 9.14.

23. Cited in Hallman, supplemental website material.

24. Cited in Hallman, supplemental website material.

25. Cited in Hallman, supplemental website material.

26. Cited in Hallman, supplemental website material.

27. Cited in Hallman, supplemental website material.

28. Bradford, Ryan, and Rothblum, 1994, cited in Hallman, supplemental website material.

29. Rosie O'Donnell, *Find Me* (New York: Grand Central Publishing, 2003), p. 71.

30. Sarah Hall, "Ellen DeGeneres Talks Abuse," *E-Online Magazine*, www.eonline.com/print/index.jsp?uuid=0869978f-048e-45b8-9214-9aede542ddf1&contentType=newsStory.

31. *The Advocate*, p. 46.

32. Allegra R. Gordon and Ilan Meyer (Mailman School of Public Health, Columbia University), "Gender Non-Conformity as a Target of Prejudice, Discrimination and Violence Against LGB Individuals," http://search.yahoo.com/search?ei=UTF-8&fr=hp-pvdt&p=gender+nonconformity+defined&SpellState=n-2757292264_q-7iAxt6CjNr7%2F%2FK45ZqHgtQAAAA%40%40&fr2=sp-top.

33. George Rekers, *Handbook of Child and Adolescent Sexual Problems* (Lexington, MA: Lexington Press, 1995), 300.

34. Cited in Hallman, *The Heart of Female*, p.76.

35. Hallman, *The Heart of Female*, p.76.

36. Hallman, *The Heart of Female*, p.76

37. Howard, p. 116.

38. Diane Mattingly, "My Path to Lesbianism," *Christianity Today* online magazine, 2/17/2005, www.christianitytoday.com/ct/2005/february/36.62.html.

39. Hallman, *The Heart of Female*, pp. 62-63, emphasis added.

40. Howard, p. 91.

41. Julie Harren Hamilton, "Homosexuality 101: What Every Therapist, Parent, And Homosexual Should Know," www.narth.com/docs/hom101.html.

42. Patton, "Working with Lesbians," pp. 96-97.

43. Lisa Diamond (University of Utah) has published "Female Bisexuality From Adolescence to Adulthood: Results From a 10-Year Longitudinal Study" in *Developmental Psychology*, 2008, vol. 44, no. 1, pp. 5-14.

44. Paulk, p. 32.

45. Cited in *Sexuality Source*, www.sexualitysource.com/presskit.php.

46. Howard, p. 57.

47. Robert Epstein, "Am I Anti-Gay? You Be the Judge," *Psychology Today*, Jan./Feb. 2003.

48. www.psych.org/MainMenu/PsychiatricPractice/Ethics/ResourcesStandards.aspx.

49. Patton, "Working with Lesbians," pp. 90-91.

50. Patton, "Working with Lesbians," pp. 125-126.

51. Patton, "Working with Lesbians," pp. 125-126.

52. See, for example, Joe Dallas, *Desires in Conflict*, rev. ed. (Eugene, OR: Harvest House Publishers, 2003).

53. Mary Beth Patton, "Essentials of Therapy," pp. 92-94.

CHANGE, GROWTH, AND THE "POST-GAY" CONCEPT

A Few Words from Someone Who's Been There

by Randy Thomas

Don't rely too much on labels, for they are often fables.

—CHARLES SPURGEON

Everyone seems to love labels. And that's true in ministry to homosexuals too. Is a person who chooses to follow Christ and walk away from homosexuality rightly called "ex-gay," or perhaps "still gay, but working on changing"… or how about "straight wannabe"?

Why is this important, you ask? If you are a counselor to men or women dealing with same-sex attractions, one thing they will want to know early on is, What does the gospel of Christ promise them? Will they indeed be ex-gay, never again to experience temptation? Will they become heterosexual? Asexual?

What will you tell them when they ask?

An Oversimplification

As the vice president of Exodus International, the most prominent "ex-gay" organization in existence, I deal with this question often. Many people likely think that I, too, claim the label "ex-gay." But to be honest, I don't know many people on this journey out of homosexuality who willingly use the "ex-gay" label for themselves. It implies that a person was once gay and now is not, and never will be again.

But this oversimplification is problematic for those of us who believe that the straight or gay paradigm is a completely false social construct. What I mean is that the labels "gay" and "straight" were created to frame a modern cultural debate over same-sex attractions and are not actually states of "being." Also, many people who have dealt with same-sex attraction have never thought and will never think of their identity as "gay." So, to say they are "ex-gay" is an incorrect descriptor.

"Ex-gay" fails on many levels, and for many reasons, but the term was an easy buzzword coined by the culture at large to describe those dealing with unwanted same-sex attractions. Think about it and you'll see why other words were just plain clumsy. "Former homosexual" is too long and may not be accurate, because if a person still has any homosexual desires, is he or she really a *former* homosexual? How un-homosexual do you have to become to reach "former" status—and if you don't reach it but don't want to be labeled homosexual, what then? So that's out. "Christian homosexual" isn't much better, because many of us don't feel the two words go together. "A believer who struggles" is too wordy, and besides, can you show me a believer who doesn't struggle with something? So ex-gay, by default, is maybe the handiest term—even if it really only works for folks in the mainstream media, who aren't exactly eager to respect our self-determination and life goals (which clash with theirs).

Reflecting the Inner Change

If you're a counselor, it's likely that you'll talk to your client about their need to repent from their homosexuality. But be aware that on some occasions people "repent" from homosexuality for wrong reasons. They may truly be homophobic and self-loathing. They might be living in fear or condemnation from an early oppressive religious experience that preached to them a false gospel of works instead of grace. They are repenting because they *have to*—because somehow, in their mind, homosexuality trumps even God's gracious atonement made available by faith in Jesus Christ.

This type of repentance might lead to some behavioral modification, but I think misses the boat. God isn't just after us acting right—He wants the very best for us. God isn't afraid or ashamed to forgive us for having acted out homosexually—either physically or in our hearts.

To be sure, a price has to be paid for our sin, but in this age of grace God doesn't exact that price from us. Instead, Christ paid for our sin Himself by His death on the cross. What an amazing amount of love! Who would ever expect someone to die so the homosexual might have eternal life? And yet Jesus did just that. Men and women with same-sex attractions can, and should, know that God knows them by name and looks upon them with great compassion and love.

God also knows that behind the homosexual's unrighteous desire there is concealed a legitimate need, and His desire is to meet that need with Himself. It's not enough to run from God promising to act right. He wants us to run *toward* Him and allow His power to transform our lives through grace, not through condemnation.

Over and over I've seen people become enlightened to the reality that they don't have to be afraid of either their sexual temptations or of God; they can walk out their repentance in confidence, humility, and peace, knowing that God will never leave them or forsake them.

My Journey

It is God's kindness, not fear, that leads to a sustainable repentance.

I know this because God's kindness is what impacted my life for change.

It's funny, though—I didn't even like Christians when I became one myself in May of 1992.

At the time, I liked only two Christians and Jesus. I didn't understand the Bible, and the only verses I knew were the ones in Leviticus that condemned homosexuality. I had read those verses on a poster somewhere and decided if the rest of the Bible was like that...I was not interested.

I was a self-avowed "gay" man and had no need to engage conservative Christians regarding my sexual preferences. But in spite of this, I couldn't resist God's tug on my heart, and I eventually came to a saving knowledge of Christ. But I didn't become a Christian to become straight or to become an "ex-gay." In fact, I was determined to be gay and a Christian at the same time.

It was a few months later during a time of prayer that I had what I've come to call a *ka-pow!* moment. I didn't get up from that prayer time "straight," but I did come out of it forever changed in how I viewed homosexuality. And that's one of many changes people like me really do experience—a change in attitude and perspective.

One Saturday afternoon I was bored and trying to listen to Christian music. I didn't like most of what I heard, but I did discover a tape by Dennis Jernigan called "Break My Heart, O God." Knowing that Dennis had once struggled with homosexuality, I related to a few of the lyrics. I still didn't understand why or how anyone could "overcome" homosexuality (or even what that meant), but his tape was the only one I wanted to listen to more than once.

Then at some point it struck me that I really didn't understand why we called Jesus "Lord." I did know it meant that He owned everything and that He supposedly had the last say in my life's details, so that was my starting point. Half thinking out loud and half praying I said, "Jesus, why do we call You 'Lord'? I know what a landlord is and I know that England has a House of 'Lords,' but why do we call *You* 'Lord'?"

Before I could even finish the question I was overwhelmed with a flood of emotion. Tremendous sadness and grief consumed me. I burst into tears, with my eyes squeezed tightly together. My heart was wrenched with pain and my mind was saying, *Randy, you've lost it. You're a crazy person.* Then unbidden, the Holy Spirit showed me a picture. Some might call it a vision, others would say the Spirit utilized my imagination…others will deny any spiritual cause. All I know is that God brought the following picture to my mind.

I pictured the first man I ever loved. Not my first sexual experience but the first man I had ever given my "everything" to. His name was Ron and I had given him my heart, my love, my mind, my body…whatever he wanted, I willingly gave to him. In this picture that the Lord put before me, Ron and I were in a lovers' embrace. Also in this picture, completely uninvited, was the Lord Himself, standing beside our bed. And He was weeping with tremendous sorrow over us.

The grief I was overwhelmed by was *His* grief. The Lord spoke to me and said, "This is just a very small taste of My sadness." Then He asked very calmly and quietly, "Randy, what is the sin here?" At first I had no answer because I hadn't even thought of Ron in a long time. I didn't want to be reminded of our relationship…much less with Jesus standing there. Again, very quietly the Lord spoke to my heart and asked me, "Randy, what is the sin here?"

I told the Lord I didn't like the verse that came to mind. It was the only scripture I knew—Leviticus 18:22: "When one man lies with another as a woman it is an abomination before the LORD."

Again, the Lord asked me, "What is the sin, Randy?"

I repeated the scripture and still He wouldn't let it go.

I repeated it several times until finally I got stuck on the word "it." The Lord prompted me again, "What is 'it'?"

Confused that the Lord would be giving me a grammar pop quiz, I said, "'It' is a gender-neutral pronoun."

The Lord said, "EXACTLY!"

Then the light came on and I finally understood. *I* was not the abomination. *Ron* was not the abomination. It was *what we were doing* that grieved the Lord. Neither of us knew Him, and that broke His heart. Ron and I were trying to accomplish something in the only way we knew how, and God knew it would never satisfy us. He wanted to be our satisfaction, but of course we had no clue that we were to look to Him for our fulfillment.

God also knew that Ron was HIV-positive and didn't know it. I, too, was therefore at risk. Ron would pass away not much more than a year later.

More emotions of amazement and love overwhelmed me as I realized that God had seen every single act Ron and I had ever done. But instead of sending hellfire and brimstone, He had sent a grieving Savior to take the penalty of my sin on Himself instead of condemning me.

In my past, that verse in Leviticus felt like death, despair, condemnation, and alienation. And now, it has become a reminder not just of my sin, but also of the immensity of God's love for a sinner such as me.

Love drew me, broke my heart, then drew me even closer. That worked for me. Thus, my goal has never been to become "straight." My only goal has been to be like Christ.

So What Changed?

I think the biggest change in my life regarding men was this: I was much more intentional with what I spent my time thinking about and focusing on. I was much less "cruisy," no longer sexualizing men immediately upon seeing them. And having sex with other men immediately stopped. I had thrown out what little porn I had just before that prayer time with the Lord when He changed my mind concerning homosexuality. It had just occurred to me one day that those people in the pictures were real people, with real lives and concerns, and God knew every single one of them. So I remain, as of this writing, single and celibate. (And after a 16-year dry spell I could totally appreciate meeting my future wife soon!)

That's not to say temptation doesn't rear its head, especially in this age where we've seen a massive increase in the sexualization and objectification of the male body in almost every facet of society. Women, unfortunately have suffered under this and are more exploited, but men are starting to catch up. So, where formerly one had to be in search of male pornographic images in order to find them, nowadays all you have to do is walk past an Abercrombie and Fitch store or watch every fourth commercial on television. What was once considered taboo or soft porn is now considered good marketing, and it floods people like me with images we don't want or need to see when we are least expecting it. I've had to deal with that, and when you think about it, I guess that puts me in the company of most Christian men. We see things every day that may be enticing, but are also forbidden. So we exercise restraint and a little common sense, turn our heads, and keep walking. No mystery there.

The spiritual changes were profound too. I knew theologically that I was born again, but oh, how I felt it now too! My spiritual gifts also came alive, and where my life had been enclosed in a hard shell of self-sufficient survival...spiritually the door opened to a much larger world full of mystery and dependence on the Holy Spirit for wisdom, grace, and understanding.

Looking at myself in those early days, I was definitely a "nuclear man" as Henri Nouwen described it. I was not aware of my past, had no context for my present, and certainly did not think much about the future. Even so, by God's grace I'm able to tell the world that God is good and that freedom from a life defined and determined by homosexuality is possible.

Which leads me to the subject of the criticism of me and others like me and, by extension, the work we do. Some of these critics call themselves "ex-ex-gays," meaning they tried to change, and when change didn't happen (or didn't happen the way they thought it would) they became vocal in their belief that no one should reject their homosexual attractions, but rather accept them and even act on them.

From what I have seen of and heard from these people, it is hard to generalize about them. I've always believed people should be listened to in order to

determine if they have something legitimate to offer or if they have a true griev-
ance that needs to be addressed. And in my experience with these critics, I've
found that some of them have stories that are heartbreaking, while others are
simply seeking notoriety.

There can be issues of legitimate disagreement or conflict...but there can
also be the people who are just seeking justification not to go back to their support group, counselor, or church. In such people there isn't anything "ex" about
their "gayness" at all.

Most of the time I have found that these critics had (or had placed upon
them) either unrealistic expectations or unreasonable demands that were unmet,
which then led to their eventual disappointment and their decision to not pursue
a life beyond homosexuality. That this happens to certain people is a clarion call
for people and leaders like me to be very clear, careful, and gracious in explaining ourselves and what has happened in our lives. We must also be very careful
to love our critics, even as we disagree with them.

In every case, I wish they could experience what I've experienced. They
would see that being "ex-gay" isn't the goal at all. Becoming spiritually mature
and more Christlike is our goal.

When trying to describe all this, I actually like the word "change," but it's
important to say that change occurs at every level when we come to Christ, no
matter what our proclivities are.

We who've repented of homosexuality experience change in going from gay
culture or a double life to a life devoted to Christ as His disciple. We change in
the way we identify ourselves. We no longer identify as gay or even ex-gay. We
are simply Christians trying to live up to what the name "Christian" implies.
We also change our entire relational worldview. We seek God in entirely new
and deeply intimate ways. We learn and rejoice in God's perfect intent for creating the opposite sex, and we embrace and are grateful for our own sexual
identity. We simply don't identify ourselves as gay, and many of us prefer not
to even slap the label "ex-gay" on ourselves; rather we've come to appreciate a
concept that transcends the limitations of both terms.

Post-Gay: A New Paradigm

In the sixteenth episode of the television show *Nip/Tuck*, Liz Cruz, a lesbian
character, describes being "gay" as something similar to picking a political party

because they align with your thinking. You then of course vote for that party's candidate. Then Liz goes on to state that every once in a while a candidate from the other party comes along that really interests you. You vote for them and then all of a sudden the labels no longer fit, and that's when the questions start. I am not a fan of the show, but this one scene showed an eloquence and depth of thought that finally approached the subject of what I and thousands of others live out every day: Labels don't fit anymore, so we are seeking answers to the questions that arise. We are tired of reducing our love, life, faith, and identity to polarized stereotypes. We are seeking to speak up in a world effectively silenced by high stigmatization for far too long.

As calls for "change" have erupted around the world as of late, how about those of us who are constantly called on to defend *our* personal choice to change our lives out of a gay mind-set and articulate it in a way the culture can understand? I think it's time for a new paradigm where people of good will move beyond the limiting, predetermined conflicts of a vocal few. We are not "gay," we are not "ex-gay," we are not "straight." We are people who live, love, and believe in the power of freedom toward self-determination for all, including those who live in a post-gay reality.

So this is my problem with "ex-gay." It seems to suggest a bipolar, ontological model of sexual attraction—gay or straight. In doing so it unfortunately sets up men and women for a fall when that bipolar model doesn't seem to fit their experience.

So what's an alternative model for those of us who want to affirm the redemption of same-sex attraction and broken sexuality? I find "post-gay" a useful alternative. It isn't an *ontological* statement, it's a *vectorial* statement. A vector is simply a description of a direction and magnitude. It describes a movement, not a position (ontology). "Post-gay," then, is less about being straight or gay and more about a choice of a journey.

Perhaps a personal example will clarify this. I'm post-gay because I chose to leave "gay" behind. I chose to no longer accept "gay" as an explanation of who I am and instead began a journey away from it. I chose to do so because I was convinced from the Scriptures that "gay" wasn't a suitable way to describe myself—that it isn't a valid ground for a Christian to establish his or her identity upon. I was compelled not just by reading the normal Scripture passages on the subject but also from the story in John 8:1-11 of the woman caught in adultery. Jesus' last words to her, I noticed, were "Go now and leave your life of sin."

He doesn't magically transform the woman from a harlot to a saint, but rather simply gives her an instruction of direction—leave this place you're at (adultery) and move on from it. His command is vectorial, not ontological. It is the call of discipleship—it says, "Follow Me to wherever I take you—I don't promise you riches or immediate perfection, but I do promise you hope."

Following God Toward Reality

This is why I personally find "post-gay" a far better description for those of us who have left homosexuality behind. It describes a journey away from a false identity constructed around one's emotions into an identity grounded in following Jesus. For some of us that journey involves changes in our sexual orientation, perhaps marriage and children. For others they may see no change in their sexual attractions, but they still are choosing to leave behind the false identity, that of seeing themselves as "gay," which defines an unchangeable aspect of their being.

Stated another way—while some may experience complete change in sexual orientation, and others have partially shifted from homosexuality toward a more bisexual response, and others would say they are still 100 percent homosexually attracted—the term "post-gay journey" is still appropriate because we do not choose to identify with gay culture or the gay ideology. Instead, we've chosen to walk by faith wherever God leads us. This also casts off the false notion that if a person is not fully heterosexual there's something wrong with his or her testimony of leaving behind the "gay" life.

I don't think that the post-gay concept will create a common ground among people with different moral opinions on homosexual behavior and relationships. However, it will bring much-needed clarity on how people like me and tens of thousands of others view our same-sex attractions in the context of our faith. That in and of itself, I pray, will bring a level of peace that hasn't existed between people with different views on same-sex attraction. I believe it has the potential to create common ground—especially with the younger generation—but that common ground is a benefit. The goal is clarity.

Because of the mainstream media and entertainment world's embracement of the "gay" aesthetic, there is much more of a brand value these days to being "gay." We have gay-centered shows, cable channels, entertainment, and celebrities, and even a gay denomination and theology.

When I lived life as a gay man it came naturally for me to buy products or visit stores that were gay-friendly. I voted for pro-gay politicians without much concern for the other views they represented. My artistic and entertainment tastes centered around gay culture, and my relational outlook was locked into other men being my only option for love and romance. Women were at most good friends. As for God, He was just a vague far-off figure who undoubtedly was pro-gay. Being gay was a "life-filter."

But post-gay is indicative of a life journey beyond gay, not necessarily an identity brand. While those of us who have dealt with same-sex attraction are in agreement that those attractions were and are not a choice, we were wrong in believing that we didn't have a choice to live our lives outside of the false social construct of gay vs. straight. We were wrong to allow society to go from stigmatizing us to ghettoizing us. We are all also wrong by allowing our attractions to be used to keep us perpetual victims who rebel against authority and seek to redefine the world around us in light of our gayness or ex-gayness. The totality of life and the afterlife transcends this one aspect of our souls.

I can promise that anyone walking this path will be studying the above topics and their nuances for the rest of their lives. It's not an easy journey, but it is a "worth it" journey. It's worth every painful step and every joyful leap. To embrace a gay worldview would ultimately have been a cop-out for me. And while I would love to have more answers than I do have…I've come to a place of contentment in Christ no matter the circumstance. That's why I can see exactly what Robert Louis Stevenson meant when he wrote:

To know what you prefer,
instead of humbly saying "Amen"
to what the world tells you ought to prefer,
is to keep your soul alive.

CHAPTER THIRTEEN

Change, Growth, and the "Post-Gay" Label

○—Key Points—○

1. It's difficult to find a single term that accurately describes the experience of a person who has repented of homosexuality, and for that reason it may be advisable to avoid such a label.

2. To cease homosexual behavior does not necessarily mean one will also experience no homosexual temptations. In fact, those temptations are likely to continue, in degrees that vary from person to person, since temptation is a predictable part of the Christian life.

3. People repent of homosexual behavior for a number of reasons, but normally a primary motive is a desire to know God and live within the parameters He has set.

4. Strong friendship and community are critical for people struggling against homosexuality.

5. Changes that people struggling with homosexuality experience include changes in behavior, identity, priorities, worldview, and sexual-emotional responses.

Resources

God's Grace and the Homosexual Next Door by Alan Chambers, general editor, Harvest House Publishers, 2006.

Desires in Conflict, rev. ed., by Joe Dallas, Harvest House Publishers, 2003.

Restoring Sexual Identity: Hope for Women Who Struggle with Same-sex Attraction by Anne Paulk, Harvest House Publishers, 2003.

TIPS FOR MINISTRY TO HOMOSEXUAL STRUGGLERS

by Alan Chambers

Above all we must show our zeal for the truth by continually, in season and out of season, endeavoring to maintain it in the tenderest and most loving manner, but still very earnestly and firmly.

—CHARLES SPURGEON

Ministry to homosexuals is cutting-edge work. It's vibrant and relevant, and the need for it grows every year.

I should know. I serve as the president of Exodus International, headquartered in Orlando, Florida, which is the largest and most established organization ministering to homosexuals and their families. As of this writing, Exodus is over 30 years old, with referral ministries across the United States and around the world. I've been associated with Exodus since 1992, first as a staff member with a local support-group ministry, then as a ministry leader, then finally as their president since 2001.

Every day we serve people who are touched by homosexuality in one way or another—people whose homosexual desires are at war with their desires to serve and obey God; parents whose sons or daughters have just "come out" to them and are wondering what to do next; pastors who want to know how to counsel those who come to them for help with their same-sex attractions; gay activists who wonder (and at times hate) what we're all about; community leaders who want to better understand the Christian view on homosexuality. We're there to educate, up-build, and comfort all of them. And over the years we've learned a few lessons along the way.

That's what this chapter is about. I want to pass on some ministry do's and don'ts that I've picked up along the way. I'd like to help you avoid the potential pitfalls, and I'd like to offer some guidelines for dealing with some of the situations you're sure to run into as a pastor, lay leader, or concerned Christian who will be dealing with gay and lesbian people, and with the people who love them.

I've been there. I began my own transition from homosexuality to heterosexuality in 1991, and am now a happily married father and husband. But the road from *there* to *here* needs to be re-examined if you want to really understand my story, and the stories of countless men and women like me.

A Case in Point: Me

I always felt different, and trust me, that's something you'll hear time and again from people who've wrestled with homosexuality. It's not that we necessarily felt *homosexual* from early in life, but we sure felt *different*! Different came to mean a lot of things, but mostly it meant feeling different from those I should have been most similar to: my dad, my brothers, and my same-sex peers. They all seemed to possess qualities, interests, and feelings that I didn't.

These differences became a point of contention as I got older. Others noticed those differences and teased me for such things as not participating in sports, for not being "one of the guys," and for being "one of the girls." I felt most at ease with my mom, sisters, and girl friends—being a boy wasn't something I wanted or understood. The teasing I experienced, mostly from my same-sex peers and father, only alienated me further from all things male. I wanted nothing to do with the reality of being a boy or a man; although I did crave good male attention and affirmation, which occasionally led me to "dream" about it.

At first my "dreams" were of my being accepted by guys, but the dreams quickly turned into my wishing I was a girl so that guys would really like me—not sexually, as I was just a kid and didn't understand this component yet. I only knew that boys liked girls, and I wanted boys to like me.

Then when I was nine years old, a teenage boy molested me. For the first time a popular, good-looking guy liked me, or so I thought. I didn't like what he was doing, but he was paying attention to me. My innocence was stolen by that incident and my craving for simple camaraderie was hijacked and became confused with sex.

As I went through puberty and into early adulthood, my sexual attractions became exclusively homosexual, though I did experience crushes on girls. However, the strength of what I felt for guys could not be matched. They possessed something I had to have, and my desire for them was almost emotionally cannibalistic. I would see a guy that I wanted to look like, act like, and be liked by, and my sexual fantasy temporarily satisfied that longing.

But the older I became, the less "fantasy" sufficed. So in middle and high school, I embarked on some sexual encounters and then during college went full force into an active homosexual lifestyle. My activities ranged from sexually anonymous to emotionally committed. I was a sexual addict, as was every other homosexual person I was involved with. Homosexual life was all about sex.

I grew up conflicted over my sexuality. I never wanted or chose to have same-sex attractions. Like every other gay person I met, I wanted to change. The difference for me was I heard about the possibility and decided to act on it.

I had experienced enough of the emptiness of gay life to know I wanted more than a life of sexual encounters. I tried attending a "gay-affirming" church, but it was the same as everything else, only with the added twist of trying to force myself to believe God liked what I was doing.

Transformation seemed impossible, immeasurable, and improbable. But, the alternative was even less appealing. I did not want to continue in what I had experienced in gay life—the hopelessness, instability, and superficial existence I had almost come to accept.

So at age 19, I went to a local Exodus International Member Ministry for help. Not too long after, I remember going out to dinner with friends from my new support group. We ran into a group of my gay friends and one of them said to me, "Are you out with your straight-wanna-be friends tonight?" I laughed and blushed on the outside, but I was crushed on the inside and wondered, *Will this alternative really work? Should it even be tried? What if I fail and then my old friends want nothing to do with me either? Am I just forever gay and should own up to it and just be true to who I really am? Should I just be gay and ask for forgiveness daily for the rest of my life? Is celibacy the answer—realize I'm gay and have all the fun without all the sex? Can I call that "diet homosexuality"?*

Ultimately, my misgivings diminished and I settled into some real security. In a setting with other struggling men I was able to, for the first time in my life, connect on a level deeper than mere physical and sexual attraction. For me, the major benefit of this group was the camaraderie that I was looking for in childhood, but on a more adult level. For the first time ever, I was able to establish friendships with guys that didn't cause me to "want" them inappropriately, and those relationships never ended with us in bed doing something that didn't end up satisfying the ache anyway.

Of course, this didn't miraculously cure me, but I learned that my desire for men was at its core a desire for friendship, acceptance, and affirmation from other males. Homosexuality, on the other hand, was an immature and selfish drive meant only to satisfy one's own desires and needs, not a mutual relationship based on meeting each other's needs.

I quickly learned that the opposite of homosexuality wasn't heterosexuality, and that simply not engaging homosexually wouldn't "cure" or "fix" me; ceasing all homosexual behavior didn't make me straight.

Homosexuality had taken a lifetime to develop. I discovered that heterosexuality was developed also, but only did so as the psychological stages of development, essential for every human, were successfully gone through. Funny, I learned about this in high school psych class, but it seemed no one paid much attention to the validity of this.

My journey into heterosexuality was difficult, but successful as I persevered. At this time I also recognized that I didn't feel like a man and didn't perceive myself as a male. I was, at best, a man who would always be less than other men, or, at worst, a woman trapped in a man's body. I realized I had to change my thinking.

Thankfully, an older heterosexual man (I was 20, he was 35) at my church befriended me—he took it upon himself to mentor me. This man listened to me, affirmed me, hugged me appropriately, and treated me (despite my past) as his equal—like a man. He was kind of a father figure to me, and I relied on him in that role for a time. I began to notice as time went on that I needed him less, and that my confidence in my ability to be a man grew even when I wasn't with him.

This confidence led me to build friendships with other men my age. As I did, I grew even more confident and secure in my masculine identity. I noticed that the more healthy friendships I developed, the more normal I felt and even became. Where I once only developed deep friendships with girls, I was now friends with only healthy heterosexual guys.

Several years into this process, I began to want more than just friendships with guys; I also wanted a friendship with a girl, but not the same kind of friendship I had with them before, and not necessarily like the kind I had with guys currently. So, I looked for what I wanted—tried a few times to develop this "new" type of relationship, but struck out.

Then, one evening I was sitting in a room with about 50 other singles at a Bible study when a girl walked in who caught my eye. I didn't lust after her or want to date her, but I did want to get to know her. She was beautiful, obviously a lot of fun, and smart. I tried to get to know her, but she didn't give me the time of day.

Eventually though we became friends, then exclusive friends, and then started dating. Today, she is my wife and the mother of my two beautiful kids.

I say all this not just to tell the story about a man who was involved in homosexuality, but rather, to tell a story about what *worked* to help a man out of his involvement in homosexuality. My story isn't unique, and I also hope you're wanting to be a source of help and healing to someone who is where I was. You'll meet someone like that, if you're in any form of leadership. So let me offer five tips for effective ministry to homosexual people.

Keep It *Biblical*

Some who are called upon to counsel homosexuals—often pastors—get sidetracked into thinking they have to be up on psychology to minister to a homosexual, but let's take Paul at his word when he says, "All scripture is inspired by God, and is profitable for doctrine, for reproof, for correction, for instruction in righteousness" (2 Timothy 3:16). The social sciences are helpful, but the minister who's well versed in the Word can do a lot of good addressing the human condition from a biblical perspective, so don't shy away from doing so. Here's a quick sampling of what you already know from Scripture regarding homosexuality:

1. God created human sexuality (Genesis 2:18-25).

2. We're a fallen race and the fall has affected all parts of our life, so it's no surprise we experience all sorts of sexual brokenness we were never meant to endure (Genesis 3:16-17; Galatians 5:19-21).

3. We're dead in sin until Christ gives us life, no matter what our particular sins may be (Romans 3:23; 1 Corinthians 15:21-22).

4. Sexual behaviors apart from monogamous heterosexual marriage fall short of God's will (Leviticus 18; 20; 1 Corinthians 6:9-10; 1 Timothy 1: 9-10).

5. Once we're born again we're given the power to turn from sinful behavior (Romans 6:12-14).

6. There's still a struggle between the flesh and the spirit throughout this life, so some amount of temptation toward old behavior is guaranteed (Galatians 5:17).

7. Growing in prayer (1 Thessalonians 5:17) and the study of the Word (2 Timothy 2:15); deep and healthy relationships within the church (2 Peter 1:22); and striving to serve others (Mark 9:35) are three key elements to healthy living and overcoming struggle.

8. Former homosexuals are nothing new (1 Corinthians 6:11).

9. Happiness in this life is desirable, but not at the expense of eternal life (Matthew 5:29-30). So we're running a race, putting our sins aside, with an eye toward eternal rewards (Hebrews 12:1-4).

Pretty basic, right? But these principles are so helpful to someone who's struggling with homosexuality. Sometimes professional counseling is also very helpful, and psychiatry, medicine, therapy, and support groups can all be terrific resources that should be utilized when necessary. But if you're a pastor, please realize how much impact you already have in your role as a shepherd. By all means, when it comes to complicated issues surrounding the why's and wherefore's of human sexuality, admit what you don't know. But also proclaim, and boldly, what you *do* know. The Word is still living, powerful, and sharp, so first and foremost, let's keep it biblical.

Keep It *Clear*

Paul said, "If the trumpet makes an uncertain sound, who will prepare himself for battle?" (1 Corinthians 14:8). All who are in leadership should take note of that, because when we call people to purity, we call them to literal battle with the world, the flesh, and the devil himself. So if we're not clear in our guidance and standards—our battle plan, so to speak—how can we expect anyone to fight well? Godly warfare is an undeniable part of godly living. So strive for clarity in your teaching and counsel.

When someone is emotionally broken, for example, call it a *wound*, the remedy for which is healing and grace. We don't call people to repent of wounds, after all. We call them to be healed.

But when someone commits a deliberate sin, let's not call it a "struggle." It's a *transgression* (a deliberate act of rebellion) and needs to be dealt with as such.

When someone is wrestling with and resisting temptation, let's call that a *struggle*, and encourage the struggler to continue to resist.

When someone turns from sin, let's clarify to them that at times there will be temptations to return to that sin. So when someone asks "Can I really change?" the answer is "yes." But the biblical concept of "change" isn't a complete and permanent relief from struggle. (See Galatians 5:15 cited above, for example, or Paul's agonizing description of ongoing struggle in Romans 7.) In other words, let's be clear that the power of sinful temptations is greatly reduced through obedience and sanctification (Romans 6:14; 2 Corinthians 3:18) but the presence of sin and temptation, to some degree, is a fact of Christian life in this fallen world (1 John 1:8). Change, then, is definite, incomplete, and ongoing.

Keep It *Honest*

I've met pastors who actually seem afraid to tell homosexuals that homosexuality is a sin, fearing they'll somehow damage them by telling the truth. Granted, our speech should be grace-filled, but that's no reason to shy away from an honest assessment of someone's behavior. So please be honest when discussing what's right or wrong, and let's make sure that whoever hears us, whether they agree with us or not, will at least walk away knowing where we stand. Let's be honest about homosexual sin.

But let's also be honest about homosexual *people*. Untold numbers of lies have been spread about them—sometimes by Christian leaders—and for that we should all be ashamed. Homosexuals are not by nature child molesters, nor are they all promiscuous, violent, drug-abusing, or alcoholic. Any destructive trends you find in the homosexual population (like casual sex, addiction, suicide, and domestic violence) can be found in the heterosexual one as well; and while some studies indicate higher rates of these behaviors among homosexuals, it would be unfair and dishonest to ascribe them to gays and lesbians in general. We can preach against a sin without slapping stereotypes onto the persons practicing it. So whether we're talking about homosexual behavior, or homosexual people, let's keep it honest.

Keep It *Wise*

Remember the Lord's admonition to be "wise as serpents, and innocent as doves" (Matthew 10:16), along with James's promise that if we ask for wisdom, we'll receive it (James 1:5). So if you're ministering to homosexual people, when asking for wisdom, order a venti-sized portion.

That's because this type of ministry requires you to know when to rebuke, when to weep, when to be silent, when to confront, when to encourage, when to persevere with a struggler, and when to turn an unrepentant rebel over to his or her own ways. So God help you (and He will!) to know *when* to do *which*.

When a homosexual woman or man is repentant, she or he will be willing to abstain from homosexual sex, and to take steps necessary to walk away from that behavior, identity or both. Wisdom calls you to offer that person encouragement and discipleship.

When a homosexual person is militant and argumentative, showing more of a desire to debate than to be discipled, then you may feel manipulated, investing time and energy into conversations and confrontations that go nowhere. Wisdom may call you to stop striving and be a better steward of your efforts by investing them where they're received.

And when you start ministering to homosexual people through pastoral care, support groups, seminars, or other outreaches, at times outside pro-gay groups will want to engage you in debate. Or, on the other end of the spectrum, Christian political groups may try to get you to align yourself with them and their goals. I have often felt called to align myself with social action groups, and to discuss or debate with gay activists, so I'd be the last one to say you shouldn't do either! But let me caution you to always weigh an outside group's request for your time and energy against your primary responsibilities. I've learned the hard way that I've only got so much time and strength, and if I say "yes" to everyone who wants to argue with me or get me on their team, I'll never have time for the people and responsibilities God's given me! Wisdom calls you to be about your Father's business, which is, of course, whatever primary calling He's given you. Let nothing interfere with or distract you from that.

Keep It *Relevant*

If you're a pastor, lay counselor, youth minister, or Christian leader of any sort, you're serving people who probably know someone who is homosexual, or someone who is himself or herself attracted to the same sex. Your people need answers and tools, and to meet their needs and the times we live in, you must be relevant. Relevance requires that the ministry we offer matches the genuine needs of the people we serve.

Where to start? Here are a few ideas.

1. Encourage your church to host a seminar to your congregation on homosexuality, covering topics such as what Scripture says about it, how the gay rights movement impacts the church, and how to witness to and love homosexual people. Invite a guest speaker who's knowledgeable on the subject. If you need some referrals, check the Exodus International website Speaker's Bureau,[1] and encourage your congregation to attend and support this effort.

2. Work cooperatively with ministries in your area that already provide group support or Christian counsel to people struggling with homosexuality. If no such ministries exist, consider starting one yourself by first checking Exodus International's resources for churches.[2]

3. Consult regularly with people who've been doing this sort of work, to glean insights and practical suggestions along the way.

4. If you're a pastor, spend some pulpit time addressing human sexuality from the biblical perspective. Not just homosexuality, but sexuality in general, including sex within marriage, how to manage sexual desires before or apart from marriage, the joy and value of sexuality contrasted with the damage done by sexual sin, and so on. One of the most crying needs of the church today is biblical literacy, and one of the greatest tragedies in the church today is the high number of believers who are ignorant as to what God has said about the gift of sexuality. Speak about sex plainly and openly, and you'll be relevant.

In the film *Field of Dreams*, an ethereal voice instructs a farmer to build a baseball diamond on his land, mysteriously promising, "If you build it, he will come." I've often thought the same could be said of ministry to homosexuals. If you put a ministry in place, the people will come.

Responding Biblically

Along with those who come, any number of situations, challenges, and victories will come as well. Here are the ones pastors and Christian leaders most often describe to me.

"Pastor, we want to keep coming to your church but we're a gay couple. Can we still attend and participate in church activities?"

Suggested response: There's a difference between church attendance and church membership. Provided people don't disrupt church services or behave inappropriately during them, of course we'd want them to attend, saved or unsaved, homosexual or heterosexual. That usually can include church activities apart from worship services, though at times you may need to weigh the desire to serve the homosexual couple against the needs and comfort levels of others in your congregation. Case by case wisdom is certainly called for, but in general, openly homosexual people coming to church services should be welcomed and prayed for, just like any other visitors who are either unsaved or significantly living outside God's will.

But church membership is another matter. When someone joins a church they are stating that they're committed believers in, and followers of, Jesus Christ. If they have no clear profession of having been born again and put their trust in His finished work, then their conversion should obviously precede their membership in the church.

Church membership also, though, calls for a willingness to live by the moral standards the church sets. Your church hopefully has a clear standard regarding sexual behavior which precludes, among other things, homosexual behavior. Joining your church would mean submitting to that standard, and if they're not willing to do that, whether out of disagreement or simple refusal, then they shouldn't apply for, or be given, membership. They may profess to be believers, but that alone should not be sufficient for membership. Adherence to the biblical standards the church follows should also be required, or else membership makes little sense.

"A teenager in our youth group just came out as a homosexual. Should we let him keep coming? What do we say to the other kids?"

Suggested response: Since this will no doubt come up more frequently in churches as more teenagers are "coming out," more and more youth pastors will be faced with this. And as I stated above, if someone wants to attend a church, they should be welcomed and encouraged, provided their presence or their behavior is not interfering with the general work the church is trying to accomplish. So if an openly gay or lesbian teenager is wanting to continue attending the youth group, it seems wise for the pastoral staff to first meet and discuss whatever boundaries they may need to establish with the young person (regarding appropriate speech, conduct, and whatever influence the person may have on the group) then discuss these boundaries honestly and respectfully with the youth. If he or she seems cooperative and willing to abide by these boundaries, there's no reason to limit her or his participation. It should be obvious, though, that there's a huge need for our young people to be clearly taught what their Creator has to say about human sexuality. Sound teaching will go a long way toward equipping them to love, dialogue with, and hopefully win over a friend in their group who's involved in any kind of sexual sin.

"Pastor, we were in a same-sex relationship but we realized it was wrong, so we've stopped having sexual relations. But we still want to live together and be committed to each other without any sex involved. Is that okay?"

Suggested response: This is a fairly new phenomenon, often referred to as "covenant relationships," in which two people of the same sex live and function as a nonsexual couple, committed and, for all intents and purposes, married without sex. Normally these arrangements are made because the couple realizes homosexuality is wrong, but wants to also enjoy the closest thing they can to a homosexual relationship without actually calling it one.

Which, to my thinking, sells God short in the "I will supply all of your needs" category. What about abstaining from all appearances of evil, as commanded by 1 Thessalonians 5:22? And how about *fleeing* from sexual sin (instead of flirting with it) as commanded by 1 Corinthians 6:18? Two same-sex-attracted people pledging their lifelong love and devotion to one another, with or without sex, seems nothing less than a homosexual relationship, even if only emotionally so. After all, it isn't only the sex that makes homosexuality sinful, it is choosing to live outside of God's best. He did not create two men or two women to meet the needs of one another in a spousal capacity. Loneliness isn't grounds for trying to meet your own needs outside of His will, sexually or otherwise. Sanctioning such a relationship, to my thinking, is a collusion with compromise.

"I realize I'm gay and I feel okay with it, but I still want to hold on to my leadership position in the church."

Suggested response: If members are expected to live by the standards the church teaches, church leaders, whether they're worship leaders, pastors, elders, or volunteers, obviously can't do less. Now, if by saying "I'm gay," the leader is simply saying he's attracted to the same sex but not acting on those attractions, and he realizes that acting on them can never be an acceptable option, then no discipline or action needs to be taken. He may or may not want to discuss with a pastor or counselor how to best manage his feelings for the same sex when they arise, but I see no reason to require that of him, provided his life is chaste.

But if he's asking to engage in behavior that conflicts with church teaching, then there's no justification for him continuing in leadership. This does, though, bring up the need for local churches to make sure their position on homosexuality is clarified (in writing, preferably) to anyone in a paid or voluntary position of leadership, to avoid potential lawsuits or controversies that can erupt when someone on a church staff says, "You never told me homosexuality was grounds for dismissal!" Your church attorney should be able to advise on the best ways to prevent this. I'd suggest you also consult with the Alliance Defense Fund, a Christian legal organization devoted to protecting churches and ministries, with any questions you may have about homosexuality and church policy.[3]

Effective ministry to homosexual people brings us back to the basics of the faith, as it causes us to revisit concepts of discipleship, church discipline, resisting the drift of the world, and extending grace and support to people who struggle with their unique weaknesses. And this, I think, may be the most attractive feature of this kind of work: It calls us to basic Christlikeness. Because when I think of being His voice and hands to the homosexual, I'm reminded of His public announcement when, in Luke's Gospel (4:18-19) He made it known who He was, and what He was about:

And He said,
"The Spirit of the Lord is upon Me
Because He has anointed Me
To preach the gospel to the poor
He has sent me to heal the brokenhearted
To proclaim liberty to the captives
And recovery of sight to the blind
To set at liberty those who are oppressed
To proclaim the acceptable year of the Lord."

As we minister to the homosexual people He so deeply loves, and to whom He would proclaim liberty and recovery, may His words and His mission be our own.

CHAPTER FOURTEEN

TIPS FOR EFFECTIVE MINISTRY TO HOMOSEXUALS

○—KEY POINTS—○

1. While ministry to homosexuals can be enhanced by clinical, sociological, and scientific insights, it should be based primarily on biblical principles. A working knowledge of Scripture equips a pastor or lay leader to offer discipleship principles and practices to homosexual people seeking to live sanctified lives.

2. Clarity is called for in this type of work, as it is necessary for people to receive clear instruction and guidelines. Ambiguity in ministry renders it ineffective. Those wanting to serve should be committed to clear speech, guidelines, and principles.

3. Statements about homosexuals should be accurate and free of unwarranted generalizations. It is possible to preach against a person's sin without misrepresenting the person.

4. Wisdom is called for when dealing with the many situations associated with ministry to homosexual people. Different ministry opportunities call for different ministry approaches, and the best approach often can only be determined by prayerful consideration and petitioning for godly wisdom and guidance.

5. Our efforts should be measured by, among other things, the relevance

of what we're doing and how we're doing it. Since homosexuality is a growing concern, ministry to homosexual people, or people affected by homosexuality, should strive to be relevant to the needs and situations of the people we serve.

RESOURCES

God's Grace and the Homosexual Next Door by Alan Chambers, gen. ed., Harvest House Publishers, 2006.

101 Frequently Asked Questions About Homosexuality by Mike Haley, Harvest House Publishers, 2004.

Loving Homosexuals as Jesus Would by Chad Allen, Brazos Press, 2004.

Welcoming But Not Affirming by Stanley Grenz, Westminster John Knox Press, 1998.

"Church Membership, Repentance and the Transformed Life" by Robert J. Gagnon (online article on church discipline), www.presbyweb .com/2006/Viewpoint/0703—Robert+Gagnon—Repentance.htm.

NOTES

1. http://exodus.to/content/view/192/77/0.
2. http://exodus.to/content/view/29/39/.
3. www.alliancedefensefund.org/main/default.aspx.

CHAPTER FIFTEEN

SEXUAL ADDICTION

by Nancy Heche, DMin

It is with our passions, as it is with fire and water,
they are good servants but bad masters.

—AESOP, GREEK SLAVE AND FABLE AUTHOR

Sexual addiction is defined as a progressive intimacy disorder character-ized by compulsive sexual thoughts and acts. Its negative impact on the addict and on family members increases as the disorder progresses; and there is recurrent failure to control the sexual behavior despite significant harmful consequence. The Sexual Recovery Institute (SRI) defines sexual addiction by the escalating negative consequences of sexual behaviors that are acted out compulsively and impulsively, often without regard to personal or relational consequences.

Homosexuality and sexual addiction are not the same. Many homosex-ual men and women are not sexually active, and thus could hardly be labeled "sex addicts." Others may be sexually active, but display none of the symptoms associated with sexual addiction. But because sexual addiction does show itself prominently in the gay male community, it's a subject we need to address when discussing the broader subject of homosexuality.

The definition of sexual addiction is based not on the type or frequency of sex-ual acts in which one engages, but upon the "escalating negative consequences" and the disregard for the effects on one's personal life. If that is the case, then one may or may not be addicted to homosexual sex, just as one may or may not become addicted to heterosexual sex.

Dr. Harry W. Schaumburg, author of *False Intimacy: Understanding the Struggle of Sexual Addiction*, writes:

> Sexual addiction exists when a person practices sexual activity to the point of negatively affecting his or her ability to deal with other aspects of life…and becomes dependent on sexual experiences as his or her primary source of fulfillment…regardless of the consequences to health, family and/or career. A probable sex addict exhibits the following—compelling and consuming behavior, behavior leading to negative consequences, out-of-control behavior, and denial of the seriousness of the behavior. The primary goal of sexually addictive behavior is to avoid relational pain—essentially to control life. S/he feels that life isn't fulfilling, experiences disappointment in intimacy, loses hope, and lacks self-confidence.[1]

Dr. Lance Dodes, sex-addiction specialist and author of *The Heart of Addiction: A New Approach to Understanding and Managing Alcoholism and Other Addictive Behaviors*, writes that it is the nature of addiction to be compulsive, to be driven by internal purposes and drives, and to tend not to be responsive to external factors.

Consequently, just as the internal psychology of addiction drives it to continue despite loss after loss, this compulsive psychology also drives it past the objections, concerns, and even threats of one's family and acquaintances. "The drive behind addiction," he states, "is a psychological compulsion to perform a particular action."[2]

The SRI says that sex addicts are more likely to define their sexual behavior with words like "driven," "secretive," or "shameful" than "fun," "playful," or "intimate." Dr. Patrick Carnes, author of the now-classic book on sexual addiction *Out of the Shadows: Understanding Sexual Addiction*, defined sexually addictive behavior as sexual activity most often involving shame, secrecy, or abuse.[3]

The information from the SRI describes the feelings and activities that surround addictive sexual behaviors as:

- *shameful*—feels inner worthlessness or despair about ever being worthy or lovable; experiences reinforcement of an inner core of negative feelings that ends up sabotaging relationships, careers, and self-esteem.

- *secretive*—finds her/himself wrapped in a web of lies and manipulations, consistently hiding from those close to them while using justifications, rationalizations, and outright denial to lie to themselves.

- *abusive*—manipulates someone or uses one's power over them to get sex; employs exhibitionism, voyeurism, and sex with minors and/or rape to get sex.

It's usually understood that sexual addiction is used as a means to tolerate emotional stress, distract one from past trauma, or to feel more important or powerful. This is borne out by Melissa Fryrear in her chapter on lesbianism in *God's Grace and the Homosexual Next Door* when she notes that "at its core… lesbianism is about emotional intimacy."[4]

David Kyle Foster, author of several books on sexual issues from a Christian perspective, writes,

> For sex addicts, intimacy, for one reason or another, is not worth taking any chances for. For the addict, it is better to pretend than risk the hurt and rejection of attempting true intimacy. The life of a sex addict is usually saturated with a profound sense of unworthiness, disbelief in the idea of being acceptable to anyone on any deep and meaningful level, and a history of attempted compensation through substitution and fantasy. The pain of believing that they are unlovable or unredeemable drives many people to engage in compulsive behaviors that provide a jolt of pleasure so that for a brief while they can forget that they are hopeless, lost, or destined for the trash bin of humanity. But the more they are driven to find stronger jolts of pleasure in even more perverse behaviors, the more convinced they become that they are indeed worthless human beings who God could never love and would never redeem.[5]

The SRI, along with the American Psychological Association, acknowledges that homosexual behavior or lifestyle choice does not imply or suggest any form of mental illness or pathology. Yet in the gay men's community there are higher rates of sexually transmitted diseases (STDs), higher rates of alcohol and substance abuse, and higher reports of mental depression. Many gay men report addictions to pornography and masturbation.

It is widely believed that sexual addiction among lesbian women has been underreported and cannot be accurately determined. Yet, again, all the same risks are present for lesbians except for higher rates of STDs.

In *The Heart of Addiction* Dr. Dodes describes one man's sexual addiction "as an effort to reverse the helplessness of his loss, the loneliness and emptiness into which he had been thrust" after his mother died and his father became depressed. "The intensity of the drive behind his addiction reflected the kind of basically healthy insistence on not being helpless, not being left alone."[6]

Dodes goes on to explain that feeling helpless and alone will often lead to addictive behaviors that essentially have little to do with sexuality. On the other hand, since sex is such a meeting ground for feelings, it is to be expected that sometimes the emotions that give rise to addictions have a significant sexual component or may be expressed through sexual means.

Dodes writes that sexual addiction

> may be the most private and most shameful addiction...However, in sexual addiction, as with other addictions, although the focus is on sex, it is the meaning of sex that is important.[7]

Because there is no valid research that has discovered a homosexual gene, it is clear that there are many complex conditions that can indirectly influence the susceptibility to live homosexually. There may be an indirect genetic factor for some people that when combined with numerous other factors may produce a sexual addiction, and particularly addictive homosexual behavior. Medicinenet .com claims that the risk of addiction is in part inherited.[8]

A Christian Position

Author David Kyle Foster rightly observes:

> The ironic thing is that the sexual addict uses what God intended as a primary means of intimacy (sexual relations) to achieve just the opposite...the sex addict will depersonalize the object of his or her lust and use sex as a flight from intimacy rather than a means of intimacy...A great rebellion against God and the created order of things is going on within the psyche of the person.[9]

Dr. Harry Schaumburg writes,

> Sexual addiction is not a disease over which the sex addict has no control. Sex addicts make significant choices and must be held accountable for those choices…Only God can help a person overcome sin. Treatment programs can influence a person to stop committing certain sexual acts, but the programs can't address the root cause of those behaviors without bringing the power of Christ to bear on the issue of the heart. Sexual addiction primarily stems from the sinfulness of the human heart and a reluctance to be in a passionate, dependent relationship with God.[10]

Foster writes,

> There are other dynamics at work as well. For example there is always a neurochemical component. Irregular synaptic patterns are often found in the brains of addictive personalities. Imbalances of chemicals like serotonin that provide a sense of well-being also contribute to the impulse to seek out a substance or behavior that will make one feel better. What is not known, however, is whether these conditions precede the initial behavior or whether the behavior generates the brain irregularities that then precipitate further dysfunctional behavior…
>
> Most addictions have their genesis in early childhood trauma, where self-esteem and self-worth have been significantly compromised…The perception of being inherently bad or defective creates an obsession with self. Sexual addicts are often narcissistic or in some other way hooked into unhealthy and habitual introspection. Their biggest battle is turning from a focus on "self" to a focus on God…with God's help there comes a dawning of a new self-image and healing can occur.[11]

There is a heart-wrenching sadness that could overwhelm us when we read about the pain and shame one experiences as an addict to sex. I am reminded of one psychologist's healing remark to his borderline personality disorder patients—"You must have had a very good reason for doing [it]." There are reasons for one's sexual addiction, and even though the reasons may not be the same reasons that we get stuck in our seemingly less vulgar sins, they are valid reasons in the mind of the addict. We are called out to show compassion and understanding just like Jesus does.

We should also keep in mind the powerful words of the apostle Paul in 2 Corinthians 5:19: "God was in Christ reconciling the world unto Himself, not imputing their trespasses unto them, and hath committed unto us the word of reconciliation" (KJV).

In that same spirit of reconciliation, pastors, Christian therapists, and mentors can be invaluable as they walk alongside the sexual addict, offering guidance and encouragement.

Helping the Sex Addict

As someone who's known many people affected by addiction, let me offer five points to consider when helping the sexual addict. (These are only brief points, since this book was not intended to address sexual addiction in a comprehensive manner. For more detailed treatments of the subject, please see the references listed at the end of this chapter.)

1. The addict needs to *reject* the addictive behavior by *separating* himself from it. The first step to renouncing the behavior is to put distance between the addict and the behavior, and, as much as possible, remove access to the behavior. A practical example is Internet pornography. If a man has become addicted to it, he'll need to remove access by putting a filtering device on his computer, or giving someone else his password, or removing the computer entirely.

2. The addict needs to *establish* himself in *daily fortifying.* He needs to commit to daily prayer and Scripture reading, reflection, and a mental review of the reasons he is motivated to stay sober. This builds his mind up daily with concepts that keep him motivated to stay on track.

3. The addict needs *weekly accountability.* He needs to know that he will be asked, on at least a weekly basis, whether or not he has indulged in the addictive behavior that he's committed to abstain from. Secrecy is one of the most empowering influences that keep addictions alive; accountability diffuses that influence and its power.

4. The addict needs to make amends to those affected by his behavior. In most cases, there's a wife, a family member, a friend, or

parishioners suffering from a man's addiction and the damage it's done to his relationship with others. Part of real repentance is a willingness to address the damage a sin has done, and, as much as possible, repair that damage through consistent sobriety and consistency.

5. The addict needs to accept the fact that, to some extent, the addictive behavior he's renounced will have some attraction to him for the rest of his life. That is not to say he's doomed to keep repeating that behavior, but the history and testimony of most addicts points to the reality of lifelong temptations. These temptations can, of course, be resisted, and there's no reason the addict shouldn't be expected to resist them. But he can hardly do so unless he accepts the fact that they will remain, and should be both expected and prepared for.

My friend and neighbor in Michigan, Sue, who is a new follower of Jesus asked me if I thought God could speak to her. She had a hunch that what she heard in the shower one day was the Lord's "voice" and wanted me to confirm it…So here's what Sue told me: She was in the shower, moaning about her children, about her life. Her unmarried daughter was pregnant again by the same man who was the father of her four-year-old son. Their relationship was on again, off again, and Sue was feeling discouraged and hopeless…Everyone was already overwhelmed and overloaded. Now this. What were they thinking? Where was there room for a new baby? It seemed to her as if this baby would come into the world with a lot of strikes against him. *All the more reason to love him*, was what Sue heard in the shower that morning.

"Now tell me," she said, "would anyone but God say something like that? *All the more reason to love him.*"

I believe this is God's response, and ours, to someone who is struggling with sexual addiction.

CHAPTER FIFTEEN

SEXUAL ADDICTION

◦—KEY POINTS—◦

1. Sexual addiction is defined as a progressive intimacy disorder characterized by compulsive sexual thoughts and acts, and escalating negative consequences without regard to one's personal life.

2. Homosexuality as an orientation does not constitute sexual addiction. Likewise, a homosexual man or woman who is sexually active is not necessarily sexually addicted. A large number of homosexual men do, however, display sexually addictive tendencies and behavior.

3. A sex addict becomes dependent on sexual experiences to feel worthwhile, to avoid relational pain, to feel important and powerful, and/or to distract from past trauma.

4. The life of a sex addict is usually saturated with a profound sense of unworthiness, disbelief in the idea of being acceptable to anyone on any deep and meaningful level, and a history of attempted compensation through substitution and fantasy.

5. There is therapeutic help and spiritual help for sexual addicts, and a number of programs exist, both secular and Christian, addressing this addiction.

6. Shame is one of the most common emotional elements associated with sexual addiction, often causing the addict to avoid admitting his problem and getting the assistance he needs.

7. The sex addict is not helpless to address his condition. While the condition itself may be overwhelming, he has the capacity to make the decision to get the help and take the steps necessary to remain sober.

8. Sexual addiction often involves a confusion of erotic pleasure for love, thus the sex addict may frequently report "falling in love" but display a limited capacity for sustaining intimacy.

9. Treatment for sexual addiction should include counseling from someone who specializes in treating sexual addiction, group support and accountability, and spiritual disciplines.

10. Sexual addiction is best viewed as a long-term condition that needs to be perpetually managed, but that need not dominate the addict's life. The person who is sexually addicted should expect ongoing temptations and strong pulls toward sexual "acting out," but he can also choose to manage and resist those temptations.

RESOURCES

Out of the Shadows: Understanding Sexual Addiction by Dr. Patrick Carnes, Hazelden, 2001.

False Intimacy: Understanding the Struggle of Sexual Addiction by Harry Schaumburg, NavPress, 1997.

The Final Freedom: Pioneering Sexual Addiction Recovery by Douglas Weiss, Strang Communications Company, 1998.

NOTES

1. Harry Schaumburg, *False Intimacy: Understanding the Struggle of Sexual Addiction* (Colorado Springs, CO: NavPress, 1997), p. 22.

2. Lance Dodes, *The Heart of Addiction: A New Approach to Understanding and Managing Alcoholism and Other Addictive Behaviors* (New York: Harper Paperbacks, 2002), p. 170.

3. Patrick Carnes, *Out of the Shadows: Understanding Sexual Addiction* (Center City, MN: Hazelden, 2001), p. 126.

4. Melissa Fryrear, "Ministry to Lesbian Women," in *God's Grace and the Homosexual Next Door*, gen. ed. Alan Chambers (Eugene, OR: Harvest House Publishers, 2006), p. 176.

5. David Kyle Foster, *Sexual Healing: A Biblical Guide to Finding Freedom* (Franklin, TN: Mastering Life Ministries, 1995), p. 184-185.

6. Dodes, p. 221.

7. Dodes, p. 210.

8. See "Sexual Addiction Index" at medcinenet.com, www.medicinenet.com/sexual_addiction/index.htm.

9. Foster, p. 186.

10. Schaumburg, p. 205.

11. Foster, pp. 189-190.

PART FIVE

THE PARENT'S DILEMMA

by Nancy Heche, DMin

*Making the decision to have a child is momentous. It is to decide
forever to have your heart go walking around outside your body.*

—ELIZABETH STONE

To any parent reading this, please believe me: I've been there, and I know. I know what it's like to have your beloved child (grown or still young, that's *still* your child!) say to you, "I'm gay." I've heard those words; I've felt the pain. And out of my own experience with the dilemma Christian parents face when homosexuality hits home, there's much I'd like to share in the way of encouragement.

So let me offer some case studies and stories, along with commentaries from voices across the very broad spectrum of issues related to sexual brokenness in families, mine included. Through these, I hope you'll be more informed, gain deeper insight into the subject in all its facets, and be equipped for intelligent, informed discussion. Some of this information is encouraging, certainly, and some may be discouraging. But hopefully all of it prepares you for a loving, caring, empathic response to your loved one.

Before we begin, let's remember that we are constantly overwhelmed by the abundance of information and dialogue about homosexuality in the media—press, TV, web, talk shows. The topic is open for discussion almost everywhere you turn. It seems everything around us is saying, "Pay attention. Be prepared." And with good reason.

After all, the earliest family histories recorded in Scripture reveals Satan's plan to kill and destroy children and families: Cain kills Abel; Pharaoh kills Israel's infants; David's sons die; families are torn apart by sexual sins and wars and disease; Herod kills more babies when Jesus is born; Paul persecutes Christians.

Satan is still the prince of the power of the air. His seduction of children, spouses, parents, siblings, into the killing fields of sexual sin should not surprise us. But it does. It shocks us. We were not expecting anything like *this*.

What Happened?

The November 19, 2007, issue of *People* magazine relayed a tragic story:

> Mary Lou Wallner rejected her lesbian daughter—and paid a terrible price. Today she has a simple message for Christian parents: Embrace your gay children. A devout Christian, Mary Lou Wallner grew up believing homosexuality was a sin. So she was devastated when, in 1988, her older daughter Anna, 21, told her she was a lesbian. Wallner's reaction—and Anna's subsequent suicide—haunt her to this day.[1]

What a tragedy. We may reject Mrs. Wallner's belief that embracing our children means approving of their homosexuality as well, but we can certainly weep for and with her in her loss. After my own daughter—actress Anne Heche—came out to me (as detailed in this book's introduction) I, too, wondered if my own Christian convictions might have been seen by her as rejection.

I thought of all the times I wished I had blessed her. Instead, I'm sure I made many mistakes. I remembered the first time she and her partner at the time, Ellen DeGeneres, came to Chicago and we had dinner together—how awkward and helpless I felt; how coldhearted and scared I may have seemed. Then there was the time I visited them in their gorgeous *Architectural Digest* designer home and they invited some girlfriends to come to their pool and swim naked. (Talk about a situation a mother isn't prepared for!) And the time we played badminton on their lawn, and I beat Ellen (at least that's the way *I* remember it!). And the time we had a really difficult political discussion in their kitchen about gay preachers and gay marriages.

I loved Anne so; I loved them both! But when it came to beliefs about right and wrong, we were worlds apart. I felt awful. I really didn't know what to do.

What We *Can* Do

But now I know at least one thing I could do. I could confess my own sin. And I could bless her…to bless is to ask God to interfere, to take action in one's life to bring them to the desired relationship with Himself so that they are truly blessed and fully satisfied. When God blesses He releases His power to change the character and destiny of the one being blessed.

Sure, there's a place for discussing things, speaking the truth in love, and putting boundaries in place when you need to. But when it's all been said and done, you still don't have the power to change another person's mind. But you can bless them. "God bless you." It's amazing what a release and relief it can be just to say that.

Let's look at another situation where a mother had some hard lessons to learn.

Judy: A Mother's Story About Her Son's Estrangement

My middle son is adopted. We brought him home from the hospital when he was nine days old.

Two months before his graduation from high school, he went to a rehearsal for his senior musical. He was long overdue returning home. Consequently I was waiting in the living room for his return. When at last he came home, he sat down in a chair opposite me. I was angry and said, "What's going on? Are you and your girlfriend having sex?" (My worst fear!)

He just looked at me with a very cynical look and said, "You have no clue!"

After a few minutes of just looking at me, he said, "For the past four years I've been living a homosexual lifestyle."

I couldn't speak for several moments. While my husband was peacefully sleeping just a room away, I was having my life turned upside down. I didn't understand how this could be happening in our son's life and our home. I tried to reason with him, but he was very antagonistic and got up and headed for the door to leave.

He announced that he was going to his best friend's sister's house. She had told him that he could stay there if things didn't go well here tonight.

"You're not going anywhere until your father knows what's going on," I said. "Stay right here until I get him!" I woke up my husband and quickly told him what was happening. When he came into the living room, he said to our son, "Get out of here, and don't come back until you've got your life straightened out!"

"Think what you're saying!" I shouted.

My husband just continued to look at our son and then calmly said, "Well, that's what I'd like to say, but you're my son and will always be my son. Since I can't agree with what you're doing with your life, can we sit down and talk about this?"

"No," our son answered, and walked out the door saying that he would be back the next day for his things.

The next day I contacted a friend who gave me a phone number for a ministry to families affected by homosexuality. The woman was very comforting and put me in contact with another mother in my area who was in my position but further down the road in dealing with it...I pray daily for his life to be touched in some way that will bring him back to where he belongs. I pray that he will have a right relationship with God and come out of a very deceptive and dangerous lifestyle.[2]

Now, let's look at what went right in this situation, what went wrong, and what can be done about it.

What went right. The mother listened, which was one of the best things to do at a time like that. She insisted the father be brought into the situation, which was also critical, and when her husband initially reacted in all the wrong ways, she intervened. When her son left, she sought out support for herself, and has continued to stand in the gap, prayerfully, for her son.

The father, too, had the integrity to admit he was wrong after his initial outburst, and he showed real consideration when he asked the son to please sit down and talk it over. And when his son refused, he didn't resort to violence or more name calling. Since his son was an adult or near adult, it seemed there was little he could do but allow him to leave, much as the Prodigal Son's father had to do. (If his son was still technically a minor he might have tried legal intervention, but since it's not clear in this case what his exact age was, it's also not clear whether or not that would have been advisable.)

What went wrong. Clearly, the father's first words were hurtful and damaging. Like wounds, they must have gone deep into that boy's soul, making a bad situation worse. Still, he did take responsibility for what he'd said and tried to make things right.

It might be possible for both of them to meet with the son, whether in the home or a more neutral place, to talk about the future. Even if the son can't be persuaded that homosexuality is wrong, at least the parents can try to re-establish some contact with him and rebuild their relationship, with an agreement that they may disagree on this issue, but that there's no reason to let it destroy their relationship.

Standing in the Gap

Sometimes that's hard to do, I know. My own hard heart had created a huge gap in my relationship with my daughter (and her friends). We tried, she tried. I tried to talk about my schoolwork, her projects, her sisters, and her nieces and nephews, but we always ended up arguing about our disagreements and convictions. We couldn't agree to disagree. We were both so adamant about our beliefs. So the conversations became more abusive and the distance grew greater, every word eroding the edge of the cliff on which our relationship teetered. We ended with her saying that she never wanted to talk to me again. Then she would call, unexpectedly, a year or so later, out of the blue, and we would begin the whole process over again.

I saw a picture in my mind of something like the Grand Canyon. I'm on one side (the heterosexual side), with a large, proud, familiar heterosexual crowd. She's way across the canyon on the side with a smaller but nonetheless proud homosexual crowd.

My hard heart was keeping me inaccessible and unapproachable to anyone on the far side of that great canyon between us. So how would we ever be able to close the gap—the avowed heterosexual mother and the avowed homosexual daughter?

It occurred to me that this heterosexual/homosexual canyon scenario was not just my problem. Yes, it was about me and my daughter, but it was also about all of us proud heterosexual, Bible believers on that one far side of the canyon separating ourselves from the homosexuals—professing believers or not—on the far side.

Who would stand in the gap? In the Hebrew Scriptures the prophet Ezekiel hears these words from the Sovereign Lord: "I looked for [someone] who would...stand before Me in the gap on behalf of the land so I would not have to destroy it, but I found none."

When the Israelites were wandering and complaining in the wilderness on their way to the Promised Land, Moses stood in the gap—he negotiated before God on behalf of the Israelites—many times: "He said He would destroy them—had not Moses, His chosen one, stood in the [gap] before Him to keep His wrath from destroying them."

What are we doing? Why am I—why are we—not standing in the gap? Why are we comforting ourselves with our safe but unapproachable friends on one side of the canyon when others *whom we do not want to see "destroyed"* stare incredulously and defensively from the other side? Many of them know the gospel of Christ. They must wonder what gospel we know that causes many of us to distance ourselves and act so hateful toward them. When will I stand in the gap? When will I become a negotiator, a chosen one, to stand in the gap before God, before the gay community, so that *we* are not destroyed?

I don't know exactly what that might look like for you. But for me it means that I stop separating the world into two spheres, the heterosexual and the homosexual, when I read John 3:16, and I read it as Jesus spoke it: God so loved the *whole world—all the people in the world*—"that He gave His one and only Son, that whoever believes in Him shall not perish but have eternal life."

It means I "go and make disciples of *all* the world," not two separate worlds.

It means that I "do not forget to entertain strangers, for by so doing some people have entertained angels without knowing it."

It means I stop living my life with an "us versus them" worldview. And I stop holding my loved ones and the gay community hostage to my judgment and condemnation. Instead, I can live like Jesus, not counting their sins against them every time I think about it...the same Jesus who said, to my hardened (but still teachable) heart: "Run, Nancy! Run to the other side of the canyon and take as many people with you as you can! Stand in the gap, fill it up—way up."

Please hear me. I know there's a stand to take. I know there's a need to clarify to your son or daughter what's right or wrong, especially if your child is still a minor and you need to enforce your values in your home. Likewise, even with an adult son or daughter, you sometimes have to make it clear where you stand, and what you can or can't go along with. That's true. But let's start the process by looking at our own hearts, making sure they're softened with His love, and then, from that position of humility, we can proceed to deal with our loved ones.

Let's look at another family's situation and see what we can learn from it.

Saralee: A Mother and Her Son Re-Establish Their Relationship

Our son became very close to me and to my mother. I guess we were what you would call his heroes. If only I had known the importance of a relationship between a son and his father, I might have [reconsidered divorcing my husband].

When our son began school, it was hard for him—overwhelming in fact—to detach from my mother and me. Most days he went to school crying. Of course the other kids made fun of him. Kids can be very cruel. They began to call him names. "Fag" was at the top of the list.

There was never any true male role model for my son...If I had only known all the pain he was feeling...I will never forget the day I came right out and asked him if he was gay. My heart broke when he said yes.

From that day forward my mind was consumed with nothing else. I began to go over every little detail of his life. What did I do to cause this to happen? What could I have done to prevent this? I blamed myself for all of it...Our relationship had changed from best friends to what seemed like enemies.

All I could do was pray. And that's what I did. Once again, God was speaking to me through my pain and heartache. I spent many months on my knees...I picked myself up and started working on what I could do to better understand my son. I started reading. The first book I read was *When Homosexuality Hits Home* by Joe Dallas. This book gave me a whole new view of where I fit into all of this. I had to go back and walk in B.'s shoes—feel the pain he felt for so many years, understand the scars he carries with him on a daily basis. I must say that the pain was unbearable.

After a time, I was ready to talk with him. I called him and we met for dinner. I prayed the whole time I was traveling to meet him that God would give me the words to say. When I sat down, I was just about to burst inside; then we started talking. I told him about the book I had read and that I had put myself in his shoes and had felt his pain. I told him that I was so sorry for causing any part of his pain. This was the beginning of a whole new relationship for us. Just hearing my acceptance of him opened the door. I told him that I didn't agree with what he was doing, but I felt more understanding about the fact that he was gay. I let him know that he had a family who loved him and wanted to see him. I told him that he had a little sister who thought he hung the moon, and she deserved to see her brother.

Since that talk we have been able to have a better relationship. I know now that I can once more talk to him about anything. I know that more answers will come in time. I will not push. I will just pray—and never stop praying—that someday my son will see the light that I have seen.[3]

Can we learn something from Saralee's experience? Let's try.

What went right. Saralee certainly cared, didn't she? She made no bones about loving her son, and his deep attachment to her speaks of the affection and nurturing she no doubt showed him. She had the sensitivity to detect something was wrong, which led her to ask him if he was gay. And once she got the answer, she began looking for help, trying to identify anything that could be corrected.

She took the time to read and make use of resources that were available to her, and as she learned more about her son and herself through her reading, she began to empathize with him ("walk in his shoes," as she puts it). Then she planned out a time to have a serious talk with her son about the situation. She made it clear where she stood, and made her love and support clear as well. And she wisely realized that, having made herself clear where she stood on homosexuality, she couldn't force her grown son to agree with her, so she continues to pray for him, while building a good relationship with him.

What went wrong. It's understandable that she started asking herself, "What did I do wrong to cause this?" But that often leads to a lot of speculation and second-guessing, not to mention needless guilt over "what might have been." The truth is, it's really hard to say exactly why, in every case, someone becomes homosexual. Certainly, it would have helped if she had arranged for more male role models to be in her son's life. But no one can say that that, alone, would have kept him from becoming attracted to men. So needless self-blame is one thing we want to avoid. Take responsibility when you know you've done something wrong, but don't go scrambling to try to figure out what *unknown* thing you may have done.

Answering Some Questions

When a parent faces the fact that their son or daughter is homosexual, that parent is also facing questions they have never before considered. Lots of them! So here's a list of the questions I hear most often from parents, along with my answers.

"My teenager just told me he's gay. There's a gay student club at his school he wants to join, and I know he's already met some other kids who say they're gay as well. I don't approve, so what can I do?"

You can't tell him what to feel, so don't bother saying, "You can't be gay! I won't allow it!" But you can tell him what you, as his parent, will or won't allow him to do.

When he's an adult he can decide for himself whether or not to be involved in pro-gay groups, or form a relationship with another man. But for now, you've the right and responsibility to set terms and boundaries—just as you would for a heterosexual son. Let him know, for example, that he can't be a part of something that's morally and spiritually wrong. That would include joining a gay club, or a gay online chat room, or, for that matter, any form of pornography or material you object to. And don't be afraid to exercise your authority when deciding which friends he's allowed to hang out with, either.

But try to keep the conversation going too. Ask him lots of questions: When did he first realize he felt this way about men? What's it been like for him? How does he feel about it? How does he think God feels about it, and about him? These are all important questions, and they can get a good conversation going. Let him know that while you're not going to compromise when it comes to his behavior or his activities, you really do care, and want to better understand him. Especially, try to find out more about where he is spiritually. Ask about his relationship with Christ, his beliefs, his feelings about God and eternity. Make sure he still participates in the life of your church. And if he's open to it, try to find a good Christian counselor for him to meet with to discuss this more. A good youth pastor or minister may be available too.

"My daughter just came out to us. I want her to go for counseling, but she doesn't think her lesbianism is a problem. Should I make her get into counseling?"

If your underage child is showing serious emotional or behavioral problems, it's fine to insist on counseling whether she wants it or not. But if she has simply said, "Mom and Dad, I'm gay," then you should *offer* counseling, but not *force* it. (I would apply this whether your daughter is a minor or an adult.) Forcing her to get into counseling for her homosexuality will feel like a huge violation to her, and will almost certainly not produce any good results. I know, from my own work as a pastoral therapist, that the counseling relationship is a very personal, delicate one. It requires willingness and high motivation on the part of the person being counseled, and if that isn't there, not only does it usually not work (causing a lot of time and money to be wasted) but it can also hugely damage the relationship between parent and child.

"I can't believe my son is really gay. I think he's just confused. Am I wrong?"

Maybe he's confused. Some people, especially teens and young adults, go through phases when they're not sure what their sexuality really is. But before assuming it's just confusion, remember that he's the one who can best say what he does or does not feel. Often when we hear something about our child that we don't want to hear, we tell ourselves it's something else; something easier to accept. And for you, it's probably easier to accept the idea that your child is confused, rather than the idea that he's homosexual. But don't argue over whether this is a confusing stage in his life. Instead, let him tell you what he's feeling.

Take his words at face value. You don't have to use the words "gay" or "homosexual" as labels for him. But don't put the "confused" label on him either. He'll have to decide for himself, as an adult, both what he feels and what he's going to do as a result.

"My daughter is marrying another woman, and wants me to come to the ceremony. I don't feel at all right about it, but I also don't want to insult her. What can I do?"

Paul said that "whatever is not done of faith is sin" (Romans 14:23). It doesn't sound like you could in good faith celebrate a homosexual union, and there's a reason for that. It's one thing to have a relationship with a son or daughter who's openly gay or lesbian. I think in most cases, it's best to keep that relationship in good working order, spend time together, and basically "agree to disagree." But it's another thing to go to a same-sex wedding ceremony, because attending a wedding is a way of saying, "I bless, approve of, and support this union." It's not just socializing; it's affirming. And that's probably why you feel the way you do. Hard as it is, sometimes we have to let someone we love know that they're asking us to do something that violates our conscience. Tell her that you'd never push her to do something she truly doesn't believe in, and ask her to show you the same respect and grace.

"My adult son wants to bring his partner to our home for dinner and stay the weekend with us. How should we respond?"

I see nothing in Scripture that tells me I can't, as a Christian parent, host my son or daughter and their partner, even if their relationship is outside God's will. To be with them is not to make a statement of approval, no more than Jesus socializing with sinners meant He approved of their sin. He loved them and enjoyed them as people without in any way compromising, and we can do the same.

That doesn't mean in all cases it's the best thing to do, though. If you or your own spouse really feel there will be too much tension, or that you really can't handle meeting the person your son is with, then you don't have to put yourself in that position. But if you feel you can, then there's nothing wrong with spending time with both of them.

One thing you can reasonably ask is that they not sleep together in your home, which may mean asking them to either room elsewhere, or for both of them to stay in separate rooms. He may refuse; he may even find the idea absurd. But remind him that you're only asking that he respect the beliefs you hold to in your home, and that you would not ask him to host anything in his home that he didn't believe in, either.

"My daughter was raised Christian, and she knows what Scripture has to say about homosexuality. So what can I say to help her rethink her present pro-homosexuality position and lifestyle choices?"

The question is based on the assumption that you can influence her on this matter, and that may not be so. If she has decided that she is a lesbian, and that she feels comfortable with that, then there's a good chance that no words from you would change her mind. That's not to say her mind won't ever change. Rather, I'm saying that unless and until she feels convicted that homosexuality isn't what God intended for her, and unless and until she feels ready to abandon that behavior, your ability to change her mind is very, very limited.

It's somewhat like the principle of witnessing. You can sow the gospel seed, but you can't convict another person of their sins, nor can you give them the faith to believe in the Savior's promises. You sow the seed in the hope other people or events will water it, and God will give the increase.

Having said that, I do think asking her the right questions, then listening carefully and respectfully to the answers, are two powerful tools God can use to open her heart. So let her know you want to understand better. When did she first realize she felt this way? What's it been like for her? Did she feel she needed to hide it? How did she think you and the family would react? What are her hopes, and her fears? How does she think God feels about it, and about her? These are all helpful questions, and if you think it over and pray on it, I'll bet you can come up with more of your own.

"My grown son and I are trying to work out how to relate, now that he's told us about his homosexuality. What sort of agreement do we need to have if we're going to go on relating well?"

You need to talk honestly about the family situations that usually come up in these cases. Here are the ones you're likely to face:[4]

1. *Telling other family members.* Your adult son or daughter should be the one to decide who is told about his/her homosexuality, and should assume the responsibility to tell them in his/her own time.

An exception would be underage children. You should be the one to decide under what terms they should be told, and by whom.

2. *Arguing about the issue.* If you're having ongoing discussions about what the Bible does or does not say, what psychology or science says or doesn't say, or what laws should or should not be in effect regarding homosexuality, and if you feel these discussions are constructive, fine. But if you're feeling as though all you're doing is arguing and if the arguing is doing more harm than good to all involved, then call a moratorium on it, agree that you're going to disagree, and find other things to discuss when you're together.

3. *Displays of affection.* At family get-togethers, you may want your son or daughter to attend with their partner, but you may also want to let them know your feelings about physical affection between them. To them, perhaps, holding hands or embracing in your family's company may seem reasonable, but to you it probably won't. You'll need to discuss this in advance, and come to an understanding of what is or isn't a workable approach.

"But meanwhile, what can I do?"

After we've said our piece to our son or daughter, established whatever boundaries we may need to put in place, apologized for whatever wrongs we may have done, and determined to keep our relationship with them intact even as we disagree, we're still left with some unmovable facts: We love our child; we can't make our child think, believe, or feel what we want him to think, believe, or feel; but even though we know we can't change what is, it still hurts to see someone we love outside of God's will. That, too, is a place I've been. But God is still at work in that loved one! So let me close with these encouraging thoughts from a woman who reached a point where she realized her own brokenness. As you read this, remember that the person you love is no more beyond His reach than she was:

> As I continued to cry out to God and read His word, I came across the story of the woman at the well recorded in John 4. Jesus said to that woman that if she drank the well water she would thirst again; but if she drank of the water He would give her, it would become in her a spring of living water. Finally I saw a ray of hope. I clung

to that passage and God showed me two things: 1) that she had to drink of the well water to live. Translation: It's not wrong to satisfy a felt need (in God-approved ways of course); and 2) that if I only satisfied my felt need, I would continue to become thirsty; in fact, my thirst would be ever increasing because there is a deeper need that only God can fill by His Holy Spirit.[5]

I guess the one thing I want to communicate to the homosexual is that his or her needs are real and they deserve to be met. But if God isn't allowed to meet those needs in the depths of the person's soul, and in the way He intended them to be met, then he or she will always thirst and never be satisfied.

CHAPTER SIXTEEN

The Parent's Dilemma

○—Key Points—○

1. When an *underage* son or daughter announces his or her homosexuality a Christian parent should exercise parental responsibility by setting terms as to what the child may or may not participate in, and who the child may or may not socialize with. But the parent cannot dictate to the child what the child may or may not feel, or believe. On this point the parents should make their beliefs and hopes clear, try to initiate discussion, and, when appropriate, get good counsel and support for the child and the parents.

2. When an *adult* son or daughter announces their homosexuality, the parents will have to recognize their limitations. Their goal should be to preserve the relationship as much as possible, without compromising their own integrity. In most cases this is possible.

3. A son or daughter may say "I'm gay" when, in fact, he or she is simply confused. But in most cases it should be assumed that if he or she says "I'm attracted to the same sex," he or she is the best judge of his or her true feelings.

4. Forcing a son or daughter to get counseling, or join a program or ministry against their will, is not advisable, unless that son or daughter is displaying severe emotional problems, or is engaged in self-destructive behavior.

5. Christian parents who find out about their child's homosexuality should take steps to get help for themselves, by way of support and education, to help them deal with their own emotions and questions.

6. Christian parents who learn about their child's homosexuality will need to decide what boundaries need to be set, especially during family gatherings, and regarding what they will or will not continue to discuss or debate. Then they need to discuss these boundaries with their children, and, in some cases, negotiate them and come to some mutually agreed on terms for maintaining their relationship.

7. While it's important to be clear in our own positions, endless arguing over the rightness or wrongness of homosexuality tends to do more harm than good to families. At some point it can be advisable to "agree to disagree" and not let this issue become a wedge between parents and child.

8. Parents may still have influence in their adult child's life, but that influence is limited. Christian parents with a homosexual son or daughter should be especially prayerful that the Holy Spirit will do the work in their child's conscience that they themselves cannot do.

9. Asking relevant questions of a homosexual son or daughter can be a very useful way of opening up dialogue that's redemptive, and that helps both parties better understand each other.

10. God is still very much at work in the life of the prodigal, even when his parents are unable to do more than watch and pray.

RESOURCES
BOOKS FOR PARENTS

The Truth Comes Out by Nancy Heche, Regal Books, 2006.

When Homosexuality Hits Home by Joe Dallas, Harvest House Publishers, 2004.

Someone I Love Is Gay by Bob Davies and Anita Worthen, InterVarsity Press, 1996.

Where Does a Mother Go to Resign? by Barbara Johnson, Bethany House Publishing, 2004.

SUPPORT FOR PARENTS

Living Stones Ministries: education, seminars, support groups

114 North Glendora Ave.
Glendora, CA 91741
877-963-6683
www.livingstonesministries.org

PFOX (Parents and Friends of Ex-Gays and Gays): education, seminars, support groups

PO Box 510
Reedville, VA 22539
804-453-4737
www.pfox.org

NOTES

1. "One Mother's Tragic Lesson," *People* magazine, November 19, 2007.
2. Nancy Heche, *The Truth Comes Out* (Ventura, CA: Regal Books, 2006), pp. 171-173. Used by permission.
3. Heche, pp. 183-185. Used by permission.
4. For a more thorough discussion of terms and boundaries to set with a gay loved one, see Bob Davies and Anita Worthen, *Someone I Love Is Gay* (Downers Grove, IL: InterVarsity, 1996); and Joe Dallas, *When Homosexuality Hits Home* (Eugene, OR: Harvest House Publishers, 2004). Both of these books include suggestions and approaches that I think you'll find helpful.
5. Heche, pp. 174-175. Used by permission.

THE SPOUSE'S DILEMMA

by Nancy Heche, DMin

*One should rather die than be betrayed. There is no deceit
in death. It delivers exactly what it promised. Betrayal,
though…betrayal is the willful slaughter of hope.*

—Playwright Steven Dietz

A tearful, middle-aged man edges down beside me in the front row of the auditorium and says, "I never knew how much I hurt my wife until I heard your speech tonight." He hangs his head and weeps. This conversation and confession is hard for me. I had never heard those words from my husband about his double life with homosexuality, and it's hard for me to keep forgiving him, even now, 25 years later. I take comfort in hearing Jesus say I have 490 times to forgive. I'm probably close to 213 or 214 today.

This emotional exchange with the guilty, sad-eyed man brings up a lot of ambivalence for me. Maybe I could take out all my old hurt and anger on this poor unsuspecting man by asking him (with a jab to the ribs), "How could you be so stupid! What did you think she would feel when she found out? Jerk!" (Sorry, I'm still a work in progress—but don't worry, I didn't actually say it.)

Instead, I asked him, "How would it be for you to talk to her about your feelings and your new insight?" That's better. I take a deep breath. If the Holy Spirit can convince this man of the pain resulting from his hurtful, adulterous choices and turn him around and forgive him, then I can too. I peel off and discard one more layer of anger toward my late husband.

Isn't that how God works? I think I'm helping someone, and instead I probably get more of what I need than he does.

Sadly, I'm not alone in my experience. Because in so many cases, when a man "comes out of the closet," he brings a bewildered and heartbroken wife right along with him. Listen to another woman's story:

> After many years of marriage, many years of struggle, many years of pain, I had come to acknowledge that my own marriage was dead. The pain of realizing that my hopes and dreams wouldn't come to pass is something I'm still working through. I thought the struggles were finished when we married. But for many reasons, the marriage was difficult from the start. After a number of years I found out that my husband had experienced repeated falls. This devastated me. I took the blame, telling myself that if I had been a better wife, if I had prayed more, and so on, this wouldn't have happened. At the same time, I kept the issue to myself. Although God didn't want me to bear it alone, I did. I didn't want to deal with the judgment that would likely come from the church.
>
> I've taken a lot of comfort in the words of Isaiah 43. God says, "When you pass through the waters, I will be with you; and when you pass through the rivers, they will not sweep over you. When you walk through the fire, you will not be burned; the flames will not set you ablaze." Notice that He didn't say *if* I pass through the waters, but rather *when* I pass through the waters. I never wanted the deep struggles of life to touch my family. But they did. I knew of my husband's struggles with homosexuality from the beginning, but I didn't have much understanding with that knowledge. I didn't understand the roots and the deep pain and difficulty in overcoming those issues.
>
> As I have opened up a little, I find that I am not alone. Now I am holding on to God's promise that He has a plan for me, for my future, for hope (Jeremiah 29:11). God is faithful. He is meeting all my needs. Even through the waters, the river, and the fire God has been with me, they have not swept over me nor set me ablaze.[1]

No indeed, they haven't and they won't. But what a time of sorrow and confusion a spouse goes through when learning of a partner's homosexuality! Here's another one of many examples:

> During the past several years, my marriage had been dying a slow, agonizing death. I kept thinking that things would improve, but they didn't. Last year, on the week of my birthday, my husband came out of the closet and moved out. I could never have dreamed that this would happen to me, to us, or that I would be living alone at this time in my life, with this betrayal and pain. Those things happened to other people, not to me. Not to my family. We were the perfect family, with the perfect children. We were supposed to live happily ever after. How were we going to get through this? How do we go on with our lives when everything we've known for so many years is taken away?
>
> I can't tell you how many times I prayed for the Lord to wrap His arms around me, comfort me, and put me to sleep. And He did. He gave me the strength to keep going. Let me tell you about some things I have learned that have helped me:
>
> I learned that I can have a new dream for my life.
>
> I learned to be more thankful for my children.
>
> I learned that I can make my own decisions.
>
> I learned that I don't have to be angry about my situation.
>
> I learned to live each day and be thankful for it.
>
> Several months before the separation I decided that my greatest desire was to get through this separation with as much grace and dignity as possible. Most days I have succeeded. My hope is that if anyone reading this is experiencing a difficult time right now, he or she will find encouragement to keep moving forward.[2]

The Spouse Comes Out Too

According to the Centers for Disease Control, more than 3 million women are or have been wives or girlfriends of men who secretly have sex with other men. The Straight Spouse Network cites similar statistics. And according to the Family Pride Coalition, 20 percent of America's gay men are in heterosexual marriages, and at least 50 percent of the gay men in America have fathered children.[3] And while most of these situations involve everyday people, there are more than a few familiar faces who've been through it too.

In 1998, former California congressman Michael Huffington, husband of commentator Arianna Huffington, publicly disclosed his homosexuality. Six years later, in August of 2004, former New Jersey Governor Jim McGreevey announced his closeted homosexuality and the double life he'd been leading, unbeknownst to his wife and two sons. And in 2006, the Reverend Ted Haggard, one of America's most prominent pastors, was exposed by a male prostitute he'd been visiting, sending shock waves through the church, the culture, and his own wife and children.

Nearly 20 years earlier tennis champion Billie Jean King's husband endured a similar dilemma when Ms. King's former female lover forced Billie Jean to acknowledge their lesbian affair. And before partnering with rock star Melissa Etheridge in a well-publicized lesbian relationship, Julie Cypher had been married to movie star Lou Diamond Phillips. Clearly, then, the experience of a spouse discovering a partner's homosexuality is a painfully common one. In fact, the popularity of the 2005 film *Brokeback Mountain*, which portrayed a decades-long homosexual relationship between two married men, spoke to themes that, sadly, all too many spouses could relate to. Let's consider another woman's story:

> I was so worried about his drastic changes. All I could think about was that he was going crazy—something very awful was happening to my husband. Until just two years prior I thought we had a nearly perfect marriage! Our friends wished their marriages were like ours. We were best friends, we talked about everything. He was charming, a complete extrovert, wonderfully fun. He loved to go shopping with me. We did everything together. We helped couples with their marriage problems, even counseled friends who were struggling with homosexuality.
>
> But in the space of two years, all of that changed. He started being cool to me; he was not at home as much as usual; and then one day he told me he wanted to be single...
>
> When things started getting very strange, I asked him to go to counseling with me. He said he would go, but only one time. He

would go on the condition that he could tell the therapist what was wrong with me and what I needed to do. It wasn't to be about him. When I went back the next week by myself, the counselor asked me about our sexual relationship. I knew she must be probing to see if I had thought of homosexuality. Then she said it. "Have you considered the possibility that he is a homosexual?"

I felt ashamed and guilty of my thoughts. What a terrible accusation. What if it weren't true and I hadn't waited to see if he were proven innocent. I was horrified to think that I would ever think such a thing. We had been married for 20 years. Surely this couldn't be true![4]

But so often it *is* true, and we leave a partner wondering how such a thing could have ever come to be.

"How, and Why, Did This Happen to Me?"

Given that every marriage is unique, I won't presume to say why, in every case, a person who is homosexual marries and, often, keeps his or her homosexuality hidden. But I can tell you what I've often seen, which is a progression of events and experiences.

1. Prior knowledge. A person usually knows he or she is attracted to the same gender early in life and prior to marriage. While in some cases—mostly involving women—a person may really not realize their sexual preference until later in life, it is usually something that shows itself early enough so that a person knows, by the time they marry, which sex they are primarily attracted to.

2. Conflict over homosexuality. There are several reasons a person will choose to marry someone of the opposite sex in lieu of partnering with someone of the same sex. Cultural taboos against homosexuality are still largely intact in many states (and certainly in other nations as well), leaving many homosexuals feeling compelled to enter a heterosexual marriage, seeing that as the only way to enjoy a family life. Others may have looked at the homosexual population and concluded that a heterosexual marriage offers more stability than a homosexual partnership, so they opt for traditional marriage. More common than either of these first two scenarios, though, is religious conflict. Many Christians (and

Orthodox Jewish people, Mormons, Jehovah's Witnesses, and Muslims) view homosexuality as being incompatible with their beliefs, so they marry, often hoping that marriage will eliminate, or at least alleviate, their conflict with their homosexuality.

It should be noted that in many (probably most) cases, there's a deep love involved. Most men and women who admit their homosexuality later in their married life also report they genuinely care for their spouse, and did not marry them for convenience sake, or as a façade. Generally, they report entering into the union gladly and, even if their erotic desire for their spouses wasn't as strong as they hoped for, their love and affection were. "We loved each other or we would never have tried so hard," writes gay activist Mel White of his marriage and his ultimate decision to leave his wife and embrace his homosexuality. "It wasn't just pathology that kept us in a relationship...it was also love. We fought and cried and held on because we loved each other."[5]

3. Ongoing homosexual attractions in spite of marriage. It usually doesn't take long for the homosexual spouse to realize that marriage, with its availability of legitimate sexual outlet with a partner who's loved and respected, does not nullify his or her homosexual desires. Erotic attractions for the same sex can remain intact, despite deep emotional ties to the partner of the opposite sex.

4. Stressors weaken resolve. The homosexual spouse will usually retain a resolve to resist her or his homosexual attractions, and focus sexual energy and attention on her or his partner. Homosexual behavior or fantasy, then, is something the person feels tempted to default to, but is committed to resist. But with time, any number of routine pressures and stresses can weaken that resolve, and "defaulting" to the behavior that offers a primary sexual gratification becomes an increasingly attractive option.

5. Outside intimacy weakens resolve. At times, perhaps innocently, the homosexual spouse will enter into a relationship that begins as a friendship but evolves into an adulterous affair. One of the original board members of Exodus International, a network of ministries devoted to helping people overcome homosexual behavior, found himself deeply attracted to and ultimately in love with another man who had volunteered for the organization. Both were married; both divorced their wives and formed a homosexual partnership. And back in 1959 (long before this subject was discussed so openly as today) popular

Christian author Eugenia Price wrote what I consider to be an accurate description of how this can play out among Christian women:

> Many of you would be shocked at the number of heartbroken and troubled letters I receive from Christian women who are deeply embroiled in "inordinate affection" for each other...they have permitted another person to get into God's place in their lives. One woman's husband was threatening to divorce her...her heart was so smashed she turned to a woman. Another woman I know writes to her woman friend every day! And if there is stormy weather and the air mails are not on schedule, she is panicky...she is lovesick.[6]

6. Accessibility weakens resolve. When the thing a person is committed to resisting becomes more readily available, inevitably it's harder to resist. The Internet has made all forms of pornography, homosexual included, available in ways no one would have dreamed possible. It has also opened up communication, so that the person curious about his or her own homosexual feelings—a person who would never have ventured into a gay bar to discuss those feelings with others—can now, in safety and anonymity, chat with others who are homosexual, exploring their feelings and their options. This, too, has weakened the resolve of many married homosexuals who were initially committed to fidelity. Now, in light of ongoing life stressors, they have easy accessibility to other lesbians or gay men, and the eroding of the cultural taboos against homosexuality itself, make it harder to keep resisting.

What to Do?

All of the above lead to the decision to experiment, explore, engage. Then when the truth comes out, and the betrayed spouse realizes the gravity of the situation, and some course of action has to be taken. That brings us to the critical question: What's a spouse to do when discovering that the partner they know and love is homosexual? Let me offer some ideas that will, hopefully, cover the most important bases.

1. Ascertain where your spouse stands on homosexuality. When a husband tells his wife "I'm gay," or when a wife tells her husband "I'm lesbian," that raises important questions, such as:

1. Have you been sexually active outside our marriage, or when you say, "I'm gay," are you only describing your sexual attractions?

2. Are you currently involved with, or in love with, another man or woman?

3. Where do you stand on homosexuality? Do you think your feelings are something to be resisted, or are you considering "coming out" and acting on them?

4. Where do you stand on our marriage? Now that you've declared yourself gay, are you still committed to this marriage, or are you undecided, or are you considering ending it?

5. If you are still committed to our marriage, are you willing to get into counseling with me to learn how to best deal with this?

These are the initial questions a spouse needs to ask, and the sooner they're asked, the better.

2. Remember the difference between orientation and behavior. If your spouse's orientation is homosexual, that's a completely involuntary condition which he or she didn't choose, nor can he choose to simply "change" it. If, on the other hand, he or she has engaged in homosexual behavior, that is indeed a choice, one that your partner is morally responsible for. Either way, neither your spouse's orientation or behavior are a reflection on you, and there's nothing you could have done to prevent or cause either of them.

3. Consult with a qualified third party. Immediately set an appointment with your pastor, or a Christian counselor, or a trusted mentor. As a couple, sit down with this third party and clarify what steps need to be taken at this point. These steps should include:

1. *Ongoing counseling* to address your options as a couple, depending on what your spouse chooses to do about his/her sexual feelings.

2. A *safe place*—a support group, for example, or your own counselor—for you to work out your own feelings, fears, and needs while you're dealing with this.

3. An *agreement* on the terms under which you'll continue to live together. In some cases, if a spouse is unwilling to remain monogamous, a separation can be advisable. In most cases, terms should

include commitment to fidelity, ongoing counseling with either a professional Christian counselor or a pastor, and whatever ongoing attempts to rebuild and preserve the marriage are needed.

4. Consider immediate medical concerns. If you're a wife married to a man who's admitted his homosexuality, and if your husband has been sexually active, then consult with your doctor and discuss the various tests you should have for sexually transmitted diseases and HIV. While there's no reason to panic or jump to conclusions, it would be foolish not to deal with your own health and deal with whatever medical problems may arise from your situation.

5. Avoid knee-jerk reactions. The initial shock of discovering a husband or wife's homosexuality can lead to extreme, abrupt actions. Try to avoid these, and put on hold extreme measures (separation, for example, or discussion of divorce) until both of you have had time to think, consider your options, and consult with a competent third party.

The Story Hasn't Ended

In many cases, the shock of discovery and the hard work of rebuilding is only the first part of the story. Listen to, and gain hope from, this woman's experience:

> I didn't know anything about homosexuality, but I trusted the promises of the Bible that the Lord can change anyone. I also knew that I had sought the Lord in regard to our relationship from our very first date, and that the Lord did not want our marriage to end in divorce. With the help of our parents and a few close friends, I began looking for a counselor, a book, or a program to fix the situation and to get Mike to change his mind. In spite of these efforts, [he] left and jumped completely into the gay lifestyle...
>
> The only times I found true comfort and peace were when I was reading my Bible and when I was on my face before the Lord in prayer. Nothing I did seemed to be working to bring Mike home. Finally I realized that I was worrying about Mike when the Lord wanted to change me. I realized that my life would never be the same...God would have to do a work in my own heart. I began to submit myself to the Lord for His work in me.

One evening in April 1997, he came to our house and offered to mow the lawn for me. That evening he came inside and asked to come back home…I had a choice, and out of obedience to the Lord, I chose to recommit myself to the marriage. We stood in the kitchen at opposite corners of the room and stared at each other. We were both hurt and wounded. We had no loving feelings for each other and we didn't even know where to start; but we both believed that the Lord would honor our commitment…

We joined a Bible-teaching church. We also had a godly counselor who poured into [him] what it means to be a man in Christ. We worked through the struggles of giving and receiving forgiveness; we learned how to communicate, rebuild trust, and make our marriage and home a safe place. People often ask me how I was able to forgive him. It was simply obedience to God…He has given us a love for one another beyond our understanding, and certainly beyond anything we could have imagined. He has restored trust and intimacy between us. He has blessed us with three beautiful children. And He has given us opportunities to minister to others—to comfort others with the comfort we have received. He has shown Himself to us as powerful and gracious and loving—keeping all of His promises.[7]

The spouse's dilemma is indescribable; the pain at times seemingly unbearable. But when we look beyond the obvious options—end the marriage and let the homosexual spouse "come out," or pretend the problem doesn't exist and just "go on"—we see Curtain Number Three. Behind it is an option that unveils God's grace and restorative power, as we accept the challenge to face the issue, deal with it realistically and biblically, and see the redemptive power of Christ yet again work its miracle.

CHAPTER SEVENTEEN

The Spouse's Dilemma

○—Key Points—○

1. A number of husbands and wives learn, with time, that they are married to someone who is homosexual. Their spouse's homosexual orientation is usually something that developed early in life, is deeply ingrained, and is involuntary in nature.

2. Homosexual orientation (the condition by which one is sexually attracted to the same sex) does not constitute deliberate sin, therefore the spouse's orientation does not constitute adultery.

3. Unlike the homosexual orientation, a homosexual act with another person on the part of a married man or woman does constitute adultery, and is a chosen act of immorality.

4. Most women and men who are homosexual and married were aware of their homosexuality before they married, but chose not to embrace it due to cultural taboos, a preference for the stability of married life or, more often than not, a religious/worldview conflict over homosexuality.

5. Most women and men who are homosexual and married did not marry with the intention of using or deceiving their partners. In most cases they felt heterosexual marriage was their only option, and hoped it would resolve their conflict over homosexuality.

6. Most women and men who are homosexual and married to a heterosexual report a deep love and concern for their spouse, and do not label their marriages as "shams" or "marriages of convenience."

7. Most women and men who are homosexual and married retain an erotic preference for the same sex, even though they emotionally love and prefer the spouse they are married to.

8. When a spouse discovers his or her partner's homosexuality, the couple needs to then determine the homosexual spouse's beliefs and intentions regarding homosexuality before deciding what actions to take.

9. When a marriage has been impacted by homosexuality it almost always requires some counsel and guidance from a pastor or professional Christian counselor.

10. The discovery of homosexuality on the part of a married spouse need never signal the end of a marriage, though the marriage's future will be largely determined by the willingness on the parts of both partners to do the work necessary to rebuild and enhance the relationship.

RESOURCES ON MARRIAGE AND HOMOSEXUALITY

The Truth Comes Out by Nancy Heche, Regal Books, 1996.

Boundaries in Marriage by Henry Cloud and John Townsend, Zondervan, 2002.

When Homosexuality Hits Home by Joe Dallas, Harvest House Publishers, 2004.

ONLINE RESOURCES

"Roadsides Toward Hope: A Wife's Response to her Husband's Sexual Addiction" by Penny Freeman, http://exodus.to/content/view/268 /53/.

Wifeboat: A Blog/website for Women Impacted by a Husband's Sexual Sin, hosted by Renee Dallas, www.wifeboat.com.

NOTES

1. Nancy Heche, *The Truth Comes Out* (Ventura, CA: Regal Books, 2006), p. 176. Used by permission.

2. Heche, pp. 180-182. Used by permission.

3. "Why Wives Like Dina McGreevey Don't Know Their Husbands Are Gay," PR Web News Release Newswire, May 5, 2007, www.prweb.com/releases/2007/05/prweb523170.htm.

4. Heche, pp. 186-187. Used by permission.

5. Mel White, *Stranger at the Gate* (New York: Simon & Schuster, 1994), p. 185.

6. Eugenia Price, *Woman to Woman* (Grand Rapids, MI: Zondervan Publishing House, 1959), pp. 123-124.

7. Heche, pp. 192-193. Used by permission.

THE ADULT CHILD'S DILEMMA
One Woman's Firsthand Thoughts
by Nancy Heche, DMin

> *In law and culture, the new idea is that children are fine with*
> *any one or more adults being called their parents so long as*
> *the appointed parents are nice people. But how do children*
> *feel about the brave new world of parenthood? Do fathers*
> *and mothers matter to children? Does how they feel matter?*

> —"How Redefining Marriage Redefines
> Parenthood" by Elizabeth Marquardt

In 2000 (ten years prior to this writing) the U.S. Census Bureau reported over a million American couples surveyed had identified themselves as homosexual,[1] a number that has certainly grown significantly since then. Some well-known celebrity same-sex couples are raising or have raised children, such as Melissa Etheridge, singer Clay Aiken, and Rosie O'Donnell and her partner. Others have openly homosexual parents, such as the comic actor and screenwriter Mike White, whose father Mel White is an openly gay activist. Each year growing numbers of children learn that one of their parents is homosexual; each year growing numbers are being raised by same-sex couples.

What, then, should we assume about kids being raised in a home headed by a same-sex couple? Do they suffer in any way as a result, and if so, is the suffering directly related to their parents' homosexuality, or other problems the parents may have that are unrelated to sexuality, or to society's viewpoints…or all three?

The child's dilemma in these cases is largely determined by the child's view, the nature of the home, and the community they live in:

> A host of parental problems can challenge children raised by those who act out same-sex attraction, according to Dale O'Leary, a writer and researcher for the Catholic Medical Association and author of *The Gender Agenda: Redefining Equality.*[2]

If the home the child's being raised in is essentially unhealthy in overt ways, then the atmosphere of the home, not the parent's sexuality, is the primary dilemma. Dawn Stefanowicz, for example, grew up in a homosexual household during the '60s and '70s in Toronto, and describes her upbringing by a gay father as being largely dysfunctional and damaging:

> Unfortunately, my father, as a child, was sexually and physically abused by older males. Due to this, he lived with depression, control issues, anger outbursts, suicidal tendencies, and sexual compulsions. He tried to fulfill his legitimate needs for his father's affirmation, affection and attention with transient and promiscuous relationships. He and his partners were exposed to various contagious STDs as they traveled across North America. I was at high risk of exposure to contagious STDs due to sexual molestation, my father's high-risk sexual behaviors, and multiple partners. Even when my father was in what looked like monogamous relationships, he continued cruising for anonymous sex. My father's (ex) partners, whom I had deep caring feelings for and associated with, had drastically shortened lives due to suicide, contracting HIV or AIDS. Sadly, my father died of AIDS in 1991.[3]

If the community the child interacts with largely disapproves of homosexuality, the child's dilemma is less over her or his parent's status as gay or lesbian, but more over the way the community perceives gay and lesbian people. Terrance McGeorge, a 20-year-old adult male whose father was openly homosexual, recalls such a challenge. When his father first came out, children in his neighborhood "cut me no slack whatsoever. They all knew about it. He looked different, acted different, and they made sure I knew it."[4]

So what effect does same-sex parenting have, in the long run, on adult children raised by a gay or lesbian couple? Reports so far seem contradictory. Some say that being raised by a lesbian or gay male couple might influence the future sexual orientation of the child; others say there's no evidence of any harm done to the child whatsoever and there may even be some benefits to being raised in a same-sex-couple household; while others say the jury is still out on the matter.[5] (See chapter 22 on gay parenting for a more detailed discussion of studies on the issue.)

Herein lies a tough dilemma for any child, small or grown. Small children bond with the adult raising them, whether biological or adoptive. And if the adults they bond with happen to be homosexual, that's not likely to change their love for them. In the 1996 documentary *It's Elementary: Talking About Gay Issues in Schools*, a young child is shown discussing her love for her two mothers,[10] a love we have no reason to believe isn't real and, in many ways, deserved. However strongly we feel about homosexuality, we've no reason to believe homosexual parents don't love and care for their children. So it's a given that, provided the home is a reasonably safe place, the child raised by a homosexual couple will love both adults involved. McGeorge makes no bones about this when, in describing his gay father, he declares,

> My dad has been my best friend since I was a kid. He always encouraged me and was there for me, for whatever it was, graduations, performances, he was there, immediately.[7]

Many will say, as adults, that they were raised by a wonderful gay couple whom they remain grateful to and well bonded with. I have no argument with that, because, as is obvious by now, people hold different views on homosexuality. So if a man or woman raised by a gay couple sees nothing wrong with homosexuality, we could hardly expect them to have expressed experiencing any "dilemma" in their upbringing over their parent's sexuality. One such woman is Rebecca Meiksin, who was 12 when her mother moved in with a lesbian partner, and who says she "rarely felt any kind of discomfort growing up"; is "very comfortable talking about growing up with a lesbian mother" and says her life "always felt normal to me."[8]

But for those who do adopt a biblical perspective, or who feel their upbringing was less than it could have been had their parents been a heterosexual couple, the subject is fraught with frustration and the inevitable conflict between loyalty to one's parent and a gnawing belief that their upbringing suffered because of what that parent chose to yield to. "I came to deeply care for, love, and compassionately understand my dad. He shared his life regrets with me," Dawn Stefanowicz recalls. And yet,

> My father prized unisex dressing, gender-neutral aspects and a famous cross-dressing icon when I was eight years old. I did not see the value of biological complementing differences of male and female or think about marriage. I made vows to never have children since I had not grown up in a safe, sacrificial, child-centered home environment. I sought comfort looking for my father's love from boyfriends starting at 12 years old.[9]

Mary, a Catholic from New York City who was also raised by a homosexual father, reflects on Dawn's comments:

> Dawn's story breaks my heart yet somehow heals those wounds. She and I have so much in common. I recognize the girl whose identity as a woman was blurred in the mire of homosexuality. For years we were silent because society had no idea we existed, and now a deaf society won't allow our voices to be heard.[10]

So who's got it right? Mary and Dawn, who state their upbringing under same-sex parents left unmet needs in their lives, or Terrance and Rebecca, who sing their gay parents' praises? Research on the issue is still new, with experts on both sides of the issue claiming the scientific and moral high ground.[11]

But it remains certain that adult children raised by same-sex couples will have experienced a host of challenges unique to their situation, the severity of which only time and experience will prove since research on the subject is relatively new. (Again, for more information on same-sex parenting see chapter 22, "Gay Parenting: Plus, Minus, or Equal?") Still, as the question mark hangs over the "long-term effects of gay parenting" issue, Dawn's remarks set a cautionary tone:

> My biggest concern is that children are not being discussed in this same-sex marriage debate. Are my childhood experiences unique? According to a growing number of personal testimonies, experts,

and organizations, there is mounting evidence of strong common-alities to my personal experiences.[12]

CHAPTER EIGHTEEN

THE ADULT CHILD'S DILEMMA

◦——KEY POINTS——◦

1. The long-term impact of being raised by parents of the same sex varies from person to person, and no one profile will fit all cases. Some adults raised by same-sex couples report a very satisfactory upbringing; others report feeling deprived of a better, more norma-tive environment.

2. In even the best of circumstances, some unique challenges will be faced by children raised by same-sex couples; challenges that will be remembered and perhaps continue to have impact into the child's adulthood.

3. Three primary ways in which being raised by a same-sex couple presents a dilemma to a child are: If the home the child is raised in is inherently dysfunctional; if the child feels personal conflicts over his or her parent's homosexuality; and if the child's environment is overtly negative toward the child and parents because of the par-ents' sexuality.

RESOURCES

Out from Under: The Impact of Homosexual Parenting by Dawn Stefano-wicz, Annotation Press, 2007.

Support for adult children raised by same-sex couples: www.dawn stefanowicz.com/dawntest.htm.

Meta studies on homosexuality and parenting: www.futureofchildren .org/usr_doc/06_FOC_15-2_fall05_Meezan-Rauch.pdf.

NOTES

1. Margie Mason, "Census Figures on Same-Sex Couples," Associated Press, August 8, 2001, as quoted at www.speakout.com/activism/apstories/10044-1.html.

2. Quoted in "Caring Friends Support Ministry" website at www.caringfriends.hk/index.php?id =10.

3. Personal testimony of Dawn Stefanowicz, www.dawnstefanowicz.com/dawntest.htm.

4. Mackenzie Carpenter, "What happens to kids raised by gay parents? Research suggests that they turn out about the same, no better, no worse and no more likely to be gay than other kids," *Pittsburgh Post-Gazette*, Sunday, June 10, 2007.

5. Respectively: Warren Throckmorton, "Do Gay Parents Influence the Sexual Preferences of Children?" www.narth.com/docs/influence.html; "Gay Parenting Does Affect Children Differently, Study Finds...Authors Believe Gay Parents Have 'Some Advantages,'" February 8, 2008, www .narth.com/docs/does.html; and see, for example, a comprehensive study done by Meezan and Rauch at www.futureofchildren.org/usr_doc/06_FOC_15-2_fall05_Meezan-Rauch.pdf.

6. From the documentary "It's Elementary," available at www.imdb.com/title/tt0116659/.

7. Carpenter.

8. Carpenter.

9. Stefanowicz.

10. Stefanowicz.

11. See a sampling of both sides of the debate represented in Carpenter.

12. Stefanowicz.

CHAPTER NINETEEN

GAY TEENS

by Nancy Heche, DMin

The appearance of so many gay adolescents has, predictably, worried social conservatives, but it has also surprised gay activists, who for years did little to help the few teenagers who were coming out. Both sides sense high stakes.

—FROM "THE BATTLE OVER GAY TEENS,"
TIME MAGAZINE COVER STORY,
OCTOBER 2, 2005

G ay teenagers may be more visible than ever, but they're nothing new. As long as there have been homosexual people, there have been teenagers who were aware of their sexual desires for the same sex.

We may object that an adolescent is too young to embrace the label "gay" or "lesbian," and with good reason. The label may be premature at least; inaccurate at worst. A 1992 survey of 34,707 adolescents ages 12 to 17, published in the journal *Pediatrics,* reported that 10.7% of the students overall were uncertain whether they were homosexual or heterosexual. The "uncertain" figure jumped to 25.9% among the 12-year-olds, indicating that between ages 12 to 17 there was "an unfolding of sexual identity during adolescence, influenced by sexual experience and demographic factors."[1] This alone provides a strong argument against premature gay/lesbian labeling, as noted by physicist and psychiatrist Dr. Jeffrey Satinover:

The experience of pleasure creates powerful, behavior-shaping incentives. For this reason when biological impulses—especially the sexual ones—are not at least partially resisted, trained and brought under the civilizing influence of culture and will, the pressure to seek their immediate fulfillment becomes deeply embedded in the neural network of the brain. [2]

Concerns about labels notwithstanding, some teens are, in fact, quite aware of their sexual desires, and that those desires are specifically directed to the same sex. They are aware of this because, when they fantasize sexually, or are erotically aroused by a person or image, the fantasy and arousals are homosexual in nature. Traditionally, many of them have needed to hide their sexual preferences, facing enormous levels of ridicule, rejection, and potential violence if they revealed themselves. But *secret* doesn't mean *nonexistent*. Gay teens have always been with us, as indeed they always will be.

There have always been confused teens as well, who aren't sure what their sexual preferences are, so they experiment with both sexes. Or teens who, out of curiosity, engage in sex play with each other and wonder if that means they're homosexual. Or teens who don't fit the culture's standards of masculine or feminine—teenage boys who are quiet and bookish; girls who are aggressive and tomboyish—who wonder if their gender nonconformity makes them homosexual. Calling them gay would be premature at least; presumptive at best. They're undecided, undefined, confused.

Both groups—the decidedly homosexual and the undecided and confused— had no option in the past other than to hide their feelings, no matter how sophisticated their city, state, or culture. Not so today. In many communities, public junior high and high schools (and even some elementary schools) have school-sponsored Gay-Straight Alliance clubs, where openly homosexual, bisexual, and heterosexual students can meet for discussions and understanding. The youth culture is hugely influenced by MTV, television shows, popular music, and young celebrities, and most of these influences have taken an aggressively pro-gay posture. A gay activist, educator, and advisor to President Obama, Kevin Jennings of the Gay, Lesbian and Straight Education Network told *Time* magazine:

We're gonna win because of what's happening in high schools right now...this is the generation that gets it. [3]

The *Time* article continues by noting,

> The popular media is helping teens who believe they are gay to openly express their homosexual attractions without the "loneliness and longing" that characterized the childhoods of so many gay adults…gay teens can now watch fictional and real teens who have come out on shows like *Desperate Housewives*, the dating show *Next* on MTV and *Degrassi High*.[4]

Educational institutions have largely adopted a similar position, with many teachers openly declaring their homosexuality and still more declaring their approval of it. The Internet offers access to chat rooms for gay teens, which are numerous and common, offering yet another means for homosexual youth to connect with each other.[5] With so many elements influencing the adolescent population toward a pro-homosexual viewpoint, the "coming out" of more teens is predictable and inevitable. In fact, according to *The New Gay Teenager*,[6] the average gay person now comes out just before or after graduating high school, and the mean age at which lesbians first have sexual contact with other girls is 16; it's just 14 for homosexual boys.[7]

But that doesn't mean the world at large welcomes gay teens. In many cities, states, and families, "coming out" and "being hurt" are synonymous. While there are people who disapprove of homosexuality out of conviction, there are sadly many—family members, even—who react to gay teens with hostility.

The *Columbia Spectator* of Columbia University, New York, for example, detailed the heart-wrenching story of a teenage boy named Drew who admitted his homosexuality to his parents, only to be beaten, threatened with death, and thrown out:

> "My dad just freaked out and started screaming. Then he started hitting me. He'd never hit me before, never, but when I told him who I was, that I was gay, he just got so mad. He said he was going to kill me and I believed him, so I ran."
>
> After spending a few nights sleeping at a friend's house, Drew returned home, hoping that things might have calmed down. "I tried to open the door, but my key didn't work anymore. So I started knocking and eventually my dad came to the door and told me that I was no longer his son and he never wanted to see me again. He said

if I ever tried to get in touch with him or my mom again he'd find me and kill me," he explained. He now lives on the streets of New York's Upper West Side, where he begs strangers for food and money. He often has to exchange unsafe sexual favors for it.[8]

Helpful Categories

The above example is, to be sure, extreme—atypical of what most same-sex-attracted teens experience. In fact, just as we recognize there's no such thing as a typical adult homosexual, the same should be said of teens wrestling with their orientation. One size doesn't fit all; one story doesn't represent each. But when examining the subject we do see same-sex-attracted teenagers in general as being *conflicted, questioning,* or *gay-identified.*

The conflicted teen is in serious anxiety over his same-sex attractions. His anxiety may spring from the disapproval he knows he'd face if his immediate culture, family, or ethnic group knew of his attractions. It may likewise come from religious conflicts he has over homosexuality, creating a moral/spiritual crisis. In any event, he's in a lonely and difficult position. In extreme cases he may resort to running away from home, adopting destructive behaviors, and experiencing severe physical and emotional traumas as a result. In less serious cases he'll at least feel isolated and possibly depressed. As 17-year-old Vance Smith commented to *USA Today* regarding the tension between his sexuality and environment, "I was so scared I didn't even tell my parents because this is just not a good place to be gay." [9]

The questioning teen, represented by the 10.7% figure cited above, isn't certain where she or he fits on the homosexual-heterosexual continuum. She may feel deep longings for female intimacy without being able to ascertain whether they're sexual or emotional; he may attracted to certain other boys while wondering whether the attractions constitute admiration or desire. While other teens might know beyond doubt which sex they're attracted to, the questioning teen can feel like a citizen in a sexual no-man's-land, lacking a category into which he or she can comfortably fit. Adding to the dilemma is pressure that may come from either pro-gay or conservative voices, both of which might sound as though they're demanding that the teen make a decision to announce or renounce homosexuality.

The gay-identified teen has embraced his or her orientation and has probably announced it to significant people in her or his life. While conflicted or questioning teens are nothing new, gay-identified teens represent a recent and growing phenomenon in the adolescent landscape. Far from being intimidated into silence, they make their identity known by attending proms with same-sex dates and holding hands in public, and they often find support not only from gay-affirming parents, but through school-sponsored clubs and alliances, countless chat rooms and websites dedicated to gay teens, and a variety of books, films, and television shows encouraging their choice to embrace their sexuality.

A patchwork response, then, awaits teens who come to self-identify as homosexual. In some parts of the country, their school, families, and communities welcome them and approve both of their homosexuality and their decision to embrace it. In other cases, hostility and rejection, even from loved ones, might be their lot. And virtually every response in between these extremes can be expected as well. So while we may bemoan the nation's growing acceptance of homosexuality, even among our young, we should note that it is still generally not an easy thing to be adolescent and experience same-sex attractions.

A number of studies over the past decade have indicated that rates of suicide attempts, depression, and unhealthy behaviors are higher among gay teens than among their heterosexual counterparts,[10] and some studies suggested that early identification as lesbian or gay, gender nonconformity, and early sexual experimentation were linked to teenage suicide attempts.[11] Some would argue that society's "homophobia" accounts for their trauma; others insist homosexuality itself is their inherent problem. What is certain, though, is that many homosexual teenagers are hurting. So the question we face is not "Where's the blame?" Instead, it's "Where's the church?"

Well, we're here, of course, but that doesn't mean we're paying attention. In our communities we have hurting teens; in our own families we have kids who struggle and parents who react, not to mention heterosexual teens who don't have a clue as to where they stand or should stand on this issue! So what do we do? Here are some ways we can be more present, and more effective, in our response to homosexuality among teenagers.

We Can Speak to Parents

In our sanctuaries, Bible-study classes, and seminars, we have regular opportunities to teach our people how to respond biblically to challenges they face in the culture and in their own homes. Why, then, shouldn't we be teaching parents how to respond to this issue?

We can first make certain that the parents in our churches have a clear understanding of what Scripture has to say about homosexual behavior, and about loving our neighbor, and about God's grace, and about the power of love and community when it comes to drawing people out of sinful behaviors.

All of these are equally important, so let's not teach one without the other. If all our parents know is that homosexual behavior is a sin, they're not likely to offer much warmth and compassion to a homosexual teen, even if it's one of their own. Conversely, if all they know is compassion without convictions of right or wrong, all they'll have to offer is sentiment. It's critical that pastors and church leaders make certain the mothers and fathers who support their churches are getting a biblically based education in godly standards and compassion. This alone will do much to make our ministry to gay teens effective.

But that's not enough. Parents need to be taught to face the very real possibility that one of their own may step outside the parameters they've been taught as children. What will they say and do if a teenage daughter or son says to them, "Mom, Dad, I've lost my virginity," or "I've looked at porn," or "I'm pregnant."

Or even, "I'm gay."

Doubtless we hope no parent in our churches will ever hear these words, but experience shows that, indeed, some will. Wouldn't it be better if they were prepared to respond lovingly, clearly, redemptively? We don't plan on earthquakes happening, but we prepare for them. And there's no reason we shouldn't be prepared for familial earthquakes as well, since they happen to the best of us.

We Can Speak to Our Teens

We also have a responsibility to prepare our kids to deal with people who hold different views and live differently as well. It's naïve not to realize our kids are very likely to know someone who's homosexual. Wouldn't it be better if they knew how to dialogue with, relate to, love, and respect such a person? On the one hand, the culture is making a case to our children against everything we're teaching them about love, sex, and marriage. Shouldn't we work to preempt that presentation by making our own to our kids before the culture beats us to the punch?

But on the other hand, while we teach our kids to know where they should stand on moral issues, heaven forbid they join the chorus of cruel, callous kids who taunt, heckle, and terrorize their gay schoolmates. Let's teach love, respect, and conviction in equal measures to our kids, making sure, through our youth curricula and Sunday school classes, that they're prepared to deal with their homosexual peers in a Christlike manner. My question to every church leader and Christian parent is this: Has your church provided your young people with any teaching that prepares them to address this subject? Do they know the biblical guidelines for human sexuality? Do they know what Scripture teaches about homosexual behavior? Have they a clue how to witness to a gay friend?

If so, great. But if not, then let's do it now.

We Can Stay Relevant

Christians are called many things, like bigoted, homophobic, backward, uneducated. Usually we let the words roll off our backs, as we should. But one word we hope we will never be rightfully charged with is *irrelevant*. The gospel is, after all, always relevant, as is God Himself. If we're His followers, can we afford to be anything less than relevant to a hurting culture?

So are we prepared for the gay teenager who will come to our youth groups? Shawn Harrison, youth leader at Exodus International, reminds us,

> The days of wondering if a gay teen might show up to your youth ministries are now over—gay teens are coming to youth ministries. Therefore, youth workers need to become aware of what to do and how to do it.[12]

Are the youth leaders among us ready to explain to that teenager the following?

- the claims of Christ and the gospel
- their value in God's sight and in ours
- our invitation to them (gay teens) to be part of the church activities
- our position on homosexual behavior
- our request that if they disagree with that position, they will at least respect it while being with us

- our hope that they'll feel free to come to us with any questions they may have about this, and to talk with us anytime they want to pursue a walk with Christ

- what they can expect if they reject homosexual behavior and embrace a lifestyle of abstinence before marriage

If we can't explain these points to a gay teenager who walks into our church, we're not operating in relevance. And relevance is, today, more critical than ever. This subject is surely not going away. If anything, it's forcing itself on the church more and more, and nowhere is that pressure showing itself so keenly as it is among our young.

Shawn Harrison explains this well in an article written to help youth workers recognize the needs of homosexual teenagers. In his essay titled "Ministry to Gay Students," he offers the following crucial ministry tips:[13]

1. *Be ready to deal with your own stereotypes and prejudices.* If you are tense about discussing this issue, if you are uncomfortable around gay people in general, you must deal with these things before any gay student will trust you and open up to you. They want (and need) to feel safe. Youth workers need to continuously be informed about the issues surrounding homosexuality!

2. *Be willing to pray for wisdom, understanding, and for God's pure love to flow through you.* When dealing with students who struggle with their sexual identity, many straight students and youth leaders may feel unsure about themselves and about being around their same-sex peers. Many have several layers of "stuff" built around wounded hearts. The more you pray for God's Spirit to pour from you into students, the better prepared you'll be in this journey.

3. *Be aware: This is a journey, not a walk in the park.* Do not bail out on a student once you have begun this journey with them—unless you already have someone to take your place (one that the student already knows and trusts). Please determine to stay the course. Too many times, too many people have started to walk with gay teens and have left them standing alone when the going gets tough. Given that most gay teens have unhealthy relationships, the last thing they need is their youth worker walking out on them too.

4. *Be advised: Same-sex attraction is mainly about broken relationships*

between the sexes. Students need to find and connect with healthy same-sex relationships. This needs to be done with great discernment and prayer. Those connected to gay teens should be people who are spiritually mature in their faith. It would be beneficial to use men and women who have gone through some (or all) the struggles the teen is facing. However, make sure that those adults can handle walking alongside a gay teen.

5. *Be ready to offer counseling* as a means to help your students open up about the pending issues. Refer students to outside support groups and counseling when needed—and it will be needed. Also, besides finding the students resources, be sure to find resources for the parents too. Family support groups are a big plus in helping parents stay connected with their struggling teen.

6. *Be ready to set strict guidelines in your ministry:* No gay jokes, no gay puns, no gay anything…it isn't cool, and it does major damage to those within the group…Gay students are looking for a safe place to plug into…Change your vocab—the students follow by example; teach about all sin, not just the gay verses; God hates all sin, and no sin is higher than another.

7. *Be ready to pray.* And when you have finished praying, pray again. As said before, the more you invite the Spirit into your situation to lead and direct you, the greater the results.

To which I can only add, God help us to recognize, relate, and respond. For all of our sakes.

CHAPTER NINETEEN

GAY TEENS

○——KEY POINTS——○

1. Though there's more openness than ever among teens regarding homosexual behavior, being a teenager and experiencing same-sex attractions is still very difficult for many gay teens.

2. Not everyone who experiments with homosexual behavior is in fact homosexual, and many teenagers may have a homosexual experience and incorrectly conclude that this alone makes them gay.

3. Studies indicate that gay teens are at higher risk for suicide attempts, drug abuse, and other emotional or behavioral problems.

4. The church has a responsibility to educate Christian parents, who in turn educate their own children about homosexuality and teach them how to speak both love and truth to the homosexual.

5. The church has a responsibility to educate Christian parents how to respond if their own children stray outside biblical boundaries of sexual behavior.

6. The church has a responsibility to be relevant by being prepared to deal with gay teens who are very likely to come to our churches and seek community and ministry.

RESOURCES

Exodus Youth at http://exodusyouth.net/youth/.

Groundswell Conference on Youth and Homosexuality, http://ground swell2006.org/groundswell/.

NOTES

1. Gary Remafedi, Michael Resnick, Robert Blum, and Linda Harris, "Demography of Sexual Orientation in Adolescents," *Pediatrics,* vol. 89, no. 4 (April 1992), pp. 714-721.

2. Jeffrey Satinover, *Homosexuality and the Politics of Truth* (Grand Rapids, MI: Baker Books, 1996), p. 111.

3. *Time* magazine's cover story for October 10, 2005, is "The Battle Over Gay Teens" by gay journalist John Cloud.

4. Cloud.

5. Cloud.

6. Ritch C. Savin-Williams, *The New Gay Teenager* (Cambridge, MA: Harvard University Press, 2005).

7. See, for example, the Gay Lesbian Straight Educators Network at www.glsen.org/cgi-bin/iowa/student/student/index.html.

8. Cited on *Box Turtle Bulletin* blog, April 7, 2008.

9. Marilyn Elias, "Gay teens coming out earlier to peers and family," *USA Today,* February 7, 2007.

10. Richard Fitzgibbons, "Gay Teens: Studies on Emotional/Relational Health," October 17, 2005, www.narth.com/docs/instability.html.

11. Dale O'Leary, "Gays and Attempted Suicide," September 3, 2008, www.narth.com/docs/inst ability.html.

12. Shawn Harrison, "Ministry to Gay Students," http://exodusyouth.net/2009/08/20/ministry-to-gay-students/#more-421.

13. Harrison.

PART SIX

SAME-SEX MARRIAGE

by Bill Maier, PsyD

*Marriage, like money, is still with us;
and, like money, progressively devalued.*

—"Real Women," *Ladies' Home Journal*, January 1964

Currently American society is undergoing what I believe is the most radical social experiment ever proposed in our nation—redefining the institution of marriage. This experiment was forced on the people of Massachusetts in 2004 by four judges on that state's Supreme Court. Four judges on California's Supreme Court did the same in 2008, when they overruled the will of the citizens of California and legalized gay marriage there, introducing a polarizing election in which Californians voted 54 percent to reaffirm the traditional definition of marriage.

Because we don't, as of this writing, have a marriage protection amendment in the United States Constitution, we're really just one Supreme Court decision away from legalizing same-sex marriage in this country. Given the current makeup of the Court, it's anybody's guess how they would rule on the issue.

When we consider the same-sex marriage experiment, it's important to remember that what we're talking about here is a *radical redefinition of the human family*. Up until the last few "milliseconds" of human history, no society anywhere in the world, at any time in recorded history, has ever affirmed homosexual marriage. Until very recent history, homosexual unions have never officially been considered a normal, morally equal part of any culture. If you were to spin a classroom globe, stop it, and put your finger on any inhabited land mass, you would find that marriage is, and has always been, about men and women committing themselves to each other and to raising the next generation.

It doesn't matter whether you visit the remotest part of Siberia or a tiny Polynesian island, you will not find *any* culture where the basic family unit is headed by two men or two women.

But in the past few years, a few Western countries (and a few state judges and politicians) have been arrogant enough to believe that we can take marriage and reconfigure it, dismantle it, and dismember it, and not suffer any negative consequences.

When we're discussing same-sex marriage, it's critical that we clearly articulate what this debate is really about and what it's *not* about.

- It's *not* about whether gays and lesbians are nice people or good citizens. Some are, some aren't, just like heterosexuals.

- It's *not* about whether gays and lesbians can form loving relationships—of course they can. (We might argue that they are not experiencing love as God intended for it to be experienced, but they certainly share feelings of affection.)

- It's *not* about whether gays and lesbians can be loving parents. There are nurturing, caring gay couples raising children all across this country. (Whether they are providing their children with what they truly need is another matter, which we'll talk about in just a bit.)

- It's *not* about whether gays and lesbians should be treated with respect and dignity. Every member of the human race should be treated with respect and dignity.

Here's what I believe this debate *is* about:

- It's about whether we have the right to redefine marriage so it is elastic enough to include any grouping of adults.

- It's about whether we acknowledge the wonderful human diversity expressed in the two sexes, male and female.

- It's about whether men and women complement and complete each other in their differences.

- It's about whether mothers and fathers play unique and irreplaceable roles in the lives of children, precisely *because* of their sex.

- It's about whether there are compelling societal reasons to define marriage as one thing and not as another.

The Institution of Marriage

Let's take a look at the institution of marriage for a moment. As Christians, we believe that heterosexual marriage was established by God. Genesis 1:27 tells us: "God created man in His own image; in the image of God He created him; male and female He created them."

We could spend an entire seminary course unpacking that statement, but let's focus on the second half of the verse. God created human beings as two distinct, complementary sexes.

Some theologians like to use the term "co-humanity." In other words, male coupling cannot display the complete image of God, and female coupling cannot display the complete image of God.

Jesus made that clear to the Pharisees in Matthew 19:4:

> "Haven't you read," Jesus replied, "that at the beginning the Creator 'made them male and female,' and said, 'For this reason a man will leave his father and mother and be united to his wife, and the two will become one flesh'? So they are no longer two, but one" (NIV).

Here Jesus clearly and powerfully spells out God's intent for marriage: God created human beings as male and female...marriage unites the two complementary sides of humanity into "one flesh."

C.S Lewis makes a beautiful and relevant statement about marriage in his book *Mere Christianity*.

> The Christian idea of marriage is based on Christ's words that a man and wife are to be regarded as a single organism—for that is what the words "one flesh" would be in modern English. And the Christians believe that when He said this He was not expressing a

> sentiment but stating a fact, just as one is stating a fact when one
> says that a lock and its key are one mechanism, or that a violin
> and a bow are one musical instrument. The inventor of the human
> machine was telling us that its two halves, the male and the female,
> were made to be combined together in pairs, not simply on the sex-
> ual level, but totally combined.[1]

I love his analogy of a violin and a bow. Have you been to see a symphony orchestra at some point? You've probably noticed that the various "sections" of musicians are seated in a particular order in the stage. Typically the string section is near the front, and leading the string section is the "first violinist," often the most experienced, competent violinist.

As the symphony is about to begin, the conductor makes his way to the plat-form, raises his baton, and *voilà!* Beautiful music!

But think about a violin—a beautiful Stradivarius, worth tens of thousands of dollars. That violin cannot be completed by another violin. And a bow can-not be completed by another bow. The violin needs the bow and the bow needs the violin…and *together* they fulfill the purpose *for which they were created.*

Since marriage was created by God, it naturally follows that it is a universal human institution. Even a non-Christian can pick up an anthropology text-book, examine any culture at any time in history, and find that families look remarkably similar.

While a few societies have practiced polygamy, the core of the family has always consisted of men and women raising the next generation in a cooper-ative way.

And marriage is not just a Christian institution—don't get caught up in that debate. Every one of the major world religions upholds and honors marriage between a man and a woman.

The Benefits of Marriage

In the public debate over same-sex marriage, pro-gay spokespersons often argue that same-sex couples should be given the same status and recognition that is given to heterosexual couples. But it's critical to remember that the *rea-son* society provides benefits to married couples is because *marriage provides benefits to society.*

There is a virtual mountain of social science data showing how marriage benefits *adults, children,* and *society.* Let's take a look at some of that research for a moment. Bear in mind that these findings apply to natural, heterosexual marriages, where children are being raised by their biological mother and father. There is no evidence that homosexual marriage would provide these things... in fact in some ways, homosexual relationships are qualitatively different from heterosexual relationships. I'll explain how in just a moment.

How does marriage benefit adults? Here are a few ways:

- Married people have better emotional and physical health and live longer than unmarried people.
- Married couples have greater incomes than single adults, and the longer they stay married, the more wealth they accumulate.
- Married couples enjoy greater sexual satisfaction than unmarried people.
- Married women are safer than unmarried women. Never-married, cohabiting, separated, and divorced women experience higher rates of domestic violence than married women.

The research also tells us that marriage benefits children:

- Children living with married parents are much safer than children living with single parents, because they are less likely to be aborted and less likely to be abused or neglected.
- Compared to children in single-parent families, children raised in married-parent homes have better emotional and physical health and engage in fewer risky behaviors, such as premarital sex, substance abuse, delinquency, and suicide.
- Children with married parents do better academically and fare better economically.
- Children raised in intact homes are also less likely to cohabit and more likely to view marriage positively and maintain life-long marriages themselves.

And here are some of the benefits that marriage provides to society.

- Marriage makes homes safer places to live, because it curbs social problems such as domestic violence and child abuse.

- Communities with more married-parent families are safer and more attractive places to live, because they are less likely to have substance abuse and crime among young people.

- Marriage is the best antidote to poverty and welfare dependency. In fact, almost every dollar we spend on social programs can be traced to out-of-wedlock childbearing, fatherlessness, and the negative impacts of family breakdown.

- Married people are more likely to be healthy, productive, and engaged citizens, benefiting businesses and, ultimately, the economy.

Research findings like these never cease to amaze me, as a Christian psychologist. We can see so clearly that God is the great architect of creation. When we follow His blueprint for human relationships, things work the way they are supposed to. However, when we defy God and live in ways that are contrary to His design, we often reap a harvest of pain and suffering.

The Results of Same-Sex Marriage

One of the claims you'll hear from same-sex marriage supporters is that gay marriage will provide these same good things to society. In fact, the more conservative gay activists (like Andrew Sullivan) claim that same-sex marriage will cause gay men to "settle down" and become monogamous. But recent research from the Netherlands doesn't support that belief.

Stability

Civil unions and same-sex marriage have been legal in the Netherlands for several years. Researchers in Amsterdam recently conducted a long-term study of male homosexual relationships which was published in the journal *AIDS*. The fact that the subjects were HIV positive must be taken into account, but nonetheless, here's what they found:[2]

- Gay men in "steady partnerships" stay together for an average of 18 months.

- Gay men with a "steady partner" have an average of eight "additional" sexual partners per year.

Research here in the United States mirrors those findings. Sociologist Edward

Laumann and his colleagues at the University of Chicago have found that monogamy and fidelity are virtually nonexistent in the male homosexual community.[3]

Michelangelo Signorile, a gay activist and writer, is more realistic about the nature of male gay relationships. Here's what he says:

> For these men the term "monogamy" simply doesn't necessarily mean sexual exclusivity...The term "open relationship" has for a great many gay men come to have one specific definition: A relationship in which the partners have sex on the outside often, put away their resentment and jealousy, and discuss their outside sex with each other, or share sex partners.[4]

So as our children and grandchildren observe the marriages of gay men on their block or in their neighborhood, what will they learn?

They'll learn that marriage no longer means being faithful and committed to one person for life. Monogamy and fidelity will simply become outdated concepts that no longer apply to marriage.

We don't have to look further than Cody Rogahn and Jonathan Yarbrough. Cody and Jonathan were the first couple in line when Massachusetts began issuing gay marriage licenses two years ago. When a reporter from the *Boston Herald* asked them about their relationship, Jonathan said this:

> I think it's possible to love more than one person and have more than one partner...In our case, it is. We have an open marriage.[5]

Unlimited Redefinition?

As we face the prospect of same-sex marriage in California, we need to consider the other possible ramifications of such an untested social experiment. It's critical for each of us to look at what may lie ahead. If we redefine marriage in one way, there is no logical reason for us not to redefine it in other ways.

We're already hearing demands for equality from those who advocate polygamy or group marriage, known as "polyamory." They argue that if marriage can be redefined to include two men or two women, what's to stop us from redefining it to allow marriage between a man and four women, or a group of six or seven adults and their various children?

If you don't believe this is a very real possibility just look at the Netherlands.

Two years ago, newspaper headlines declared the first polygamous wedding there, as *one man married two women* in a civil union ceremony.[6]

Many groups and academics here in the United States are arguing for the legalization of group marriage.[7] If you don't believe it, just go on the Internet and enter the word "polyamory" into a search engine.

What about age restrictions or prohibitions on marrying close blood relatives? If marriage is simply about a person's right to marry the person they "love," there is no logical reason why those restrictions should be in place. If a father wants to marry his 14-year-old daughter, on what grounds can we deny him? Wouldn't that be discrimination?

Government Enforcement

Same-sex marriage will also teach our children that the words "male and female" and "mother and father" are simply meaningless, outdated ideas. If same-sex marriage is the law of the land, our public schools and textbooks will be required to reinforce those concepts.

Shortly after same-sex marriage was legalized in Massachusetts, Boston teachers were sent a memo from the superintendent of schools threatening them with disciplinary action if they did not present same-sex marriage to their classes in a positive light.[8]

According to National Public Radio, a lesbian teacher in Brookline, Massachusetts, named Deb Allen now openly teaches her eighth-grade students about gay sex. She says she does it "thoroughly and explicitly, using a chart." If parents complain, Ms. Allen says, "Give me a break—it's legal now."[9]

As Christians, we should realize that nationwide same-sex marriage could mean a very real threat to our religious freedom. Christians who dare to suggest that gay marriage is somehow wrong or immoral may be cited for a hate crime. It's already happening in Sweden and Canada.

A pastor in Sweden, Rev. Ake Green, was arrested in his own church for quoting Bible verses dealing with homosexuality.[10] And a Catholic bishop in Calgary, Alberta, was hauled before a human rights tribunal, accused of "hate speech." What did he do? He dared to suggest in a pastoral letter that same-sex marriage was contrary to God's will.[11]

And we're already seeing the clash between same-sex marriage and religious freedom in the U.S., with the case of the Methodist Camp Meeting Association in Ocean Grove, New Jersey. This is a historic church camp on the New Jersey shore—and they have a beautiful pavilion overlooking the Atlantic. A lesbian couple wanted to hold their civil union ceremony there, but the association turned down their request because a gay civil union would violate their religious beliefs. The lesbian couple filed a complaint with the state, and as a result, the Methodists lost a state tax exemption for part of their property.[12]

Perhaps the saddest thing about same-sex marriage is that it places adult desires above the best interest of children. Why? Because it intentionally creates motherless or fatherless families. That's probably the most important thing to remember when you are discussing same-sex marriage with those on the other side of this issue.

Children Need Mothers *and* Fathers

Same-sex marriage intentionally creates motherless or fatherless families. *Permanently* motherless or fatherless families. Gay activists will tell you that all children need is two "caring adults." But children need more than that…They need a mommy and a daddy.

That's because mothers and fathers parent differently and provide very different things to their children. There are numerous academic studies[13] demonstrating that kids do better on *every measure of well-being* when they are raised by their married, biological parents.

So what does the research *really* say about the effects of same-sex parenting on kids? We don't have a lot of hard data on this, because gay parenting is a fairly recent phenomenon. The research is also complicated because of a host of methodological problems—for example, a married woman with children decides to divorce her husband and move in with her lesbian lover. Not only are the kids being raised by two women, they are also impacted by the effects of divorce.

One the most comprehensive reviews of the same-sex parenting literature to date was conducted by sociologists Judith Stacey and Timothy Biblarz at the University of Southern California. Stacey and Biblarz reviewed 21 of the most significant studies in the field—they crunched the numbers and examined the research methodology. Their analysis was published in the journal *American Sociological Review.*

You should know that Dr. Stacey and Dr. Biblarz both personally support same-sex marriage and parenting, and Dr. Stacey regularly advocates for gay marriage in academic circles and in the media.[14] And yet, in their review of the research, they noted some significant differences in children raised by gay couples.[14]

- They are more likely to engage in behavior that is non-normative for their gender. (These are Stacey and Biblarz's words—the way I read the research, the little boys aren't really sure what it means to be male, and the little girls aren't really sure what it means to be female.)

- The girls are more likely to be promiscuous. (Stacey and Biblarz spun the language a bit with this finding and said, "Well, the girls tend to be *less chaste.*" Sorry, but the research clearly shows that these girls are *more promiscuous.*)

- And finally, both the boys and the girls are more likely to experiment with homosexual behavior. That doesn't mean they will ultimately self-identify as gay adults, but it does mean they are more likely to "give it a try"—to experiment with same-sex relationships as teens and young adults.

Stacey and Biblarz aren't concerned about these differences, but as a child psychologist, I'm very concerned about them.

Complementary Contributions

Gay marriage advocates will tell you that what children really need is "two loving adults in their lives" and that the sex of those adults doesn't matter. The assumption is that mothers and fathers are optional and interchangeable.

But many leading scholars believe that mothers and fathers provide unique contributions in the lives of their children precisely *because* of their gender. Sarah McClanahan at Princeton, Kyle Pruett at Yale, and David Popenoe at Rutgers have done extensive research on how children benefit from growing up in a home with their married, biological parents. These researchers and others have examined the parenting styles of men and women and found that mothers and fathers actually parent differently:[15]

- For example, when it comes to child discipline, fathers tend to be "rule-based," stressing justice, fairness, and duty; mothers tend to be "relationship-based," stressing sympathy, care, and help.

- Mothers and fathers also have different communication styles. Fathers tend to be more brief, directive, and to the point, while mothers tend to be more descriptive, personal, and verbally encouraging.

- Mothers and fathers even play differently with their kids. In their play, fathers tend to encourage competition, while mothers tend to encourage equity.

- Fathers tend to wrestle and tickle more, and they throw their children into the air. In fact, one study found that 70 percent of father-infant games were more physical and action-oriented, while only 4 percent of mother-infant play was like this.

Child Trends, a nonprofit, nonpartisan research organization dedicated to improving the lives of children, set out to discover what type of family structure best contributes to child well-being. Here's how they sum up the literature:

> An extensive body of research tells us that children do best when they grow up with both biological parents…Thus, it is not simply the presence of *two parents*, as some have assumed, but the presence of *two biological parents* that seems to support children's development.[16]

I want to conclude with a real-life story about same-sex parenting, and a member of a same-sex couple we're all familiar with.

One of Hollywood's most famous lesbians is comedienne Rosie O'Donnell. Years ago, the ABC Television news program *Primetime* did a two-hour special on gay adoption.[17] Host Diane Sawyer interviewed Rosie, who spoke glowingly about her lesbian relationship and the three children she and her partner Kelly have adopted.

During the program, Sawyer asked Rosie if her then six-year-old son, Parker, ever asks why he doesn't have a daddy. Rosie replied, "Oh yes, all the time." Diane seemed surprised by this admission, so she asked Rosie what she told him.

When Parker asks why he can't have a daddy, Rosie said she tells him this: "Because I'm the kind of mommy who wants another mommy."

A just, compassionate society should always come to the aid of motherless or fatherless families. But a just, compassionate society should never, ever, intentionally create motherless and fatherless families. And that's exactly what same-sex marriage does.

CHAPTER TWENTY

SAME-SEX MARRIAGE

○—KEY POINTS—○

1. The concept of same-sex marriage constitutes more than an adjustment to our current understanding of marriage. It constitutes a radical redefinition of the human family, unprecedented in human history.

2. To disapprove of the redefinition of marriage is *not* to discount the capacity of same-sex couples for love, intimacy, or the capacity to love and care for children. It is, rather, to recognize same-sex marriage as not being in the best interest of children.

3. The role of both a father and mother in the lives of children are irreplaceable, and are absent in even the most ideal of same-sex unions.

4. Marriage as created and defined by God in Scripture is a universal institution, historically identifiable in virtually all cultures, among people of all beliefs.

5. Studies indicate that marriage as traditionally defined provides maximum physical and emotional benefits, higher income, and greater sexual satisfaction.

6. Studies indicate that children living with traditionally defined married parents are physically and emotionally healthier, academically perform better, and are financially more successful as adults.

7. Marriage as traditionally defined benefits the community at large, as communities with higher ratios of married-parent families have lower incidents of substance abuse, crime, and poverty.

8. Where same-sex marriage has been initiated, studies indicate that its definition changes, especially as it pertains to monogamy.

9. The redefinition of marriage virtually guarantees a further redefining, as other changes to its traditional definition will logically follow.

10. The revision of the definition of marriage to include same-sex couples has serious implications for the future of freedom of speech and religion, as religious individuals and institutions objecting to same-sex marriage are likely to experience restrictions and repercussions.

BOOKS ON SAME-SEX MARRIAGE

Marriage on Trial by Glenn Stanton and Bill Maier, InterVarsity Press, 2004.

Same-sex Marriage: Putting Every Family at Risk by Mathew Staver, B and H Publishing, 2004.

Marriage Under Fire by James Dobson, Multnomah Press, 2004.

ONLINE RESOURCES

"Same-sex Marriage: A Selective Bibliography of the Legal Literature," compiled by Paul Axel-Lute (a comprehensive online bibliography of legal decisions regarding the definition of marriage, articles for and against same-sex marriage, and state-by-state synopsis of court decisions, regularly updated). See at: http://law–library.rutgers.edu/SSM.html.

NOTES

1. C.S. Lewis, *Mere Christianity* (New York: HarperCollins, 2002), p. 61.

2. "Study finds gay unions brief," *Washington Times,* July 11, 2003, www.washingtontimes.com/news/2003/jul/11/20030711-121254-3711r/.

3. Adrian Brune, "City Gays Skip Long-term Relationships: Study Says," *Washington Blade,* February 27, 2004, p. 12.

4. Michelangelo Signorile, *Life Outside* (New York: HarperCollins, 1997), p. 213.

5. "Same-sex couple flaunts 'open marriage'" World Net Daily, May 18, 2004, www.wnd.com/news/article.asp?ARTICLE_ID=38537.

6. "First trio married in the Netherlands," *The Brussels Journal,* September 27, 2005, www.brusselsjournal.com/node/301.

7. See, for example: "Legalize Polygamy," *The National Post,* www.nationalpost.com/story.html?id=8451dc17-5b5f-4ea4-a05f-71f7c758662a; John Tierney, "Who's Afraid of Polygamy?" *New York Times,* March 11, 2006, http://query.nytimes.com/gst/fullpage.html?res=9C04EEDA1331F932A25750C0A9609C8B63&sec=&spon=&pagewanted=all; "Lawsuit uses repeal of sodomy laws to support Utah polygamy," *The Advocate* magazine, August 6, 2004, cited at www.glapn.org/sodomylaws/usa/utah/utnews026.htm.

8. "An examination of the constitutional amendment on marriage": transcript from hearing before the Subcommittee on the Constitution, Civil Rights and Property Rights of the Committee on the

Judiciary, United States Senate, 109th Congress, First Sessions, http://bulk.resource.org/gpo.gov/hearings/109s/24661.txt.

9. Transcript of National Public Radio broadcast, September 13, 2004, cited at Mass Resistance website, www.massresistance.org/docs/a8a/general/NPR_091304.htm.

10. Cited at the Ake Green website, www.akegreen.org/.

11. Cited on the Religious Tolerance website, www.religioustolerance.org/hom_marb45.htm.

12. "Gay Rights, Religious Liberties: A Three-Act Story," National Public Radio broadcast, June 16, 2008, www.npr.org/templates/story/story.php?storyId=91486340.

13. See chapter 22 of this volume: *Gay Parenting: Plus, Minus, or Equal?* for citations to studies regarding same-sex versus opposite-sex parenting.

14. Judith Stacey and Timothy J. Biblarz, "(How) Does the Sexual Orientation of Parents Matter?" *American Sociological Review,* vol. 66, no. 2 (April 2001), pp. 159-183.

15. See Sara McLanahan and Gary Sandefur, *Growing Up with a Single Parent: What Hurts, What Helps* (Cambridge, MA: Harvard University Press, 1994); Claudia Quigg's remarks on Kyle Pruitt in "What Dads Do for Kids," www.babytalk.org/whats-new/Lets-talk-columns-2006/20060617-What-Dads-do-for-Kids.html; David Popenoe, "Life without Father," http://mensightmagazine.com/Articles/Popenoe/nofathers.htm.

16. Kristin Anderson Moore, Susan M. Jekielek, and Carol Emig, "Marriage from a Child's Perspective: How Does Family Structure Affect Children, and What Can We Do about It?" *Child Trends Research Brief,* June 2002, www.childtrends.org/files/MarriageRB602.pdf.

17. Quoted in Gary Palmer, "The Defining Issue of our Time," *The Hawaiian Reporter,* May 28, 2004, www.hawaiireporter.com/story.aspx?d8567e33-c327-40ba-bf9c-ce8442e47405.

GAYS IN THE MILITARY

by Joe Dallas

The military is not popular culture. Those who favor
personnel policies grounded in notions of fairness to the
individual must be required to demonstrate beyond any
doubt that military discipline, unit cohesion, and combat
effectiveness will not be diminished one iota by adoption of
their preferred policy. Otherwise, it elevates the individual
over the mission and that is the antithesis of military service.

—PROFESSOR OF LAW WILLIAM A. WOODRUFF

In 1993 newly elected President Bill Clinton learned the hard way just how contentious the subject of gays in the military could be. Having assured the homosexual population, "I have a vision and you're part of it,"[1] he began his presidency with sleeves rolled up to make good on his promises to them, including his commitment to lifting the existing military ban on homosexuality. But the opposition was swift and startling, coming from the Joint Chiefs of Staff, members of Congress in both parties, and a considerable segment of the U.S. public.

Polls indicated that 67 percent of Republicans and 45 percent of Democrats were against changing the policy.[2] Democratic Senator Sam Nunn of Georgia organized congressional hearings and conducted well-publicized interviews with military personnel adverse to lifting the ban, two Department of Defense reports were published defending the ban and arguing for its preservation, and congressional phone lines were soon jammed with calls from constituents opposing Clinton's plan. Clearly, the new president's hope for an immediate change in policy was unrealistic and a compromise was called for. "Don't Ask, Don't Tell"—a policy under which military personnel would no longer be asked if they were homosexual, and under which homosexual personnel were under no threat of discharge unless they volunteered such information—was born.

Why such a reaction? Was it warranted, and how different would the outcome be today? A brief look at the history of homosexuality and the military may help explain, while shedding light on both traditional and current views on the subject.

Homosexuality and the Military Ideal: A Changeable Status

It should first be observed that while Scripture condemns homosexual behavior, it says nothing of the general characteristics of homosexual people. So Leviticus forbids the male homosexual act (Leviticus 18:22 and 20:13), Paul describes same-sex eroticism as unnatural to the Romans (Romans 1:26-27) and, writing to both the Corinthians and Timothy, he places it alongside a number of other vices, both sexual and nonsexual (1 Corinthians 6:9-10; 1 Timothy 1:9-11).

None of these verses describe the mannerisms or personalities of homosexual people. They don't declare homosexual men to be culturally effeminate, nor lesbians to be masculine, so holding a biblical position doesn't require us to do so either. If anything, the Bible's refusal to pigeonhole homosexuals into one stereotypical image calls us to a similar refusal, so we do well to acknowledge that some homosexual males are masculine, some feminine; some lesbians conform to the stereotypical "butch" image, others are markedly "ladylike"; and many homosexuals of both sexes fall between the two extremes. One can know a behavior to be wrong while assuming little else about the person involved in it.

The error of stereotyping leads a number of believers to assume an openly gay man would be "swishy," obnoxious, and sexually aggressive. That, in turn, makes the idea of working alongside a homosexual (much less living and fighting alongside one in close quarters) abhorrent to some people. Comments sometimes heard from men when asked about gays in the military include, "Who wants to fight next to a fairy?"; "I don't wanna sleep beside some guy who's gonna make passes at me"; or "Gays can't fight! Everyone knows they're sissies who couldn't handle combat."[3] And while there are valid concerns raised by the question of openly homosexual service men and women, stereotypes like these tend to weaken arguments that might otherwise have merit.

To those assuming a homosexual male cannot be masculine (that is, physically strong, aggressive, and unafraid), the idea of such a man engaged in conventionally masculine activities is far-fetched. Many a man working the rodeo, running the scrimmage, or laboring in the construction site does so with certainty that his rugged partner or co-worker is heterosexual. Those roles are for "real men," after all, so gays need not apply. But history shows that such a limited view hasn't always been the dominant one.

Ancient Greece is an easy and obvious case in point, where warriors in openly sexual relationships with each other were often held in high regard. One of many famous examples is found in the Sacred Band of Thebes, an army of 500 soldiers literally and selectively paired as couples, who defeated a Spartan army three times their size in 375 BC. Then four years later, they won a decisive battle at Leuctra, again vanquishing the Spartans and establishing Thebes' independence from Sparta, commemorated as a battle by which "all Greece won independence and freedom."[4] Some have suggested the idea of forming an army of lovers came from remarks made in Plato's *Symposium*, in which the character Phaedrus suggests their battle-worthiness:

> For what lover would not choose rather to be seen by all mankind
> than by his beloved, either when abandoning his post or throwing
> away his arms? He would be ready to die a thousand deaths rather
> than endure this. Or who would desert his beloved or fail him in
> the hour of danger?[5]

Aristogeiton and Harmodius, a male couple who plotted assassination against the tyrant brothers Hippias and Hipparchus in 514 BC, were revered as martyrs to the cause of freedom in Athens.[6] And a popular account that may be part fable centers on Antileon and Melanippus, two lovers so appalled at the sadism of the tyrant Phalaris they plotted to overthrow him. They failed in their attempt, but popular fifth-century Greek legend has them showing such bravery under Phalaris's punishment of torture that the tyrant was moved to not only release and pardon them, but to praise them as well.[7]

Similar accounts from Ancient Greece, Rome, and medieval times are easily found[8] to reinforce the point that homosexuality and masculinity, even the masculinity of the battlefield, have not always been seen as mutually exclusive. And while earlier cultures were by no means unanimous in their views on sex between men—some pro, some con, some conceptualizing it very differently than we do today—there's ample evidence that it was not always seen as a deficit of manliness.

Prohibitions and Stigma

But in Western culture, largely influenced by Judeo-Christian values, same-sex relations have traditionally been prohibited, and those involved stigmatized. The prohibitions were and are primarily founded in Scripture, but the stigmatization often has roots in less noble prejudices.

Both prohibitions and stigma, then, have coexisted in American society for some time. The prohibitions have been reflected in laws, moral consensus, and public policy, including military policies, but the stigma has been less official, though widespread. Homosexuals portrayed in films from the 1930s through the 1970s were generally unbalanced, flamboyant, self-hating, or weak, or behaved more like the opposite sex than their own. "Queer" jokes were acceptable stand-up comic fare until recently; students not conforming to gender norms were and sometimes still are subject to relentless teasing and bullying. And while society has considered many sexual behaviors to be sinful, fornicators and adulterers have seldom experienced the social contempt historically reserved for homosexuals. Prohibition says, "That's wrong"; stigma says, "You're disgusting." Along with *disgusting* come concepts like predatory, sick, sissy, or butch or mannish, all of which have been ascribed by many heterosexuals to all homosexuals.

That being the case, it's easy to see why objections to gays and lesbians serving openly in the military have been a mixed bag of moral conviction, prejudice, and legitimate concerns about military readiness and effectiveness, all of which have played into past and current policies.

The first recorded discharge for homosexual conduct within American troops occurred during the Revolutionary War in 1778, the first of many citing oral or anal intercourse under the term "sodomy."[9] In fact, the term dishonorable discharge came to be so closely associated with homosexuality that to be dishonorably discharged, unless the specific cause of the discharge was clear, invited suspicion of deviancy.

In early America, homosexuality being a vice seldom mentioned in polite company, it was easy to maintain bans against something so universally disapproved of. Since the lesbian woman or homosexual male was considered an aberration, it was unthinkable to allow one to share barracks, meals, and showers with other women and men. The combination of legitimate moral conviction and stigmatization was solid.

The Shift in Opinion

It remained so until the 1980s, with occasional challenges reflecting the slow but steady changes of public opinion regarding homosexuality. The most famous of these concerned decorated Air Force sergeant Leonard Matlovich, who, after revealing himself to his commanding officer shortly before the fall of Saigon in the mid 1970s, was discharged in a widely publicized case featured on the cover of *Time* magazine.[10]

Public opinion was just beginning its decades-long shift toward a more lenient view, evidenced by the support for a change in military policy among some Democratic presidential candidates in the 1980 primaries. The traditional view still held firm, though, and the Department of Defense in 1981 clarified and strengthened its position on homosexuality with DoD Directive 1332.14, citing homosexuality as "incompatible with military service," and the presence of homosexuals as something that would "adversely affect the ability of the armed forces to maintain discipline, good order and morale" making the ban necessary to "prevent breaches of security." The wording of 1332.14 solidified reasons traditionally unquestioned in the military:

- Homosexuality was considered immoral by most, so openly homosexual servicewomen and men would be an offense to others in the service, affecting morale.

- Since homosexual acts were still illegal in some states, and since homosexuality itself still carried a stigma, homosexual soldiers and ranking officers could be subjected to blackmail, making them security risks.

- Heterosexual servicewomen and men would find it intolerable showering and sharing bunks with others whom they knew to be homosexual.

- Prejudice against homosexuals would create tensions disruptive to morale and troop cohesion.

But by then the gay rights movement had made significant advances, some of which called these reasons into question. The American Psychiatric Association had removed homosexuality from its list of diagnosable disorders, antisodomy statutes were struck from the books of many states, gay pride parades were common events in some of America's biggest cities, and openly gay public figures—most notably the recently assassinated San Francisco supervisor Harvey Milk, pro football running back David Kopay, and tennis champ Billie Jean King—had put celebrity faces onto the issue. The stigma, so prevalent and powerful in the past, was starting to fade, and with it faded the strength of some, though not all, arguments for changing military policy.

After all, if the trend toward decriminalizing sodomy continued, and if social disapproval of homosexuality decreased correspondingly, concerns about gays and lesbians being blackmailed and becoming security risks had to lessen as well. The image of the "sissy-man" who'd be such an offense to fellow soldiers was being challenged by the likes of Kopay, as the notion of lesbians being uniformly mannish and abrasive was by King. And if general prejudice against homosexuals was waning, the concern about prejudiced soldiers clashing with homosexual comrades lost strength as well. Soon, those advocating reform in this area would point to the military's segregation policies of a few decades past, when African-American soldiers were considered by many white soldiers to be unsuitable bunkmates, and would argue that the issues were essentially the same.

That couldn't be said of other concerns immune to social trends. Heterosexual men and women could still be uncomfortable undressing, showering, and sleeping alongside those finding the same sex attractive, no matter how discreet the homosexual soldier might be. Moral objections to homosexuality, deeply held by many in the service, could create tensions no matter how politely they were voiced. And the specter of recruiting preferences and sensitivity training, both commonly enacted when a particular group is recognized within the service as a viable minority, was a real and (to some) dreaded possibility.

Broader issues came into play as well. By the 1980s, homosexuality had become a playing field on which conservatives and liberals fought, and hard. Many liberals came to see any success for gay rights as a victory for tolerance, a rejection of conservative thought and (at times) of conservatives themselves, and as increased acceptance of progressive ideas. Many conservatives likewise saw the defeat of gay rights as a moral imperative, each defeat reassuring continuation of important mores, and (at times) they viewed gay success, on any issue, as a setback. In short, the acceptance or rejection of pro-gay efforts became a barometer of the strength or weakness of the Left or the Right.

Military standards represent high ideals to the citizenry, so where the armed forces stand on an issue sends a message to the public at large, affecting, at some level, public opinion and mood. That being the case, a showdown between traditionalists and reformers over gays in the military was inevitable.

Clash and Open Debate

The conviction that homosexuality was incompatible with military service remained a policy cornerstone throughout the Reagan and Bush Sr. administrations, but a series of challenges kept revisiting it, both within the military and in the public arena. Publicized cases of lesbians or homosexual men being discharged received generous and, in most cases, sympathetic coverage from a media largely supportive of gay rights.[11] And while the military debate was important in and of itself, it should also be viewed as part of the broader struggle between liberal and conservative factions. No wonder, then, it became a prominent hot potato in 1992 when the first liberal Democratic president to occupy the White House in 12 years became commander in chief.

While running for office, Clinton had made no secret of his commitment to overturn the ban on gays in the military. It was a campaign promise, made at first without a clear timetable since he wanted to seek consensus and advice.[12] But upon taking office he launched into efforts to change the longstanding policy, and the resistance he encountered, indicating how many people still held the traditional view of homosexuality, provided a balance to the obvious shift in favor of gay rights that had emboldened him to push for this reform.

Rejecting Clinton's initial attempts to completely lift the military ban, Congress voted, after 12 legislative hearings and field trips, to essentially confirm existing policy. Questions regarding an inductee's sexual orientation would no longer be asked, and so long as the homosexual kept her or his orientation private, there'd be no reprisals. So while "Don't Ask, Don't Tell" was touted by the president as a compromise (and thus a step forward), it was, in fact, mostly a codification of existing law. And people on both sides were displeased with it.

Some on the pro-gay side felt he'd reneged on a promise he could have kept, despite his assertion that Republicans had forced him from his initial plan to the compromise of Don't Ask, Don't Tell.[13] Many on the other side saw DADT as an insult to the military leaders and service persons who'd expressed their clear desire to keep existing policy intact. The arguments on both sides of the debate were crystallizing, and to this day many of them are essentially the same.

Common Arguments for Allowing Homosexuals to Serve Openly

1. It's an established fact that lesbian women and homosexual men have honorably and effectively served in the military.

2. The cost of investigating charges against homosexuals in the service is exorbitant and unnecessary.

3. Qualified and needed military personnel are discharged because of this policy and the armed forces suffer as a result.

4. Surveys indicate strong public support for overturning DADT.

5. Other countries that allow openly gay and lesbian personnel to serve have suffered no damage to troop cohesion or morale.

6. Concerns about troop cohesion if homosexuals are allowed to openly serve are similar to those raised when the military racially integrated, and those concerns were found to be invalid.

Common Arguments for Banning Homosexuals from Serving Openly

1. Heterosexuals are likely to feel uncomfortable bunking and showering with those attracted to the same sex, for the same reason women would feel uncomfortable bunking and showering with men, and men would feel uncomfortable doing the same with women.

2. In cases of sexual harassment from someone of the same sex, the victim may feel that any report of such behavior will be viewed as homophobic and result in damage to their military career.

3. A majority of military personnel favor the ban.

4. Sensitivity classes and quotas may be implemented if homosexuals are treated as a protected class.

5. Civil rights comparisons are unfair when those objecting to homosexuality are objecting on grounds of modesty, not prejudice.

6. Discussions on sexual ethics that are likely to arise between soldiers if openly homosexual people serve are likely to create serious tensions and disruption of troop morale.

In the interest of developing a response and establishing a position on the issue, let's begin by expanding on both sets of arguments.

Expanding on Common Arguments for Allowing Homosexuals to Serve Openly

1. It's an established fact that lesbian women and homosexual men have honorably and effectively served in the military. This is inarguable, and is unchallenged by those favoring a continuance of the ban. History has shown that many of the women and men discharged over their homosexuality were decorated, competent, respected. The question hasn't been whether or not a homosexual is capable of serving honorably and effectively, but rather, whether or not a person's known homosexuality would affect morale and combat readiness.

2. The cost of investigating charges against homosexuals in the service is exorbitant and unnecessary. To better understand the numbers involved, both in discharges and costs, this table shows us the number of military women and men discharged just since 1993 once Don't Ask, Don't Tell was established. As shown below, from 1994 to 2006 there were nearly 12,000 known cases and undoubtedly more during the years discharge figures aren't available.

	Coast Guard	Marines	Navy	Army	Air Force	Total
1994	0	36	258	136	187	617
1995	15	69	269	184	235	772
1996	12	60	315	199	284	870
1997	10	78	413	197	309	1,007
1998	14	77	345	312	415	1,163
1999	12	97	314	271	352	1,046
2000	19	104	358	573	177	1,231
2001*	—	—	—	—	—	1,273
2002*	—	—	—	—	—	906
2003*	—	—	—	—	—	787
2004	15	59	177	325	92	668
2005	16	75	177	386	88	742
2006	—	—	—	—	—	612
Total	113	655	2,626	2,583	2,139	11,694

* Breakdown of discharges by service branch not available. Figures taken from Leo Shane, "Obama Wants to End 'Don't Ask, Don't Tell,'" *Stars and Stripes*, January 16, 2009, www.stripes.com/article.asp?section=104&article=60043.

Regarding financial impact, a University of California blue ribbon commission including former members of both the Reagan and Clinton administrations reported in February 2006 that $363 million has been spent on investigations and discharges, including $14.3 million for "separation travel" once a service member is discharged, $17.8 million for training officers, $252.4 million for training enlistees, and $79.3 million in recruiting costs.[14]

It may be that these figures indicate an unfortunate but necessary expense for retaining a sound policy, and one can logically hold the position that unit cohesion and sound morale is worth the price. But for such a position to be informed, it needs to consider the numbers and costs involved, and then still determine that the benefit of the one outweighs the liabilities of the other.

3. **Qualified and needed military personnel are discharged because of this policy and the armed forces suffer as a result.** This argument is bolstered by a fairly recent example. In 2005, among the military women and men discharged over their homosexuality, 55 were Arabic-language specialists. Because of the obvious advantages of intercepting and understanding terrorists'

communications, language specialists' skills are critical and not easily replaced. It could be argued that these specialists knew of the ban before enlisting, then speculated that had they opted not to enlist it's likely that other specialists who were heterosexual would have enlisted in their place. The speculation is not unreasonable, but as with the above issue of financial impact, the cost of losing valuable staff needs to be considered and weighed into the position one holds.

4. Surveys indicate strong public support for overturning DADT. As of February 2008, both Gallup and Pew polls showed public support for lifting the ban and allowing openly gay and lesbian people to serve was somewhere between 60 and 65 percent.[15] It's fair to ask, though, to what extent public opinion should influence military policy, and whether or not it should defer to the opinions of the men and women who are themselves in the military.

5. Other countries that allow openly gay and lesbian personnel to serve have suffered no damage to troop cohesion or morale. A University of Southern California Santa Barbara study indicated that "the presence of openly gay and lesbian personnel in the multinational units in which Americans serve has not had a negative impact upon cohesion or military performance."[16] Additionally, experts from NATO and the UN have come to similar conclusions.[17]

Similar results were found in a study done of Canadian troops after the ban on homosexuals in the service was lifted in 1992,[18] showing, among other results, that "lifting restrictions on gay and lesbian service in the Canadian Forces has not led to any change in military performance," and that homosexual service members polled "describe good working relationships with peers in supportive institutional environments where morale and cohesion are maintained."[19] It could be argued that research on the effect of openly homosexual military personnel is scant, and that much more needs to be done before it can be conclusively said that no significant, long-term negative impact comes from more open policies. Likewise, the Canadian study relied largely on the reporting of homosexual personnel, who, it's fair to say, had no small stake in its outcome.

It's also fair to ask to what extent personnel who are privately uncomfortable in close quarters with homosexuals are willing to say so openly, even in a survey. In an environment where open homosexuality is officially permitted, it's easily assumed that, at least according to the powers that be in that environment, "enlightened" people are comfortable with homosexuality and "unenlightened" people are not. Survey results could thus easily be affected, as those who are uncomfortable with the new policies may feel inhibited and reluctant to admit it.

6. Concerns about troop cohesion if homosexuals are allowed to openly serve are similar to those raised when the military racially integrated, and those concerns were found to be invalid. Opposition to President Truman's executive order to integrate the U.S. military in 1949 came from majorities inside and outside the armed forces. A Gallup poll taken at the time showed that only 26 percent favored integration. Troop cohesion, morale, and close quarters were all cited as reasons for objections to Truman's order.[20]

Yet the fairness of this comparison can be called into question. Servicemen opposed to close quarters with African-Americans based their opposition on who African-Americans were, not what they were attracted to. In other words, to compare unreasonable prejudices against someone of another race with inhibitions about sleeping and showering with someone who may be sexually attracted to you is quite akin to comparing apples to oranges.

Expanding on Common Arguments for Banning Homosexuals from Serving Openly

1. Heterosexuals are likely to feel uncomfortable bunking and showering with those attracted to the same sex, for the same reason women would feel uncomfortable bunking and showering with men, and men would feel uncomfortable doing the same with women. In a compelling statement read by Elaine Donnelly of the Center for Military Readiness to the House Armed Services Committee, Ms. Donnelly described cohabitation between heterosexuals and homosexuals in the barracks as being "tantamount to forcing female soldiers to cohabit with men in intimate quarters...on a 24/7 basis...(forcing) persons to live with persons who might be sexually attracted to them."[21] Cadet Jennifer Speeckaert offered a similar observation (as do numerous individuals who've blogged or written on the subject) when she stated:

> Personally, I would not feel comfortable showering in front of men. Reasonably, I would know that just because they were men and I am a woman, it wouldn't mean they were checking me out. Emotionally,

however, most women would agree that it would not be a comfortable position to be in. How is this different, then, than showering in front of a gay woman?[22]

While it would be inaccurate and unfair to presume homosexual persons would sexually harass fellow soldiers, the problem is not sexual predators, but sexual privacy. One can know that a gay or lesbian soldier is not overtly harassing, but still realize that soldier is in fact sexually attracted to the people he or she is showering and sleeping with. This is a legitimate and common concern.

2. In cases of sexual harassment from someone of the same sex, the victim may feel that any report of such behavior will be viewed as homophobic and result in damage to their military career. Donnelly raises this point when she suggests that, should the military revise its policy and regard homosexuality as a civil rights issue, it will implement policies and programs accordingly, as it has done regarding other civil rights issues:

> This means that any military man or woman who expresses concerns about professed homosexuals in the military, for any reason, will be assumed "intolerant," and suspected of harassment, homophobia, "bullying," bigotry or worse.[23]

3. A majority of military personnel favor the ban. In a 2006 poll announced by the *Military Times* newspapers, in response to the question "Do you think openly homosexual people should be allowed to serve in the military?" 30 percent answered "yes," 59 percent answered "no," and 10 percent answered "no opinion." The same percentage—59 percent in opposition—was reported by the *Military Times* survey in the previous year, and the figure for 2007 was 57.4 percent.[24] These figures have to be seriously considered and weighed, as they represent the views of those whose lives are directly affected by military policy far more than the general public, who can much more casually approve policy changes they themselves don't have to live with.

4. Sensitivity classes and quotas may be implemented if homosexuals are treated as a protected class. It can be shown that where minority status is newly recognized, a certain amount of indoctrination often follows. And it is already evident the military is seriously considering placing sexual orientation in the same category of protection as race and sex. A report from the Santa Barbara–based Palm Center states:

> In recent years, military leaders have further emphasized the notion that gay men and lesbians are worthy of anti-discrimination protection by analogizing sexual minorities to racial minorities and women.[25]

This introduces the very real possibility of special programs aimed at eradicating deeply held views based on religious premises neither the military nor the government has the right to challenge. For example, in Israel, after bans on open homosexuality were lifted, an openly gay soldier describes the benefits that followed:

> After discrimination against gays in the Israeli Defense Force was prohibited in 1993, people began to come out because they knew they were protected. The army had created channels to report rights violations. Affirmative action programs were established, such as sensitivity training in the national police department, and a special pre-military service training program that stresses affirmation and rights.[26]

A similar description comes from Canada, detailing changes some will no doubt applaud, but others will find ominous:

> The policy (of allowing openly homosexual enlistment) later evolved to recognize protection for transgender volunteers as well; and encompasses perhaps the world's most thoroughly inclusive armed force affirmation of rights. In Canada, it seems, there are no caveats or exceptions nor pragmatic excuses or arguments for exclusion. The military has ongoing training regarding respect and dignity and a policy of zero tolerance for harassment. It is the first nation to have held a same-sex wedding of uniformed military personnel.[27]

In light of programs like these being enacted where bans on homosexuality were lifted, it's fair to ask to what extent intimidation plays into the responses of soldiers who are polled regarding their feelings on the subject. This, in turn, calls into question surveys purporting to prove that, where bans were lifted, there have been few problems with cohesion. Indeed, the phrase "no caveats or exceptions nor pragmatic excuses or arguments" seems in line with Elaine Donnelly's fears regarding what she considers the inevitable retraining service people will be subjected to:

> Anyone who resists the program could be accused of "harassment" and punished with denial of promotions—particularly to high rank.[28]

5. Civil rights comparisons are unfair when those objecting to homosexuality are objecting on grounds of modesty, not prejudice. As mentioned above, the comparisons between racial prejudice and discomfort over sleeping and showering with those attracted to the same sex don't seem apt. Racial prejudice says, in essence, "I dislike those people because of who they are." Discomfort over sexual attraction says nothing about liking or disliking the person in question. It's about disliking intimate proximity to someone who's attracted to your gender, even if you generally like that someone. So a male co-worker may like a female co-worker as a person, but still feel very uncomfortable undressing in her presence. That says nothing about a prejudice on his part toward women, but it does speak to a normal, deeply ingrained modesty. That's why, when testifying before a Senate hearing on the issue, sociologist Charles Moskos said:

> I think the black/white analogy vis-à-vis gays/straights...really is the misleading one. It really is the male/female analogy.[29]

6. Discussions on sexual ethics that are likely to arise between soldiers if openly homosexual people serve are likely to create serious tensions and disruption of troop morale. Given the intimidation factor mentioned above, if the ban on homosexuality is lifted and sensitivity training and re-education programs are implemented, those who privately hold a traditional view on human sexuality will be placed in an untenable position. Conversations about critical issues are likely to arise among servicemen and women, and all should be free to express their views without fear of retaliation. But in an atmosphere in which objections to homosexuality seem increasingly frowned upon, it may now be the traditionalist who will feel bound by a Don't Ask, Don't Tell policy. If he or she states an objection to homosexuality on moral or religious grounds, reprisals and tensions could follow. Yet if she or he keeps silent about such objections, even if they might be part of the normal course of a conversation, the person holding the traditional view will feel censored and repressed. This sets up a no-win situation no enlisted person should have to experience.

How Then Should We Respond?

As of this writing (January 2009) U.S. president Barack Obama is on record as intending to overturn the established policy of "Don't Ask, Don't Tell," thereby removing any ban on openly homosexual enlistees or service persons. This would put the United States in the company of Australia, Canada, the United Kingdom, Germany, Israel, Italy, and Switzerland, all of whom have removed similar bans. That being the case, by the time this book is published the decision may already have been made to dismantle current U.S. military policies regarding homosexuality. Yet only the most naïve would assume that will end the controversy, both culturally and interpersonally.

How, then, should Christians respond?

First, let's clarify that when Scripture calls a behavior a sin, it doesn't necessarily call us to also oppose everything those practicing that behavior may want. So we're not required to automatically resist every political or social goal the homosexual community has. There's room, in fact, for disagreement among Christians over the best approach to take in the public arena. We may agree that homosexuality falls outside God's will, yet differ over which laws to support or oppose regarding gay rights. On some issues—same-sex marriage, for example, or hate-crime laws restricting freedom of religion—the right stand to take seems clear and will be shared by most of us. On others, a "correct" Christian position is not so easily arrived at.

Gays in the military may well be such an issue, so the position advocated in this chapter will be presented with conviction, but without the adamancy we'd reserve for other issues. Granted, they're all related. Gays in the military, gay adoption, same-sex marriage, and pro-gay student clubs are separate but connected, with today's acceptance or rejection of one affecting tomorrow's acceptance or rejection of the other. Yet one issue can be urgent, with only one clear biblically based response; others may be important but less clear, the right Christian response being debatable. That, I believe, correctly describes this subject, so this chapter's position is written from that perspective.

All factors involved should be considered, including the fact that homosexuals

are unquestionably capable of exemplary military service, the cost of discharging gay and lesbians soldiers is high, and the loss of such discharged personnel is
significant. It's also true that some object to homosexual soldiers out of pure prejudice, or false ideas of what a homosexual is or isn't, and that some comparisons
between this controversy and the integration struggles of the 1940s can be made.
Finally, studies indicating success when lifting bans on homosexuality in other
nations' militaries have to be considered. All these points matter, and ignoring
them would a violation of Proverbs 18:13, which warns us that "he who answers
a matter before he hears it, to him it is folly and shame."

Having considered these points, though, it still seems that a ban on openly
identified homosexuals in the military is the better policy. And if this is true, it
will remain true, whether or not such bans are being lifted in all nations. This
position is reached for five primary reasons:

1. The roles of the individual soldier and the collective military are biblically recognized as honorable (1 Timothy 2:3, for example) and
   are at times used as examples to illustrate godly resistance, aggression, and duty (1 Corinthians 9:7; 2 Corinthians 10:4; Ephesians
   6:11-17; 1 Timothy 2:4). Military service, then, is praised and
   praiseworthy; a noble calling and a necessity in a fallen world.

2. Military policy should be dictated by what is in the best interest of the military, rather than the preferences of the individual.
   Military service is not a right, nor is exclusion from it a govern-
   mental wrong. A number of qualifications or exemptions may be
   employed by the military that may be unwarranted in most civil-
   ian occupations.

3. Troop cohesion is in the best interest of both the military and the
   nation it serves. Its maintenance should be considered above individual interests in most cases, and when a contest between the two
   arises, the priority is clear.

4. While openly homosexual-identified women and men can and do
   serve well, their presence could well create ruptures in morale and
   cohesion among those who feel discomfort in the day-to-day inti-
   macies associated with military life. This is significantly different
   from the less intimate interactions one would have with a co-worker
   or associate with whom one does not shower, sleep, and reside.

5. Because forms of social engineering via sensitivity training and punitive measures often accompany recognition of minority status, and since trends within and outside the military lean toward awarding homosexuals such status, programs intended to promote a "correct" view of homosexuality are likely to be implemented in the military should it lift its ban. These programs could damage cohesion and morale by intimidating personnel and discouraging future recruits.

For these reasons a ban seems to be an increasingly unpopular but still expedient policy. Time will tell, of course, to what extent the concerns raised in this chapter will be realized. Should all major nations allow homosexuals to serve, and if their service does no damage to troop unity or national concerns, then so much the better. One wonders if we'll ever be able to measure whatever damage such a change creates, but we can hope for the best of outcomes. Still, whatever else may be said of the rights, contributions, and qualifications of individuals, we're left with the less quantifiable but very real thing we call *morale.* When referring to this essential element of a viable, ready national defense, columnist Thomas Sowell offers both a description and a warning when he writes,

> Military morale is an intangible,
> but it is an intangible without which
> the tangibles do not work.[30]

CHAPTER TWENTY-ONE

GAYS IN THE MILITARY

○—KEY POINTS—○

1. Stereotypes about lesbians and homosexual men as soldiers don't hold up well. They are generally as capable as heterosexuals of all responsibilities inherent in military service, and are often not easily identified and, in fact, may conform strongly to stereotypical standards of masculinity of femininity.

2. While America retains restrictions on openly identified homosexuals' ability to serve (as of this writing, January 2010), other nations

have lifted similar bans, and many report varying degrees of success when doing so.

3. Many arguments for lifting such bans are compelling and should be considered, since resistance to lifting them may be based more on prejudice or misinformation than sound reasoning and facts.

4. Compelling reasons for considering a lifting of the ban include reports from other countries that have done so and report no or few ill effects; the high cost of investigating and discharging homosexual personnel; the opinions of military leaders who support policy change; public opinion in general; and the general wrongness of keeping exclusionary policies in place when there's no compelling reason to do so.

5. Compelling reasons for keeping the ban in place include the need to preserve troop cohesion; the discomfort many personnel would feel during the intimate interactions (communal showering, sleeping, and living) inherent in military life; the restrictions on freedom of speech and religion that can accompany policy change when a group is granted minority status; and the opinions of military personnel themselves who, in contrast to public opinion, show resistance to this change in large number of polled responses.

RESOURCES

Don't Ask Don't Tell: Debating the Gay Ban in the Military, ed. Aaron Belkin and Geoffrey Bateman, Lynne Rienner Publishers, 2003. Authors on both sides of the issue contribute to this debate providing perspectives from both camps.

Conduct Unbecoming by Randy Shilts, Ballantine Books, 1995. A largely pro-gay but comprehensive, finely detailed account of the U.S. military's historical debate and struggle over this issue.

Elaine Donnelly, President of the Center for Military Readiness: Testimony made before the House Armed Services Committee July 23, 2008, http://armedservices.house.gov/pdfs/MilPers072308/Donnelly_Testimony072308.pdf. Well-defined objections to lifting the military ban presented with ample documentation and useful for anyone discussing or debating the issue.

NOTES

1. Eleanor Clift, "How the Candidates Play to Gays," *Newsweek*, Sept. 14, 1992, www.newsweek .com/id/119196.

2. "After 15 years, it is alright to say that you are gay in the US armed forces," www.andhranews.net/ Intl/2008/July/19/After-years-54836.asp.

3. See Randy Shilts, *Conduct Unbecoming: Gays and Lesbians in the U.S. Military Vietnam to the Persian Gulf* (New York: St. Martin's Press, 1993) for a historical overview of such attitudes toward homosexual servicemen.

4. Louis Crompton, *Homosexuality and Civilization* (Cambridge, MA: Belknap Press, 2003), p. 73.

5. *Symposium* by Plato, see http://classics.mit.edu/Plato/symposium.html.

6. Thucydides, "On Aristogeiton and Harmodius," *The History of the Peloponnesian War*, 6th book, written c. 431 BC, tr. Richard Crawley. See www.fordham.edu/halsall/pwh/thuc6.html.

7. Crompton, p. 30.

8. See, for example, B. Burg, *Gay Warriors: A Documentary History from the Ancient World to the Present* (New York: NYU Press, 2001).

9. Shilts.

10. "The History of Gay Soldiering," www.reason.com/blog/show/120965.html.

11. See "Media Bias Basics" on the Media Research website at www.mediaresearch.org/biasbasics/bias basics.asp for some telling statistics on reporter's political leanings and positions on key issues like homosexuality. Also see Shilts for details of key legal challenges to military policy.

12. Lisa Keen, "Clinton stands firm on vow to repeal military's gay ban," *The Washington Blade*, November 13, 1992, www.washblade.com/2007/11-9/news/blast/11529.cfm.

13. "Clinton Blames GOP for Gay Policy," *San Francisco Chronicle*, December 8, 2000, www.sfgate .com/cgi-bin/article.cgi?f=/c/a/2000/12/08/MN72681.DTL.

14. "Report: 'Don't Ask, Don't Tell' costs $363M," *USA Today*, February 14, 2006, www.usatoday.com/ news/washington/2006-02-14-dont-ask-report_x.htm, accessed on 2007-05-25.

15. Paul Waldman, "Will the Next President Lift the Ban on Gays in the Military?" www.prospect.org, accessed February 26, 2008.

16. Palm Center Study on Don't ask Don't Tell, www.palmcenter.org/files/active/0/Executive%20Order %200n%20Gay%20Troops%20-%20final.pdf.

17. www.palmcenter.org/files/active/0/2004_02_BatemanSameera.pdf.

18. See "Effects of the 1992 lifting of restrictions," www.palmcenter.org/publications/dadt/effects_of_ the_1992_lifting_of_restrictions_on_gay_and_lesbian_service_in_the_canadian_forces_apprais ing_the_e.

19. "Effects of the 1992 lifting of restrictions."

20. "Service Interests Versus Presidential Intent," www.history.army.mil/books/integration/IAF-13.htm.

21. See Elaine Donnelly, President of the Center for Military Readiness: Testimony made before the House Armed Services Committee July 23, 2008, http://armedservices.house.gov/pdfs/MilPers 072308/Donnelly_Testimony072308.pdf.

22. Jennifer Speeckaert, "Sound Off! A Cadet Defends ROTC," *upROAR!* March 6, 2008, see *The Cornell Daily Sun*, http://cornellsun.com/node/28559.

23. See Donnelly.

24. Robert Hodierne, "Down on the War," *Army Times*, Dec. 29, 2006, pp. 12-14.

25. www.palmcenter.org/node/274.

26. Denny Meyer, "A Gay Soldier: Captain Avner Even-Zohar, Israeli Defense Forces," /www.thegay militarytimes.com/0805Zohar.html.

27. "OH CANADA! Michelle Douglas' struggle in ending discrimination in Canada's military," www .thegaymilitarytimes.com/0901Douglas.html.

28. Donnelly.

29. Donnelly.

30. Thomas Sowell, quoted by The Center for Military Readiness, www.cmrlink.org/HMilitary.asp? DocID=287.

GAY PARENTING
Plus, Minus, or Equal?
by Joe Dallas

We made radical changes in the family without realizing how it changes the experience of growing up. We embarked on a gigantic social experiment without any idea about how the next generation would be affected.

—DR. JUDITH WALLERSTEIN,
DESCRIBING THE DIVORCE DEBATE OF THE 1970s

The first critical thing God ever said about man proved the value of emotional and sexual intimacy. Adam was created magnificently incomplete, despite being in union with his Creator and his exquisite surroundings. "Still," God declared, "he's alone, and this is not good." So Eve was created, a couple united, and marriage was born. In the only true Age of Innocence, it was all quite sexy and astonishingly beautiful. They were unashamed, monogamous, and united with a fully acknowledged sense of mutual need. It was, just as God said, "Good, very good." And from this "very good," children and family were meant, by design, to grow and thrive.

Sadly for all of us, what happened in Eden stayed in Eden. When Adam went along with Eve's disobedience, allowing sin to enter and decimate the environment, one of the first noticeable signs of the Fall was its impact on marriage:

> Your desire shall be for your husband, and he shall rule over you
> (Genesis 3:16).

Where there'd been cooperative harmony there would now be power struggle and deterioration. Within the next chapters of Genesis, the results—fratricide, prostitution, rape, homosexuality, and incest—glaringly underscore how far we've fallen from what we were meant to be.

Marriage as an institution and experience is certainly included in that fall. Among our finest patriarchs, including Abraham, Jacob, King David, and Solomon, we see disregard for the monogamy God intended, and in Moses' law, permission to divorce is granted to men for grounds as vague and subjective as "displeasure" with one's wife. And while this was all allowed by God, in an indictment against men's reluctance to bridle their passions, Jesus explained that Moses granted a bill of divorce only to accommodate man's hardness of heart, not God's ideal (Matthew 19:8). Indeed, a clear message woven through Scripture is God's view of marriage as typifying His relationship with His people, one marked by fidelity and permanence.

But world history shows a frequent and ongoing disregard for that standard; understandably so, considering that the world at large is not, nor is it meant to be, the church. So there will often be a contrast between the way secular cultures view marriage versus the way it's viewed by the church. We've seen, in different centuries, cultures, and trends, marriage defined as a property arrangement by which a man purchases a wife, or a prearranged political alliance, or a polygamous institution, or one prohibiting intermarriage between races. We've seen divorce laws enacted, dismantled, strengthened, and amended as different generations grapple with the ethics of terminating a civil agreement that normally is entered into with permanence in mind. Clearly, our definition and concept of marriage has morphed regularly throughout history, and if history itself were our guide as to what constitutes marriage, we'd be a very confused people indeed.

Of course, in Western culture we did seek guidance from the Bible when developing laws and expectations for married couples. But that guidance took some strong hits in the 1960s, when no-fault divorce, cohabitation, and "swinging" began to be seen as alternatives to the traditional definition of a loving partnership. And considering the number of heterosexual couples who embraced these changes, it's really no surprise that homosexual couples eventually came forward saying, "Us too!"

Still, our conviction that marriage is by definition a contract between one man and one woman remains stubbornly intact. In California, where Hollywood, the rock-and-roll industry, San Francisco liberalism, and all things hedonistic thrive, the state's citizens still voted in 2008 by 52 percent, via the controversial Proposition 8, to retain the traditional definition of marriage.

Other states have passed similar laws, and where such decisions are left to the general population, the population so far has taken, in most cases, a decidedly traditional turn. Many (perhaps most) of us still believe that a lifelong union between two sexes is not only the best way to create children, but to raise them as well. Something, whether knee-jerk, learned, or inherited, tells us that while two people of the same sex can love each other deeply, care for children diligently, and contribute to society significantly, such a pairing still doesn't constitute a marriage. A relationship, certainly, and often a committed one. But not a marital one. And the testimony of Scripture, always the key guide to Christian thinking, bears this out.

At this point same-sex marriage advocates may rightfully and vehemently charge traditionalists with hypocrisy, citing the high divorce rate, prevalence of live-in relationships, and appallingly common use of pornography among Christians. And who could argue with them? A growing disrespect for marriage *has* seeped from the culture into the church, and the evidence is there for any casual observer to comment on. The Christian population exhibits inexcusable levels of sexual sin and a cavalier attitude toward wedding vows (see statistics on sexual sin among Christians cited in chapter 2) so when we protest the redefinition of marriage, based on our contention that it's meant to be permanent, monogamous, and heterosexual, a cynical response ("Well, you've got the heterosexual part down, but you could sure use some help with monogamy and permanence!") is understandable and, to a point, deserved.

But charging someone with hypocrisy only discredits their *character*, not their *position*. If a doctor advises his patients not to smoke, then lights up once he leaves the office, what's he guilty of—the wrong message, or the wrong behavior? His refusal to take his own advice surely doesn't negate the advice itself. And neither does a prevalence of shortcomings among Christians negate the Christian message itself. We should practice what we preach, but if our preaching goes unpracticed, the problem lies with our behavior, not our preaching. So it's reasonable to ask if our drift away from biblical standards should be continued, just because so many ignore them, or if we should instead adjust our actions, not the standards that condemn them. That general line of questioning will lead us to more specific queries about marriage itself.

Should We Change the Standard?

The most important of those specific questions is this: Is it in the best interest of children and society for us to broaden the definition of marriage to include same-sex coupling?

Some say yes, confidently, and with all the right credentials to back their assertions. The American Psychological Association, for example, takes this official position:

> Overall, results of research suggest that the development, adjustment, and well-being of children with lesbian and gay parents do not differ markedly from that of children with heterosexual parents.[1]

The American Psychiatric Association concurs, having this to say about same-sex parenting:

> Gay and lesbian couples and individuals should be allowed to become parents through adoption, fostering and new reproductive technologies, subject to the same type of screening used with heterosexual couples and individuals.[2]

The American Academy of Pediatrics agrees, as do the National Association of Social Workers and the American Psychoanalytic Association.[3]

Relying on a number of studies that have examined the general health and well-being of children raised by same-sex couples, all these organizations have concluded there's little or no difference between the development of children raised by gay couples and those raised by heterosexuals.

But some studies have gone even further, claiming children raised by same-sex couples may actually be healthier, instead of "as healthy," than kids reared by a male and female. Two University of California sociologists re-examined 21 studies and concluded that daughters of lesbians had higher aspirations to male-dominated occupations, and that sons of lesbians were more likely to be more nurturing than those of heterosexuals. (Interestingly enough, when also finding that daughters raised by lesbians tended to be more "sexually adventurous" and that children raised by homosexual partners were themselves more likely to at least experiment with homosexuality, those findings were either seen as positive or neutral.)[4]

At first glance, many would be satisfied with these positions, considering the stature of the organizations and individuals holding them. But a growing number of dissenters are still unsettled.

Just How Sure Are We?

In their 2004 publication *Getting It Straight: What the Research Says About Homosexuality*, editors Peter Sprigg and Timothy Dailey cite no less than 16 researchers, analysts, and academics (some of whom were either openly homosexual or holding pro-gay sentiments) who reviewed numerous studies purporting to find no difference between the parenting effectiveness of gay couples versus heterosexual ones. But not only did they find methodological flaws in these studies, they also expressed concerns that conclusions about the benign nature of same-sex parenting, based on these studies, were being drawn prematurely.

Openly lesbian Charlotte J. Patterson of the University of Virginia, for example, in the official statement on homosexual parenting by the American Psychological Association declared, "In summary, there is no evidence that lesbians and gay men are unfit to be parents or that psychological development among children of gay men or lesbians is compromised in any respect..." Yet having made such a broad statement in favor of gay parenting, she then adds, "It should be acknowledged that research on lesbian and gay parents and their children is still very new and relatively scarce...Longitudinal studies that follow lesbian and gays families over time are badly needed."[5]

David Cramer, in the *Journal of Counseling and Development*, reviewed 20 studies on homosexual parenting and found them lacking control groups, and using sample groups that were either too small or too uniform.[6] Other concerns raised by analysts of pro-same-sex parenting studies included "lack of external validity"; "major deficiencies in sampling"; difficulty obtaining accurate representative samples; and the personal investment of subjects (as gay parents) in the outcome of the study being positive, possibly diminishing the accuracy of their statements when being interviewed.[7]

But academics aren't the only ones questioning the methods and pace by

which we're re-engineering an established institution. In 2003, the Massachusetts Supreme Judicial Court issued its ruling *Goodridge v. Department of Public
Health*, a decision that led to legalized same-sex marriage in that state. Both the
plaintiffs and defendants cited studies of same-sex parenting. Yet in her dissent-
ing opinion, Justice Martha Sosman echoed the concerns of researchers cited by
Sprigg and Dailey, especially regarding the lack of long-term studies on same-sex
households, the inconclusive nature of what research *had* been done in the matter, the political bias and agendas often influencing such research, and the verified
differences in child raising styles observed in men and women. She noted:

> Conspicuously absent from the court's opinion today is any acknowl-
> edgment that the attempts at scientific study of the ramifications
> of raising children in same-sex-couple households *are themselves in
> their infancy and have so far produced inconclusive and conflicting
> results.*

She continues by explaining:

> Studies to date reveal that there are still some observable differences
> between children raised by opposite-sex couples and children raised
> by same-sex couples…Interpretation of the data gathered by those
> studies then becomes clouded by the personal and political beliefs
> of the investigators, both as to whether the differences identified
> are positive or negative, and as to the untested explanations of what
> might account for those differences. Gay and lesbian couples living
> together openly, and official recognition of them as their children's
> sole parents, comprise a very recent phenomenon, and the recent-
> ness of that phenomenon has not yet permitted any study of how
> those children fare as adults and at best minimal study of how they
> fare during their adolescent years.

Finally, she comes to the crux of the matter, verbalizing reservations many
Americans, whether liberal or conservative, are still wrestling with when the
subject of gay parenting comes up:

> The Legislature can rationally view the state of the scientific evi-
> dence as unsettled on the critical question it now faces: Are families
> headed by same-sex parents equally successful in rearing children

from infancy to adulthood as families headed by parents of opposite sexes? Our belief that children raised by same-sex couples should fare the same as children raised in traditional families is just that: a passionately held but utterly untested belief. *The Legislature is not required to share that belief but may, as the creator of the institution of civil marriage, wish to see the proof before making a fundamental alteration to that institution.*[8]

We, too, wish to see the proof that children raised by same-sex couples fare as well as children raised by parents of the opposite sex. Because so far, the weight of evidence seems to favor the traditional view, an opinion held by some who normally stand on the pro-gay side of social issues.

A case in point is David Blankenhorn, president of the New York–based Institute for American Values and a self-defined "liberal Democrat," who criticizes the rush to legitimize homosexual parenting when he notes:

> Marriage is a gift that society bestows on its next generation. Marriage (and only marriage) unites the three core dimensions of parenthood— biological, social, and legal—into one pro-child form: the married couple. Marriage says to a child: The man and the woman whose sexual union made you will also be there to love and raise you. Marriage says to society as a whole: For every child born, there is a recognized mother and father, accountable to the child and to each other.

Aligning himself with the traditional view, he acknowledges plainly:

> All our scholarly instruments seem to agree: For healthy development, what a child needs more than anything else is the mother and father who together made the child, who love the child and each other.

And touching on the two issues same-sex parenting raises—the rights of adults to have children versus the rights of children to be raised in an optimal environment—he poses a relevant question, easy to answer but not asked nearly often enough:

> Reducing homophobia is good. Protecting the birthright of the child is good. How should we reason together as a society when these two good things conflict?[9]

We reason together as a society by recognizing that we're not required to choose between the two, that's how. We can and should reduce unwarranted prejudice against homosexuals, but it doesn't take a redefinition of marriage to do so. And if studies attempting to prove that such a redefinition is benign are widely disputed (which they are) then we're left with an overarching, uncomfortable question mark hovering over our children's future. Granted, no one, not even the most conservative apologists, are arguing that same-sex couples are destructive to children. Focus on the Family, for example, one of America's most conservative Christian organizations, begins its research paper on same-sex parenting by affirming:

> Few would deny that most gay and lesbian couples raising children
> are loving people who work tirelessly to provide the best possible
> life for children.[10]

So the question is not "Do homosexual couples damage children?" By and large, all evidence says they don't. The better question is, "Which provides a more *optimal* environment for children—a home headed by a homosexual couple, or a heterosexual one?" In a sense, we could ask the same regarding single parenting—"Do single mothers or fathers damage children?" Generally, no. But would we then conclude that there's no difference between single and dual parenting? Surely not, because the better question is, "Do children benefit more from a two-parent home than a single-parent one?" All of which leads to two critical questions to be asked and answered when considering same-sex parenting:

1. Are children better off being raised by both a father and a mother?
2. Are children better off being raised by their *biological* father and mother?

After all, even if we object morally to homosexuality, if there's no difference in the way children are raised by a same-sex couple versus an opposite-sex one, then our objections to homosexuality don't compel us to resist redefining parenthood to include same-sex couples. But if, in fact, it can be shown that it's in children's best interest to be raised by both of their biological parents, then that, and that alone, should settle the argument.

An *Optimal* Versus a *Permissible* Environment

Sotirios Sarantakos, an Australian sociologist, reported his findings in the journal *Children Australia* after studying 174 primary school children, 58 of whom were being raised by heterosexual "co-habiting" (unmarried) couples; 58 by same-sex couples; and 58 by a married heterosexual couple. Measuring the children's functioning in twelve areas—language, math, sports, sociability, learning attitude, parent-school relation, gender role, school related support, and parental aspirations for the child's achievement—children of the married couples did the best; children of homosexual couples showed the poorest results.[11]

Fearing that his findings might invoke "homophobia," Sarantakos revealed two things simultaneously: The fear of "encouraging homophobia" that often pervades allegedly neutral research, and the inevitable conclusion that opposite sex parenting is the most effective, as he says:

> Before one jumps to conclusions encouraging homophobia and traditionalism, other relevant factors must be considered." Yet, he goes on, "In this study, *married couples seem to offer the best environment for a child's social and educational development.*[12]

But his findings actually say little against homosexuality per se. The fact that two caretaking adults may be homosexual in their orientation doesn't preclude their ability to love, instruct, and protect their kids. The problem, rather, is in the nature of their *coupling*. A team of two men or two women, no matter how loving and responsible, cannot provide the same diverse unit, with its complementary parenting and communication skills, that a heterosexual pair can. Likewise, as Sarantakos shows, children perform better when raised not only by two parents of the opposite sex, but by *their* two parents of the opposite sex. (Notice the children raised by unmarried heterosexual couples did more poorly than those raised by married couples.) You simply cannot beat the inherent instincts, skills, and commitment that come with both marital status and biological parenthood.

Fathers Count

When analyzing over 100 studies examining the impact of biological fathers on the children, Ronald Rohner and Robert Veneziano concluded:

Overall, father love appears to be as heavily implicated as mother love in offspring's psychological well being and health.[13]

And active father figures have a key role to play in reducing behavior problems in boys and psychological problems in young women, according to a review published in the February 2008 issue of *Acta Paediatrica:*

> Swedish researchers also found that regular positive contact reduces criminal behaviour among children in low-income families and enhances cognitive skills like intelligence, reasoning and language development. Children who lived with both a mother and father figure also had less behavioural problems than those who just lived with their mother. The review looked at 24 papers published between 1987 and 2007, covering 22,300 individual sets of data from 16 studies; 18 of the 24 papers also covered the social economic status of the families studied.[14]

Dr. Anna Sarkadi from the Department of Women's and Children's Health at Uppsala University, Sweden, remarked on these findings by noting:

> We found various studies that showed that children who had positively involved father figures were less likely to smoke and get into trouble with the police, achieved better levels of education and developed good friendships with children of both sexes. Long-term benefits included women who had better relationships with partners and a greater sense of mental and physical well-being.[15]

These findings aren't unique. Studies cited by The National Center for Fathering, Father Love: Keeping Fathers Connected, and the NYU Child Study Center conclude that fathers contribute uniquely to their children's development in ways that cannot be replicated or substituted.[16] The NYU Child Study Center notes that according to a number of writers, quoting research to support their position, the following functions are best performed by biological fathers married to biological mothers who live together:[17]

- Fathers provide role models for their sons to learn how to be a man; girls need fathers to learn how to relate to a man.

- Fathers are better able than mothers to constrain and correct boys headed toward violence and other antisocial behaviors.

- Fathers teach sons and daughters better lessons than mothers regarding assertiveness and achievement, and provide better formative experiences for daughters in terms of developing the capacity for heterosexual intimacy, trust, and even femininity.

- Fathers play differently with young children—they are more physical, they challenge and foster independence more than mothers, and young children prefer fathers' form of play.

In summary, proponents of the essential-father point of view see *the parenting contributions of mothers and fathers as linked to their sex*, with mothers generally emphasizing connection, relatedness, safety, and care, and fathers emphasizing autonomy, action, risk-taking, and following rules.[18]

Mothers Count

Just as research confirms the unique role of fathers in child raising, it predictably has similar points to make regarding motherhood. For example, the NICD Early Child Care Research Network found that nonmaternal care of babies and preschool children, as opposed to early bonding with their biological mothers, has been linked to behavioral problems at older ages.[19]

Likewise, a study released in the *Journal of Family Issues* concluded that maternal employment (during a child's adolescent years) significantly decreases grades, underscoring the specialized nature of maternal care.[20]

And in addition to the emotional and behavioral losses incurred in a mother's absence, her parenting style is complementary to, but distinct from, a father's. To requote the NYU Child Study Center:

> Mothers generally emphasize connection, relatedness, safety, and care, and fathers emphasize autonomy, action, risk-taking and following rules.[21]

All of which led David Popenoe to conclude, regarding the importance of both parents:

> We should disavow the notion that "mommies can make good daddies," just as we should disavow the notion of radical feminists

that "daddies can make good mommies." The two sexes are different to the core, and each is necessary—culturally and biologically—for the optimal development of a human being.[22]

Biology Counts

When comparing the ties between stepparents and stepchildren to those between biological parents and their offspring, the results are clear and unsurprising: Where childrearing is concerned, biology counts. Examples abound:

- An extensive body of research tells us that children do best when they grow up with both biological parents in a low-conflict marriage…Thus, it is not simply the presence of two parents, as some have assumed, but the presence of two biological parents that seems to support child development.[23]

- It has been consistently found that stepfamilies are not as close as nuclear families (Kennedy, 1985; Pill, 1990) and that stepparent-stepchild relationships are not as emotionally close as parent-child relationships (Ganong and Coleman, 1986; Hetherington and Clingempeel, 1992; Hobart, 1989). Many clinicians and researchers assume that stepfamilies tend to become closer over time. However, previous longitudinal studies conducted on stepfamilies have found little empirical support for this (Hetherington and Clingempeel, 1992; Kurdek, 1991).[24]

- Most researchers now agree that together these studies support the notion that, on average, children do better when raised by two married, biological parents who have low-conflict relationships.[25]

- Children that are deprived of frequent contact with both their mother and their father have a greater risk of drug abuse, dropping out of school, teenage pregnancy, and many other behavioral and emotional problems. Children whose parents are divorced are at the greatest risk because court-ordered visitation does not provide enough contact with the noncustodial parent to reduce the risk of deviant behavior.[26]

- Children living in stepfamilies are also likely to have significantly greater emotional, behavioral, and academic problems than children living with their biological mother and father.[27]

So Is Gay Parenting a Plus, a Minus, or Equal to Straight Parenting?

If research consistently shows that children function best when raised by their two biological parents, provided the parents are reasonably high functioning, then gay marriage could hardly be considered a "plus" for the child, nor could it be called "separate but equal" considering that it denies children the benefit of being raised by a union of the two sexes, with each parent's unique gender capacities in play. It can only be, in fact, a "minus," in that it lacks what only the Creator's original design can supply.

One can of course compare a seriously unhealthy heterosexual marriage— one featuring drug addiction, for example, or violence—to a relatively healthy same-sex relationship, and easily conclude that a child will fare better under the care of a stable homosexual couple than with an unstable heterosexual one. But pitting the worst case scenario of one against the best case scenario of the other hardly proves the point. One could also argue that a child is better off with a healthy single mother than with an abusive couple, but we'd still conclude that a two parent home is generally more desirable.

And so we return, repeatedly, to the conclusion that while a homosexual couple may offer love, warmth, and care to a child, the optimal environment for child raising lies in a two-parent home headed by the child's biological mother and father. Arguing for the right of same-sex couples to have children, rather than the right of children to be raised in homes best suited to their maximum growth, shows how far the discussion has veered from what matters most, as Elizabeth Marquardt points out:

> The growing emphasis is on meeting adult's rights to children, rather than children's needs to know and be raised, whenever possible, by their mother and father.[28]

As for the contention that happy and well-adjusted children often come from homes headed by homosexual couples, that point is inarguable. But the question isn't whether or not such homes can produce happy children, but rather, whether those same children got the maximum of parenting benefits. Dale O'Leary points this out when commenting on APA studies suggesting a father's place in the home is secondary:

Several years ago, I met a 16-year-old boy named Charley, who had lost his foot many years ago in an encounter with a lawn mower. Charley was a great kid—happy, joking, and fully adjusted to his prosthesis. Should Charley's ability to cope with his traumatic loss lead us to conclude that "one foot is as good as two"? Of course not.[29]

All of which leaves us concerned about the gay parenting trend, primarily because it speaks to a longstanding, lamentable willingness to elevate our wants over the emotional and mental needs of our children. Glenn Stanton and Kjersten Oligney remind us of this when they admonish:

We can learn a great deal by comparing these early days of the same-sex family experiment with the early days of a previous and national experiment with the family. When our nation's first no-fault divorce law was passed in 1969, it was assumed that children, being flexible and resilient, would quickly recover from the shock of divorce and, in the long run, if their parents were in happier marriages, they too would be happier.

These parents had the support of some early studies and child development professionals...but no scholars really knew for sure, since divorce had not been experienced by large, diverse populations over long periods of time, like the same-sex family experiment today.[30]

If marriages are broken, then let them be fixed. There are few things we could do that would be as worthwhile. But if the definition of marriage works, then it needs no repair, whether by redefinition or amendment. The Creator Himself presided over the first marriage, calling it *good*. And we, the creation and eventual offspring of that first union, dare not call it anything else.

CHAPTER TWENTY-TWO

GAY PARENTING

o———KEY POINTS———o

1. The definition of marriage has historically changed from culture to culture, largely depending on the worldviews and practical concerns of

each culture. But the original definition of marriage articulated in Genesis is a pairing of one man and one woman in permanent union.

2. That definition has been challenged recently by those proposing that homosexual unions offer the same benefits to children as heterosexual ones.

3. A number of professionals and professional organizations—including the American Psychiatric Association, the American Psychological Association, and the American Academy of Pediatrics—have stated their support for same-sex unions, and have contended children raised under such unions suffer no ill effects.

4. That assumption, in turn, has been challenged by a number of professionals across the political and philosophical spectrum, who believe that research and common sense tell us that heterosexual parenting provides the optimum benefit to children.

5. Research indicates that both fathers and mothers play critical and unique roles in their children's development, and that neither can be replaced.

6. Research also indicates that the bonding inherent between biological parents and children cannot be replicated, and provides the best scenario for a child to grow and develop in.

7. The Christian argument against same-sex parenting is not based on the belief that homosexuals are inherently damaging to children. Rather, it's based on the belief that a same-sex couple cannot, by its very nature, provide the benefits a heterosexual couple can.

Books on Same-Sex Marriage

Marriage on Trial by Glenn Stanton and Bill Maier, InterVarsity Press, 2004.

Same-sex Marriage: Putting Every Family at Risk by Mathew Staver, B and H Publishing, 2004.

Marriage Under Fire by James Dobson, Multnomah Press, 2004.

ONLINE RESOURCES

"Same-sex Marriage: A Selective Bibliography of the Legal Literature," compiled by Paul Axel-Lute (a comprehensive online bibliography of legal decisions regarding the definition of marriage, articles for and against same-sex marriage, and state-by-state synopsis of court decisions, regularly updated). See at http://law–library.rutgers.edu/SSM.html.

NOTES

1. APA Policy Statement on Sexual Orientation, Parents and Children, www.apa.org/pi/lgbc/policy/parents.html.

2. American Psychiatric Association's position on gay adoption, adopted November 2003, see www.hrc.org/issues/parenting/1592.htm.

3. Respectively: Committee on Psychosocial Aspects of Child and Family Health, "Co-parent or Second-Parent Adoption by Same-Sex Parents," http://aappolicy.aappublications.org/cgi/content/full/pediatrics;109/2/339; www.hrc.org/issues/parenting/1598.htm; www.apsa.org/portals/1/docs/about%20apsaa/positionpapergaymarriage.pdf.

4. "Gay Parenting Does Affect Children Differently, Study Finds—Authors Believe Gay Parents Have 'Some Advantages,'" www.narth.com/docs/does.html.

5. Charlotte J. Patterson, "Lesbian and Gay Parenting," *American Psychological Association Public Interest Directorate*, 1995, p. 8, cited in Peter Sprigg and Timothy Dailey, *Getting It Straight: What the Research Says About Homosexuality* (Washington, DC: Family Research Council, 2004), p. 96.

6. As cited in Sprigg and Dailey, pp. 96-97.

7. As cited in Sprigg and Dailey, pp. 95-102.

8. Cited in "How do children fare in families led by same-sex parents?" Religious Tolerance website, www.religioustolerance.org/hom_mar13.htm, emphasis added.

9. "Protecting Marriage to Protect Children," Op-ed, *Los Angeles Times*, September 19, 2008.

10. Cited in Glenn T. Stanton and Kjersten Oligney, "Refuting Points No One Is Making: A Response from Focus on the Family to the American Academy of Pediatrics July 2006 on Same-Sex Parenting," www.citizenlink.org/pdfs/fosi/marriage/AAP_Analysis.pdf.

11. As cited in Sprigg and Dailey, pp. 109-110.

12. As cited in Sprigg and Dailey, pp. 109-110, emphasis added.

13. Ronald Rohner and Robert Veneziano, "The Importance of Father Love: History and Contemporary Evidence," *Review of General Psychology* 5:4 (2001), 382-405, cited by Stanton and Oligney, p. 5.

14. "Children Who Have an Active Father Figure Have Fewer Psychological and Behavioral Problems," *ScienceDaily*, Feb. 15, 2008, www.sciencedaily.com/releases/2008/02/080212095450.htm.

15. "Children Who Have."

16. Respectively: http://fatherfamilylink.gse.upenn.edu/org/ncf/importnc.htm; www.fatherlove.com/ articles/riskfactors.html; www.education.com/magazine/article/Ref_Many_Meanings_Family/.

17. www.education.com/magazine/article/Ref_Many_Meanings_Family/.

18. www.education.com/magazine/article/Ref_Many_Meanings_Family/.

19. Jay Belsky et al., The NICHD Early Child Care Research Network, "Are There Long-Term Effects of Early Child Care?" *Child Development* 78 (2) (2003), pp. 681-701.

20. Baum, Charles L., "The Long-Term Effects of Early and Recent Maternal Employment on a Child's Academic Achievement," *Journal of Family Issues*, vol. 25, no. 1, pp. 29-60 (2004), http://jfi.sagepub .com/cgi/content/abstract/25/1/29.

21. www.education.com/magazine/article/Ref_Many_Meanings_Family/.

22. Cited in Stanton and Oligney.

23. Kristin Anderson Moore, et al., "Marriage from a Child's Perspective: How Does Family Affect Children, and What Can We Do About It?" *Child Trends Research Brief*, June 2002, cited in Stanton and Oligney, p. 12.

24. "Exploring the Stepgap: How Parents' Ways of Coping with Daily Family Stressors Impact Stepparent-Stepchild Relationship Quality in Stepfamilies," by Melady Preece, University of British Columbia, 1996, www.psych.ubc.ca/~mpreece/compdoc.pdf.

25. Mary Park, "Are Married Parents Really Better for Children?" Center for Law and Social Policy brief May 2003, cited in Stanton and Oligney, p. 12.

26. Judy Jones, "Children Missing Contact with Both Biological Parents at Risk," 24/7 Press Release, June 22, 2005, www.24-7pressrelease.com/view_press_release.php?rID=6509.

27. Zill, "Understanding Why Children in Stepfamilies Have More Learning and Behavior Problems Than Children in Nuclear Families," cited in Stanton and Oligney, p. 12.

28. Elizabeth Marquardt, "How Redefining Marriage Redefines Parenthood," talk given at the Ion Institute, Dublin, January 30, 2008.

29. Dale O'Leary, "APA Study Says: 'Who Needs Dad?'" www.narth.com/docs/whoneeds.html.

30. Stanton and Oligney, p. 15.

PRO-GAY EDUCATION IN SCHOOLS

Why Is What They're Teaching So Dangerous?

by Mike Haley

The philosophy in the classroom of this generation is the philosophy of government in the next.

—ABRAHAM LINCOLN

Change. To paraphrase Mark Twain: Everybody talks about it, but nobody does anything about it. Business gurus write about methods for managing it. Some observers, like Winston Churchill, suggest "to be perfect is to change often." But in the final analysis, most of us (grudgingly) agree with A.P. Gouthey: "There is nothing permanent in life but change."

Some change is natural—such as aging or growing—but much of change is induced, like technological advances, fashion tastes, and most prevalently, social phenomena. Homosexuality has become today's leading example of societal change. So in this chapter, we highlight how this change has and is occurring and why, as the German proverb concludes, "To change and to change for the better are two different things."

Two Types of Change

Many leaders in our nation's history believed social change resulted from new or revised laws: what we call political change. In many ways their belief in the power of political change has been borne out. Yet, there remains a problem with such change—laws often can be easily overturned or amended beyond recognition, thereby invalidating the desired change.

But there is another way to effect change, and some believe it is more powerful and more significant than political change. We refer to it as cultural change, which comes about by changing what people believe about something; changing what and how they talk about it; changing what people accept and what they value.

The power of such change is that, unlike political change, it is not easily overturned, because it's not dependent upon or sacrificed to the whims of elected leaders. And concerning homosexuality, cultural change is turning out to be the more powerful of the two.

Yes, political change abounds on this issue, such as new national, state, and local pro-gay laws (for example, gay marriage). But the significant, substantive, lasting change happens not in state houses but in our houses, the homes in our neighborhoods.

Take, for example, a 2001 Reuters news story, which concluded:

> U.S. high school seniors hold more liberal views on gay issues than the rest of the country's adult population...Eighty-five percent of seniors thought gay men and lesbians should be accepted by society [and] two-thirds of those surveyed said gay marriages should be legal.[1]

Let's consider for a moment how such dramatic change has occurred.

In 1987, two gay activists, Marshall Kirk and Erastes Pill, outlined how homosexuals could effect cultural change in American society. In a *Guide* magazine article entitled "The Overhauling of Straight America," Kirk and Pill wrote:

> The first order of business is desensitization of the American public concerning gays and gay rights. To desensitize the public is to help it view homosexuality with indifference instead of with keen emotion...
> You can forget trying to persuade the masses that homosexuality is a

good thing. But if only you can get them to think that it is just another thing, with a shrug of their shoulders, then your battle for legal and social rights is virtually won.[2]

Later in their article, Kirk and Pill recommended a more detailed plan of action.

Any campaign to accomplish this turnaround should do six things: 1. Talk about gays and gayness as loudly and as often as possible; 2. Portray gays as victims, not as aggressive challengers; 3. Give protectors a just cause; 4. Make gays look good; 5. Make the victimizers look bad; 6. Solicit funds.[3]

In this chapter we'll focus primarily on the first and second points, but the third through sixth deserve brief mention.

"Give protectors a just cause" is linked to "Portray gays as victims," for once gays are seen as victims, society and societal leaders see a reason for changing laws, policies, and procedures—political change. As a result, we now see nondiscrimination laws based on sexual orientation.

"Make gays look good" is clearly evidenced in today's popular media. Once we saw in the media unflattering, stereotypical images of gays and lesbians. Men and women dressed either in outrageous or very little clothing and demonstrated egregious behavior in gay pride parades and other gatherings. Now we see well-dressed, mainstream, educated, well-spoken gays and lesbians.

Meanwhile, those who say anything negative about homosexuality are made to look bad. The easiest method is to take the truly worst among us on this issue, like the controversial Rev. Fred Phelps, and associate him with all Christians who oppose homosexuality.

Fred Phelps identifies himself as a pastor but devotes much of his time to a hateful campaign against homosexuals. Phelps typically loiters outside the funerals of gays and lesbians displaying signs reading "God hates fags." He sponsors a virulently anti-gay website containing similar messages. Predictably, and successfully, homosexual activists associate radicals like Fred Phelps with all conservative Christians to fulfill Kirk and Pill's strategy.

Of course, no social movement could succeed without monetary support, and gay activists seem particularly adept at filling their coffers. Many professional people—doctors, lawyers, and so on, both gay and straight—donate faithfully to gay causes. Well-placed, wealthy foundations fund gay and lesbian endeavors. One of the more prominent, the Gill Foundation, operates in Colorado Springs, Colorado. Some large, well-known corporations whose services or products you likely buy also support homosexual activism: Levis, IBM, American Airlines, Nike, Google, Starbucks, and Apple, to name a few.[4]

But relative to pro-gay education in the public school system, let's consider numbers one and two.

Strategy 1—Talk About Gays and Gayness as Loudly and as Often as Possible

In describing this strategy, Kirk and Pill wrote,

> The principle behind this advice is simple: Almost any behavior begins to look normal if you are exposed to enough of it at close quarters and among your acquaintances.

The two most effective vehicles for normalizing homosexuality "at close quarters" and "among...acquaintances" have been through popular media and in school.

Media

Once upon a time, most television shows looked like the popular 1950s and 1960s sitcom *I Love Lucy* when portraying marriage. If you watched that show, you may remember that Ricky and Lucy, although married, did not sleep in the same bed. And when Lucy was pregnant the first time, they avoided showing her stomach. To do so required acknowledging, even implicitly, how she got that way.

Jump ahead a little more than a decade to *The Brady Bunch*. Mike and Carol, the married couple in that show, may have slept in the same bed, but the most topics—teenage acne, boyfriend problems, homework distress—remained noncontroversial, and saw resolution in 29 minutes with a return to domestic bliss.

Now leap ahead a few more decades to today, and we see a decidedly different TV environment. Over this time, standards gradually sank regarding sexuality, violence, and profanity, and along the way we shrugged our shoulders and began "slouching toward Gomorrah," as Judge Robert Bork described it. The same is now true with homosexuality.

Today, we find no shortage of gay and lesbian television characters. In fact GLAAD, the Gay and Lesbian Alliance Against Defamation, tracks the number of homosexual roles on TV, encouraging networks to not only include such characters, but to portray them in the best light.[5] And to simply view the prevalence of openly gay and lesbian characters during a given television season is to see their success.

During the 2001–2002 television season, for example, NBC featured seven homosexual characters on *Providence, ER, Friends,* and *Will and Grace.* An actor on the latter show, Eric McCormack, revealed the show's mission: "When old ladies out there say, 'Oh, I hope he meets a nice man,' that's when we'll know the show has succeeded."[6]

During that same period ABC featured two gay characters on *Spin City* and *NYPD Blue.* CBS included two homosexual characters on *The Ellen Show* and *The Education of Max Bickford.* The latter show also featured the first transgender character.

Fox had two gay characters on *The Simpsons* and *Dark Angel,* and WB carried four homosexual characters on *Dawson's Creek, Felicity,* and *Buffy the Vampire Slayer.* While premium cable networks operate with greater content freedom, Showtime broke new ground with the show *Queer as Folk,* featuring a gaggle of homosexual characters and graphic gay sex.

But television isn't the only popular media effecting change on this issue. Music does as well. As the old saying goes, "If I can write a nation's songs, I care not who writes its laws." Musicians, both gay and straight, sing about homosexuality from a pro-gay perspective.

For example, the Indigo Girls, a duo made up of lesbian musicians who were popular in the early 2000s, sang openly about their sexuality. Janet Jackson glorified homosexuality in some of her songs, and George Michael, a gay man, following his arrest for lewd conduct in a public restroom, had a hit song and video based on the incident. In a well-publicized event, lesbian singer-songwriter Melissa Etheridge and her partner wanted to have a child. They used the services of David Crosby of Crosby, Stills, and Nash to get pregnant. Now, Etheridge and her partner have separated. And more recently, in 2008 former Christian musician

Katy Perry enjoyed huge success with her song "I Kissed a Girl," detailing the joys of an experimental lesbian encounter.

Schools

With a heavy dose of the "all gay all the time" message at home through popular media, many kids head to school and encounter more of the same. Beginning as early as kindergarten, students learn about homosexuality in different school settings, such as curricula and assemblies. To get an idea of the success of pro-gay advocates have enjoyed through the public school system, consider just a few of the sweeping developments that have occurred between 1978 and 2008:

1. In 1978, homosexuality was still largely unaddressed in the public school system, and that fall a California state senator, John Briggs, sponsored an initiative that was placed on the ballot. If passed, the Briggs initiative would have prevented any public school teacher from promoting homosexuality as normal, or gay rights as desirable.[7]

2. Six years later, in 1984, openly lesbian teacher Dr. Virginia Uribe established Project 10, a public school–sponsored and –supported program aimed at educating school teachers and students on the normality of homosexuality and the wrongness of homophobia. Her program became a pilot and model for similar programs in schools across the country.[8]

3. In 1989, the first of many children's books on homosexuality came out. Titled *Heather Has Two Mommies*, it described a girl who spoke glowingly of her two lesbian mothers, and was followed in 1991 by *Daddy's New Roommate* (a young boy's account of his father's decision to leave his mother and form a union with another man); *Gloria Goes to Gay Pride* (also released in 1991, describing a child's positive experience participating in a local gay pride parade), and *King and King*, a 2002 fairy tale in which a prince falls in love with another prince.

4. In 1997, the National Day of Silence was established by GLSEN (Gay, Lesbian and Straight Education Network) designed to remind students how many homosexual people feel the need to

remain silent about their sexuality. In this student-led event, observed annually by hundreds of schools across the nation, students and teachers may choose to not speak for the entire school day, in recognition of, and support for, gay rights.[9]

5. In 2008, shortly after the California State Supreme Court decreed that same-sex marriage was a right guaranteed in the state's constitution, elementary school students in San Francisco were taken out of class to attend their lesbian teacher's same-sex wedding ceremony.[10]

Dr. Uribe once publicly remarked:

> The State Courts must be used to force the school districts to disseminate accurate information about homosexuality. Starting in the kindergarten, again, and working its way all through high school. This is war.[11]

Taking her challenge literally, it's clear, in our nation's public school system, who's winning the war. For example, many primary-age students read children's books such as *Daddy's New Roommate* or *Heather Has Two Mommies*. *Jesse's Dream Skirt* features the story of a young boy who dreams of wearing a dress to school. However, the story's antagonist, played by his close-minded father, won't allow it.

Other schools sponsor assemblies featuring pro-gay skits students find entertaining. The assemblies end with actors or school officials moralizing about "normal" families and "accepting" homosexuality.[12] Still other schools organize "Diversity Week" celebrations or encourage teachers to "come out" to their students.[13]

Often, events like these occur without parental knowledge or permission.

On the West Coast, parents of kindergarten students at Elementary School of Hayward, California, discovered their children were being taught to be "allies" to gays and lesbians. And unbeknownst to these parents, the school was participating in National Coming Out Day by offering readings of stories with a gay or transgender twist, such as "Jane and the Beanstalk."[14]

In the 1990s, National GLBT History Month began to be observed in a number of public schools. Sponsored by Equality Forum, which describes itself as "a national and international GLBT civil-rights organization with an educational focus,"[15] National GLBT History Month is celebrated in schools internationally. It features lessons on various prominent homosexuals, pro-gay guest speakers, a history of the gay-rights movement, and related issues. The event's goals is to "send an important message to our nation's teachers, school boards, community leaders, and youth about the vital importance of recognizing and exploring the role of gay, lesbian, bisexual, and transgender people in American history."[16]

While some applaud these goals, many parents have objected. In some cases, their objections have not only been dismissed but found to be grounds for potential legal action. Parents in the UK, for example, pulled their children from school during National GLBT History Month, not wishing them to be exposed to teaching and materials running contrary to their religious and moral values. In response, they were informed their children would be considered truant, which could carry criminal charges.[17]

Of course, most parents taking issue with pro-gay education programs don't wind up in jail. But the heavy-handed way anyone who disagrees with the pro-gay view gets treated is best summed up in this dialogue taken from the documentary "It's Elementary." In this recorded discussion among teachers at a school that's about to sponsor a Gay and Lesbian Pride Day for its students, a young African-American woman asks the gay and pro-gay organizers of the event whether or not respect for differing opinions is allowed:

> **Question:** As a school, are we saying that kids have to support this? That's what it sounds like to me...if a child comes from a background that says that homosexuality is not correct, are we telling that child that they're supposed to [support it]?
>
> **Response:** I don't know if this works for you, but I think that we are asking kids to believe that this is right...We're educating them, and this is part of what we consider to be a healthy education.[18]

Considering these remarks, the next goal Kirk and Pill suggest takes on real irony.

Strategy 2—Portray Gays as Victims, Not as Aggressive Challengers

Despite the draconian measures mentioned above, homosexual activists continue to act on Kirk and Pill's second recommendation and cast themselves as victims. Just as with the first strategy, this manifests itself both in media and in schools.

Media

One of the most stark examples came after the death of Matthew Shepard. Gay activists and sympathetic media exploited (and continue to exploit) this terrible incident, attempting to create a victimization mentality around homosexuality. Television and print media covered the story far longer than the normal news cycle, and the made-for-TV movie, *The Matthew Shepard Story*, created a spirit of martyrdom.

Yet, when homosexuals aggressively victimize someone else, the story goes unreported. Take, for instance, the case of young Jesse Dirkhising, who was brutally raped and murdered by two gay men. Matthew Shepard's case was no more brutal than this young boy's, but Jesse went unacknowledged by gay activists, civil rights groups, and the mainstream media.[19]

Schools

In schools, activists tend to pass over such gratuitous victimization, favoring, instead, "research" that "proves" it. One of the more popular "findings" states, "Gay youth account for 30 percent of all teen suicides." Paul Gibson, himself a gay man, published this finding in the paper "Gay Male and Lesbian Youth Suicide."[20] Although this became an oft-quoted figure in schools, it's a spurious statistic.

As it turns out, Gibson harvested his numbers primarily from biased homosexual sources. As a foundation for his study, Gibson used the now widely discredited Kinsey study, which states 10 percent of the population is homosexual (the real figure is around 2 to 3 percent). Gibson reported that 3000 gay youth commit suicide each year, when the 1998 Statistical Abstract of United States states there were only 2200 suicides among all youth.

Gibson also built his study on unacknowledged assumptions. He assumed homosexual orientation is normal and natural and presupposed that homosexuality is unchangeable and fixed at birth. Moreover, in seeking to explain his findings, he failed to acknowledge other psychological factors that could contribute to homosexual youth suicide, such as family problems or abuse.

But Gibson isn't the only activist fond of skewed statistics. The popular pro-gay school curriculum Project 10 is built on the 10 percent figure first perpetuated by Kinsey. In fact, the name comes from that statistic. And while gay activists know the 10 percent number to be inflated, they continue to use it. As one gay activist admitted,

> I think people probably always did know that it was inflated, but it was a nice number that you could point to, that you could say "one-in-ten," and it's a really good way to get people to visualize that we're here.[21]

Such cavalier mischaracterizations only compound the already murky message fed to children and the rest of the American public about a lifestyle fraught with harmful physical, spiritual, emotional, psychological, and sociological implications. The result is a dramatic change in what we understand and believe about homosexuality.

Perhaps Paula Ettelbrick, former legal director of the pro-gay Lambda Legal Defense Fund described it best:

> Being queer is more than setting up house, sleeping with a person of the same gender, and seeking state approval for doing so. Being queer means pushing the parameters of sex, sexuality, and family, and in the process transforming the very fabric of society.[22]

To effect lasting, significant change, nothing is more powerful than cultural change. And this is the type of change we see when we question the very definition of our sexuality, behavior, and how we are created in God's image.

So why is what they are teaching so dangerous? As Italian novelist Umberto Eco concludes, changing everything results in a society where ultimately nothing matters.

CHAPTER TWENTY-THREE

PRO-GAY EDUCATION IN SCHOOLS

○—KEY POINTS—○

1. For society as a whole to normalize homosexuality, it will be necessary for the public school system to promote that normalization via pro-homosexual class curriculum and special programs to which children will be exposed.

2. Cultural change tends to be more permanent and potent than mere political change, as cultural change cannot simply be "voted out."

3. Pro-gay education programs tend to portray homosexuals as a minority group, often victimized, and those who support parental rights and religious freedoms as being oppressive and bigoted.

4. The first official and widely recognized pro-gay education program in the United States is Project 10, founded by lesbian teacher Dr. Virginia Uribe.

5. Gay-Straight Alliances are student-initiated and student-led groups, meeting on campus, formed to combat homophobia in the schools.

6. The National Day of Silence is an annual event during which students and teachers may opt, for an entire school day, to remain silent in recognition of the number of homosexuals who fear openly declaring their orientation.

7. One of the most common arguments posed in favor of pro-gay education is the argument that homosexual students are at high risk for suicide, violence, or academic and social difficulties.

8. The indoctrination of children toward a pro-homosexual viewpoint begins as early as kindergarten, and books portraying homosexual couples as normal, and homosexual parenting as legitimate, are available to help in this process.

9. Pro-gay education programs work in concert with other sources that highly influence children and youth—television, media, and popular music—to normalize homosexuality in the minds of upcoming generations.

10. While the degree to which a public school promotes gay rights varies from state to state, the success of the gay-rights movement in influencing public educators and administrators is undeniable.

BOOK RESOURCES

The Homosexual Agenda by Alan Sears and Craig Osten, Broadman and Holman, 2003. In particular, chapter 3 ("Stupid Parents, 'Enlightened' Kids"), chapter 4 ("The Lavender Tower"), and chapter 8 ("The End of Tolerance"), all of which document important information regarding pro-gay education.

Getting It Straight: What Research Shows About Homosexuality by Peter Sprigg and Timothy Dailey, Family Research Council, 2004.

The New Tolerance by Josh McDowell and Bob Hostetler, Tyndale House, 1998.

ONLINE RESOURCES

The Alliance Defense Fund website, www.alliancedefensefund.org. This website posts regular updates on court cases involving religious freedom and the public square, including the public school system. Deeply involved in many cases involving homosexuality and public school controversies.

National Association for the Research and Treatment of Homosexuality (NARTH) website, www.narth.com. See, especially, section titled "Gay activism in the public schools" for updated information.

Focus on the Family's site for parents trying to counter promotion of homosexuality in schools is www.truetolerance.org.

NOTES

1. Christopher Michaud, "U.S. students hold mostly pro-gay views," August 27, 2001, www.boston.com/news/daily/27/students_views.htm.

2. Marshall K. Kirk and Erastes Pill, "The Overhauling of Straight America," *Guide* magazine, 1987, Mass Resistance website, www.article8.0rg/docs/gay_strategies/overhauling.htm.

3. Kirk and Pill.

4. "10 Pro Gay Companies to Go and Spend All Your Money With" *Queeried*, November 3, 2009, www.queeried.com/10-pro-gay-companies-to-go-and-spend-all-your-money-with/.

5. See GLAAD's mission statement at www.glaad.org/mission.

6. Christopher Michaud, "Show with gay male lead deemed ready for prime time," Craven's Movie Vortex, http://members.tripod.com/~zero_sum/index-2.html.

7. Hugo Schwyzer, "When Reagan was Right," History News Network, http://hnn.us/blogs/entries/5539.html.

8. See Project 10 website at http://project10.0rg/index.htm.

9. "Day of Silence" website, www.dayofsilence.org/index.cfm.

10. "San Francisco first grade takes trip to 'gay wedding,'" www.christianexaminer.com/Articles/Articles%20Nov08/Art_Nov08_11.html.

11. From the video "Gay Rights, Special Rights," produced by Jeremiah Films. Transcript available at www.christian-apologetics.org/html/Gay_rights_Special_rights.htm.

12. Linda P. Harvey, "Homosexual Agenda Escalates in Public Schools," July 15, 2001, Public Schools Commentary, NewsWithViews.com, www.newswithviews.com/public_schools/public_schools1.htm.

13. Harvey.

14. "School holds surprise 'Gay' Day for kindergartners," World Net Daily, October 22, 2008, www.wnd.com/index.php?fa=PAGE.view&pageId=78829.

15. "October is National GLBT History Month," www.gayagenda.com/tag/glbt-history-month/.

16. "October is National GLBT History Month."

17. "Parents could face criminal charges for opposing gay history month," April 11, 2010, 365gay.com website, www.365gay.com/news/parents-could-face-criminal-charges-for-opposing-gay-history-month/.

18. Excerpted from the documentary film *It's Elementary,* cited in "Homosexual-oriented education espouses error, confuses children,'" March 28, 2002, Baptist Press website, www.bpnews.net/bpnews.asp?ID=13025.

19. Allyson Smith, "The tragic story of Jesse Dirkhising: How confused 13-year-old died brutal death as a sex toy," September 23, 2002, WorldNetDaily.com, www.wnd.com/news/article.asp?article_id=29026.

20. Paul Gibson, "Gay Male and Lesbian Suicide," www.lambda.org/youth_suicide.htm.

21. "Gay Rights, Special Rights."

22. Paula Ettelbrick, quoted in William B. Rubenstein, "Since When Is Marriage a Path to Liberation?" *Lesbians, Gay Men, and the Law* (New York: The New Press, 1993), pp. 398, 400, as quoted in Timothy Dailey, *The Bible, Church and Homosexuality* (Washington, DC: Family Research Council, 2004).

HATE CRIME LEGISLATION

by Nancy Heche, DMin

> *All Christians should take note. In numerous cases…*
> *human rights tribunals and the courts have made clear*
> *that in their opinion, the equality rights of homosexuals*
> *trump the ostensible guarantees of freedom of religion*
> *in the laws and the Constitution of Canada. Thanks to*
> *these judicial rulings, Canadians no longer have a legal*
> *right to make a public statement that is liable to expose*
> *homosexuals to hatred or contempt, even if the statement is*
> *true and reflects the Christian convictions of the speaker.*
>
> —CANADIAN WRITER RORY LEISHMAN

Hate is not a crime, but when a criminal act is motivated by particular hatreds—hatred of someone's religion, gender, or sexual orientation, for example—many people believe that the hatred motivating the act makes the crime all the more serious. It becomes what's known as a hate crime, a legal term that's one of the most contentious issues associated with gay rights.

Definitions and Descriptions

The Federal Bureau of Investigation defines a hate crime as "a traditional offense like murder, arson, or vandalism with an added element of bias."[1] Congress in turn defines it as "a criminal offense against a person or property motivated in whole or in part by an offender's bias against a race, religion, disability, ethnic origin or sexual orientation."[2] So if a gang of young men damaged a family's home by defacing the property and scrawling graffiti on their walls, they would have committed the crimes of trespassing and vandalism. But if the family also happened to be African-American, the graffiti the gang painted on the walls included racial epithets, and the gang was found to have targeted the family because of their race, then the vandalism would also be deemed a hate crime, making it more serious and warranting stiffer penalties. The gang's demonstrated hostility toward the family's race would, in this case, be seen as motivation for the crime, and motivation is what largely determines and defines a hate crime.

Hate crimes, then, are crimes motivated by hatred and prejudice, ranging in nature from lynchings to cross burnings to vandalism of synagogues. Laws against hate crimes should not be confused with antidiscrimination or equal opportunity laws prohibiting discrimination based on sexual orientation. And although the term "hate crime" did not enter the nation's vocabulary until the 1980s when emerging hate groups launched a wave of bias-related crime, the FBI actually began investigating what we now call hate crimes as far back as the early 1920s, when they opened the first Ku Klux Klan case.[3]

Hate crimes or bias-motivated crimes are ones in which the perpetrator targets a victim because of his or her membership in a certain social group. A federal law passed in 1994 (Public Law 103-322) defines a "hate crime" as a

> crime in which the defendant intentionally selects a victim, or in the case of a property crime, the property that is the object of the crime, because of the actual or perceived race, color, religion, national origin, ethnicity, gender, disability, or sexual orientation of any person.[4]

Hate-crime legislation has expanded in recent years to include crimes perpetrated against homosexuals and transgender persons due to their sexual orientation. The main event was the horrific assault, robbery, and murder of a gay University of Wyoming student Matthew Shepard in 1998. Although this murder was marketed as a hate crime against a homosexual male, later news reporting by ABC's *20/20* has revealed that Shepard's murder was likely motivated less by hatred and more by a desire to rob, combined with the influence of methamphetamines.[5]

After that, however, President Bill Clinton included homosexuals in the Hate Crimes Act, and hate crimes have been expanding to include more people and to cover more specific thoughts and words. Any time a crime can be proven to have the intent of hate toward a certain social group, it is a hate crime. Also if words incite hatred or harm, they are considered a hate crime as well.

The purpose of hate crime legislation is to deter such crimes through harsher punishment and to eliminate disempowerment and victimization of the various groups covered by these laws.

Concerns and Dangers

The danger with categorizing a crime as a hate crime is its attempt to discern intent. While intent has always been present in law (for example premeditated murder vs. manslaughter), there is a danger that motives not present may be ascribed to the perpetrator of a crime. In addition, there is an advantage in being considered as part of a group which deserves "special protection" as opposed to being covered under the Constitutional provision that "all men are created equal." Thus homosexual and transgender groups could use this legislation to silence the church from speaking out against homosexuality and transgenderism.

There are concerns in the U.S. Supreme Court with defining hate crimes. It finds that the statutes can create a conflict with free-speech rights.[6] Those who are against hate crime legislation fear for a court to define a person's intent behind his behavior believing that then the thoughts are being penalized or governed. Some call the legislation involving *intent* "thought crimes." This leads some to believe that we are beginning the step toward penalizing opinions. Others believe that such encoding into the law gives some groups greater rights and more privilege.

On the other hand there are many who say legislation on hate crimes protects classes of people such as Jews, Muslims, African-Americans, women, children, and those in the GLBT community, all of whom are considered by some to be at risk within society. It is hoped by hate crime legislation supporters that tougher penalties for hate crimes will deter violent acts against women and children, homosexuals, and even religious groups, including Christians.

There are sound reasons for criticizing hate crime legislation. But before doing so, we should consider the horrors inflicted on certain groups by individuals, organizations, and, at times, whole nations.

The twentieth century alone witnessed the lynching of African-Americans, the genocide of Armenians in Turkey and Hutus and Tutsis in Rwanda, millions murdered by Pol Pot in Cambodia and Stalin in Russia, and Europe's wide-scale annihilation of Jews, Gypsies, and others—including some homosexuals. And if the past 100 years are peppered with such atrocities, ancient history abounds with them as well. Likewise, individual acts of hate inflicted on one citizen by another (or on one citizen by several others) are easily cited and voluminous, representing, sadly, the tip of hate's iceberg.[7] So to say acts of violence against individuals based on race, gender, sexual orientation, or religion are incidental or unimportant is factually and morally wrong.

Still, many who oppose hate crime legislation do so for two primary and valid reasons. First, such legislation unfairly elevates the worth of one individual over another, through stronger penalties for crimes committed against certain classes. Second, hate crime laws are likely to evolve into "thought crime laws" limiting freedom of speech and religion.

Around the Globe

Some international cases in point have been chronicled by Robert Knight, President of Coral Ridge Ministries, and posted online by Concerned Women of America:

- In June 2004, Swedish pastor Ake Green was arrested and sentenced to one month in prison for preaching against homosexual behavior from a biblical perspective in his pulpit at his church in Kalmar in 2003. Green was the first pastor prosecuted for a "hate crime" after the Swedish government added "sexual orientation" to its "hate crime" law in 2003. The public prosecutor, Kjell Yngvesson, justified the arrest by saying, "Collecting Bible [verses] on this topic as he does makes this hate speech."[8]

- The Scottish Parliament has banned criticism of homosexuality by religious guest speakers during the four-minute slot in its proceedings called "A Time for Reflection," in which representatives of different religions are invited to speak. On December 22, 2004, Cardinal Keith O'Brien, the Catholic Archbishop of St. Andrews and Edinburgh, gave a Christmas message that included a vague mention of "sexual aberrations" as a form of human captivity. A leftist

Parliament member immediately proposed a motion to prohibit religious ministers from speaking against homosexuality during the reflection time. The motion, which passed, called Cardinal O'Brien's reference a "gratuitous insult."[9]

- The Anglican Bishop of Chester, England, Dr. Peter Forster, was investigated by police for saying that homosexuals "could and should seek medical help to 'reorient' themselves." The Lesbian and Gay Christian Movement (LGCM), among others, accused him of advocating a "scandalous" and "offensive" argument from a "bygone age." [10]

- A Christian group called Living Word made two videos that questioned "safe sex" slogans by exposing the link between AIDS and homosexual behavior. The New Zealand Film and Literature Board of Review banned the films for encouraging "hate speech." A parliamentary committee also attempted to have censorship laws changed so that all Christian videos critical of homosexuality would be banned.[11]

- C-250, Canada's new "hate crimes" law, reads: "Everyone who, by communicating statements, other than in private conversation, willfully promotes hatred against any identifiable group is guilty of...an indictable offense and is liable to imprisonment for a term not exceeding two years." The law specifically states that those who practice homosexual behavior are an "identifiable" group. On New Year's Day 2004, Canadian Internet journalist Robert Jason received a visit from two plainclothes police officers. They were there to investigate a possible "hate crime" after a homosexual activist complained that he didn't like Jason's pro-family website and felt personally threatened by it... The officers felt it was necessary to investigate Jason, 70, a retiree who supports himself by caring for handicapped people in his home.[12]

- Hugh Owens, a resident of Regina, Saskatchewan, took out a small ad in the Saskatoon *StarPhoenix* newspaper on June 30, 1997, that had a stick figure of two men holding hands, with a circle and a line through it, and a brief list of Bible verses on homosexuality. The Saskatchewan Human Rights Tribunal ruled on June 15, 2001, that both Owens and the newspaper publisher had to pay a total of $4,500 in damages to three homosexuals ($1,500 each) who were "offended" by the ad. The "inquiry adjudicator," Valerie Watson, wrote that the plaintiffs "were exposed to hatred, ridicule and their dignity was affronted on the basis of their sexual orientation."[13]

In the United States of America

In the U.S., where freedoms of speech and religion have been historically celebrated and protected, trends continue to slant against both freedoms. Below are only a handful of cases in which hate crime legislation, civil law, antidiscrimination regulations, or official censure have been wielded against Christians holding to the traditional view.

New Mexico: Christian photographer sued for not photographing same-sex commitment ceremony. In September of 2006, Vanessa Willock and her lesbian partner sought the services of Elaine Photography, owned and operated by Elaine Huguenin of Albuquerque. Huguenin, an evangelical Christian, declined the request on religious grounds. In response, Willock filed a complaint with the New Mexico Human Rights Division, citing human-rights violations and seeking a ruling that would prevent Huguenin from refusing to photograph same-sex ceremonies in the future. The court ruled in the plaintiff's favor.[14]

New Jersey: Methodist church sued for not allowing facilities to be used for same-sex civil union ceremony. An Ocean Grove boardwalk pavilion owned by a local church association has lost its tax-exempt status for refusing to rent the property for same-sex civil union ceremonies. The state ruled the location no longer met the criteria of being open to all members of the public.

The issue arose after two lesbian couples were not allowed to rent the pavilion for a civil union ceremony. They filed a complaint with the State Division of Civil Rights, which then began a discrimination investigation. The church association "sued the state, claiming that the investigation violated its First Amendment rights." However, the federal district court judge in charge of the case did not stop the investigation.[15]

California: Oakland employees disciplined for "hate speech" for referring to family values. The Pro-Family Law Center challenged the 9th Circuit Court of Appeals and district court rulings that found the terms *marriage, natural family,* and *family values* to be hate speech.

The case involved two employees of the city of Oakland who were threatened with termination for using those terms on an employee bulletin board. The employees were concerned about the homosexual-activist material being circulated in the workplace. They attempted to raise awareness and support for the "natural family." They were also concerned about "Bible-bashing" in the workplace. They sought to establish the Good News Employee Association in response to this alleged Bible-bashing, which had supposedly been committed by ranking city officials and other groups who were granted open access. The employees tried to express their views through a flyer they posted on an open city bulletin board, and were allegedly censored. Other groups were still allowed to post materials.[16]

California: Christian event condemned. An evangelical youth event called "Battle-Cry for a Generation" was met with an official condemnation from the City of San Francisco when they came to the city. The two-day rally held at AT&T Park was intended to energize and motivate evangelical youth, and to decry sin in the culture. The rally drew over 25,000 teens, and a group of protestors as well. These protestors represented abortion activists, antiwar activists, gay-lesbian rights activists, and atheistic groups.

Mark Leno, openly gay city assemblyman, denounced the evangelicals, saying that "they're loud, they're obnoxious, they're disgusting, and they should get out of San Francisco." The openly gay author of the city resolution, Tom Ammiano, said of the event, "Even if it is done by a Barnum & Bailey crowd with a tent and some snake oil, I think we need to pay attention to it...we should not fall asleep at the wheel."[17]

The City of San Francisco Board of Supervisors passed an official city resolution "condemning the 'act of provocation' by what it termed an 'anti-gay,' 'anti-choice' organization that aimed to 'negatively influence the politics of America's most tolerant and progressive city.'"[18]

Pennsylvania: Christian activists arrested and charged with "hate crime." On October 10, 2004, 11 Christians peacefully carried signs, handed out literature, and sang hymns at "Outfest," a Philadelphia homosexual street fair taking place on public grounds. The Christians were confronted by the "Pink Angels," who blocked the 11 by interlocking arms, shouting obscenities, and shoving large Styrofoam angels in their face. The homosexual activists also used shrill whistles to drown out the message of the 11.

Police arrested all 11 Christians but none of the Pink Angels. The Christians were charged with three felonies and five misdemeanors (criminal conspiracy, possession of instruments of crime, reckless endangerment, ethnic intimidation, riot, failure to disperse, disorderly conduct, and obstructing highways), totaling a possibility of 47 years in prison. The charge of "ethnic intimidation" fell under the state's hate crime law, to which "sexual orientation" was recently added. After a long legal process, all charges were eventually dismissed on February 17, 2005.

A lawsuit was later filed in May 2006 on behalf of the "Philadelphia 11" when it became known that Philly Pride Presents, the homosexual activist group responsible for "Outfest," had conspired with the Philadelphia police department to prevent the "religious right" from interfering with the event.[19]

Colorado: Court orders Christian mother to refrain from teaching child anything that could be deemed "homophobic." A Denver County Circuit Court judge has ordered Dr. Cheryl Clark to "make sure that there is nothing in the religious upbringing that the minor child is exposed to that can be considered homophobic." Dr. Clark is a Christian and a former lesbian. The case stemmed from a problem Dr. Clark's former partner, Elsey McLeod, had with Focus on the Family and Promise Keepers material on display in Dr. Clark's church.

Prior to this case, McLeod had been awarded "psychological parent" status and, as a result, was awarded joint custody even though she had no official tie to the child and Dr. Clark was the child's adoptive parent. The court gave no orders to McLeod that would prevent her from speaking against Dr. Clark's new way of life.[20]

Wisconsin: Christian father discusses homosexuality; gets fined and re-educated for his "hate crime." David Ott, a self-described former homosexual living in Madison, approached a practicing homosexual and engaged in conversation. David, holding his toddler at the time, was making no threats but merely disagreeing. A few months later he got a knock on the door and a court summons. He was charged and convicted of a "hate crime" and sentenced to a re-education class led by a lesbian whose opening premise was, "Homosexuality is normal." Ott was sentenced to one year probation, 50 hours of community service, and "sensitivity training" taught by two lesbians at the University of Wisconsin. He also incurred more than $7,000 in legal fees in fighting the alleged "hate crime" of trying to tell a gay-identified man about the sin and dangers of living homosexually.[21]

The extremity, heavy-handedness, and injustice displayed in cases like these, where seemingly noble hate crime laws have evolved into unreasonable restrictions, led *National Review* magazine's editors to express publicly what millions of skeptical citizens (privately?) think:

> We want to deter and punish crimes against blacks, women, homosexuals, and everyone else. But we do not want to open the door to legal punishment for harboring incorrect thoughts about controversial issues—especially when those incorrect thoughts are part of the historic teaching of our major religions.[22]

A Christian Response

To the Christian this is especially problematic. We value human life; we value freedom of speech and religion. But if exercising those rights literally endangers another human being, as some hate crime apologists suggest, how should we then respond? A few guidelines are called for:

1. *Hear the matter.* Proverbs 18:13 tells us that "he who answers a matter before he hears it, it is a folly and a shame to him." Too often, Christians or social conservatives have a knee-jerk reaction to hate crime laws, dismissing them without first considering them. Yet Scripture encourages us to hear a matter before rejecting it. At the least, we should consider, then, the claims and arguments of those who support hate crime legislation.

2. *Examine the claims.* Having heard the claim that hate crime legislation is necessary to protect the lives and well being of certain groups, we should then examine their merit. We will readily agree that homosexual and transgender citizens deserve legal protection from assault and mistreatment, and many believe that existing laws already provide them with such protection. So when we're told that additional state and federal laws are statutes are now needed, we should request the facts and documentation proving the point.

3. *Watch our speech.* While we value free speech, we also recognize the responsibility it carries, particularly for the Christian. If we stand against hate crime legislation, let us also take a stand against hate itself, and let that stand be shown in the way we address all people, including (and especially) those we disagree with. So we take

Paul's admonition to heart: "Let your speech always be with grace, seasoned with salt" (Colossians 4:6).

4. *Resist and oppose oppressive laws.* When legislation is being considered that will demonstrably restrict cherished freedoms without reasonable cause, then respectful Christian resistance is called for.

The author George Orwell, whose classic novels *1984* and *Animal Farm* described the evils of totalitarianism, left a warning on the matter that anyone valuing basic freedoms should note:

> If large numbers of people believe in freedom of speech, there will be freedom of speech even if the law forbids it. But if public opinion is sluggish, inconvenient minorities will be persecuted, even if laws exist to protect them.[23]

CHAPTER TWENTY-FOUR

HATE CRIME LEGISLATION

○—KEY POINTS—○

1. Legislation on hate crimes is intended to protect certain classes of people who may be considered at risk within the society, including individuals in the GLBT community.

2. The implied purpose of hate crime legislation is to deter crime through further punishment and to eliminate disempowerment and victimization of specified groups.

3. Hate crime legislation is considered by many to be "thought crime" legislation because it "penalizes politically incorrect beliefs, attitudes, and thought rather than actual crimes."

4. The big danger with hate crimes is the attempt to discern intent.

5. One of the worries behind hate crime legislation is that individuals in the GLBT community will view certain preaching as inciting rage against that community.

NOTES

1. "Hate Crimes—Overview" from the Federal Bureau of Investigation (FBI) official website. See www .fbi.gov/hq/cid/civilrights/overview.htm.

2. "Hate Crimes—Overview."

3. "Hate Crimes—Overview."

4. 103rd Congress, 2nd Session. See www.legalmomentum.org/assets/pdfs/vawa1994.pdf.

5. "New Details Emerge in Matthew Shepard Murder," *20/20* broadcast, November 26, 2004.

6. See U.S. Supreme Court decision *RAV v. City of St. Paul* at www.bc.edu/bc_org/avp/cas/comm/ free_speech/rav.html.

7. See, for example, "The Human Face of Hate Crimes" at www.civilrights.org/publications/hate crimes/human-face.html.

8. Swedish Minister Acquitted of Hate Speech Charges," WorldNetDaily.com at www.wnd.com/ news/article.asp?ARTICLE_ID=47633; Lars Grip, "No Free Speech in Preaching," *Christianity Today*, August 9, 2004; "Swedish Court Reviews 'Hate' Case," BBC News World Edition, May 9, 2005, at http://news.bbc.co.uk/2/hi/europe/4530209.stm. Cited by Robert Knight in "'Hate Crime' Laws Threaten Religious Freedom" 12/12/2005 at www.cwfa.org/articledisplay.asp?id= 9672&department=CFI&categoryid=papers.

9. "Scottish Parliament Bans Criticism of Homosexuality by Religious Guest Speakers," LifeSiteNews .net, May 4, 2005, at www.lifesite.net/ldn/2005/may/05050407.html. Cited by Knight.

10. Will Batchelor and Suzanne Elsworth, "Bishop to Face Quiz by Police," Liverpool Daily Post, November 10, 2003 at http://iccheshireonline.icnetwork.co.uk/0100news/0100regionalnews/tm_ objectid=13608857%26method=full%26siteid=50020-name_page.html. Cited by Knight.

11. *Living Word Distributors Ltd v. Human Rights Action Group* (2000) 3 NZLR 570 at www.world lii.org/int/cases/ICHRL/2000/63.html; Janet Folger, *The Criminalization of Christianity* (Sisters, Oregon: Multnomah Publishers, Inc., 2005), p. 8; David McLoughlin, "Bid to Ban Christian Films," *The Dominion Post*, Wellington, New Zealand, March 6, 2003; and "Human Rights in New Zealand Today," New Zealand Human Rights Commission at www.hrc.co.nz/report/chapters/ chapter08/expression03.html#10. Cited by Knight.

12. Rory Leishman, "Canadian Human Rights Tribunals Should Be Ditched," London (Ontario, Canada) Free Press, as reprinted on July 11, 2001, at www.cwfa.org/articles/110/CFI/cfreport. Cited by Knight.

13. Leishman, cited by Knight.

14. "Proposition 8 and the Right to Marry," http://prop8legalcommentary.blogspot.com/2009/12/new -mexico-district-court-judge-rules.html.

15. "Civil Union Dispute Pits Methodist Retreat against Gays Who Aided in Its Rebirth," *New York Times,* September 3, 2007.

16. "US Court Rules It's OK to Censor the Terms 'Natural Family,' 'Marriage,' and 'Family Values,'" LifeSiteNews.com, March 8, 2007, www.lifesitenews.com/ldn/2007/mar/07030805.html.

17. "Youth Rally in San Francisco," *San Francisco Chronicle,* March 25, 2006.

18. "Youth Rally."

19. "Philly Group to Protest Outfest Again," World Net Daily, April 6, 2010, www.wnd.com/news/ article.asp?ARTICLE_ID=46731.

20. "Ex-Lesbian Couple Use Court in Custody, Homophobia Spat," *Washington Times,* November 17, 2003, www.washingtontimes.com/news/2003/nov/17/20031117-104249-1352r/.

21. "Hate Crime Legislation Added to Defense Bill," JBS.org, April 12, 2010, http://jbs.org/jbs-news -feed/1540-hate-crimes-legislation-added-to-defense-bill.

22. "Hating Hate," *National Review* online, May 1, 2007, http://article.nationalreview.com/.

23. George Orwell, cited at Liberty Tree website, http://quotes.liberty-tree.ca/quotes_by/george +orwell.

TRANSGENDER ISSUES

by Nancy Heche, DMin

> *God grant me the serenity*
> *to accept the things I cannot change;*
> *courage to change the things I can;*
> *and wisdom to know the difference.*
>
> —REINHOLD NIEBUHR

In June of 2009, Chastity Bono, daughter of the singing duo Sonny and Cher, made public her decision to undergo sex-change, female-to-male surgery. "Yes, it's true," her spokesman, Howard Bragman, reported. "Chaz, after many years of consideration, has made the courageous decision to honor his true identity."[1]

And though relatively few celebrities have so publicly announced and acted on their desire to change sexes, Bono does join a handful of well-known figures that are still a part of the public's consciousness. Christine Jorgensen (formerly known as "George") was perhaps one of the most famous, having been a male who underwent sex-change surgery abroad in 1952 and becoming a prominent spokesperson for pro-gay and transgender causes. Dr. Renee Richards, a physician formerly named Dick who underwent sex-change surgery, became a professional tennis player. And Brandon Teena, a female-to-male transgender murder victim who did not undergo surgery but lived as a male nonetheless, was portrayed in the Oscar-winning film *Boys Don't Cry.*[2]

Transgender people may be somewhat rare, but as part of the Gay Lesbian Bisexual and Transgender population (GLBT) it plays an increasingly prominent role in the gay rights movement. And as the GLBT movement ushers in more tolerance for its members, churches will undoubtedly be confronted with the issue. John W. Kennedy, a writer for *Christianity Today*, proposes that advocates and critics of the transgender movement seem to have come to the same conclusion: More transgender people will be showing up at American churches and will be open about their controversial lifestyle.[3]

Clearly, the subject is as unavoidable as homosexuality, as transgender advocates follow the course mapped out by their gay predecessors. From the 1970s onward, the gay rights movement advanced itself through films, television characters, sympathetic journalists, the American Psychiatric Association, antidiscrimination laws, and the educational system. The national debate shifted accordingly, the question eventually morphing from "Is homosexuality normal?" to "Are objections to homosexuality normal?" Those who hold such objections now find themselves (and their churches) subject to intense pressure and scorn.

The gay rights movement's success is emulated by its transgender cousin, undoubtedly the next wave of sexual revolution.[4] Consider the following:

- Popular films such as the Oscar-winning *Boys Don't Cry*, *The Crying Game*, and *Normal* (starring Jessica Lange as a wife who comes to terms with her husband's need to live as a woman) portray transgenders not as unnatural, but as victims of prejudice and circumstance.

- Television characters such as the transgender in the highly popular show *Ugly Betty* use the likability factor to educate the public on the inherent "normality" of transgenderism and the ignorance of those who disapprove of it.

- And sympathetic journalist Barbara Walters in a *20/20* piece titled "My Secret Self," first aired in the spring of 2007, invited viewers to "open [their] hearts and minds" to "courageous and loving parents" who allowed their transgender children to live as the opposite sex, promising, "most of you will be moved" by their stories.[5]

- As gay activists did in 1973, transgender advocates are pressuring the American Psychiatric Association to revise its *Diagnostic and Statistical Manual* to eliminate transgenderism (or gender identity disorder) as a classifiable disorder.[6]

- Antidiscrimination laws and educational reforms that cite transgender people as a protected class have swept through high school and college campuses, as well as corporations and small businesses.[7]

The predictable outcome—increased acceptance of transgender variations and increased pressure on those who dissent—forces us to articulate a biblical response.

Terms and Definitions

Transgenderism is a broad term, defined by the Oxford English Dictionary as "relating to, or designating a person whose identity does not conform unambiguously to conventional notions of male or female gender, but combines or moves between these." It serves as an umbrella term covering a number of sexual and gender variations, including:

- *Cross-dressers (or transvestites):* People who enjoy wearing clothing of the opposite sex, though in general they are identified as and with their assigned sex (such as men who are unambiguously male but who also enjoy dressing in women's clothing).
- *Drag queens or drag kings:* Men or women who dress in the clothing of the opposite sex for the purpose of entertainment. When someone is "in drag," he or she is temporarily adopting clothing and mannerisms that he or she would not normally adopt in daily routine.
- *Transsexuals:* Most transsexuals seem to feel, from early in life, "trapped" in the wrong body, hence the American Psychiatric Association's definition of transsexualism as "strong and persistent cross-gender identification…and…persistent discomfort about one's assigned sex."[8] Historically, transsexuals were distinguished from transgender individuals by virtue of having undergone an actual sex-change surgery. This was later expanded to include those in the preparatory stages of surgery.

Intersex is a condition in its own category, referring to those who are either born with both sets of genitals or with genitalia that are at least ambiguous. This constitutes more of a medical condition than a psychological one, and it will often be approached via surgery or other forms of medical intervention.

With time, it is common for people who self-identify as transgender or transsexual to develop a form of depression called *gender dysphoria*—as in, a depression over the sex one has been *assigned* as opposed to the sex one feels most comfortable *being*.

"I'm so mad at God," a seven-year old laments in the Barbara Walters special. "He made a mistake."[9] The torment of gender dysphoria expresses itself in the question, "How can I be one way yet feel another?" Lest anyone dismiss the seriousness of this depression, it should be noted that suicide attempts, drug abuse, and horrendous efforts at self-mutilation are commonly reported among young transsexuals.[10]

The solution, many conclude, is a process called sex reassignment, through which the person's body is hormonally and surgically altered. The sex a transsexual wants to be is the target sex, as opposed to the assigned sex with which he or she was born. Reassignment can include injections of hormones, facial reconstruction, breast implants or removal, and reconstruction of genitals. This process is widely available, although most clinics require a person to live (dress, work, and self-identify) as a member of the opposite sex for a prescribed period before undergoing surgery, accompanied by extensive psychological counseling to determine suitability for the procedure.

The impossibility of truly becoming the opposite sex may seem obvious, but so does the desperation a person must feel to make such an attempt. Surely, castration, implants, and hormones still leave a man unable to ovulate; penile implants and breast reduction likewise won't delete a woman's womanhood.

Knowing all this and more, thousands still attempt reassignment, believing that they were born not for the body they inhabit, but for the one they're trying to create. At one time such a belief held little sway, the testimony of the body overriding that of the mind. But as we move further from the influences of Scripture and Judeo-Christian tradition, embracing a more subjective grid for decision making, feelings often trump facts.

Traditionally, if a man felt like a woman yet inhabited a male body, his feelings, not his body, were viewed as the problem. They were considered something to be resisted, modified if possible, and contrary to what was. Currently, what one is is being determined by what one feels—an ominous trend when one considers its implications. It is, in essence, an attempt to redefine reality by desire, knowledge by intuition.

Transgenderism's increased acceptance, combined with its early developmental appearance, leaves many professionals and laity convinced that it is an inborn trait. The jury, after all, is still out on the question of homosexuality's origins—inborn, acquired, or a combination of the two?—and compelling arguments are made on all sides. Biological or genetic factors thus may create, or at least contribute to, this mystery as well. (As of this writing, there is no single, universally accepted theory of the origins of transgenderism.)

The Work of the Church

Christian therapist Warren Throckmorton, past president of the American Mental Health Counselors Association, says he has advised transgender people who are in absolute agony over their state. Typically, such individuals are desperately in search of hope and acceptance, he says. It may be uncomfortable to tell transgender individuals that their desires don't align with the Bible, but pastors must do so.

> Even if science does determine differentiation in the brain at birth, even if there are prenatal influences, we can't set aside teaching of the Bible because of research findings.[11]

Yet, the pressure to do just that is growing. Homosexuality used to be considered an unnatural tendency that was to be resisted, not expressed. Today, it's widely viewed as something the homosexual should default to, lest he deny his true feelings and do himself damage. "Homophobia" is the word now applied to traditional disapproval, making the disapproval, not the sexual preference, the problem.

Transgenderism is in a similar metamorphosis. Barbara Walters, for example, commended the parents of young transsexuals for granting their children's desire to live as the opposite sex, thus "sparing them a lifetime of misery."[12] The new word for disapproval of transgenderism and transsexualism—"transphobia"—takes an obvious cue from the oft-used term "homophobia."

Defaulting to the conviction that one is trapped in the wrong body is touted as the answer to the conflicts inherent in transsexualism. Recent studies indicate that this may be a premature assumption, however. "There is no conclusive evidence that sex change operations improve the lives of transsexuals," one such study reports, "with many people remaining severely distressed and even suicidal after the operation."[13] As for the growing belief in reassignment surgery's efficacy, Chris Hyde, director of the University of Birmingham's Aggressive Research Intelligence Facility (ARIF), found that "most of the medical research on gender reassignment was poorly designed, which skewed the results to suggest that sex change operations are beneficial."[14]

In this light, Paul's writings to Corinth regarding one's calling seem both a commandment and a caution:

> As God has distributed [in Greek, "apportioned," "dealt," or "divided"] to each one, as the Lord has called each one, so let him walk. Let each one remain in the same calling in which he was called (1 Corinthians 7:17,20).

In this, the transgender person will surely need the church to walk alongside.

Recently I came across the testimony of a pastor who discipled a transsexual who had had reassignment surgery. "Mandy" originally presented himself as a woman, was converted and baptized, and then disclosed his secret to the pastor. The pastor, while making it clear that the assigned gender was the one to strive for, nonetheless continued to care for Mandy, encouraging him to disclose the truth to others gradually and pursue God's will.

As he did so, his masculine characteristics became more apparent, surgery notwithstanding. His church gathered around him, supportive and accepting, until Mandy decided to live openly as a man. As the pastor describes it,

> Mandy became "James." Great was the rejoicing when a fine, besuited young James walked to the front on the first Sunday of the year to be "introduced" to the church. Fifteen months later, James announced his engagement to a girl in the church, but that's another story.[15]

Mandy was blessed; his church was Christlike.

Other churches should take a cue, and respond likewise to those with this struggle who will no doubt be joining other congregations as well. As the transgender movement picks up steam, the church as a whole must be prepared to articulate and defend the biblical position, while offering support and discipleship to repentant transgender individuals. The transsexual dilemma demands a response, as the culture and the church wrestle with its many ramifications.

CHAPTER TWENTY-FIVE

Transgender Issues

○—Key Points—○

1. Homosexuality and transsexualism are entirely separate. A homosexual is sexually attracted to the same sex; a transsexual feels that he or she is a member of the opposite sex, but "trapped" in the wrong body.

2. The modern gay rights movement is generally supportive of transgender and transsexual individuals, believing they should be allowed to undergo sexual reassignment surgery if they desire, and that the stigma often associated with transsexualism should be removed.

3. GLBT is an acronym for Gay, Lesbian, Bisexual, and Transgender. There are a number of definitions of transgenderism. It is defined as a gender-identity disorder and mental illness on one end of the spectrum, and a gender that transcends the binary gender system inherent within the patriarchal social structure on the other end. Others say it is a social movement seeking transgender rights. This broad diversity of definitions leads to strong polarization in the culture as well as the church around the issue.

4. Many believe that more transgender people will be attending American churches and will be open about their controversial lifestyle.

5. Transgender advocates have become more vocal and active in the last four to five years.

6. There are varying degrees of transgender behavior and expression.

7. There are reasons to believe that transgender individuals who choose sex-reassignment surgery may experience ongoing psychological, emotional, physical, professional, and social problems.

Resources

"Transsexuality Explained" by Sander Breiner, National Association for the Research and Treatment of Homosexuality Online Journal, www.narth.com/docs/transexpl.html.

NOTES

1. Stephen M. Silverman, "Chastity Bono Undergoing Sex Change," *People* magazine, Thursday, June 11, 2009.

2. Respectively: www.christinejorgensen.org; "The Lady Regrets," *New York Times*, 2/1/2007, www .nytimes.com/2007/02/01/garden/01renee.html?ex=1327986000&en=5de83aa236e6d59b& ei=5088&partner=rss; "The Story of Brandon Teena: A Life That Should Have Been Lived," www .justicejunction.com/judicial_injustice_brandon_teena.htm.

3. John Kennedy, "The Transgender Movement" *Christianity Today*, February 12, 2008, www.chris tianitytoday.com/ct/2008/february/25.54.html.

4. The pro-transsexual public health website "Public Health Seattle and King County" (www.metrokc .gov/health/glbt/transgender.htm#mh), for example, makes assertions about acceptance of transsexualism that parallel those that homosexuals made 30 years earlier when it reports, "Although societal acceptance of transsexual and transgendered people is far from complete, there is a growing and active community of transgendered people—particularly in the coastal areas of the United States. There are also increasing numbers of books and online information and support for transgendered people."

5. Barbara Walters, "My Secret Self," *20/20*, April 27, 2007.

6. Kelley Winters, "Issues of GID Diagnosis for Transsexual Women and Men," GID Reform Advocates, www.gidreform.org/gid30285.html.

7. See a listing of such reforms and proposals in Francisco Forrest Martin, "Breaking New Ground in International Law Protecting Transsexual Rights: Rights International's Amicus Curiae Brief in *X., Y., and Z. v. United Kingdom*," *The National Journal of Sexual Orientation Law* 3, 1 (1997), www .ibiblio.org/gaylaw/issue5/transbre.html.

8. See "DSM IV: Gender Identity Disorder," Diagnostic Features, Gender Identity Disorder Today, MH Today, www.mental-health-today.com/gender/ dsm.htm.

9. "My Secret Self."

10. George J. Wilkerson, "What We Don't Know: The Unaddressed Health Concerns of the Transgendered," Trans-Health.com, www.trans-health.com/displayarticle.php?aid=7.

11. Kennedy.

12. "My Secret Self."

13. David Batty, "Sex Changes Are Not Effective, Say Researchers," *Society Guardian*, July 30, 2004; cited at http://society.guardian.co.uk/print/0,,4982009-105965,00.html.

14. Batty.

15. "Transsexualism in the Church: A Pastor Responds," Proverbs 27:7 Issues, New Hope Outreach, www.newhopeoutreachtoronto.org/A_pastor_responds.html.

HIV AND AIDS

by Nancy Heche, DMin

> *The AIDS epidemic has rolled back a big rotting log and revealed all the squirming life underneath it, since it involves, all at once, the main themes of our existence: sex, death, power, money, love, hate, disease and panic. No American phenomenon has been so compelling since the Vietnam War.*
>
> —Edmund White, American author

Because HIV/AIDS most noticeably struck the gay male community in the early 1980s, it's impossible to adequately address homosexuality without addressing AIDS as well. While it was initially considered by many to be a "gay disease," it's now common knowledge that AIDS does not discriminate, and is transmitted through many avenues, not merely homosexual activity. Its most common forms of transmission are through sexual intercourse (anal or vaginal), shared hypodermic needles, blood transfusions, and from mother to child in the womb. In this chapter we'll discuss HIV/AIDS, its origins, and the challenges and opportunities it presents to the church. Let's begin by clarifying our main terms:

- HIV—Human Immunodeficiency Virus is the forerunner to AIDS. It can be transmitted through blood, semen, pre-ejaculate, vaginal fluid, or breast milk. Transmission can occur through unprotected sex, sharing needles during intravenous drug use, from mother to child in the womb or through breastfeeding, and via blood transfusions (although blood screening procedures may help to reduce this).

- AIDS—Acquired Immunodeficiency Syndrome is a "set of symptoms and infections resulting from the damage to the human immune system caused by the human immunodeficiency virus (HIV). It progressively reduces the effectiveness of the immune system, leaving the victim susceptible to any number of opportunistic infections."[1]

There are various explanations of how HIV and AIDS began in the United States. HIV and AIDS were officially defined 18 months after five completely healthy people came down with a unique form of pneumonia in June 1981. Some sources suggest that the original source of HIV was from a type of chimpanzee native to West Africa. A plasma sample that predates any occurrence in the United States was taken in 1959 from an infected adult male from what is now the Democratic Republic of Congo. Since that time AIDS has spread throughout the world.[2]

In the United States, AIDS was first identified in 1981, although no name had been given to the new disease that was primarily affecting gay men. It was called the "Gay Plague," GRIDS (Gay Related Immune Deficiency), and ARC (AIDS Related Complex) before AIDS became its official name.

GLBTQ (Gay/Lesbian/Bisexual/Transgender/Queer) communities have played an important role in AIDS activism. They were among the first groups affected by the disease, and their collective response has directly impacted the course of the epidemic and greatly influenced AIDS treatment and advocacy. Currently, access to treatment has increased, but new technology reveals a higher number of new HIV infections in the U.S. than previously known.

The Current Situation

Some recent newspaper and magazine articles citing statistics and developments are worth noting:

David Baltimore, a Nobel-winning biologist, sounded a note of despair in an address to the American Association for the Advancement of Science in February 2008. He noted that the virus has evolved in a way that makes it virtually impossible to attack by priming the immune system, the usual goal of a vaccine…"The best hope may lie in the biological equivalent of a 'Hail Mary' pass—a wholly new approach that would combine gene therapy, stem cells and immunologic therapy to thwart the disease."[3]

South Africa's finance minister has announced the government will spend more than a quarter of a billion dollars over the next three years to double the number of people receiving AIDS medication.[4]

Deborah Jack, Chief Executive of the National AIDS Trust in the United Kingdom, said, "In recent years we have witnessed knowledge and understanding about HIV decline and at the same time the HIV diagnoses have reached an all time high. By 2010 there will be over 100,000 people living with HIV in the UK if current trends continue. We cannot afford to be complacent about HIV education. Ignorance about HIV increases vulnerability to infection and also contributes to stigma and discrimination."[5]

A Christian Response

An interview with Rev. Bruce Sonnenberg, founder and executive director of the ministry He Intends Victory, reveals a redemptive approach to the AIDS epidemic that deserves study and emulation.[6] This interview tells the story of how Rev. Sonnenberg became active in the church's global response to the HIV/AIDS pandemic.

> **Q:** Pastor Sonnenberg, you've been working in AIDS ministry as a pastor and the founder of He Intends Victory for over 20 years now. How would you define effective AIDS ministry?
>
> **A:** The key to effective AIDS ministry is hope. We have to first know that our hope lies in Christ, and then be able to communicate that hope to the people we serve. When someone gets a test result saying they're HIV positive, or when a doctor tells a patient he has AIDS, the patient can feel pretty hopeless, like he's lost all value and there's no future left. Effective AIDS ministry reminds a person like that of two things: First, that they have tremendous value in this life

and still have so much to contribute. Second, that there's hope in Jesus Christ, who's invited this person to know Him and thereby know eternal life. That's hope, and when you're ministering to people affected by AIDS, hope is the key.

Q: That sounds like an evangelical pastor talking. But before you got into this ministry, did you know much about AIDS?

A: Not much at all. In fact, I remember watching the news with my wife, way back in the early 1980s when so many news stories centered on AIDS, and saying, "I'm sick of hearing about AIDS all the time!" Pretty ironic, huh? Because nowadays, I not only hear about it all the time, but I talk about it all the time as well.

Q: Then what got you involved in this work?

A: I'm an evangelical pastor. Years ago, a young man in my church, who I knew very well and whose parents had been with our congregation for years, came to me and said, "I've got to tell my parents two huge things. First, I've been involved with men. Second, I have AIDS." All of sudden all the things associated with this seemed to fall on me—homosexuality, secret sin, heartache, medical problems, mortality, grace, everything. Then, believe it or not, two other similar situations came up in my church. That's when my perspective on this changed hugely. It wasn't any longer a problem a few people out there had. It was in the church. My church! And I knew if that was true of me and my church, it was also true of churches around the world. I knew I needed to respond—and out of that, He Intends Victory was birthed.

Q: To help us understand what constitutes AIDS ministry, can you tell us a bit about what He Intends Victory actually does?

A: We're a Bible-believing ministry offering practical care, support, education, and evangelism to people who've been impacted by AIDS. We try to operate on the model of the Good Samaritan, who didn't care so much how the man he helped got into his condition, but rather, that he was able to give him the help he needed.

And believe me, there's a lot of need out there. We currently have chapters in 23 countries around the world, with 422 volunteers worldwide. We try to serve according to need. For example, in third-world, poverty-stricken areas, the primary need regarding AIDS may be food or clothing, medical outreach, emotional support, and shelter. Remember, we're dealing both with people who've been *affected* by HIV and those *infected* with it as well. So while caring for the person with AIDS, we address the needs of the family also. In some countries we offer agricultural outreach to help families and villages develop and nurture their own crops to keep their families alive. In other areas we provide medical referrals, or support groups, or education as to how people can protect themselves from becoming infected. You see, to do AIDS ministry properly, you have to figure out what the greatest specific need is, and respond accordingly.

Q: Do you talk to people about sexual sin? After all, you are a Bible-believing ministry and you're dealing with many people who got the virus through sexual contact apart from marriage.

A: That's partly true, but you'd be surprised how people are infected who aren't guilty of any overt sexual sin. In Africa, for example, many men have multiple wives, or engage prostitutes. And since a wife is often deemed to be their "property," they see no need to warn or inform her. Such a woman has no sexual sin to repent of. Likewise, there are places in India where parents become so destitute they honestly believe the only way their children will survive is through prostitution. Some sell their ten-year-old girls into sexual slavery, where they are at huge risk of becoming infected. What sin do these children have to repent of?

Of course, we don't make any bones about where we stand. When appropriate, we fully disclose that we believe any sexual behavior apart from heterosexual marriage is wrong. But our main goal isn't to tell people where they've gone wrong, but rather, to help them by meeting their needs where they are right now.

Q: But surely, when you are clear about your position on homosexuality, you get criticized by people who call you "homophobic." How do you respond?

A: We're not here to argue. If people disagree with us, fine. But a number of pro-gay folks have come to see we're not here to judge, but to serve. And sometimes we've developed friendships with them and had terrific talks about Christianity and sexuality. I guess a lot of gay people have misconceptions about Christians, just as a lot of Christians have misconceptions about gays.

Q: Speaking of misconceptions, what's a common misconception our culture has about HIV/AIDS and people with AIDS?

A. The most common misconception people have is that this epidemic is somehow over, or not very serious. People hear so much about treatment and effective drug therapy that they figure HIV is no big deal, just a chronic condition. And it's not!

Q: But tremendous progress has been made, right?

A: Certainly, but there's still no cure, no vaccine—and the average life expectancy for someone with HIV may be 20 to 30 years. Or more, perhaps—but no one should assume it's "no big deal" to get infected. And remember, while there are medications available, the side effects of those medications can be pretty rough. Decreased or redistributed body fat, nausea, or neuropathy—degeneration of the nervous system—are a few of the common ones. And sometimes the side effects get so rough that a person has to take medications to relieve the side effects! And that's not to mention the fact that, after about five years or so, the body can develop resistance to these drugs, making newer, perhaps stronger ones necessary. So you see, infection is still very, very serious. Not a death sentence, sure, but serious.

Q: What about the church? Are there common misconceptions people in the church have today about HIV/AIDS and people with AIDS?

A: Many Christians still seem to think AIDS is a "gay disease," whatever that means. They think it only affects homosexuals, which of course isn't true. Some still even cling to the idea that it's God's judgment for sexual sin. Some also still think it can be very casually transmitted through things like shaking hands or other casual contacts.

Q: Where do you think the church could improve when it comes to dealing with AIDS?

A: A friend of mine once said, "The church is miles wide, but inches deep." Meaning, of course, that we can be quite shallow, even when we've got big congregations and numbers. I agree with him. On the one hand, there's not nearly enough teaching in our churches about holiness and about taking Paul seriously when he said our bodies are temples of the Holy Spirit. The amount of sexual sin in the church is discouraging, as is the lack of sound, clear biblical teaching on the subject. That makes us all the more vulnerable to all sorts of problems, including AIDS. And we sure could improve in our ability to love. My gosh, the horror stories I could tell you about people who were judged, shunned, and looked down on by Christians because they had AIDS. So in those two areas—clear biblical teaching about sexual purity, and nonjudgmental love for all people—we really could improve.

On that point, Kay Warren, wife of internationally renowned pastor and author Rick Warren, seems to agree:

Pastors and church leaders, Christians, all of us need to take a fresh look at Scripture. Look at Scripture and ask: What do I think God's response is to people who are sick?

Read the Old Testament, the New Testament, to see a God who is deeply compassionate about people who are sick. You'll see in Ezekiel where God said to the shepherd of Israel, "You have not bound up the wounded; you have not gone after the sick or the weak sheep; you have not taken care of their wounds. You have taken care of the fat sheep and driven the thin sheep away"...

Then when you take a look at Jesus' response in the New Testament, everybody knows a third of His ministry was healing the sick. And if you look at it and say: Did Jesus ever ask anybody, "How did you get sick?" We get stuck on the "How did you get sick? How did you become infected?" We look at everybody with HIV and assume they did something wrong and that's why they're sick. You will not find Jesus asking, "How did you get sick?" He just said, "What can I do? How can I help you?"[7]

As mentioned in the introduction of this book, AIDS has hugely and permanently impacted my life. I retain an awareness of its seriousness combined with a hope for its eventual cure, however far-fetched such a hope may be. Meanwhile, I recognize, as does Mrs. Warren, the inroads the gospel can make when combined with compassion, concern, and practical aid given to those suffering from this devastating modern-day plague.

I long for my church—and myself—to be filled with the great love of our Father, so that we will overflow with His love toward the hurting and sick among us. We need many strategies and examples and models to help us...and here are a few of them: Bruce Sonnenberg, Kay Warren, God our Father, and Jesus our Healer, who still says to us, "Come, follow Me."

CHAPTER TWENTY-SIX

HIV and AIDS

○—Key Points—○

1. HIV is the Human Immunodeficiency Virus that causes AIDS, Acquired Immune Deficiency Syndrome. To have the virus is not the same as having the syndrome, and it is in fact possible to have the virus without ever developing the syndrome.

2. AIDS does not technically kill the body. It does, though, weaken the immune system so severely that it cannot ward off life-threatening diseases. It is these diseases, then, that can eventually kill the person infected with HIV who has developed AIDS.

3. There are currently drugs available to people who have HIV, to help keep them from developing AIDS. Likewise, there are currently drugs available to treat AIDS, in cases where the person infected with HIV has developed the syndrome of AIDS.

4. As of this writing (2010) there is no vaccination to prevent HIV transmission, and there is no cure for AIDS.

5. Because in the Western world AIDS began showing itself primarily in the gay male population in the early 1980s, it was often referred to as a "gay disease," and was initially even called Gay Related Immuno-Deficiency (GRID). That concept has been largely discarded, as there is clear evidence AIDS existed long before it showed itself in the

1980s, and has spread largely through heterosexual contact in Third World countries, most notable in Africa.

6. The best prevention of AIDS is found through sexual abstinence before marriage, and sexual monogamy within marriage; abstinence of any form of drug abuse involving needles; and blood screening to avoid transmission during transfusions.

7. AIDS became a political issue in Western nations, America in particular, as it became associated with the gay rights movement. Since the church has largely opposed the gay rights movement, it has often been assumed (sometimes correctly; sometimes not) that Christians were indifferent to the suffering of AIDS patients.

8. Ministry to AIDS patients need not include medical care, but can include visitation, education, evangelism, and practical care given to AIDS patients and their families.

RESOURCES

Center for Disease Control website: "A resource for facts, statistics and updates regarding HIV/AIDS," www.cdc.com.

He Intends Victory by Dan Wooding, Village Books, 2003. He Intends Victory, Christian HIV and AIDS Support and Education, www.hein tendsvictory.org.

NOTES

1. "What is AIDS?" www.aidsinfonet.org.
2. For statistics on the spread of HIV/AIDS internationally see the website "AIDS Around the World," www.avert.org/aroundworld.htm.
3. "Grim Outlook for an AIDS Vaccine," editorial, *New York Times*, March 30, 2008.
4. "S Africa to Increase AIDS Funds," *Boston Globe*, February 20, 2008, www.boston.com/news/world/africa/articles/2008/02/20/safrica_announces_increase_in_aids_funds/.
5. Pinknews.co.uk, 17 January 2008.
6. Interview with Bruce Sonnenberg conducted by Nancy Heche on April 15, 2010.
7. "Kay Warren—In the Front Line Fighting AIDS," *Christianity Today*, December 15, 2006, www.christianitytoday.com/article/interview.kay.warren.in.the.front.line.fighting.aids/8736.htm.

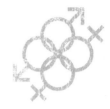

AFTERWORD
A Christlike Response
by Nancy Heche, DMin, and Joe Dallas

> *How am I, as a committed follower of Christ,*
> *supposed to make sense of all of this and respond*
> *in ways that honor Christ and bring His*
> *truths to bear on the emerging world?*
>
> —GEORGE BARNA

We began this book recognizing both the dangers and the opportunities represented in the word "crisis," and having explored the subject in these chapters we find plenty of both. There are, indeed, dangers posed to individuals, families, and the church when a behavior the Creator has forbidden is not only practiced, but openly celebrated, legally sanctioned, and publicly redefined. But there are opportunities to match the dangers as well, because controversial issues open doors for explaining worldviews, correcting misconceptions, and speaking gospel truths. In light of all we've discussed, then, we end by asking, along with Barna as quoted above, "So now what? How should we respond?"

And the clichés come tumbling in: "We should love the sinner but hate the sin"; "Speak the truth in love"; "Be salt and light"; "Fight the good fight."

Well, yes. But we've known those sayings all along, and they haven't equipped us with a response to homosexuals that's adequate, much less excellent, so a rethinking of our approach seems long overdue. In these closing pages, then, we'll concern ourselves with developing and maintaining an effective, Christ-like response.

Back to Basics

This calls us back to doctrinal basics, one of which is the purpose and role of the church. After all, a Christian response should be one that springs from, and is in line with, the church's assigned function, which we see in four parts:

1. To preach the gospel.
2. To make disciples.
3. To establish and strengthen community within the church body.
4. To be a tangible witness of God's nature, standards, and truths by our good works, our love, and our clear voice.

Let's consider each of these, then reconsider them in light of our response to homosexuals.

1. To preach the gospel. From the time Jesus commissioned the disciples before His ascension ("Go into all the world and preach the gospel to every creature"—Mark 16:15), they had an urgency about spreading the good news, accompanied with a clear understanding that people were either dead in sin or alive in Christ. So Peter's sermon on the Day of Pentecost (Acts 2:14-40); his message at Solomon's Porch (Acts 3:11-26); Stephen's defense before the high priest (Acts 6:2-53); and the scattered disciples' evangelism (Acts 8:4) all testify to a passion for calling people to recognize their mortality, their sinfulness, and the inevitable judgment they'd face if they refused the salvation God made available through Christ.

Far from ecumenical, they took the Lord at His word when He said, "No one comes to the Father except through Me" (John 14:6) and that "unless one is born again, he cannot see the kingdom of God" (John 3:3). Jesus' vivid, unsparing descriptions of hell (Matthew 18:9; 25:41; Mark 9:44) must have fueled their zeal as well, so the early church made the promotion of the only name under heaven or earth by which people can be saved (Acts 4:12) their top priority (see also Romans 10:14-15; 1 Corinthians 9:16; 2 Timothy 4:2). We cannot call ourselves serious believers if we do less.

2. To make disciples. The great commission placed discipleship alongside the preaching of the gospel itself (Matthew 28:19), making it clear that the church was to not only make believers, but followers as well. A disciple of Jesus is, according to *Easton's Bible Dictionary*, one who 1) believes His doctrine, 2) rests on His sacrifice, 3) imbibes His spirit, and 4) imitates His example.[1] The work of the church is to nurture and grow such a person.

3. To establish and strengthen community within the church body. The early church was tightly connected from its inception, marked by its members' deep mutual involvement (Acts 2:42-47). Since Jesus pointedly commanded the disciples to love each other, predicting that the whole world would recognize them as His if they did so (John 13:35), the bond among early believers isn't surprising. The spiritual gifts of different Christians were given, Paul said, for the building up of the church (Romans 12:4-8; 1 Corinthians 12:4-30; Ephesians 4:11-16), whose health is to be maintained by sound doctrine (2 Timothy 3:16–4:3), faithful leadership (1 Peter 5:1-4), deep love (1 John 4:7; 1 Peter 4:8), practical caring (1 John 3:16-17), and church discipline (1 Corinthians 5:1-12). All of these elements are necessary for healthy community.

4. To be a tangible witness of God's nature, standards, and truths by our good works, our love, and our clear voice. "We are His workmanship," Paul said in Ephesians 2:10, utilizing the Greek word *poema*, from which we get our word "poem." We are His poem, through which, in the ages to come, He will "show the exceeding riches of His grace and His kindness toward us in Christ Jesus" (Ephesians 2:7). That makes the church a visible platform by which God shows His nature, and through which He expresses His heart and mind. From the church, then, there should come a clear voice accurately expressing both God's viewpoint and His attitude.

Each element above plays into our response to the homosexual individual, the homosexual population, and the gay rights movement.

To *preach the gospel* requires recognizing that if someone is dead in sin, their sexual orientation or behavior is secondary to their unsaved status. So to the non-Christian homosexual, the church's priority must be presenting the good news, not arguments over sexual ethics. Granted, the subject may come up, and the question "Is homosexuality a sin?" should be answered plainly, but always in the context of a broader gospel message focusing on the need for redemption no matter what sins a person is bound by.

To *make disciples*, the church needs to know what's required of a believer and teach its members to conform accordingly. So what the Bible says about homosexuality, human nature, the struggle between the flesh and the spirit, and the need to present our bodies to God regardless of the passions swirling in them, all need to be taught clearly and consistently.

A healthy church community also requires involvement, mutual up-building, and discipline. So when homosexuals are born again and become part of the body of Christ, they should find involvement and encouragement among fellow believers. If they stumble along the way by relapsing back into some form of sexual sin, they should be exhorted to confess, turn from it, and receive grace from God and the brethren. Should they be unrepentant, then church discipline is in order. The requirement to *establish and strengthen the church community* calls for all of this.

And the responsibility to clearly and publicly, through whatever means available, express God's opinion and heart on a given issue cannot be ignored. While the church is not called to dominate or coerce the culture, she is called to impact it, to reason with it, to invite it to consider both its Creator and His claims. And so she becomes a *tangible witness of God's nature, standards, and truths through good works, love, and a clear voice.* Whatever cultural trends may be, let the church be vilified or dismissed, but let her never be misunderstood. If our culture rejects our message, let's be sure it has at least heard and known the message it's discarding.

Reviewing these four aspects of the church's role raises the question of performance, and what the Head of the church would say to us about how well, or how poorly, we've stewarded our responsibilities. Keeping in mind the way He addressed the churches in Revelation—praising, critiquing, or rebuking them as needed—we'd like to suggest four areas today's church must address seriously and thoroughly if we're to respond to this book's subject in an effective, Christlike manner.

Plainly put, we see four areas in which the modern church must shift:

1. From compromise to consistency
2. From contempt to compassion
3. From confusion to clarity
4. From concession to courage

In each of these areas, we feel we've fallen short—sometimes moderately, sometimes scandalously. But we're convinced that if the church will apply herself to a shift in each of these areas, she'll regain lost ground, welcome new converts, make strong disciples, and successfully offer a fitting, God-honoring response to the homosexual. We see much hope if she'll take this to heart; we see little if she doesn't. So to that end, let's prayerfully consider each of these four points.

From Compromise to Consistency

Moral compromise is the elephant in the middle of the sanctuary we'd all like to ignore but, as is true of all elephants, this one's big, messy, and unavoidable. Too many Christians, for too many years, have preached what they've refused to practice, and practiced what they've preached against.

As of this writing (late 2009) we're all familiar with the sad, well-publicized stories of Christian leaders and sexual scandal. Jim Bakker's tryst with Jessica Hahn; Jimmy Swaggart's use of a prostitute; Ted Haggard's secret homosexuality—how the mighty are fallen, how loud the thud. And as long as humans are placed in positions of trust, there'll be more. Sexual immorality among Christian leaders still makes news, but these days it intrigues more than it shocks, as scandal after scandal has brought our expectations horribly low.

But if public falls have become common, private ones among believers have become epidemic. Statistics prove that compromise in this area is a disease ravaging the entire body, leadership and laity alike, making us so much less than what we're meant to be. Consider just a few of the ugly facts:

- 1 in 5 born again Christian men and women believe that viewing magazines with nudity and sexually explicit pictures is morally acceptable.[2]

- 36 percent of Christians say cohabitation is morally acceptable, and 39 percent define sexual fantasies as morally acceptable.[3]

- A 1996 Promise Keepers survey, taken at one of their stadium events, revealed that over 50 percent of the men in attendance had been involved with pornography within one week of attending the event.[4]

- 51 percent of pastors surveyed say cyber-porn is a possible temptation; 37 percent say it is a current struggle.[5]

- Roger Charman of Focus on the Family's Pastoral Ministries reports that approximately 20 percent of the calls received on their Pastoral Care Line are for help with issues such as pornography and compulsive sexual behavior.[6]

- In a 2000 *Christianity Today* survey, 33 percent of clergy admitted to having visited a sexually explicit website. Of those who had visited a porn site, 53 percent had visited such sites "a few times" in the past year, and 18 percent had visited sexually explicit sites between a couple of times a month and more than once a week.[7]

- 57 percent of pastors say that addiction to pornography is the most sexually damaging issue to their congregation.[8]

- An article in a 1997 issue of *Newsweek* magazine noted that various surveys suggested that as many as 30 percent of male Protestant ministers had had sexual relationships with women other than their wives.[9]

- *The Journal of Pastoral Care* in 1993 reported a survey of Southern Baptist pastors in which 14 percent acknowledged they had engaged in "sexual behavior inappropriate to a minister." It also reported that 70 percent had counseled at least one woman who had had intercourse with another minister.[10]

Peruse the Internet and you'll find much more of the same, pointing not only to severe moral compromise among believers, but inexcusable hypocrisy as well. And the hypocrisy may be the greater evil. It's a sin that certainly angered Jesus, who reserved His harshest words not for sexual sinners, but for religious people who said one thing and did another. (See His scathing "Woe unto you!" rebukes to the scribes and Pharisees in Matthew 23:13-26 for the most pointed example.)

And where hypocrisy goes, loss of credibility follows. That's why Nathan, when confronting David over his adultery with Bathsheba and his subsequent murder of her husband, said, "By this deed you have given great occasion to the enemies of the LORD to blaspheme" (2 Samuel 12:14). Paul made a similar point when he indicted his Jewish readers for saying "Thou shalt not," then doing the very thing they condemned, when he said, "The name of God is blasphemed among the Gentiles because of you" (Romans 2:24). Credibility cannot coexist with hypocrisy which is, perhaps, the hardest of all sins for the public to forgive.

The irony of Christians trying to impact the culture while being so compromised was not lost on pollster George Barna, who wrote:

> Christians fail to transform the culture because they are neither grieved nor humbled by their own sins.[11]

In that same vein, author and columnist Cal Thomas posed the logical question:

> Why should the majority accept something they have not seen fully lived out by those who profess to believe?[12]

Why indeed? If a man 200 pounds overweight was doing televised infomercials for exercise equipment, would anyone take him, or his product, seriously? Granted, it might be a fine product, but the man's own condition would cause people to dismiss his claims. And so it will always be—compromised holiness begets compromised impact.

How, then, should we respond?

1. More pastors could preach on the sanctity of the sexual union and the seriousness of sexual sin, defining and clarifying which behaviors are forbidden by God no matter how popular they may have become.

2. More pastors could invite members of their congregations to be honest if they've fallen into sexual sin, and to seek help and accountability within the church.

3. More churches could offer groups, in-house counsel and care, or both for people struggling with an ongoing sexual sin.

4. More Christians, especially husbands and fathers, could come clean about their own compromise and take the necessary steps to ensure that compromise ends once and for all.

5. More Christian parents could ensure that their homes aren't needlessly defiled with movies, television programs, music, and Internet input that contradict the values we say we embrace. Let the entertainment we take in reflect the standards we profess.

Peter said the time is come that judgment must begin at the house of God (1 Peter 4:17), so let it begin here, and now. Let the church first repent of whatever immorality exists in our own ranks, removing the plank from our own eyes. Then, by God's grace, we might see clearly to speak to the moral crisis of our time, and to impact the culture we hope to win.

From Contempt to Compassion

Taking a public stand against immorality is neither hateful nor unbiblical. We warn people we love if we feel they're endangered; if we love our families, our church, our nation, and the people in it, we'll do no less. There's plenty of biblical precedence for this. Lot was grieved with Sodom's brazenness (2 Peter 2:6-8); Elijah clashed openly with King Ahab over his wickedness (1 Kings 18:17-18); and John the Baptist called Herod out over his illicit marriage (Matthew 14:3-4). Certainly, Paul noted that we're not here to judge the world and that, in fact, we expect fallen humanity to behaviorally display the Fall (1 Corinthians 5:12-13). Still, being God's *poema* means expressing His heart and mind, especially on matters that are of clear public interest. The church simply isn't functioning when silent or vague about critical issues.

But saying a behavior is wrong is a far cry from also expressing undisguised contempt for the people who practice it. Moral pronouncements that are long on passion but short on humility make us sound more like Pharisees than disciples. And while we may tell ourselves the culture increasingly rejects our message because it loves darkness more than light, it may be, in fact, that we're also losing influence because the culture loves authenticity more than priggishness. Authors David Kinnaman and Gabe Lyons pointed this out in their bestseller *unChristian: What a New Generation Really Thinks about Christianity and Why It Matters*:

> The primary reason outsiders feel hostile toward Christians, and especially conservative Christians, is not because of any specific theological perspective. What they react negatively to is our "swagger," how we go about things and the sense of self-importance we project.[13]

We're not willing to concur that any hostility outsiders express toward us is a response to our own bluster, as there are many reasons non-Christians oppose the church. But we'll tearfully concede Kinnaman and Lyon's indictment is often, if not always, spot on. Too often, the more "normal" sexual sins—lust, pornography, even adultery—are preached against as wrong without the zeal, or even the wrath, expressed when homosexuality is preached against. That's why we'll also agree with historian John Boswell when he notes:

> If prohibitions which restrain a disliked minority are upheld in their most literal sense as absolutely inviolable while comparable precepts affecting the majority are relaxed or reinterpreted, one must suspect something other than religious belief as the motivating cause.[14]

Words and Actions of Contempt

Contempt, not just conviction, has too often poisoned our messages to and about homosexuals. So while we applaud Rev. Jimmy Swaggart for preaching against sin, we cringe when reading his September 12, 2008, sermon remarks in reference to same-sex marriage:

> I've never seen a man in my life I wanted to marry. And I'm gonna be blunt and plain; if one ever looks at me like that, I'm gonna kill him and tell God he died.[15]

We likewise appreciate concerns about the impact of sexual behaviors on public health, but an early statement by Dr. Paul Cameron, formerly of the Christian-based Family Research Council, discussing the future of AIDS at a conference on public policy, expresses something other than concern:

> Unless we get medically lucky, in three or four years, one of the options discussed will be the extermination of homosexuals![16]

We're grateful to the late Reverend Jerry Falwell for his immeasurable contributions to church and country, but his comments shortly after the horror of 9/11 created understandable furor:

> I really believe that the pagans and the abortionists and the feminists and the gays and the lesbians who are actively trying to make that an alternative lifestyle, the ACLU, People for the American Way, all of them who try to secularize America…I point the thing in their face and say you helped this happen.[17]

His subsequent public apology ("I would never blame any human being except the terrorists, and if I left that impression with gays or lesbians or anyone else, I apologize"[18]) showed integrity and class, so we mention his famous statements only as examples of messages from the church that have crippled, in many cases, our ability to reach the very people we claim to love.

And those messages haven't just come from well-known leaders. I (Joe) recently spoke at a church in a rural area where a large gay camping resort had just opened. Because the area was very conservative and local citizens were concerned about the impact a gay resort could have on the general moral and social climate, some members of this church purchased land next to the resort and promptly stocked it with hogs. The hog farm, with its accompanying stench, was set up to make a public statement about how its purchasers felt toward homosexuals.

The pastor of the church and many of its members were openly opposed to this. But those involved insisted God had told them to do it, no matter how much controversy and ill will it stirred. That's a contemptuous (though hardly righteous) message.

But no more so than the one I listened to the first Sunday after I'd repented of homosexuality. Fresh out of the gay community and back in a traditional church for the first time in six years, I heard the pastor begin his sermon by warning the congregation that, contrary to their claims, gays were indeed interested in children, and that when he himself had been approached by them as a young man, he beat them up. (Strong applause.) And if any of them approached his grandchildren, he'd beat them up again. (Longer applause.)

In fairness, as a father I don't even want to consider my response if one of my sons was molested. But in light of evidence and common sense, it's morally wrong and openly cruel to teach people that a homosexual is, by sheer nature of his orientation, a child predator. To hate the sin and openly rebuke it is one thing, but to "hate the sin but defame the sinner" is a strange, unholy approach.

So is the approach of openly threatening the sinner, which we heard advocated on a recent Christian talk show where we were being interviewed. One caller, concerned about the prevalence of homosexuality in her city, asked plainly, "What would be wrong with just taking these people out?"

As long as messages like these come from the church, they prove a crying need for us to shift away from contempt and toward compassion. But compassion needn't (and in fact mustn't) compromise truth.

From Disgust to Compassion

Compassion doesn't mince words about sin, but it puts the sin in its perspective, as Jesus did when talking with the Samaritan woman. She was in sin, which He made no bones about (John 4:16-18). But recognizing her sin didn't compel Him to express disgust for her, malign her as a potential child molester, or blame the world's evils on her. He was compassionate without compromise.

Commenting on contemptuous statements from Christians, blogger Joe Carter of the Evangelical Outpost notes:

> While Christians should denounce such outrageous statements, we have a duty to do much more than just issue the generic pious condemnations. We should be taking as strong a stance against violence against homosexuals as we do against same-sex marriage. Our actions should show that such enmity toward gays and lesbians goes against all that we believe. We must make it clear that such un-Biblical attitudes have no place in our community. Above all else, though, Christians must show love toward others. We must love our neighbor, even when they engage in behavior that we reject.[19]

Which brings up another troubling point. We've both observed that public speakers tend to use words, phrases, and illustrations they assume their listeners will appreciate. We both certainly do. So when I (Nancy) am speaking to a woman's group, I'll use stories or analogies I know women will appreciate, and I might even take a friendly jab or two at men, which I wouldn't normally do when speaking to a mixed audience. Most recently I have been reminded that those remarks can be "foolish jesting," not edifying, not "seasoned with salt," and most importantly, not loving. Such remarks should remain unspoken.

In other words, speakers usually know the attitudes of their listeners and modify their talks accordingly. Knowing their listeners are Christian, they wouldn't think of telling a dirty joke, or using vulgarity. Their audience wouldn't tolerate it.

So why, we have to ask, have some Christian speakers felt quite comfortable making the sort of remarks about homosexuals they wouldn't dare make about other groups? Could it be they knew that there was enough contempt for homosexuals among believers in general for remarks like that to be acceptable?

We're not sure; we're just wondering. And since the gay rights movement becomes increasingly aggressive and ambitious each year, often targeting the Christian community as a group to either be converted or intimidated, we know that the temptation to fear, loathe, and even hate homosexuals will only grow with time. In fact, later in this afterword, we'll discuss the many reasons we feel this to be inevitable. But inevitable or not, it's a temptation any serious believer has to resist.

How then should we respond?

1. We can and should clearly speak against a sin without resorting to stereotypes, sarcastic remarks, or inaccurate generalizations about the people practicing the sin we condemn.

2. Pastors especially can model for their congregations the difference between clarity and contempt. Church members absorb not only their pastor's words but their tone and attitude as well. If leaders say, either by word or tone, that contempt for homosexuals is acceptable, no doubt their parishioners will "go and do likewise."

3. We can find ways to serve homosexual people, through evangelism, respectful dialogue, and acts of kindness when possible, without compromising truth. To say "I respect and care about you" is not a compromise; to listen to and pray with a person is not to say "I condone all that you do." There's no reason to fear that our love for people will somehow negate our convictions. It will, in fact, prove them.

May this, then, be the end of anyone being able to say, as Dobson did above, that we haven't been very good about loving.

From Confusion to Clarity

As I (Joe) began writing my part of this afterword, my wife had just returned home from meeting a friend at our church. This woman was concerned because an old friend of hers, who'd been a committed Christian, had recently "come out" to her, saying, "I'm a lesbian and a Christian, and I'm trying to reconcile both parts." My wife's friend knew the Scriptures well enough to understand there was no way to reconcile sexual sin with the faith, but her friend informed her that her other Christian friends had said they were fine with her being a lesbian, and that God must have made her that way, so there was no problem.

So a Christian woman felt attracted to other women, told her friends, and they either knew so little of the Bible, or cared so little what it said, that with perhaps the best of intentions they confirmed a sister in her sin. Now magnify this lack of moral clarity among believers and you see where an epidemic of biblical ignorance, skewed priorities, and the new gospel of ambiguity has brought us. If we ourselves don't know right from wrong, then our role as salt and light seems laughable.

Paul asked, "If the trumpet makes an uncertain sound, who will prepare himself for battle?" (1 Corinthians 14:8). Good question. When the instrument that is supposed to provide guidance is unclear, then every man will have to decide for himself what's right. And that, we fear, is the relativist, uncertain direction much of the church is taking.

Consider, for example, what a professor from a conservative Christian university had to say about homosexual partnerships. John G. Stackhouse Jr., Regent College professor of theology and culture, says in his book *Finally Feminist: A Pragmatic Christian Understanding of Gender*:

> I acknowledge that in this deeply troubled world some people will find the first serious and genuine love of their lives in a homosexual relationship. I believe therefore that such relationships can be condoned, cautiously, for pastoral, therapeutic reasons as temporary accommodations to some people's particular injuries and needs. The church nonetheless does not "bless" such unions, let alone "normalize" them, but upholds scriptural sexual and relational ethics as the ideal toward which we all strive. In the meanwhile, however, we can appreciate the sad truth that some people will have to take the long way home, and a caring homosexual relationship may be a necessary part of that journey. This is clearly a difficult area of pastoral ethics and requires deep theological, psychological, and spiritual wisdom.[20]

Huh? The church must not *bless* homosexual unions, but at times (when deep theological, psychological, and spiritual wisdom are properly aligned) we *condone* what we should not *bless*, because a sexual sin that's *forbidden* may nonetheless be *necessary*? So while upholding scriptural standards as the ideal, we condone the necessary sin that we do not bless?

Professor Stackhouse's advice is symptomatic of the lack of clarity in much of the church today, and when it comes to confusion, he's hardly alone. The vagueness among prominent, popular Christian leaders cited in chapter 1 of this book needn't be rehashed, other than to say it's leaving too many believers uncertain as to what God has said, or not said, on issues as basic as the definition of the family, the sanctity of the body, and the rightness or wrongness of sexual union apart from marriage.

Contrast this with the preaching and writings of the early church. Consider again the sermons Peter, Stephen, John, and Paul preached, and ask yourself if you could have walked away from those messages uncertain as to what the speaker said, and what he wanted you to do. Certainly, you could have dismissed Peter's sermon on Pentecost without repenting, but you could hardly have done so without knowing he had *called* you to repent.

Likewise, when reading Paul's letter to the Romans (particularly the first three chapters) you might have disagreed with his views on the inherent sinfulness of human nature, but you'd hardly wonder what those views were. Clarity marked the early Christian message; clarity marks the majority of Bible passages; and clarity is a feature of any genuine revival or reformation.

But clear teaching on human sexuality in general, and homosexuality in particular, is sadly lacking, leaving us ill-equipped and unprepared. A shift is needed, from confusion to clarity, and it's needed now.

How then should we respond?

1. Pastors can recognize that many who attend churches today aren't familiar with biblical teaching on sexual behavior. No longer can a minister assume that professing Christians know they shouldn't engage sexually before marriage, view pornography, or form homosexual partnerships. While the wrongness of these behaviors may seem obvious to many of us, there's a growing number of believers to whom these behaviors seem acceptable. *Obvious* truth is not necessarily *known* truth, so more than ever, it needs to be taught in an obvious way.

2. Pastors can teach more often and plainly on the reality of temptation, ways to resist it, and how to manage the ongoing struggle between the flesh and the spirit that is experienced (but not always understood) by their congregants. A growing cultural belief seeping into the church is one that says, in essence, that if certain

feelings are ongoing and deeply ingrained, they must be God-given and should be indulged. A renaissance of teaching Pauline theology on the old and new natures would go far to counteract this trend.

3. Churches can and must lose their hesitation to invoke church discipline when necessary, whether applied to parishioners dealing with homosexual or heterosexual sins. The difference between church attendance and church membership needs to be stressed. (Anyone is welcome to attend; to become a member, one has to submit to the Lordship of Christ over all areas of life, the sexual included.) The difference between falling into a sin then repenting, versus celebrating and continuing in it, needs clarification, as the one calls for grace and restoration, while the other calls for confrontation and discipline. And the difference between judging an individual (forbidden, of course in Matthew 7:1-2) and judging behavior (mandated by the same Bible that forbids judging the person in, for example, 1 Corinthians 6:1-5) needs to be plainly stated and exercised.

Confusion must give way to clarity if the church is to have a useful voice. No doubt that will bring controversy, which is nothing to seek but something to expect. Yet if tensions rise because of the church's clarity; if truth divides and at times even offends; if the desire to get along must at times give way to our commissioned role as salt and light, then so be it. The late, formidable Christian artist Keith Green said it well: "I'd rather have people hate me with the knowledge that I tried to save them."

May we likewise prefer truth to accommodation. May our compassion be clear, but may our message and standards be equally so, balancing truth and grace in the best Christian tradition.

From Concession to Courage

When Paul preached at Ephesus, many of his listeners turned from idolatry in response to their conversion to Christianity. This was bad news for people who manufactured shrines intended for idol worship, so when the silversmith Demetrius, who specialized in producing shrines to the goddess Diana, heard about the detriment Paul's preaching was to business, he held a meeting with others in the "idol making" trade, and warned his colleagues:

> Men, you know that we have prosperity by this trade. Moreover, you see and hear that not only at Ephesus, but throughout almost all Asia, this Paul has persuaded and turned away many people, saying that they are not gods which are made with hands. So not only is this trade of ours in danger of falling into disrepute, but also the temple of the great goddess Diana may be despised" (Acts 19:25-27).

So in response to the gospel's threat to business, they started a riot, ending in a mob scene and Paul's arrest. And so it will always be—whenever the gospel in preached in clarity and power, someone will be inconvenienced.

This is not to say that all objections to Christian preaching are unfounded. As documented earlier in this afterword and elsewhere, many irresponsible, unfair, and even hateful remarks have been made by church leaders and laity. Gay or pro-gay advocates may criticize such statements, and when they do, it's hardly a form of persecution. It's an accurate assessment.

Likewise, critics may scrutinize or refute Christian teaching or statements. They may be wrong, and often are, but that's hardly in keeping with Demetrius's persecution of Paul in Ephesus. A critic, after all, is not necessarily an enemy, and even an enemy, no matter how malevolent, may still have useful things to say.

But the intolerance we often see leveled against Christians promoting the traditional view on homosexuality qualifies as neither criticism nor scrutiny, much less reasonable discourse. Rather, it indicates efforts to marginalize, and finally silence, whoever dares uphold and articulate a view which is, like Paul's call to monotheistic worship, a hindrance and inconvenience to people with a conflicting agenda. Gay writer Paul Varnell put it plainly:

> The chief opposition to gay equality is religious. We may conduct much of our liberation effort in the political sphere or even the "cultural" sphere, but always undergirding those and slowing our progress is the moral religious sphere. If we could hasten the pace of change there, our overall progress would accelerate—in fact, it would be assured.[21]

And in the interest of "hastening progress," pressure grows, nationally and abroad, for Christians to concede to the demand to either convert or be silenced. Concession is tempting, as it relieves the church of the uncomfortable repercussions that may well come if she takes an unpopular position. Many churches have already conceded, fearing to speak clearly on this issue because of the tensions clarity can cause. But Dr. Francis Schaeffer pointed out both the temptations and dangers inherent in concession:

> A part of the Good News is to take a stand; that is a part of the Good News in a broken, as well as lost, world. It must be emphasized that there is no dichotomy between preaching the Good News and taking a stand—and in fact, if there is nothing to take a stand upon there is no reason for preaching the Good News.[22]

A shift from concession to courage, then, will be one of the most difficult adjustments to make and maintain in the coming years. Indeed, facing squarely the brazen and growing trends toward silencing the biblical viewpoint on homosexuality will be one of our greatest challenges. The following look at the trends confirms this.

What Has Been Happening?

Larry Kramer is one of the nation's most influential gay leaders, with ties to celebrities, cultural leaders, and the media elite. He is also the founder of ACT UP (AIDS Coalition to Unleash Power), which gained notoriety for invading St. Patrick's Cathedral in New York City during mass and terrorizing its parishioners. Indeed, in 1987, when describing actions he felt were justified and even advisable for AIDS activists, he said:

> I think we should be tying up whole cities. We should cripple this country. We should throw bombs. We should set fires. We should stop traffic. We should surround the White House.[23]

And in remarks amazingly (but predictably) underreported by a media always ready to spotlight hateful remarks from conservatives, Kramer said, during an ACT UP meeting,

> that he wanted to set up a group to do target practice, to learn how to use guns against the police and gay bashers.[24]

Settling any doubts as to whether or not these were rare statements made off the cuff and outside the mainstream of his usual thoughts, Kramer told the *LA Times*:

> The new phase is terrorism…I don't know whether it means burning buildings, or killing people, or setting fire to yourselves.[25]

All this from one of the gay community's most celebrated, if volatile, leaders. Yet Kramer is hardly alone in his vitriol against anyone opposing him, especially Christians. The conservative Christian activist Peter LaBarbera, who heads Americans for Truth About Homosexuality (AFTAH) was recently targeted in a pro-gay blog site on which a gay activist posted LaBarbera's home address (where his wife and children live) with the following invitations for snipers to take note, and with direct threats leveled against the LaBarbera family, on January 13, 2007:

> It's across from a park in an area with cul-de-sacs. I'd bet it's a residence…and across from a park. Snipers take note…[LaBarbera] and others like him ought to know, beyond a shadow of a doubt, what future awaits them from a cadre of selected defenders willing to give up everything in order to protect the lives of gay and lesbian citizens. The greatest thing ever to happen to the [Martin Luther King] movement was the Black Panthers. Americans were shocked by an open display of firearms and Black Pride…Pushing back verbally…or with selected action isn't dishonorable, it's necessary.[26]

If a gay rights leader's call for terrorism and target practice against "homophobes" is revolting, and if a gay activist's invitation for snipers to target a Christian activist's home is frightening, then a mainstream newspaper journalist's musings about burning Boy Scouts leaders to death can only be called appalling. In response to the Scouts' position that homosexuality and scouting are incompatible, Dave Thomas of the *Orlando Sentinel*, had this helpful advice for charitable organizations:

> If I were the United Way…I'd build a big pile of wood with a pole stuck in the middle of it. Then I'd tie the leaders of the Boy Scouts of America to the pole…then I'd rub two sticks together and work on that campfire merit badge.[27]

Not to be outdone by their East Coast counterparts, gay activists on the West Coast have shown intolerance and a taste for violence that competes quite well. In November of 2008, California voters passed Proposition 8, which overturned a recent State Supreme Court decision to nullify the voter's earlier (2000) decision to limit the definition of marriage to heterosexual couples. After Proposition 8's passage, protests erupted across the state. In San Diego, a 69-year-old Christian woman experienced the dark side of the gay rights movement when she ventured out into a group of anti–Proposition 8 protestors:

> Carrying a large, foam cross, Phyllis Burgess, 69, showed up at a rally last Friday against Proposition 8, the ban on same-sex marriage approved this month by California voters. She was there to show her belief in traditional marriage, she said. Within minutes, however, angry protesters swarmed around the Palm Springs resident, yanked the cross from her hands and trampled on it.[28]

At around the same time, a group of young Christians in San Francisco were targeted for much worse antics from a crowd of angry gays. When they gathered in the predominantly gay Castro Street area for a time of public prayer and worship, a group made up largely of gay men began gathering around them. According to one of the participants:

> Then some guy (dressed in drag as a nun) took a curtain-type thing and wrapped it around us. Then a crowd started gathering. We began to sing "Amazing Grace," and basically sang that song the whole night. At first, they just shouted at us, using crude, rude, and foul language and calling us names like "haters" and "bigots." Then, they started throwing hot coffee, soda and alcohol on us and spitting on us. Then, a group of guys surrounded us with whistles, and blasted them inches away from our ears continually. Then, they started getting violent and started shoving us. At one point a man tried to steal one of our Bibles. Chrisdene noticed, so she walked up to him and said, "Hey, that's not yours, can you please give it back?" He responded by hitting her on the head with the Bible, shoving her to the ground, and kicking her. I called the cops, and when they got there, they pulled her out of the circle and asked her if she wanted to press charges. She said, "No, tell him I forgive him."

The Christian group, it should be noted, was escorted out of the area under police protection, the entire episode available for viewing on YouTube.[29]

When confronted during a taping of the *Dr. Phil* television show about this type of behavior from gays in his city, San Francisco Mayor Gavin Newsom minimized the seriousness of it by implying that both sides (pro-gay and anti-gay) were behaving the same way:

> Look, it is wrong to do those things, as it's wrong on the other side... let me assure you...there was example after example during 2004 when we were doing the wedding ceremonies, example after example in the last months when we were doing weddings, where people disrupted those weddings, disrupted real people's lives. Let's not act as victims here.[30]

Hmm—both sides are guilty? Both gays and conservative Christians are doing the same thing? The mayor seems to think so, but one wonders: Were the same-sex weddings he mentioned ("example after example") disrupted by Christian groups? Did Christians invade the churches or buildings where these weddings were taking place, surround the couple, shout into bullhorns and blow whistles, then throw objects, scream threats, and finally create such a scene that the San Francisco police had to escort the gay couple out for their own safety? Because if they didn't, then the mayor is mistaken when he asserts that both sides are guilty of the same type of behavior. And his dismissive statement "Let's not act as victims here" smacks of arrogance, considering that the young Christians who were mobbed in his city are as much his constituents as the gays who mobbed them. They weren't "acting" as victims. They *were* victims.

Then again, unpunished riots incited by gays against Christians aren't unprecedented in San Francisco. In 1993, when a conservative political activist was scheduled to speak to an evening service at Hamilton Square Baptist Church, a crowd surrounded the sanctuary, pounding on the doors, blocking the entrance, and screaming "We want your children!" Church property was vandalized and the rights of the parishioners were unmistakably violated, but when senior pastor Dr. David Innes called the police for help, he was told they could do nothing because "you have to understand, this is San Francisco."[31]

Lest anyone wonder why such bizarre and oppressive acts are committed, then condoned, by so many gays, an honest statement by Cathy Renna of the Gay and Lesbian Alliance Against Defamation makes it clear:

> People often get their views from their religions, so we don't want the pulpit saying that gay is wrong.[32]

"We don't want the pulpit saying that gay is wrong," so if the man behind the pulpit won't change his message, then we'll just take the pulpit over. Or so it seems. Just ask members of Mount Hope Church in Lansing, Michigan. On November 9, 2008, a gay "anarchist" group named "Bash Back" interrupted the church's service to fling propaganda and condoms around the sanctuary, drape a profane banner from the balcony, and feature two lesbians making out at the pulpit.[33]

In light of these displays of intimidation and anarchy, columnist Jim Pfaff raised the obvious questions of recourse and government protection when he asked:

> Will future courts ignore this brand of intimidation from groups like Bash Back!? Will they reason that the homosexual community has been "mistreated" over many years and has a right to protest for "change?"[34]

An ominous answer could be gleaned from just such a case that was heard in 2002, when members of the gay activists group Soulforce insisted on being served communion at a conference of Catholic bishops and, when refused, remained on the premises after being asked to leave and were eventually arrested. What should have been a slam dunk hearing took a stunning turn when presiding Judge Mildred Edwards in the Superior Court of the District of Columbia handed down her verdict:

> Judge Edwards refused to order the defendants to stay away from the Hyatt in the future, and declared the complete suspension of the imposition of sentence. "Terrible violence was done to you when the body of Christ was denied to you," said Judge Mildred Edwards, who also ordered the defendants to each pay $50 to the Victims of Violent Crimes Compensation Fund.
>
> "You are in solidarity with all victims of violence," Judge Edwards

continued as she addressed the three defendants. "I am terribly sorry for what happened to you. As a member of the Church, I ask you to forgive our Church. There is no way I am going to order you away from the Hyatt. You can engage in peaceful demonstration as long as it is law-abiding. Go in Peace."[35]

If the descriptions above don't convey an adequate sense of absurdity and unbridled injustice, try reversing them. Take the same events, but switch roles, replacing the gay activists with Christian activists; and Christians with gays. Use your imagination. Imagine well-respected Christian leader Rick Warren stating during an interview how displeased he was with the way so much of the world was rejecting the gospel and mistreating Christians. His answer? "I think we should be tying up whole cities. We should cripple this country. We should throw bombs. We should set fires. We should stop traffic. We should surround the White House. The new phase is terrorism, and I want to set up some target practice to use guns against gay activists."

Imagine a Christian columnist describing, in a major Christian publication, his wish to tie a homosexual to a pole and light a match.

Imagine a pro-Christian public rally, held on a street corner, into which an elderly lesbian woman walks, carrying a Rainbow Flag, the symbol of gay pride. The Christians surround her, scream in her face, and knock the flag to the ground.

Imagine a small group of gays meeting on a street corner, holding up signs promoting gay rights and exhorting people passing by to support same-sex marriage. A large group of Christians surrounds them, shouting, blowing whistles, throwing objects, and pushing one of them down. The police, rather than subdue the Christians, escort the gays out of the area while the Christians march alongside, taunting and threatening all the way.

Imagine a gay church situated in a predominantly conservative community. One night a well-known gay activist is scheduled to speak, so Christian activists surround the gay church building, pounding on the doors and blocking the entrance. When the homosexual pastor calls the police for assistance, he's told there's nothing they can do: "You have to remember, this is a conservative town!"

Imagine a gay church refusing to serve communion to a Christian activist who came there to protest the normalization of homosexuality, and the church, believing him to be wrong, bars him from the sacrament. When asked to leave he refuses, is finally arrested for trespassing, then is told by the judge that he's a victim of terrible violence and that he can go free.

Why's it so hard to imagine all of this? Because it's simply unimaginable that a Christian group would be allowed to behave that way with impunity. Yet it takes no imagination to visualize gay groups doing the same, because we're getting used to it. And maybe that's the scariest part of the story.

When Dutch Holocaust survivor Corrie ten Boom described life in Holland shortly after the German occupation, she pointed out how gradual and almost subtle the changes in daily life were:

> The true horror of the occupation only came over us slowly. A rock thrown through the window of a synagogue. An ugly word scrawled across the wall of a Jewish shop. It was as though they were testing us, trying the temper of the country, seeing how far they could go. How many Dutchmen would go along with them? And the answer, to our shame, was many.[36]

Yes, but how? How is a nation convinced a group no longer deserves its basic rights and does, in fact, deserve open and unpunished mistreatment? While we would not dare compare the treatment of any group in America to that of the Jewish population during the Holocaust, there is a common element worth mentioning: *demonizing.*

Demonize a group often and effectively enough, and the public will come to share your disdain for them, along with your belief they should be marginalized, restricted, punished. No one begins a wide-scale persecution by saying, "Let's target these people because we don't like them!" It takes subtler, more seemingly reasonable means of persuasion, and that persuasion may already be in effect.

Think for a moment about the way conservative Christians are portrayed in films, television programs, and media interviews. How often is the image of the Christian one of an unintelligent, simplistic, prejudiced, anti-intellectual, and generally unlikeable person who can be downright dangerous if unrestrained? And if such a person poses a danger, why shouldn't his rights to freedom of speech and religion be curtailed? That's exactly how current thought in America regarding Christians is being altered.

All it takes is to convince the public that a group is dangerous and hateful, and that same public will do little to interfere when that group's freedoms are dismantled. It worked in Ephesus against Paul; it's been a successful strategy ever since.

All of which makes concession very attractive. Why, after all, be on the wrong side of an issue, if doing so creates so much chaos? No reason at all, if your life is about comfort and self-interest. But for the church, commissioned to express the heart and mind of our Creator, courage trumps concession. And let us not be naïve about this—it will take God-inspired courage for laypeople and leaders to continue to speak with clarity on what is becoming the most volatile of all social issues. Yet if we've any hope of fulfilling the four basic elements of church life—the preaching of the gospel, the making of disciples, the establishing and strengthening of community, and the tangible witness of God's natures and standards—concession is a sin, not an option.

How then should we respond?

1. We can take Christ at His word when He says that hatred from the world is at times part and parcel of Christian living.

2. We can recognize that truth, while liberating, is also divisive, so a negative reaction to it is no indication that it shouldn't be promoted.

3. We can (and must) fight laws that restrict freedom of speech, conscience, and religion, and earnestly fight to see those freedoms protected.

4. We can refuse to be drawn into the sin of cowardliness in the face of intimidating forces, or the sin of hatred as we face behavior that is bullying and unreasonable. Both are un-Christian and unacceptable.

To live in consistency with the values we promote; to love when we are being reviled; to speak with authority and humility in equal portions; to present truth clearly; to stand for truth bravely—our commission, which this book has touched on but lightly, requires so much more than we possess, so we ask, as did Paul to the Corinthians, "Who is sufficient for these things?"

To both of us, and, we trust, to you as well, the answer takes us back to the basics. Because when it's all been said and done, we feel that the right response to the homosexual movement, population, and individual can be found in three simple steps, all of which we've been advocating throughout these pages:

1. Know the *Word* of God
2. Seek the *heart* of God
3. *Express* the Word and heart of God to the homosexual

If we will do this, diligently and consistently, we cannot fail.

NOTES

1. See www.blueletterbible.org/Search/Dictionary/viewTopic.cfm?type=GetTopic&Topic=Disciple &DictList=2#Easton's>.

2. Barna Research Group, "Morality Continues to Decay," 11/3/2003, www.barna.org/barna-update/ article/5-barna-update/129-morality-continues-to-decay.

3. Barna, "Morality Continues to Decay."

4. "Porn and Media Addiction," www.safefamilies.org.

5. *Christianity Today*, Leadership Survey, 12/2001.

6. "Statistics and Porn," www.safefamilies.org.

7. *Christianity Today* Leadership Survey.

8. Christians and Sex Leadership Journal Survey, March 2005. Our thanks to Be Broken Ministries for posting these figures on their website at: www.bebroken.com/bbm/network/newsletters/ news0706.shtml.

9. www.infidelity-etc.com/index.php/4.

10. www.infidelity-etc.com/index.php/4.

11. George Barna, *Boiling Point: Monitoring Cultural Shifts in the 21st Century* (Ventura, CA: Regal Books, 2003), p. 209.

12. Cal Thomas, "Religious Wing Has Too Much Faith in Caesar" *LA Times*, March 21, 1995.

13. David Kinnaman and Gabe Lyons, *unChristian: What a New Generation Really Thinks about Christianity and Why It Matters* (Grand Rapids, MI: Baker Books, 2007), p. 26.

14. John Boswell, *Christianity, Social Tolerance and Homosexuality* (Chicago: University of Chicago Press, 1981) p. 7.

15. Evangelical Outpost, www.evangelicaloutpost.com/about-me.html.

16. Cited Mark E. Pietrzyk, *News-Telegraph*, March 10, 1995.

17. www.youtube.com/watch?v=H-CAcdta_8I.

18. CNN.com http://archives.cnn.com/2001/US/09/14/Falwell.apology/.

19. See Joe Carter, The Evangelical Outpost, at www.evangelicaloutpost.com/archives/2004/09/thou -shalt-not-look-at-me-that-wayjimmy-swaggart-and-violence-against-homosexuals.html.

20. John G. Stackhouse Jr., *Finally Feminist: A Pragmatic Christian Understanding of Gender* (Grand Rapids, MI: Baker Academic, 2005).

21. See Paul Varnell, "Learning from Catholics' Change" in OutNOW! June 27, 1995, p. 15.

22. From "A Day of Sober Rejoicing," www.pcahistory.org/findingaids/schaeffer/JandR.pdf.

23. Larry Kramer, activist and playwright, responding to the AIDS crisis, 1987, www.drakkar91.com/glbthistory/history2.html.

24. "Gay Life, Gay Death," *The New Republic*, December 17, 1980, p. 24.

25. "Kramer vs. Kramer," *Los Angeles Times*, June 20, 1990, section E.

26. See entire post at Americans for Truth About Homosexuality website, http://americansfortruth.com/news/snipers-take-notelesbian-pam-spauldings-website-posts-violent-threat-against-labarbera.html.

27. See "United Way Makes Giving Not Easy," *Orlando Sentinel*, July 23, 2001.

28. "Cross-Bearing Woman Says She Was Attacked by Gay Marriage Supporters," May Press Charges, Thursday, November 13, 2008, FoxNews.com, www.foxnews.com/story/0,2933,450884,00.html. See video of this event at www.youtube.com/watch?v=VziklUbtHAE—*100k*—Cached.

29. "Anti-Prop. 8 Mob Watch: Christians in San Francisco's Castro District" by Michelle Malkin, November 17, 2008, view this on YouTube at /www.youtube.com/watch?v=DsxojbyAQGI.

30. See "Same-sex Marriage: The Prop 8 Debate," November 21, 2008, www.drphil.com/slideshows/slideshow/4796/?id=4796&slide=2&showID=1172&preview=&versionID=.

31. See official statement describing this event, which was also caught on videotape, at www.hsbchurch.org/riot1.html.

32. Michael P. McConnell, "Pro Gay Group Wants Police Chaplain Removed," *The Daily Tribune*, October 16, 2002.

33. See www.worldnetdaily.com/index.php?fa=PAGE.view&pageId=80743.

34. See "Religious liberty at stake with homosexual marriage," November 24, 2008, www.opiniontimes.com/gay-marriage-threatens-religious-liberty/.

35. See www.soulforce.org/article/594.

36. Corrie ten Boom with John and Elizabeth Sherrill, *The Hiding Place*, (New York: Bantam Books, 1984), p. 84.

BIBLIOGRAPHY

Books and Printed Articles

Allen, Chad. *Loving Homosexuals as Jesus Would.* Grand Rapids, MI: Brazos Press, 2004.

Ankerberg, John. "The Myth that Homosexuality Is Due to Biological or Genetic Causes" (research paper). Ankerberg Theological Research Institute, PO Box 8977, Chattanooga, TN.

Bailey, J., R. Pillard, M. Neale, Y. Agyei. "Heritable factors influence sexual orientation in women." *Archive of General Psychiatry,* 1993.

Bailey, J., and R. Pillard. "A Genetic Study of Male Sexual Orientation." *Archives of General Psychiatry,* 1991, no. 48.

Bayer, Ronald. *Homosexuality and American Psychiatry: The Politics of Diagnosis.* New York: Basic Books, 1981.

Bell, A., and M. Weinberg. *Homosexualities: A Study of Diversities Among Men and Women.* New York: Simon and Schuster, 1978.

Bieber, Irving. *Homosexuality: A Psychoanalytic Study of Male Homosexuals.* New York: Basic Books, 1962.

Bloesch, Donald. *The Church: Sacraments, Worship, Ministry, Mission.* Downers Grove, IL: InterVarsity Press, 2002.

Boswell, John. *Christianity, Social Tolerance and Homosexuality.* Chicago: University of Chicago Press, 1980.

Burg, B. *Gay Warriors: A Documentary History from the Ancient World to the Present.* New York: NYU Press, 2001.

Byne, W., and B. Parsons. "Human sexual orientation: The biologic theories reappraised." *Archives of General Psychiatry,* 1993.

Carnes, Patrick. *Out of the Shadows.* Center City, MN: Hazelden, 2001.

Chambers, Alan, gen. ed. *God's Grace and the Homosexual Next Door.* Eugene, OR: Harvest House Publishers, 2007.

Cloud, Henry, and John Townsend. *Boundaries in Marriage.* Grand Rapids, MI: Zondervan, 2002.

Colson, Charles. *The Apologetics Study Bible: Understand Why You Believe.* Nashville, TN: Holman Bible Publishers, 2007.

Copan, Paul. *When God Goes to Starbucks: An Guide to Everyday Apologetics.* Grand Rapids, MI: Baker Books, 2008.

Crompton, Louis. *Homosexuality and Civilization.* Cambridge, MA: Belknap Press, 2003.

Dailey, Timothy. *The Bible, Church and Homosexuality.* Washington, DC: Family Research Council. 2004.

Dallas, Joe. "Born Gay?" *Christianity Today,* 22 June 1992, p. 22.

_____. "The Transsexual Dilemma." *Christian Research Journal*, 2008 (vol. 31, no. 01).

_____. *Desires in Conflict*, rev. ed. Eugene, OR: Harvest House, 2003.

_____. *The Gay Gospel? How Pro-Gay Advocates Misread the Bible*. Eugene, OR: Harvest House, 2006.

_____. *When Homosexuality Hits Home*. Eugene, OR: Harvest House, 2004.

Davies, Bob, and Anita Worthen. *Someone I Love Is Gay*. Downers Grove, IL: InterVarsity Press, 1996.

Diamond, Lisa. "Female Bisexuality from Adolescence to Adulthood: Results From a 10-Year Longitudinal Study." *Developmental Psychology*, 2008, vol. 44, no 1.

Dodes, Lance. *The Heart of Addiction*. New York: Harper Paperbacks, 2002.

Dorner, G., W. Rohde, and F. Stahl. "A neuroendocrine predisposition for homosexuality in men." *Archives of Sexual Behavior* 4:1 (1975).

Duberman, Martin. *About Time: Exploring the Gay Past*. New York: Presses of New York, 1986.

Foster, David Kyle. *Sexual Healing: A Biblical Guide to Finding Freedom*. Franklin, TN: Mastering Life Ministries, 1995.

Friedman, Richard. *Male Homosexuality: A Contemporary Psychoanalytic Perspective*. New Haven, CT: Yale University Press, 1988.

Gallagher, Maggie. *The Case for Marriage: Why Married People Are Happier, Healthier, and Better Off Financially*. New York: Doubleday, 2000.

Gebhard, Paul. *The Kinsey Data*. Philadelphia: Saunders Press, 1979.

George, Robert. *A Clash of Orthodoxies*. Wilmington, DE: ISI, 2001.

Goldberg, Arthur. *Light in the Closet: Torah, Homosexuality and the Power to Change*. Beverly Hills, CA: Red Heifer Press, 2008.

Gomulka, Gene. *Homosexuality in Uniform: Is It Time? First Things*, 30 February 1993.

Grenz, Stanley. *Welcoming But Not Affirming*. Louisville, KY: Westminster John Knox Press, 1998.

Haley, Mike. *101 Frequently Asked Questions About Homosexuality*. Eugene, OR: Harvest House Publishers, 2004.

Hallman, Janelle. *The Heart of Female Same-sex Attraction*. Downers Grove, IL: InterVarsity Press, 2008.

Hammer, Dean, and Peter Copeland. *The Science of Desire: The Search for the Gay Gene and the Biology of Behavior*. New York: Simon & Schuster, 1994.

Harren Hamilton, Julie, and Phillip Henry, genl. eds. *Handbook of Therapy for Unwanted Homosexual Attractions*. Longwood, FL: Xulon Press, 2009.

Heche, Nancy. *The Truth Comes Out*. Ventura, CA: Regal Books, 2006.

Howard, Jeanette. *Out of Egypt: Leaving Lesbianism Behind*. Grand Rapids, MI: Monarch Books, 2001.

Isay, Richard. *Being Homosexual*. New York: Farrar, Strauss, Giroux, 1989.

Johnson, Barbara. *Where Does a Mother Go to Resign?* Minneapolis, MN: Bethany House Publishing, 2004.

Jones, Stanton. "The Loving Opposition." *Christianity Today*, July 19, 1993.

Jones, Stanton, and Mark Yarhouse. *Ex-Gays? A Longitudinal Study of Religiously Mediated Change in Sexual Orientation*. Downers Grove, IL: InterVarsity Press, 2007.

_____. *Homosexuality: The Use of Scientific Research in the Church's Moral Debate*. Downers Grove, IL: InterVarsity Press, 2000.

Kallman, F.J. "Comparative study of the genetic aspects of male homosexuality." *Journal of Mental and Nervous Disease*, 1952.

Katz, Jonathan. *Gay American History*. New York: Crowell Publishers, 1974.

Keller, Timothy. *The Reason for God: Belief in an Age of Skepticism.* New York: Dutton Adult Publishers, 2008.

King, M., and E. McDonald. "Homosexuals Who Are Twins." *The British Journal of Psychiatry,* March 1992, vol. 160.

Kinnaman, David, and Gabe Lyons. *unChristian: What a New Generation Really Thinks about Christianity and Why It Matters.* Grand Rapids, MI: Baker Books, 2007.

Kinsey, Alfred. *Sexual Behavior in the Human Male.* Philadelphia: Saunders Press, 1948.

Laurie, Greg. *The Great Compromise.* Riverside, CA: Kerygma Publishing, 2004.

LeVay, Simon. "A Difference in Hypothalamic Structure Between Heterosexual and Homosexual Men." *Science,* 30 August 1991, pp. 1034-37.

Lewes, Kenneth. *The Psychoanalytic Theory of Male Homosexuality.* New York: Simon and Schuster, 1988.

Luddy, John. "Make War, Not Love: The Pentagon's Ban is Wise and Just." *Policy Review* 64 (Spring 1993).

Marmor, Judd. "Homosexuality: Nature vs. Nurture." *The Harvard Mental Health Letter,* October 1985.

Marshall, Peter. *The Light and the Glory.* Old Tappan, NJ: Revell Publishers, 1980/

Masters, W., V. Johnson, and R. Kolodny. *Human Sexuality.* Boston: Little, Brown and Co., 1984.

Metzger, Bruce. "What Does the Bible Have to Say About Homosexuality?" *Presbyterians for Renewal* magazine, May 1993.

Minnery, Tom. *Why You Can't Stay Silent.* Colorado Springs, CO: Focus on the Family, 2002.

Moberly, Elizabeth. "Homosexuality and the Truth," *First Things* 71, March 1997.

Money, John. *Perspectives in Human Sexuality.* New York: Behavioral Publications, 1974.

Nicolosi, Joseph. *Reparative Therapy of Male Homosexuality.* New York: Jason Aronson Inc., 1991.

Park, Mary. "Are Married Parents Really Better for Children?" Center for Law and Social Policy brief, May 2003.

Paulk, Anne. *Restoring Sexual Identity: Hope for Women Who Struggle with Same-sex Attraction.* Eugene, OR: Harvest House Publishers, 2003.

Payne, Leanne. *The Broken Image.* Grand Rapids, MI: Baker Books, 1995.

Perry, Troy. *Don't Be Afraid Anymore.* New York: St. Martins Press, 1990.

Popenoe, David. *Life without Father.* New York: Free Press, 1996.

Reisman, Judith. *Kinsey, Sex and Fraud.* Lafayette, LA: Vital Issues Press, 1990.

Rekers, George. *Handbook of Child and Adolescent Sexual Problems.* Lexington, MA: Lexington Press, 1995.

Rohner, Ronald, and Robert Veneziano. "The Importance of Father Love: History and Contemporary Evidence." *Review of General Psychology* 5:4 (2001), 382-405.

Satinover, Jeffrey. *Homosexuality and the Politics of Truth.* Grand Rapids, MI: Baker, 2001.

Savin-Williams, Ritch C. *The New Gay Teenager.* Cambridge, MA: Harvard University Press, 2005.

Scanzoni, Letha, and Virginia Mollenkott. *Is The Homosexual My Neighbor?* New York: Harper and Row, 1978.

Schaeffer, Francis. *A Christian Manifesto.* Wheaton, IL: Crossway Books, 2005.

———. *The Great Evangelical Disaster.* Wheaton, IL: Crossway Books, 1984.

Schaumburg, Harry. *False Intimacy: Understanding the Struggle of Sexual Addiction.* Colorado Springs, CO: NavPress, 1997.

Schmidt, Thomas. *Straight and Narrow?* Downers Grove, IL: InterVarsity Press, 1995.

Searle, John. *Mind, Language and Society: Philosophy in the Real World.* New York: Basic Books, 1998.

Sears, Alan, and Craig Osteen. *The Homosexual Agenda.* Nashville, TN: Broadman and Holman, 2003.

Sexual Disorientation: Faulty Research in the Homosexual Debate Family. A publication of the Family Research Council, 700 13th St. NW, Ste. 500, Washington, DC 20005.

Shilts, Randy. *Conduct Unbecoming: Gays and Lesbians in the U.S. Military Vietnam to the Persian Gulf.* New York: St. Martin's Press, 1993.

———. *The Mayor of Castor Street: The Life and Times of Harvey Milk.* New York: St. Martin's Griffin, 2008.

Siegel, Elaine. *Female homosexuality: Choice without Volition.* Hillsdale, New Jersey: The Analytic Press, 1988.

Socarides, Charles. *Homosexuality.* New York: Jason Aronson, Inc., 1978.

Sprigg, Peter, and Timothy Dailey. *Getting it Straight: What the Research Says About Homosexuality.* Washington, DC: Family Research Council, 2004.

Sullivan, Andrew. *Virtually Normal.* New York: Vintage, 1996.

"The Tyranny of the Minority: How the Forced Recognition of Same-Sex 'Marriage' Undermines a Free Society," *Salvo* 6 (Autumn 2008): 17-21.

Van den Aardweg, Gerard. *On the Origins and Treatment of Homosexuality.* Santa Barbara, CA: Praeger, 1986.

Weinrich, James. *Sexual Landscapes.* New York: Scribner's Sons, 1987.

White, Mel. *Stranger at the Gate.* New York: Simon & Schuster, 1994.

Whitehead, Neil and Briar. *My Genes Made Me Do It!* Lafayette, LA: Huntington House Publishers, 1999.

Wolfe, Christopher, ed. *Homosexuality and American Public Life.* Dallas: Spence, 1999.

Wooding, Dan. *He Intends Victory.* Irvine, CA: Village Books Publishing, 1995.

Yarhouse, Mark, and Lori Burkett. *Sexual Identity: A Guide to Living in the Time Between the Times.* Lanham, MD: University Press of America, 2003.

Online Articles

"The American Gay Rights Movement: A Timeline." www.infoplease.com/ipa/A0761909.html.

"APA Leaders Respond with One Voice: Inclusion," September 5, 2008. www.narth.com/docs/apaleaders.html, accessed September 18, 2008.

"Christian History," www.christianitytoday.com/history.

"Demystifying Homosexuality." *Fridae* online magazine, March 1, 2004. www.fridae.com/newsfeatures/2004/03/01/10.demystifying-homosexuality.

Derbyshire, John. "Metaphysics, Science, Homosexuality: Are we talking biology or choice?" *National Review Online,* February 16, 2005. www.nationalreview.com/derbyshire/derbyshire200502160748.asp.

Dulle, Jason. "Dialogue with a Homosexual." www.apostolic.net/biblicalstudies/homosexualuc2.htm.

Freeman, Penny. "Roadsides Towards Hope: A Wife's Response to her Husband's Sexual Addiction." http://exodus.to/content/view/268/53/.

Gagnon, Robert J. "Church Membership, Repentance and the Transformed Life." www.presbyweb.com/2006/Viewpoint/0703—Robert+Gagnon—Repentance.htm.

————. "What Does the Bible Say About Homosexuality?" www.robertgagnon.net/ArticlesOnline .htm.

"The Gay Invention: Homosexuality Is a Linguistic as Well as a Moral Error." www.touchstnemag.com/ archives/article.php?id=18-10-036-f.

Harren Hamilton, Julie. "Homosexuality 101: What Every Therapist, Parent, And Homosexual Should Know." www.narth.com/docs/hom101.html.

"Hating Hate," *National Review Online,* May 1, 2007. http://article.nationalreview.com/?q=YWZiNjk4 ZjMxMTUzNzliMWE20DIxYzY4MjUzOThiYjY=.

"The History of Psychiatry and Homosexuality." www.aglp.org/gap/1_history/.

"The Homosexual Movement: A Response by the Ramsey Colloquium." *First Things,* March 1994. www .firstthings.com/ftissues/ft9403/articles/homo.html, accessed October 10, 2008.

Jaz, Tahir. "Homosexuality—An Analysis of Biological Theories of Causation." www.flyfishingdevon .co.uk/sakmon/year2/hormones/tahir.htm#genstudies.

Kennedy, John. "The Transgender Movement." *Christianity Today,* February 12, 2008. www.christianity today.com/ct/2008/february/25.54.html.

"The Meaning of Same-sex Attraction," www.narth.com/docs/niconew.html.

"NARTH's Amicus Brief for Hawaii's Supreme Court," March 24, 1997. www.columbia.edu/cu/augustine /arch/narth.txt>.

"Obama's Coming War on Historic Christianity over Homosexual Practice and Abortion." http://robga gnon.net/ObamaWarOnChristians.htm.

O'Leary, Dale. "Gays and Attempted Suicide," September 3, 2008. www.narth.com/docs/instability .html.

"Our Position." Focus on the Family website, www.focusonthefamily.com/socialissues/sexual_identity/ progay_revisionist_theology/ourposition.aspx.

"Palm Center Study on Don't ask Don't Tell." www.palmcenter.org/files/active/0/Executive%200rder%20 0n%20Gay%20Troops%20-%20final.pdf.

"The Problem with Pedophilia." www.narth.com/docs/pedophNEW.html.

"Reasons for Marriage" (William Raspberry's interview with David Blankenhorn). Cited at the *Institute for Marriage and Public Policy* website. www.marriagedebate.com/mdblog/2004_05_16_mdblog _archive.htm, accessed November 3, 2008.

Satinover, Jeffrey. "The 'Trojan Couch': How the Mental Health Associations Misrepresent Science." www.narth.com/docs/TheTrojanCouchSatinover.pdf, accessed February 28, 2008.

Stanton, Glenn T., and Kjersten Oligney. "Refuting Points No One Is Making." www.citizenlink.org/ pdfs/fosi/marriage/AAP_Analysis.pdf.

"Studies on the Causes of Sexual Orientation," essays 1-4. www.religioustolerance.org/hom_caus4.htm.

"Suffer the Children: What's Wrong with Gay Adoption." *Christian Research Journal* 28, no. 2 (2005). www.equip.org/free/JAH050.htm.

Throckmorton, Warren. "Homosexuality and Genes: Déjà vu All Over Again?" Oct. 30, 2003. www .narth.com/docs/dejavu.html.

The Truth Project." www.thetruthproject.org.

Wilkerson, George J. "What We Don't Know: The Unaddressed Health Concerns of the Transgendered." www.trans-health.com/displayarticle.php?aid=7.

Online Resources

Information on HIV and AIDS

Aids Infonet
   www.aidsinfonet.org

Ministries Addressing Homosexuality

Exodus International (International Referral Network)
   www.exodusinternational.org

Courage (Catholic)
   www.courage.net

One by One (Presbyterian)
   www.oneby1.org

Transforming Congregations (Methodist)
   www.transformingcongregations.ning.com

People Can Change
   www.peoplecanchange.com

Support for Parents

Living Stones Ministries
   www.livingstonesministries.org

Parents and Friends of Ex-Gays
   www.pfox.org

Support for Wives

"Wifeboat: A Blog/website for Women Impacted by a Husband's Sexual Sin" hosted by Renee Dallas,
   www.wifeboat.com.

Youth and Youth-Related Issues

"Exodus Youth"
   http://exodusyouth.net/youth/.

"Groundswell Conference on Youth and Homosexuality"
   http://groundswell2006.0rg/groundswell/.

   www.truetolerance.org

ABOUT THE GENERAL EDITORS

Joe Dallas, past president of Exodus International, lectures extensively at churches and seminars and directs a biblical counseling practice in Tustin, California. He is the author of *Desires in Conflict; The Gay Gospel?*; and *When Homosexuality Hits Home.* His articles have been featured in *Christianity Today, Christian Research Journal,* and the *Journal of the Christian Association of Psychological Studies.*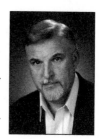

Nancy Heche is a popular Bible study teacher, author, and speaker. She holds a master's and a doctorate degree in pastoral counseling and is the author of *The Truth Comes Out.* Dr. Heche lives in Southern California.

About the Contributing Authors

Alan Chambers—Alan is the president of Exodus International, the largest evangelical organization dealing with the topic of homosexuality in the world today. His writing has appeared in *The Boston Globe, The Orlando Sentinel,* and *The Washington Times,* and he is the general editor of *God's Grace and The Homosexual Next Door: Reaching the Heart of the Gay Men and Women in Your World* and the author of *Leaving Homosexuality.*

Paul Copan, PhD—Dr. Copan is the Pledger Family Chair of Philosophy and Ethics at Palm Beach Atlantic University. He has lectured on many university campuses nationally and internationally, and is the author of a number of books, including the recent *When God Goes to Starbucks* and *Will the Real Jesus Please Stand Up?*

Melissa Fryrear, MDiv—Melissa Fryrear serves as the Gender Issues Analyst within the Legislative and Cultural Affairs Department for Focus on the Family. With over two decades of experience with gender issues, she is actively involved in public speaking, writing, and educating the church and society on a wide range of subjects related to homosexuality. Melissa is also a keynote speaker at Focus on the Family's Love Won Out conference, and served as executive director of an Exodus International Member Ministry in Kentucky. Melissa holds a Master of Divinity from Asbury Theological Seminary.

Mike Haley—As regional director for Focus on the Family's Community Outreach Department, Mike Haley oversees initiatives such as How to Drug Proof Your Kids and Thriving Families Training. In addition to being a keynote speaker at a number of Focus on the Family conferences, he also speaks frequently at churches, colleges and universities, public schools, and youth groups, and has appeared at national conventions, including the 2004 Southern Baptist Convention's Pastors' Conference. He has a degree in Christian education from Biola University and a master's degree in counseling from Liberty University. Mike and his wife, Angie, were married in 1994 and are the proud parents of two sons. The family lives in Colorado.

Bill Maier, PsyD—Dr. Maier is an author, a speaker, and a vice president at Focus on the Family. He hosts the national *Weekend Magazine* radio program and the *Family Minute with Dr. Bill Maier*. Dr. Maier received his master's and doctoral degrees from the Rosemead School of Psychology at Biola University in La Mirada, California. He is a regular contributor to *Focus on the Family* magazine, and his editorials on family issues have been published in several leading newspapers. He is co-author of the book *Marriage on Trial: The Case Against Same-Sex Marriage and Parenting* (InterVarsity Press).

Randy Thomas—As the executive vice president of Exodus International, Randy oversees more than 170 professional mental-health and church-based member agencies across North America that offer hope and help to individuals wanting to leave homosexuality. Prior to coming to Exodus in 2002, Randy was the executive director of Living Hope—an Exodus ministry in Dallas, Texas. He travels extensively, speaking on the topic of sexuality and gender, and has shared his story with members of Congress, conservative leaders, and in churches and colleges throughout the country such as Azusa Pacific College, Texas Christian University, Southern Methodist University, and University of Central Florida. His blog writing has been recognized by Family Research Council in Washington, DC, and he is also a contributing author to the book *God's Grace and the Homosexual Next Door: Reaching the Heart of the Gay Men and Women in Your World.*

INDEX

More Excellent Resources on Homosexuality
from Harvest House Publishers

DESIRES IN CONFLICT: HOPE FOR MEN
WHO STRUGGLE WITH SEXUAL IDENTITY
Joe Dallas

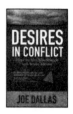

For more than a decade, *Desires in Conflict* has been the definitive "must-read" for those who wonder, "Can a homosexual change?" This new edition with updated information offers more compelling reasons why the answer is "yes!"

WHEN HOMOSEXUALITY HITS HOME:
WHAT TO DO WHEN A LOVED ONE SAYS THEY'RE GAY
Joe Dallas

The heart-wrenching declaration that a loved one is a homosexual is increasingly being heard in Christian households across America. How can this be? What went wrong? Is there a cure?

In this straightforward book, Joe Dallas offers practical counsel, step by step, on how to deal with the many conflicts and emotions parents, grandparents, brothers and sisters, or any family member will experience when learning of a loved one's homosexuality.

Drawing from his own experience and from his many years of helping families work through this perplexing and unexpected situation, Joe offers scriptural and compassionate advice to both struggling gays and those who love them.

THE GAY GOSPEL?: HOW PRO-GAY
ADVOCATES MISREAD THE BIBLE
Joe Dallas

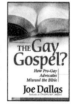

In this updated edition of *A Strong Delusion*, author and counselor Joe Dallas helps readers understand what pro-gay theology is and how to confront it. In a biblical manner, Dallas examines believers' personal responses and the need for bold love and commitment as they

- become familiar with the movement's background and beliefs
- study a clear, scriptural response to each belief
- extend Christ's love to those living the homosexual lifestyle

This resource is an important one for those who have been unsure how to respond to the growing acceptance of homosexuality in the evangelical community. It offers the balance between conviction and compassion and a practical guide to communicating with those who have embraced the pro-gay Christian movement.

101 Frequently Asked Questions About Homosexuality
Mike Haley

Almost daily we hear news reports that confirm the acceptance of homosexuality in our culture. Homosexuals are adopting children, appearing as characters on television programs, taking vacations catering to an exclusively gay clientele, and even seeking the right to "marry" their partners. But is this acceptance healthy for society?

Few topics can raise questions so quickly. And for many readers, those questions hit close to home as they learn of the homosexuality of a loved one or close friend.

Here are the answers to the most often asked questions about homosexuality, fielded by an expert on the subject and a former homosexual himself.

Restoring Sexual Identity: Hope for Women Who Struggle with Same-Sex Attraction
Anne Paulk

Restoring Sexual Identity offers answers to the most commonly asked questions from both homosexuals desiring change and friends and relatives of women struggling with same-sex attraction.

Is lesbianism an inherited predisposition or is it developed in childhood? Does becoming a Christian eliminate all desire for members of the same sex? What support is available for women who struggle with lesbianism? Can a woman be a lesbian and a Christian at the same time? How does childhood sexual abuse relate to the development of lesbianism?

These and other important questions are answered as the author draws from her own experience and that of many other former lesbians who participated in an extensive survey on same-sex attraction.

God's Grace and the Homosexual Next Door: Reaching the Heart of the Gay Men and Women in Your World
Alan Chambers and the Leadership Team at Exodus International

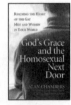

Author Alan Chambers—a former homosexual himself—and four of his colleagues at Exodus International offer practical and biblical insights on how both individuals and churches can become a haven for homosexuals seeking freedom from same-sex attraction.

> "One of the great movements in our time is that of the ex-homosexuals and ex-lesbians. These are broken people who have admitted their brokenness and found true happiness—not the so-called 'gay' lifestyle— but by living for Jesus Christ. One such man is Alan Chambers, currently president of the largest umbrella organization of ex-homosexuals, Exodus International. Alan Chambers' book provides believers with Christian and loving (but uncompromising) answers to this controversial issue."

—D. James Kennedy, PhD, Late Senior Minister, Coral Ridge Presbyterian Church

THE QUESTION OF HOMOSEXUALITY DVD:
A CONVERSATION FOR YOUTH ABOUT SAME-SEX ATTRACTION

Scott Davis

The hot-button issue of our day is addressed in this powerful DVD produced by Exodus International, the leading ministry to men and women who are tempted by unwanted same-sex attractions.

Viewers will learn from the powerful testimonies of young men and women who struggled with homosexuality as teens and will also receive biblical insights on this timely topic from Scott Davis, the director of Exodus Student Ministries.

The primary 25-minute segment answers the following questions through a dynamic mix of teaching and testimonies:

- How should we respond to friends who struggle with homosexual feelings?
- What is homosexuality really all about?
- What does God say about homosexuality in the Bible?
- Can homosexuals change?

A second 15-minute segment called "Biblical Perspectives" powerfully demonstrates that God's design for sexuality is absolutely clear throughout Scripture. It teaches that sex is a beautiful aspect of His intention for man and woman within marriage—any other sexual activity, whether premarital sex or homosexuality, goes against God's design and is destructive to their souls.

Two 30-minute bonus segments highlight the uninterrupted testimonies of former homosexuals Michelle Robinson and Mike Ensley. Their stories are sure to move hearts and connect with the life experiences of students who have same-sex attractions.

The Question of Homosexuality was specifically designed as a resource for youth groups, campus ministries, and families in an effort to ground students in the truth about homosexuality while moving their hearts to compassion for their gay-identified peers.

Leaving Homosexuality: Practical Steps for Walking Away from the Gay Lifestyle
Alan Chambers

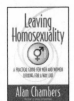

When a gay man or woman is faced with the reality that a growing and vibrant life in Jesus Christ is incompatible with their sexual attractions, what exactly does he or she *do*? What steps can be taken toward leaving the gay life and identity?

In this accessible book Alan Chambers, president of Exodus International, explains the process and clarifies the expectations for those who are skeptical of change or frustrated by an ongoing struggle with same-sex attraction.

Readers will learn how to

- enter into a new life in Christ
- set realistic and healthy expectations
- build authentic community
- learn to forgive
- overcome the power of sexual addiction

Men and women of all ages who struggle with same-sex attraction will find *Leaving Homosexuality* indispensable in their own walk of faith…and an excellent resource to give to those who haven't yet heard that there *is* a new life of freedom beyond homosexuality available to them.

Other Helpful Books on
Homosexuality and Lesbianism

THE TRUTH COMES OUT

Nancy Heche
Regal Books

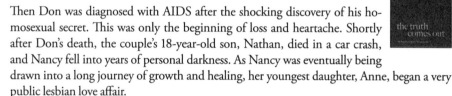

"This is the beginning of a beautiful love story," Nancy wrote in her diary after meeting Don Heche, the man she was to marry. Five children and 25 years of marriage later, it seemed as if they were the perfect family.

Then Don was diagnosed with AIDS after the shocking discovery of his homosexual secret. This was only the beginning of loss and heartache. Shortly after Don's death, the couple's 18-year-old son, Nathan, died in a car crash, and Nancy fell into years of personal darkness. As Nancy was eventually being drawn into a long journey of growth and healing, her youngest daughter, Anne, began a very public lesbian love affair.

Despite Nancy's life circumstances, she held on to what she knew of God's promises from Scripture and continues to discover how to look at people and the world from God's perspective, through eyes full of love and blessing. Her inspiring story of faith and courage will offer hope to anyone who has ever been on the brink of despair, or wondered how to respond with love to someone in a same-sex relationship.

To learn more about other Harvest House books
or to read sample chapters, log on to our website:

www.harvesthousepublishers.com

HARVEST HOUSE PUBLISHERS
EUGENE, OREGON